ONLINE LEARNING

Concepts, Strategies, and Application

NADA DABBAGH
George Mason University

BRENDA BANNAN-RITLAND
George Mason University

PEARSON

Merrill
Prentice Hall

Upper Saddle River, New Jersey
Columbus, Ohio

Library of Congress Cataloging-in-Publication Data

Dabbagh, Nada.

    Online learning : concepts, strategies, and application / Nada Dabbagh, Brenda Bannan-Ritland.

       p. cm.

    Includes bibliographical references and Index.

    ISBN 0-13-032546-5

    1. Distance education—Computer-assisted instruction. 2. Web-based instruction. I. Bannan-Ritland, Brenda. II. Title.

    LC5803.C65D33 2005

    371.35′8—dc22   2004006970

Vice President and Executive Publisher: Jeffery W. Johnston
Executive Editor: Debra A. Stollenwerk
Editorial Assistant: Mary Morrill
Production Editor: JoEllen Gohr
Production Coordination: GTS Companies/York, PA Campus
Design Coordinator: Diane C. Lorenzo
Cover Designer: Kristina D. Holmes
Cover image: *Globe:* Artville; *Computer:* Getty
Production Manager: Pamela Bennett
Director of Marketing: Ann Castel Davis
Marketing Manager: Darcy Betts Prybella
Marketing Coordinator: Tyra Poole

This book was set in Clearface by GTS Companies/York, PA Campus. It was printed and bound by R.R. Donnelley & Sons Company. The cover was printed by Coral Graphic Services, Inc.

Pearson Education Ltd.
Pearson Education Singapore Pte. Ltd.
Pearson Education Canada, Ltd.
Pearson Education—Japan

Pearson Education Australia Pty. Limited
Pearson Education North Asia Ltd.
Pearson Educación de Mexico, S. A. de C.V.
Pearson Education Malaysia Pte. Ltd.

10 9 8 7 6 5 4 3 2 1
ISBN: 0-13-032546-5

In loving memory of my father, Dr. Nassib Hammam, who was my inspiration. (Nada)

To Eric, Tristan, and Calla for all the hours spent away from you. And to my parents, Jerry and Connie Bannan, for their faith, love, and support of my efforts. (Brenda)

And to our students, who continue to promote our learning. (Nada & Brenda)

PREFACE

*O*nline Learning: Concepts, Strategies, and Application* offers a unique approach to thinking about teaching and learning in online and Web-based contexts. Beginning with a conceptualization of online learning based on the principles of learning as a social process and globalization, the book meticulously details a journey from theory to practice, informing the design of powerful and engaging online learning environments. A consistent theme in this book is the interaction among pedagogical models, instructional strategies, and learning technologies. This process is embedded in an integrative instructional design framework that is dynamic, iterative, and transformative, which enables the instructional developer, online instructor, school teacher, or educator to envision, plan for, and implement customized instructional designs for online learning.

This book was written after several years of designing, developing, researching, teaching, and implementing technology in online and distributed learning contexts. The proliferation of course management and learning management systems developed to deliver Web-based instruction and training in higher education, school, and corporate settings led us (the authors) to closely examine the instructional use of such systems on the basis of theory, research, and applied practice. The book reflects the results of this examination and our views on how course management systems and other online learning technologies can be used to design flexible and engaging learner-centered online learning environments.

The book title, *Online Learning: Concepts, Strategies, and Application,* reflects the theory-into-practice methodology we adopted when we were thinking about and presenting the content. Moving from the conceptual to the concrete, Chapters 1–3 cover the theoretical, pedagogical, and technological constructs contributing to the emergence of online learning, the online learner, and the online instructor, and the ensuing research implications. In Chapters 4–7, we discuss instructional design for online learning, providing the reader with a systematic yet flexible process that capitalizes on the interaction among pedagogical models, instructional strategies, and learning technologies. This process enables novices and experts to engage in systematic, effective, and contextualized online learning design. Chapters 8–9 provide a discussion of the evolution of authoring systems—from their use in developing computer-based instruction to Web-based instruction—and the emerging nature of course management and learning management systems. This discussion provides the reader with a thorough understanding of past, present, and future instructional technologies and a comprehensive set of tools and techniques with which to select appropriate e-learning delivery applications and implement online learning in multiple contexts.

In this book, we attempt to contextualize the content to three main educational settings: higher learning, K–12 school, and corporate training. Whether you are a teacher, an instructor, a professor, an instructional developer, a trainer, an educator, an administrator, or a graduate student, *Online Learning: Concepts, Strategies, and Application* will contribute in a unique way to your understanding, implementation, and delivery of online learning. Its nine chapters and interactive companion Web site can be consulted individually or collectively according to need and context. Briefly, Chapter 1 covers the evolution of distance education from pedagogical and technological perspectives and presents a theoretical framework for thinking about online learning based on learning as a social process and the impact of globalization on sociocultural practices. Several pedagogical and technological constructs for online learning are also discussed in this chapter. In Chapter 2, we describe the roles and competencies of the online learner and the online instructor and the learning affordances and logistical and implementation challenges that learning technologies present for the learner and the instructor in online learning. The chapter also covers institutional and administrative challenges associated with online learning, including copyright and intellectual property issues as they relate to electronic media and online courses. Chapter 3 provides an overview of the current state of research on online learning and a synthesis of specific results for application and consideration in designing, developing, and supporting online learning environments.

Chapter 4 details a systematic process of design and development for online learning environments called the *Integrative Learning Design Framework for Online Learning*. This framework is grounded in the time-tested processes of traditional instructional design as well as emerging pedagogy, the result of which is an innovative and flexible process for developing online learning environments grounded in learning theory. Based on knowledge acquisition models and learning theories that have permeated the field of instructional design and technology, Chapter 5 covers constructivist-based or learner-centered pedagogical models and includes a description of their instructional characteristics and application in online learning. Moving from models to strategies, in Chapter 6, we present 13 instructional strategies that synthesize the instructional characteristics of constructivist-based pedagogical models and describe their enactment in online learning, using specific learning technologies. Chapter 7 details a systematic process for evaluating online learning based on the developer's goals and contexts. The chapter provides a review of both formal and informal evaluation examples that can inform evaluation efforts involving online learning environments.

Chapter 8 provides an overview of authoring tools, course management systems, and learning content management systems, and their past, present, and future implications for the design and development of learning content and instructional activities. The focus of Chapter 9 is specifically on course management systems. We describe their pedagogical and technological features and provide explicit examples of how these features can be used to support instructional and learning activities in online learning. The chapter also includes guidelines for selecting course management systems from both an institutional perspective and an administrative perspective.

Pedagogical Features

Each chapter contains the following pedagogical features:

- *Learning objectives:* A set of learning objectives is provided as an advance organizer for the content. Students can use these objectives as a framework for organizing their learning and as an evaluation tool for assessing their understanding after completing the chapter. These objectives can also be used as guidelines for keeping a reflective journal.
- *Authentic scenarios:* Scenarios related to the design, development, and implementation of online learning in higher education contexts, school settings, and corporate settings are provided at the beginning of each chapter. The scenarios are designed to provide real-world relevance to the chapter content and to activate prior knowledge.
- *Prompting questions:* Questions related to the scenarios are woven into the chapter text to actively engage the reader in thinking about the concepts and issues discussed.
- *Figures and tables:* Multiple figures and tables are used throughout the chapters and at the companion Web site to provide visual aids.
- *Learning activities:* The learning activities at the end of each chapter are designed to promote reflective thinking. Some are linked to the scenarios presented at the beginning of each chapter, others are linked to previous chapter content and activities, and many are linked to the Companion Website, which contains additional examples of the concepts discussed. These learning activities engage students in applying online learning concepts and strategies in real-world contexts. Students can work on them individually or collaboratively (see also the Companion Website).
- *Resources:* Online resources are provided for each chapter at the Companion Website. These resources can be used for structuring additional learning activities based on the instructor's and/or student's need and context.
- *References:* This book integrates current theory and research. An extensive list of references is provided at the end of each chapter to support further exploration and research.

Companion Website (http://www.prenhall.com/dabbagh)

Online Learning: Concepts, Strategies, and Application has an interactive Companion Website designed to engage the student in active and reflective thinking. The Website content is related to Chapters 2, 3, 5, 6, and 9. The learning activities at the end of these chapters require the student(s) to visit the Companion Website, browse interactive tables, download portable document format (PDF) files that contain instructions on how to conduct specific activities, and examine a variety of instructional contexts and their implementation in online learning. For example, 20 scenarios or instructional challenges at the Companion Website are related to the content in Chapter 5. These scenarios are divided into three categories: higher education, K–12, and corporate. The student can select a scenario that best fits his or her context and explore a "solved" scenario, or "solve" a scenario, engaging in the design of online learning. The solution examples or "solved" scenarios are Web-based prototypes of constructivist-based pedagogical models that have been implemented by using a variety of online learning technologies. For Chapter 6, a comprehensive interactive table presents the 13 instructional strategies discussed in this chapter and their implementation using the features and components of WebCT, Blackboard, Lotus LearningSpace, and Virtual-U. A similar interactive table is designed for use with Chapter 9. This table allows the reader to browse the features and components of course management systems and to view a description of these features and related instructional examples. Tables that provide additional detail on the research studies related to online learning reviewed in Chapter 3 provide the opportunity for the reader to compare, contrast, and evaluate a sample of the research in this area. The Companion Website is designed to promote meaningful interaction with chapter content and to assist the course instructor in facilitating a variety of online learning activities.

Glossary

This book has a glossary of more than 200 words, which facilitates easy access to the pedagogical and technological concepts discussed in the chapters.

ACKNOWLEDGMENTS

Numerous students enrolled in the Instructional Technology program at George Mason University contributed in vital ways to the completion of this book. Their research skills, instructional design skills, Web development skills, and thoughtful critiques and feedback on chapter content have undoubtedly raised the pedagogical value of the book. Specifically, we thank Dianne Battle for her outstanding work on the Companion Website of this book; her contributions to the learning activities provided at the end of Chapters 2, 5, 6, and 9; her comprehensive research on copyright and intellectual property; and her insightful remarks on several chapters while they were in the making. We also thank Marcella Simon for her valuable detailed and informed editing of Chapters 4 and 7; Monique Lynch, who, with her initial research, assembly, and organization of resources, provided us with the impetus to get started; Todd Jamieson and Jennifer Korjus, who assisted in reviewing the studies for Chapter 3; and Trista Schoonmaker, who offered insights and valuable suggestions on an early version of Chapter 4. We thank Lynn Salvo for her thoughtful critique of Chapter 5; Lisa Saavedra for her book design recommendations and graphics illustrations; and Chantal Byer for her initial synthesis of the instructional characteristics of constructivist-based pedagogical models.

Thanks also to Susan Akers, Sue Sarber, Hasan Altalib, Kristin Percy-Calaff, Greta Ballard, Zeena Altalib, Margie Joyce, Nechele Hill, Paula Richardson, Lisa Prillaman, Tina Minor, Jacqueline Austin, Jennifer Korjus, Claudette Archambeault, Kate Denisar,

Richard Boyden, Ruihua Dong, Abed Almala, Patricia Gilbert, Dianne Battle, Charlotte Barner, Janie Dunfee, Kim Davenport, Pam Tiffany, Chantal Byer, LaJuanda Desmukes, and Colby Chambers Howell, all of whom contributed exemplary real-world instructional scenarios and associated Web-based prototype solutions. We appreciate the work of Maryam Al-Ali, Dana Bazin, Timothy Brannon, Karen Carter, Steve Craig, Cheryl Feldmeier, Cathy Hubbs, Frankie Jones, Elizabeth McCoy, Jill McCoy, Ansheng Qin, Cecilia Reardon, and Clare Torrans, who carefully analyzed Web-based authoring tools and course management systems products and features. Likewise, we extend our gratitude to Claudette Allen, Cindy Johannessen, Deena Mansoor, Shawn Miller, Robert Moss, Rob Parrott, Trista Schoonmaker, and Lisa Stedge, who provided outstanding examples of personae in Chapter 4 and provided much moral support. In addition, we thank Brenda Mueller for listening, understanding, and providing supportive comments.

Special thanks go to Debbie Stollenwerk, our editor, for her patience, guidance, and support as we struggled through our first experience of writing a book, and to the following reviewers, whose comments were often right on the mark: Gerald L. Gutek, Tom Bonvillain, Nicholls State University; Andrew J. Brovey, Valdosta State University; Ken Digby, Fayetteville Technical Community College; Leticia Ekhaml, State University of West Georgia; Schott Fredrickson, University of Nebraska at Kearney; Joan Hanor, California State University-San Marcos; R. Donald Hardy, Troy State University; John Hollenbeck, Old Dominion University; Nancy Knupfer, Kansas State University; Barbara Ludlow, West Virginia University; S. Kim MacGregor, Louisiana State University; Ron McBride, Northwestern State University; Carmen L. McCrink, Barry University; Sara McNeil, University of Houston; Kay Persichutte, University of Northern Colorado; Farhad Saba, San Diego State University; Shannon Scanlon, Henry Ford Community College; James A. Shuff, Henderson State University; Colleen Swain, University of Florida; and David VanEsselstyn, Columbia University.

BRIEF CONTENTS

CONTENTS

WHAT IS ONLINE LEARNING?

1

After completing this chapter, you should understand the following:

- The differences among traditional learning environments, traditional distance learning environments, and current distance learning environments

- The implications of globalization and learning as a social process on distance learning

- Pedagogical models or constructs of distance learning, such as open, or flexible, learning; distributed learning; learning communities; communities of practice; and knowledge-building communities

- The attributes and key components of online learning

- Learning technologies or delivery applications of online learning, such as asynchronous learning networks, virtual classrooms, knowledge networks, knowledge portals, tele-learning, and Web-based instruction

- The various delivery modes of online learning

CONSIDER THE FOLLOWING THREE SCENARIOS:

A Cost-Effective Training Solution: An international voice communications company that manufactures and sells cellular telephones needs to train its sales force, which consists of 1,500 employees worldwide, on the use of its newly designed cellular phone and corresponding market plan. An **electronic performance support system (EPSS)** that uses **Internet** and Web-based technologies is developed to facilitate this training event. Salespeople can access this electronic system through the Internet, as needed, to download job aids that explain the new and improved functions of this cellular phone and associated promotional marketing plans. Salespeople can also ask questions by means of e-mail, obtain expert advice through teleconferencing, view video demonstrations, and explore appropriate resources to help them effectively market the new phone at their prospective retail outlets and sales areas. What type of learning environment is this? How does it differ from traditional training settings?

Scholarly Exchange at a Distance: Three high school teachers in three geographic areas of the United States decide to collaborate on a presentation proposal for an internationally renowned conference on educational communications and technology. To facilitate this collaboration and document ideas in one accessible and shared location, one teacher sets up an exclusive **asynchronous discussion forum** using Blackboard's[1] free **courseware** site and e-mails the URL to her colleagues. The three teachers bookmark the URL and begin discussing their ideas online. After about 3 weeks, a presentation proposal outline emerges as a result of the discussion, and the writing process begins. The teachers continue to post drafts of the proposal to the site until the final proposal is complete. What type of learning environment is this? What is different about the nature of communication that was enabled by this technology?

A Tale of Two Institutions: Two faculty members teaching courses in **instructional design (ID)** at two geographically distant higher education institutions decide to conduct research on the impact of external versus internal student collaboration on solving ID cases. Group discussion and presentation areas are set up by using WebCT (a **course management system**) to facilitate this process. Students in each course are divided into groups of three or four and assigned an ID case to solve. The ID case is posted to each group's presentation area in WebCT. Each group is asked to access the case online, prepare its solution, and post the solution to the designated group area in WebCT. The groups are then randomly paired either with a group at the peer institution (outside, or external, collaboration) or with a group in their class (inside, or internal, collaboration). Each group is asked to review the other group's case solution and engage in a week-long online discussion with the other group to critique each other's solutions. Would this type of research be possible without the use of online learning technologies? Do online learning technologies promote instructional activities that differ from those typically found in face-to-face classroom environments?

---

[1] Blackboard Inc. is a Washington, DC–based company that provides Blackboard, a course management system for delivering and managing online courses and interactions.

Before proceeding, reflect momentarily on the preceding scenarios. Do you think these scenarios represent examples of online learning environments? What are some of the characteristics of these learning environments? What do you think differentiates online learning environments from traditional face-to-face instruction or training?

In this chapter, we discuss the issues evoked by these questions. We also discuss additional theoretical, pedagogical, social, and technological constructs that have been instrumental in shaping our understanding of **online learning** environments.

INTRODUCTION

Online **learning environments** have radically changed the way individuals learn. Internet connectivity and the universal browser protocol of the **World Wide Web (WWW)** have paved the way to widespread collaborative activities and information-sharing capabilities that until only a few years ago were not perceived possible. How have these new technologies impacted the way practitioners design instruction? What distinguishes online learning environments from other, more *classic,* or traditional, learning environments? To understand the concepts and principles underlying online learning, we need to look at **traditional, or conventional, learning environments,** such as face-to-face, or classroom, learning; distance education in its classic form; and earlier uses of computer technology to facilitate the teaching and learning process. In this chapter, we first discuss the general characteristics and themes that permeate traditional learning environments. Then, we focus on specific instructional models that emerged as a result of advances in **Internet-based technologies** and changes in sociocultural structures and practices, which have led to the present state of online learning.

TRADITIONAL LEARNING ENVIRONMENTS

Numerous examples of student-centered classroom learning environments can be found, in which students are actively engaged in the learning process and assume primary responsibility for their learning. However, traditional face-to-face learning environments have long been associated with classroom instruction in which the teacher is the expert, the main deliverer of knowledge, and the sole assessor of student learning. The setting centers around an authoritative and knowledgeable figure entrusted with imparting reliable knowledge to students and assessing students' mastery of knowledge through tests and other observable and measurable behaviors. Each classroom is perceived as a self-contained and isolated curricular unit, and **interaction** is limited to this unit (Kearsley, 2000). Content is generally sequenced linearly from the instructor's viewpoint, and each student receives the same instruction at the same pace within the same context (Dabbagh, 1996). Instruction therefore takes the form of a **directed approach,** in which the teacher is using methods grounded in behavioral and early cognitive **learning theory** to teach students an "identifiable body of knowledge" (M. J. Hannafin, Hill, & Land, 1997; Kearsley, 2000). The specific characteristics of the directed approach, or what is alternatively known as **directed learning environments,** are discussed next.

Directed Learning Environments

M. J. Hannafin et al. (1997) identified 10 characteristics of directed learning environments that embody conventional instructional approaches typically found in both face-to-face classroom learning and classic forms of **computer-assisted instruction (CAI).** In these researchers' view, directed learning environments reflect an **objectivist epistemology,** in which learning is driven by externally generated objectives (objectives generated independently of the learner) and by explicit activities and practice, with the goal of transmitting a discrete and well-defined body of knowledge. Content is therefore separated from the contexts in which it naturally occurs and is structured according to tasks, objectives, and prerequisites. Teaching and learning proceeds in a bottom-up manner, or what is commonly referred to as *basics first*. These characteristics suggest that directed learning environments are teacher centered and are guided by prescriptive **instructional strategies,** with the goal of mastery of content demonstrated through observable and measurable outcomes in student learning.

Characteristics of Directed Versus Web-Based Learning Environments

Traditional, or directed, learning environments can also be described as bounded (well defined), happening in real time, and relying on stable information resources (Chambers, 1997). Chambers (1997) identified seven facets of traditional learning environments and contrasted them with seven facets of Web-based learning environments that emphasize the uniqueness of the Web for learning (see Table 1.1).

Table 1.1   Characteristics of the Web as a Learning Environment Versus Those of Traditional Learning Environments

TRADITIONAL LEARNING ENVIRONMENTS	WEB-BASED LEARNING ENVIRONMENT
Bounded	Unbounded
Real time	Time shifts: asynchronous communications and accelerated cycles
Instructor controlled	Decentralized control
Linear	Hypermedia: multidimensional space, linked navigation, multimedia
Juried, edited sources	Unfiltered searchability
Stable information sources	Dynamic, real-time information
Familiar technology	Continuously evolving technology

Note. Data from *Why the Web? Linkages*, by M. Chambers, 1997. Paper presented at The Potential of the Web, Institute for Distance Education, University of Maryland University College, Adelphi, MD.

The characteristics of traditional learning environments listed in the first column of Table 1.1 are typical of a face-to-face, lecture-based (or classic) classroom setting, in which learners are passive recipients of information and the learning context is structured according to the instructor's viewpoint of the content and the stable information resources provided. Interaction is generally limited to learner–instructor and learner–content interaction, with minimal learner–learner interaction.

TRADITIONAL DISTANCE LEARNING ENVIRONMENTS

Correspondence Study

Traditional distance learning environments possess characteristics similar to those of directed learning environments, except for the face-to-face attribute, because the teacher and the learner are physically separated during the learning process. Traditional distance learning environments began with print-based correspondence courses more than 100 years ago (Galusha, 1997; Picciano, 2001; Schrum, 1999). The practice was known as **correspondence study,** or **extension courses,** and was established initially in Europe, crossing the Atlantic in 1873 (Schlosser & Simonson, 2003). "The original target groups of distance education efforts were adults with occupational, social and family commitments," and the focus was on "individuality of learning and flexibility in both time and place of study" (Hanson et al., 1997, p. 4). Guided readings, frequent tests, and free pacing of progress through the program by the student were key elements of traditional, or classic, settings of distance education.

Correspondence study courses were delivered primarily through print media, with the content segmented into manageable units to provide structure and ensure success. Correspondence study courses benefited from the planning, guidance, and pedagogical practices of an educational organization without being under the continuous and immediate supervision of tutors present with their students in lecture rooms or on the premises. Moore (1994) referred to this type of correspondence study as "nonautonomous," or "teacher determined," and gauged the degree of learner autonomy by determining how much guidance a learner needs to formulate objectives, identify sources of information, and measure objectives. Moore noted that in most conventional educational programs, resident or distance, the learner depends substantially on the teacher for guidance, and the teacher is active whereas the student is passive.

Independent Study

In another version of traditional distance learning settings, the program is more responsive to students' needs and goals, and the student "accepts a high degree of responsibility for the conduct of the learning program" (Hanson et al., 1997, p. 9). Moore (1994) and Wedemeyer (1981) preferred to use the term **independent study** for such programs, acknowledging a very important characteristic of distance education: the student's independence. The concept of student independence and autonomy continues to be a distinguishing feature between conventional and more innovative educational settings and a critical factor in designing effective distance learning environments (See Chapter 2).

The Nature of Interaction

Another distinguishing feature of traditional distance learning environments is the absence of face-to-face interaction with teachers and peers. Although several telecommunications technologies such as audio- and **videoconferencing** have enabled a simulated human interaction learning context, the absence of face-to-face interaction in classic distance education settings has been identified as one of the main causes of loss of student motivation in such learning contexts. Such loss of motivation has led to attrition, particularly in Internet-based courses (Galusha, 1997). In addition, some educators view the introduction of educational telecommunications systems as "an imposition that diminishes human interaction in instruction and learning undermining an essential element in the quality of the educational experience" (Duning, Van Kekerix, & Zabrowski, 1993, p. 19). A similar perspective on interaction is echoed by distance learning students who report feelings of alienation and isolation and believe that "the *distance* aspect of distance learning takes away much of the social interactions that would be present in traditional learning environments" (Galusha, 1997, p. 9). Nevertheless, we believe that recent advances in **telecommunications technology,** if used with a rethinking of the teaching and learning process, can help balance the human and technical considerations of distance learning environments and reach the learners who may become disinterested as a result of the lack of face-to-face interaction with teachers and peers.

EVOLUTION OF DISTANCE LEARNING ENVIRONMENTS

Along with technology, distance learning environments have changed significantly throughout the years from theoretical, pedagogical, and cultural perspectives. These changes seem to coincide with the changes and advances in learning technologies, which makes separating the impact of technology on the teaching and learning process difficult. Such coinciding changes also support the argument that technology is not neutral but brings with it its own **affordances** (possibilities for action) and implications, which open up new occasions with unforeseen consequences. Supporters of this view argue that each medium has a unique set of characteristics and that understanding the ways in which students use the capabilities of the medium is essential to understanding the influence of the medium on learning and on building media theory (Kozma, 1994). For example, telecommunications technology has shifted the educational dynamic from focusing on the individual to focusing on a group, if you look at current trends in educational uses of technology in which the emphasis is on collaborative and multicultural pedagogies (LeCourt, 1999). To better understand the current trends in educational uses of technology, we must look at how technology was first used in the teaching and learning process.

Technology, Teaching, and Learning

The development of CAI programs When computers were introduced to the teaching and learning process about four decades ago, their main purpose was to provide individualized learning experiences, to help learners progress at their own pace, and to provide empirical evidence of knowledge acquisition (Kearsley, 2000). Concern for individualized learning, self-pacing, immediate knowledge of the correctness of a response, and **reinforcement** led to the proliferation of CAI programs that followed ID patterns and methodologies grounded in principles of behaviorist learning theory. The impact of **behaviorism** on educational technology began to manifest in the 1950s, when **programmed instruction (PI)** was adopted as a pedagogical construct for implementing behaviorist principles of operant conditioning (Saettler, 1990). These principles included exposing learners to small chunks of stimulus material, requiring an overt response, and providing immediate feedback on the correctness of the response as reinforcement. Drill and practice rehearsal strategies were considered critical for achieving competent behavior, with the understanding that competency is based on mastery of the desired learning goal. Some educators described CAI as the logical offshoot of PI, identifying similar trends between the two instructional programs with respect to the underlying prescriptive instructional pedagogy (McMeen, 1985; Stevens, 1981). CAI was perceived as a more effective and efficient technology for implementing this pedagogy, and the need for carefully designed instructional materials became paramount, which paved the way for the more formal and systematic process of developing instruction known as *instructional design.*

The instructional applications of microcomputers dominated much of the ID literature in the 1980s, but positions regarding the impact of this powerful technology on teaching and learning were poles apart (Shrock, 1995). Some practitioners considered this technology as a vehicle to automate the delivery of instruction, whereas others saw it as opening up possibilities to implement the philosophies of cognitive psychology, "shifting the emphasis from a strictly behaviorist view with its emphasis on external behavior to a concern with internal mental processes and their enhancement in learning and instruction" (Saettler, 1990, p. 322). Several efforts were made to design more learner-centered CAI by capitalizing on the principle of **hypertext** to promote **pedagogical constructs** such as **learner control** and **interactivity,** and by incorporating intelligent tutoring and expert systems to design more engaging applications such as **simulations** and **microworlds.** Nevertheless, CAI continued to be plagued with the labor- and cost-intensive nature of instructional software design and development. Even with the increased availability of high-level authoring systems that simplified the development process (see Chapter 8), **pedagogical control** (the extent to which the user can meaningfully and consistently communicate with the system) has often been sacrificed. The result has been CAI described as too passive for meaningful learning (K. M. Hannafin & Mitzel, 1990; Sims, 1995). Classic forms of CAI can therefore be characterized as having attributes similar to those of traditional, or directed, learning environments. In addition, as is the case with classic forms of distance learning, interaction in classic forms of CAI was generally limited to learner–content (or learner–program) interaction, with practice and feedback activities built into the software.

The development of electronic networks   The 1990s was the age of networks: local area networks, wide area networks, client–server computing, the Internet, and, finally, the WWW. **Hypermedia, computer-mediated communication (CMC), and Web-based authoring tools** were among the innovative technologies that would ultimately change the nature of delivering instruction. With the move to Internet and Web-based technologies was a growing realization that traditional teaching techniques would not work in Internet-supported distance education settings (Thach & Murphy, 1995). In traditional distance education settings, the focus was primarily on the individual, and the "quasi-permanent absence of the learning group" was evident meaning that people were usually taught as individuals and not in groups, with only the possibility of occasional meetings for didactic and socialization purposes; (Keegan, 1990, p. 44). In addition, the learning need was based on a geographic distance that prohibited the individual from enrolling as a resident student in an academic institution.

With Internet connectivity, telecommunications technology increased the potential for interaction and collaborative work, which was difficult to achieve with previous forms of distance education (Riel & Harasim, 1994). Interaction took on a new meaning, extending beyond learner–teacher, learner–content, and learner–program modes to learner–learner and learner–group modes. Such new modes collapsed Keegan's condition of the quasi-permanent absence of the learning group in distance learning. The concept of *distance* became relatively unimportant or blurred (i.e., not limited to the physical separation of the learner and the instructor), which challenged the traditional definitions of distance education. **Pedagogical models** or constructs, such as **open, or flexible, learning; distributed learning; learning communities; communities of practice;** and **knowledge-building communities** (all of which are defined later in this chapter), began emerging. Their emergence prompted the reconceptualization of distance learning. Two underlying principles or concepts played an important role in this development: *globalization* and *learning as a social process*. We elaborate on these two principles next.

Globalization and Its Impact on Distance Learning

Globalization can be described as a psychological phenomenon that can be applied to many contexts to imply that most people are connected simultaneously with distant events, directly or indirectly, intentionally or unintentionally, which promotes a perception or an awareness of the globe as a single environment (Evans, 1995). Terms such as *the information revolution* and *the end of geography* underlie this somewhat ambiguous concept and give rise to two discrete dimensions of the concept: (a) increasing or stretching the scope of an activity, and (b) deepening the interconnectedness of an activity (Walker & Fox, 2000). For example, in multinational corporations, economic activities are stretched across the world as geographic constraints recede and economic relationships intensify, in the sense that increased interconnectedness makes the distinction between domestic and worldwide economic activity difficult to sustain and creates a new global capitalist order that exercises decisive influence over the organization

(Held & McGrew, 2002). In brief, globalization can be thought of as "the widening, intensifying, speeding up, and growing impact of world-wide interconnectedness" (Held & McGrew, n.d.).

The cultural and technological preconditions for globalization were not in place until the late 1970s and early 1980s. Evans (1995) argued that "globalization is not a technical outcome of the development and implementation of communications and transport technologies; rather it is a social, economic, political and cultural outcome" (p. 258), which has radically changed the way people view, understand, and engage the world in which they live. Therefore, both the technological and the sociocultural structures and practices of society had to evolve for globalization to take on its new meaning in the information age. With these preconditions now firmly in place, the modern meaning of *globalization* implies a global perspective of the particular area of study, a perspective that arises from the increased interdependence of technological advances and sociocultural changes.

Telecommunications technology has played a significant role in realizing this modern meaning of the concept, particularly with regard to distance learning. Recent advances in telecommunications technology have redefined the boundaries and interactional pedagogies of a traditional, or classic, distance learning environment by stretching its scope and deepening its interconnectedness. New learning interactions that were not perceived possible before can now be facilitated, such as pairing experts from around the world with novices, accessing global resources, publishing to a world audience, taking virtual field trips, communicating with a wider range of people, and having the ability to share and compare information, negotiate meaning, and co-construct knowledge. These activities emphasize learning as a function of interactions with others and with the shared tools of the community, which brings us to the second principle or concept prompting the reconceptualization of distance education: *learning as a social process.*

Learning as a Social Process and Its Impact on Distance Learning

Learning can be viewed as a social process in which social interaction plays an integral part and the emphasis is on acquiring useful knowledge through **enculturation** (understanding how knowledge is used by a group of practitioners or members of a community). The socialization of knowledge is based on the idea that knowledge is always under construction (fluid, dynamic), taking on new meanings relative to the activity and situations in which it is being explored (Brown, Collins, & Duguid, 1989). In other words, a social framework or culture surrounds a learning context, and its constituents are the learners, the interactions that these learners engage in, and the tools that enable such interactions. This social framework forms a community of practice in which knowledge is shared and distributed among its constituents.

The concept of the social framework within which knowledge is constructed is rooted in the epistemological perspective of social constructivism. **Social constructivism** is largely attributed to Vygotsky's approach to developmental psychology, in which Vygotsky argued that children develop in social or group settings, thus learning is a socially mediated activity (Maddux, Johnson, & Willis, 2001). Vygotsky emphasized that interaction with people is critically important to cognitive development and that the cognitive tools—such as the language, cultural history, and social context—that a culture gives a child to further his or her development are also important.

Knowledge in this context is perceived as belonging to, and distributed in, communities of practice or *environments of participation* in which the learner practices the patterns of inquiry and learning. The use of shared resources is part of the preparation for membership in a particular community (Firdyiwek, 1999). This view of knowledge is known as **distributed cognition** or **situated cognition.** It is also known as *cultural knowledge, social knowledge,* and *social cognition.* Rather than being thought of as an isolated event that occurs inside a person's head, cognition is perceived as a distributed phenomenon—one that goes beyond the boundaries of a person to include environment, artifacts, social interactions, and culture (Hutchins & Hollan, 1999; Rogers, 1997). Inherent in the concept of distributed cognition is the idea that "an object has a certain kind of intelligence or the context has a certain kind of knowledge" allowing learners or members of a community of practice to complete their tasks more easily (Dede, 2002).

For example, the navigational system goal of a U.S. Navy amphibious transport helicopter would be to successfully steer the ship into a harbor. Because this system is not relative to a single person but to a distributed collection of interacting people and artifacts (tools) that form a single cognitive system, it can be understood only "as a unity, the contributions of the individual agents in the system and the coordination among the agents to enact the goal" (Nardi, 1996, p. 77), which, in this case, is to achieve a successful and safe entry into the harbor. Therefore, a main principle of distributed or situated cognition is to understand the coordination among individuals and artifacts (how individuals align and interact within a distributed process) in a system or a community.

In educational settings, these distributed forms of interaction manifest in learner–instructor interaction, learner–content interaction, and learner–learner interaction (Moore, 1989; Moore & Kearsley, 1995). These types of interactions are perceived as necessary for enhancing social learning skills such as communication or group-process skills. They are also perceived as tools or activities that promote higher order thinking and sustain motivation in distance education settings (Navarro & Shoemaker, 2000). In Internet- or Web-enabled learning environments, distributed forms of interaction (or distributed learning) can occur in knowledge networks, virtual classrooms or communities, and asynchronous learning networks (all of which are defined later in this chapter), where groups of learners or professionals with a common goal congregate to share information and resources, ask questions, solve problems, and achieve goals, and, in doing so, collectively build new knowledge and evolve the practices of their community. These distributed forms of interaction are made possible by telecommunications technologies, which, as described previously, are fundamentally responsible for increasing the interconnectedness and scope of interactions and activities and providing a global perspective on a particular area of study.

The first scenario described at the beginning of this chapter is an example of a knowledge network. The 1,500 salespeople are able to download job aids and marketing plans, ask questions, and communicate with one another to coordinate efforts and fulfill the goal of selling the new cellular telephone. The second scenario, Scholarly Exchange at a Distance, is an example of an asynchronous learning network. The teachers from the three high schools are communicating asynchronously through the use of Internet-based tools to achieve a shared goal.

Distributed forms of interaction can also be used to supplement face-to-face instructional activities, which brings to the forefront an important distinction between a course as a whole that subscribes to these interactions and the notion of "distributed course events," which poses complex challenges for the course designer (Dabbagh, 2000; Dede, 2002). A *distributed course* is a course in which one or more of the instructional events that have traditionally occurred in the classroom are distributed to learners so that the events may occur while the learners are separated by either time or space from one another and the course instructor (Locatis & Weisberg, 1997). Therefore, learning can occur at the same time in different places (e.g., through scheduled videoconferencing events), at different times in the same place (e.g., meeting face-to-face in the classroom to attend guest lectures), or at different times in different places (e.g., using e-mail to communicate with the instructor and with one another). Learning is distributed across space, time, and various media (including face-to-face interaction). Unlike classic distance education settings, in which teaching learners from a distance, is specifically addressed, distributed courses are not designed solely to deliver instruction to distant learners. An example of this phenomenon is the third scenario described at the beginning of this chapter. Students meet face-to-face in their respective classrooms at each school and interact with learners at different times in different places, using various media.

Summary

In summary, learning as a social process emphasizes meaningful activity through social interaction. Telecommunications technology has increased the interconnectedness of activity and interaction and has stretched their scope, which has led to the evolution of the technological and sociocultural structures and practices of modern society and the emergence of a psychological phenomenon known as globalization. Learning as a social process and globalization are inextricably linked, which provides a viable thesis with which to rethink or reconceptualize distance learning. In essence, the principles of learning as a social process and globalization have redefined the boundaries of traditional distance learning environments and the interactional pedagogies possible.

DISTANCE LEARNING REVISITED

On the basis of the preceding discussion, we conceptualize **distance learning** as the deliberate organization and coordination of distributed forms of interaction and learning activities to achieve a shared goal. The following five attributes apply to this definition:

1. Globalization and learning as a social process are inherent and enabled through telecommunications technology.
2. The concept of a learning group is fundamental to achieving and sustaining learning.
3. The concept of distance is relatively unimportant or blurred and is not limited to the physical separation of the learner and the instructor.
4. Teaching and learning events (or course events) are distributed across time and place, occurring synchronously and/or asynchronously through different media.
5. Learners are engaged in multiple forms of interaction: learner–learner, learner–group, learner–content, and learner–instructor.

Next, we define the five closely related pedagogical models or constructs that may be used interchangeably with this operational definition of distance learning.

Open (or Flexible) Learning

Open, or flexible, learning is a new approach to describing distance education in which the emphasis shifts from delivering a preestablished curriculum to focusing on individual and local needs and requirements, and creating open learning places based on the here and now (Edwards, 1995). Key principles of open learning are student centeredness and a focus on learning rather than on teaching (The Open University, 2002). Open learning provides students with flexibility and choice in meeting their educational goals. It can include a variety of nontraditional learning opportunities, such as short courses, night courses, workshops, seminars, conferences, certificate programs, customized training packages, and degree–credit and noncredit distance education courses (University of Guelph, 2003). Examples of open, or flexible, learning environments that rely on the use of Internet-based communications technologies include **knowledge networks**, **knowledge portals,** asynchronous learning networks, virtual classrooms, and **telelearning**, which are defined later in this chapter.

Distributed Learning

Distributed learning is described as education delivered anytime, anywhere, to multiple locations, by using one or more technologies—or none (Jones Knowledge, 2000). When telecommunications media are used, distributed learning refers to off-site learning environments in which learners complete courses and programs at home or work by communicating with faculty and other students through e-mail, electronic forums, videoconferences, and other forms of computer-mediated communication and Internet and Web-based technologies. According to The California State University Center for Distributed Learning (2003), distributed learning supports a "pull" model of education, in which students engage in learning activities at their own pace and at a self-selected time, in contrast to the traditional "push" model of education, in which students must synchronize their needs and schedules to the delivery model of the institution. From a pedagogical standpoint, distributed learning environments "result in a diffuse sense of cognition—where what is known lies in the interaction between individuals and artifacts, such as computers and other technological devices" (Pea, 1990; Perkins, 1990; Salomon, 1990, cited in Bronack & Riedl, 1998, p. 3).

Learning Communities

Learning communities are groups of people who support one another with regard to meeting their learning agendas, working together on projects, learning from one another as well as from their environment, and engaging in a collective sociocultural experience in which participation is transformed into a new experience or new learning (Rogoff, 1994; Wilson & Ryder, 1998). Learning communities represent an intentional **restructuring** of students' time, credit, and learning experiences around an interdisciplinary theme to foster more explicit intellectual and emotional connections among students, between students and their faculty, and among disciplines (MacGregor, Smith, Tinto, & Levine, 1999). These communities act as academic and social support structures that allow students to learn in more authentic and challenging ways. Learning communities are considered informal learning environments; the emphasis is moved from teaching to learning. Communities of practice and knowledge-building communities are synonymous constructs. However, the term *learning communities* may be perceived as a broader or more loosely defined term that encompasses any social network or infrastructure that brings people together to share and pursue knowledge.

Communities of Practice

Communities of practice are "groups of people informally bound together by shared expertise and passion for a joint enterprise" (Wenger & Snyder, 2000, p. 139). This construct has become popular in the business community and in organizations that focus on knowledge as intellectual capital. Communities of practice differ from formal work groups or project teams in that they are defined by knowledge rather than by task, and members are self-selecting rather than assigned by a higher authority (Allee, 2000). In addition, what holds a community of practice together across time is its members' interest in maintaining the group and not project deadlines or job requirements. With time, the activity and actions of the individuals engaged in the enterprise give rise to new and specific practices and processes that all members of the community can share. When the common purpose is learning, communities of practice can be described as "shared environments that permit sustained exploration by students and teachers enabling them to understand the kinds of problems and opportunities that experts in various areas encounter and the knowledge that these experts use as tools" (Cognition and Technology Group at Vanderbilt, 1992, p. 79).

Knowledge-Building Communities

Knowledge-building communities are learning communities in which communication is perceived as *transformative* (resulting in a new experience or learning) through knowledge sharing and generation. Participants in a knowledge-building community "share a common goal of building meaningful knowledge representations through activities, projects and discussion," and the instructor or tutor "is an active, learning participant in the community" (Selinger & Pearson, 1999, p. 41). A common goal of knowledge-building communities is to advance and share the knowledge of the collective. Research teams in the scientific disciplines provide a prototypical example, although knowledge-building communities can also exist in other forms such as film societies or industrial firms. What is defining about a knowledge-building community is a commitment among its members to invest its resources in the collective pursuit of understanding (Hewitt, Brett, Scardamalia, Frecker, & Webb, 1995).

Take a moment and think of the three scenarios presented at the beginning of this chapter. Do any of the pedagogical models or constructs just defined apply to these scenarios? Perhaps the first scenario, A Cost-Effective Training Solution, is an example of open, or flexible, learning, or distributed learning. What about the other two scenarios? Do you think the second scenario is an example of a knowledge-building community? What about the third scenario? Write down your responses and rationales because this question will be revisited subsequently in the chapter.

DISTANCE LEARNING AND TELECOMMUNICATIONS TECHNOLOGIES

Distance learning in its broadest sense can be implemented through the application of various technologies, including audio; video; and computer, or digital, technologies. Of particular interest in this section are the technologies within each of these categories that foster interaction. For example, in the audio category, audioconferencing and audiographics provide interactive capabilities between instructor and student, and between student and student (Picciano, 2001). *Audioconferencing* technology connects various sites or parties simultaneously through telephone message–handling equipment. *Audiographics* can supplement this communication with **graphics** through electronic blackboards or document cameras that transmit images or drawings through the audio connection.

In the video category, videoconferencing, or teleconferencing, "provides all the benefits of [educational] television and also allows the audience or students to interact in real time with the instructor and other students," closely approximating the interaction in a traditional classroom environment (Picciano, 2001, p. 56). Videoconferencing is now also available on desktop computers so that interaction can be extended to include audiences at various locations.

Computer, or digital, technologies include several interactive technologies, such as CD-ROM software; networked software that can run on a local area network (LAN), a wide area network (WAN), or the Internet; and Internet or Web-based technologies that include various tools and applications to support the teaching and learning process.

Examples of Internet and/or Web-based technologies include the following: hypertext and hypermedia; asynchronous and **synchronous communication tools**, such as e-mail, Listservs, bulletin boards, desktop videoconferencing, virtual chat, and **groupware** (multiuser software that enables **synchronous** and asynchronous communication and document sharing and production); digital and streaming audio and video and other rich media; file transfer protocols; **search engines**; Web development tools; and course management systems. In Chapter 2, we describe these technologies in more detail.

Our focus in this book is on Internet and Web-based technologies that enable the design, development, and delivery of distance learning. We refer to these technologies as *learning technologies* or *pedagogical tools*. When several learning technologies are integrated under a single system or tool, the result is often a technological infrastructure or delivery model that supports a variety of interactions and learning activities. Examples of these broader or integrated learning technologies include knowledge networks, knowledge portals, asynchronous learning networks, telelearning, virtual classrooms, and **Web-based instruction, (WBI)** which are defined later in this chapter. We use the term *online learning* to refer to distance learning environments that use Internet and/or Web-based technologies to support the teaching and learning process. One important point to note is that *online learning* can be used synonymously with *e-learning, e-training, cybereducation*, and other similar and emergent constructs used to refer to Internet or Web-based learning, instruction, and education. We define online learning in the next section.

ONLINE LEARNING

Online learning is an open and distributed learning environment that uses pedagogical tools, enabled by Internet and Web-based technologies, to facilitate learning and knowledge building through meaningful action and interaction.

So, in addition to the five attributes of distance learning listed previously, we now add a sixth attribute to support this definition:

6. Internet and/or Web-based technologies are used to support the teaching and learning process and to facilitate learning and knowledge building through meaningful action and interaction.

To review, we provide a list of the six attributes that support the preceding definition of online learning.

The Six Attributes of Online Learning

1. Globalization and learning as a social process are inherent and enabled through telecommunications technology.
2. The concept of a learning group is fundamental to achieving and sustaining learning.
3. The concept of distance is relatively unimportant or blurred and is not limited to the physical separation of the learner and the instructor.
4. Teaching and learning events (or course events) are distributed across time and place, occurring synchronously and/or asynchronously through different media.
5. Learners are engaged in multiple forms of interaction: learner–learner, learner–group, learner–content, and learner–instructor.
6. Internet and/or Web-based technologies are used to support the teaching and learning process and to facilitate learning and knowledge building through meaningful action and interaction.

Key Components of Online Learning

Essentially, three key components of online learning work collectively to foster meaningful learning and interaction: (a) pedagogical models or constructs, (b) instructional and learning strategies, and (c) pedagogical tools, or **online learning technologies** (i.e., Internet and Web-based technologies). These three components form an iterative relationship in which pedagogical models or constructs based on learning as a social process inform the design of online learning environments, which leads to the specification of instructional and learning strategies that are subsequently enabled or enacted through the use of learning technologies (see Figure 1.1). Furthermore, as online learning tech-

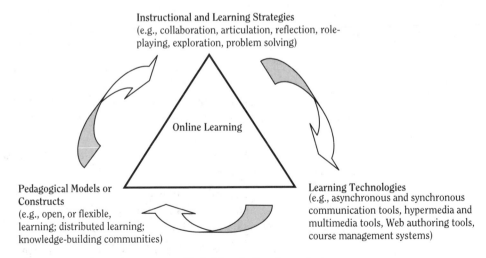

Figure 1.1   Three-Component Model for Online Learning

nologies become more ubiquitous and new technologies continue to emerge, bringing forth new affordances (possibilities for action), pedagogical practices and social structures are transformed. Therefore, the **three-component model for online learning** in Figure 1.1 suggests a transformative interaction affecting online learning. Educators and instructional designers can think of this model as a conceptual framework that guides the design of online learning environments. In Chapter 4, we specifically address how this model forms the core of the Integrative Learning Design Framework for Online Learning. In Chapter 5, we address pedagogical models and their application in online learning. Chapter 6 covers instructional and learning strategies and their application in online learning. In Chapters 2, 8, and 9, we address learning technologies from a variety of perspectives.

To help explain how the key components of online learning interact as depicted in Figure 1.1, we revisit the scenarios presented at the beginning of this chapter. The first scenario, A Cost-Effective Training Solution, can be most closely aligned with the pedagogical model or construct of open, or flexible, learning because the focus of the training is on individual and local needs and requirements rather than the delivery of a preestablished curriculum. The communications company developed a customized training package that fits the needs of its employees, delivering anytime, anywhere training. The electronic performance support system (EPSS) is essentially a knowledge network at its core with enhanced capabilities that enable users to access information, seek expert advise, view video demonstrations, and explore resources on an as-needed and just-in-time basis to perform their job effectively. The primary instructional strategies supported by this knowledge network are problem solving, **collaboration**, and exploration. The learning technologies that enable the implementation of these strategies include asynchronous and synchronous communication (e.g., e-mail and teleconferencing) and hypermedia and **multimedia** technologies (e.g., hypermedia resources and instructional videos). The scenario can also be described as a distributed learning environment because learning takes place across time, place, and various media.

In the second scenario, Scholarly Exchange at a Distance, a group of teachers are collaborating online to achieve a shared goal: writing a presentation proposal for a conference. This effort can be most closely described as a knowledge-building community. Knowledge building in this example is being supported through the use of Blackboard (a course management system). The specific feature of the system used (discussion forum) has enabled an asynchronous learning network that allows the teachers to share their knowledge through discussion and to transform this knowledge into a working product. The primary learning strategies supported are **articulation**, **reflection**, and collaboration.

In the last scenario, A Tale of Two Institutions, the pedagogical construct implemented most closely aligns with distributed learning. Course events and activities are distributed across time, place, and various media. The primary instructional strategies supported are exploration, problem solving, and collaboration. Exploration is enabled through the use of hypermedia tools, external collaboration and problem solving is supported through asynchronous communication tools, and internal collaboration and problem solving is supported synchronously through face-to-face interaction.

ONLINE LEARNING DELIVERY MODELS AND APPLICATIONS

As mentioned previously, when Internet and Web-based technologies are integrated under one system or tool, technological infrastructures or delivery platforms emerge and form specific online learning applications or delivery models that support a variety of interactions and learning activities. These applications can also be perceived to be a result of the merging of pedagogical models or constructs with learning technologies. Examples of these applications include knowledge networks, knowledge portals, asynchronous learning networks, telelearning, virtual classrooms, and Web-based instruction. These applications or delivery models constitute the infrastructure for online learning environments and span the continuum from informal and loosely defined models to formal and more tightly defined models. Next, we define each delivery model type. Figure 1.2 illustrates their relationship to one another.

Knowledge Networks

Knowledge networks are telecommunication networks initially formed by geographically separated institutions that needed to share information. Information was linked through electronic transfer or collaborative action to support the production and use of knowledge (Hudson & Davis, 1980). In today's world, the term *knowledge networks* is primarily a

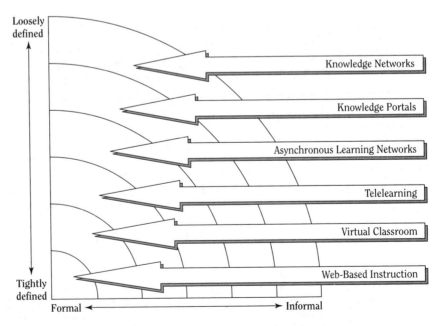

Figure 1.2 Online Learning Delivery Models and Applications

corporate concept referring to "business networks where relationships are always shifting and changing as people have need to connect" (Allee, 2000, p. 8). Knowledge networks are "loose and informal because there is no joint enterprise that holds them together" (Allee, 2000, p. 8). Their primary purpose is to collect and pass along information, unlike learning communities and communities of practice, in which there is a shared goal or a sense of mission to accomplish something. For example, the first scenario presented at the beginning of this chapter is a knowledge network designed to support a particular mission: training a sales force to market a new product. Once this mission has been accomplished, the knowledge network may dissolve unless its members or users collectively and instinctively find reason to sustain it, in which case it could evolve into a community of practice or a knowledge-building community. More often than not, however, knowledge networks serve a specific or time-bound mission or goal.

Knowledge networks can be local or global. For example, on one hand, the Internet is a global knowledge network. Its purpose is to collect and disseminate information through a network of computers and servers. On the other hand, MERLOT (Multimedia Educational Resource for Learning and Online Teaching; http://www.merlot.org) is a collection of digital resources designed primarily for faculty and students in higher education. Therefore, it is a local, or specialized, knowledge network because it serves a specific audience and a broad knowledge area—education. An added component in MERLOT supports the development of several learning communities around the available resources.

Knowledge Portals

A knowledge portal is a service metaphor adopted by the Internet commerce environment, public service education, and media organizations to imply the legitimate aggregation of others' content into a single and simplified local entry point. This entry point provides a "safe harbor" for users in a cyberworld where few local landmarks exist and where providing both a place for community discussion and trusted discussion leaders is as important as the content being discussed (Vedro, 1999). The concept of a knowledge portal began with search engines and Web **interfaces** like Yahoo, Excite, and Netscape, with the goal of providing information on a broad array of subjects and the users' ability to personalize the interface (Eisler, 2000). Other descriptions of knowledge portals include a destination and launching point; a place for self-service and nonstop learning; a perpetual learning place; a knowledge depot; a place to merge learning, knowing, and doing; and a gateway for access, information, and learning communities.

Knowledge portals are supported with electronic program guides and Web search engines. Users are expected to stay within the portal environment on the basis of the quality of the program links and the degree to which learner–learner and learner–content interactions promote a sense of belonging to a community of like-minded users (Vedro, 1999). Most universities are transforming their home pages to knowledge portals from which students, faculty, and administrators can accomplish various tasks. For example, from the knowledge portal, students can search for academic programs; apply online; download documents and forms; register for courses; check their grades, the news, and the weather; and much more. Staff and students at colleges and universities often refer to knowledge portals as *campus portals*. Corporate University Xchange (http://www.corpu.com) is another example of a knowledge portal. It provides consulting services, educational services, and membership communities for the corporate learning marketplace.

Asynchronous Learning Networks

Mayadas first used the expression *asynchronous learning networks* in 1994 to describe a distributed community of learners who, by having access to a computer network, could communicate with one another and access learning materials at any time and from any place (Oakley, 2000). Asynchronous learning networks (ALNs) capitalize on anytime, anywhere learning. An ALN supports learner–content, learner–instructor, learner–learner, and learner–group interactions. Learners in an ALN use communications technologies to interact with remote learning resources, coaches or mentors, and other learners. ALNs combine self-study with substantial, rapid, asynchronous interactivity with others (Mayadas, 1999). In this sense, ALNs are more formal than knowledge networks and knowledge portals. They offer specialized and more structured learning opportunities and activities. Turoff ("Coming to Terms," 2003) predicted that the concept of distance or distributed learning will soon become obsolete and that ALNs or learning networks will become the standard learning model in academic institutions. The Sloan Consortium (http://www.sloan-c.org), a consortium of institutions and organizations committed to quality online education, is an example of an ALN. The network offers workshops, asynchronous discussion forums, conferences, resources, scholarly publications, and various resources and activities that allow members to interact and learn.

Telelearning

"*Telelearning* [italics added] is making connections among persons and resources through telecommunications technologies for learning-related purposes" (Collis, 1996, p. 9). Telelearning can include the following instructional activities: teleaccess (use of online resources), virtual publishing (making class materials available for public distribution through telecommunication networks), telepresence (the ability to use telecommunications technologies for exploratory purposes at a remote site), telementoring, telesharing (supporting the exchange of all forms of information resources among users through telecommunications technologies), and telecollaboration (the use of telecommunications technologies for distributed **problem solving**, collaborative design, and cross-classroom collaborative inquiry; Schrum & Berenfeld, 1997). Telelearning is a more formal online learning environment because it is usually initiated by a university and is associated with credit courses and degree programs.

An example of a telelearning network is the TeleLearning Network of Centres of Excellence (TL-NCE; http://wildcat.iat.sfu.ca). In this network, an interdisciplinary research team of more than 60 faculty members from the areas of education, the social sciences, computer science, and engineering, representing 28 Canadian universities, are working with client communities to achieve the TL-NCE mission, which is to enhance and expand lifelong learning opportunities. In this example, telelearning can be considered similar to ALNs with the added features of synchronous communication and real-time collaborative activities.

Virtual Classrooms

A **virtual classroom** is a formal online learning environment. It resembles a classroom environment but without face-to-face interaction.

> Students in the virtual classroom share their thoughts with professors and classmates, using computers and software that enables them to send and receive messages, interact with professors and classmates, read and comment on lecture material, take tests, and receive feedback without having to attend scheduled classes.   (Hiltz, 1990, p. 133)

Examples of virtual classrooms can be found at the Virtual High School (VHS) Web site (http://www.govhs.org). The VHS is a collaborative effort in which high schools from across the United States participate and offer courses online. The VHS was made possible in part by the U.S. Department of Education, and in the 2000–2001 school year, more than 150 schools and 3,000 students participated. A VHS course, known as a *NetCourse,* is a course in which all learning activities occur online, primarily asynchronously, through **computer conferencing** or bulletin board systems (Riel & Harasim, 1994). As many as 20 students may enroll in a VHS NetCourse, and the participants may be from across the United States, which creates a learning environment that is content rich, diverse, and collaborative.

Web-Based Instruction

"*Web-based instruction* [italics added] encompasses the integrated design and delivery of instructional resources via the World Wide Web, promoting student engagement with text-based, hypermedia, multimedia, and collaborative resources for the purposes of teaching and learning" (Bannan-Ritland, 2004, p. 638). Web-based instruction (WBI) takes many forms and incorporates various types of delivery technologies, ranging from the posting of instructional resources for students, such as syllabi and instructor course notes, to the use of text-based communication tools to promote collaborative discussion and shared activities and documents among learners and instructors. In addition, multimedia resources, including **streaming video and audio**, and **animation** capabilities, can provide engaging components for inclusion in WBI.

These and other capabilities have been integrated into specialized software for Web course development, known as *course management systems* (*CMSs*) such as WebCT and

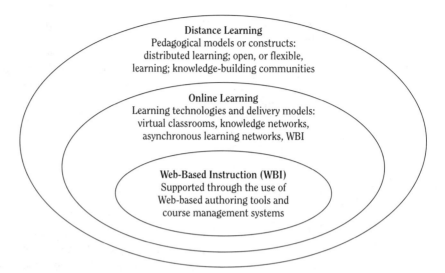

Figure 1.3 Relationship Among Distance Learning, Online Learning, and Web-Based Instruction

Blackboard, which provide the nonprogrammer with templates for easily posting resources and providing collaborative activities. In the context of this book, WBI is considered a derivative or subset of online learning in which Web-based technologies, primarily Web-based authoring tools and CMSs are used to design and deliver more formal online learning environments such as credit-bearing online courses. Figure 1.3 illustrates the relationship among distance learning, online learning, and WBI.

According to Figure 1.3, distance learning, as conceptualized in this chapter, is an overarching, or broad, pedagogical model or construct in which learning is described as distributed forms of interactions occurring across time, place, and various media. Online learning is a specific application of distance learning that uses Internet and Web-based technologies to support distributed forms of interactions. WBI is a specific application of online learning that uses Web-based authoring tools and CMS to deliver instruction.

Take a moment and revisit the scenarios presented at the beginning of this chapter. Perhaps you would say that all three scenarios are examples of online learning because they use Internet and Web-based technologies to foster meaningful action and interaction. However, if you examine the scenarios more closely, perhaps you can now convincingly say that the first scenario is an example of a knowledge network, the second scenario is an example of an ALN, and the third scenario is an example of WBI. Do you agree? Why or why not?

In the last section of this chapter, we discuss the various delivery modes (or methods) of online learning. This discussion will provide you with another important dimension of online learning and a different perspective with which to classify the scenarios presented at the beginning of this chapter.

DELIVERY MODES OF ONLINE LEARNING

Online learning delivery modes range from Web-supported or Web-enhanced instruction—in which Internet and Web-based technologies are used to support face-to-face instruction or course events—to the administration of fully online courses or learning environments in which all instruction, learning, and interaction occurs virtually. In Web-supported or Web-enhanced instruction, also known as *hybrid*, or *blended*, *courses*, online learning works hand in hand with classroom instruction, combining online and face-to-face activities. The Sloan Consortium (http://www.sloan-c.org) defines hybrid, or blended, courses as courses for which 30 to 80% of course content and events is delivered online. Classes continue to meet face-to-face either on a regular basis (as scheduled by the institution) or on a variable basis, depending on the extent to which Web-based technologies are used to support learning activities. For example, the use of Web-based technologies can range from minimal or supplemental use—such as posting a course outline, facilitating electronic submission of assignments, and providing links to resources and downloadable text material—to integral or central use—such as facilitating online discussions of reading assignments and administering online practice quizzes with tutorials to help students review concepts covered in class (Gandell, Weston, Finkelstein, & Winer, 2000). The Web-supported or Web-enhanced delivery mode of online learning facilitates the organization of course materials by the instructor, provides continuous student access to these materials, facilitates student–student and student–instructor communication, and offers students a richer and more **self-directed learning** experience.

In the fully online, or Web-only, delivery mode, Web-based technologies are exclusively used to deliver instruction, learning, and interaction. Gandell et al. (2000) referred to this delivery mode as "exclusive Web use," which implies that the course is conducted fully online, with no face-to-face component. In this case, the network (Internet or **intranet**) serves as the primary environment for course discussions, assignments, and interactions. The fully online, or Web-only, mode can be used on a micro (course or faculty) level or a macro (curriculum or institutional) level. On the micro level, CMSs (e.g., Blackboard and WebCT) have taken the lead in facilitating the implementation of Web-based courses. On the macro level, virtual universities; virtual campuses; and comprehensive, off-the-shelf e-learning and e-training solutions are continuously emerging to fulfill this need. Examples of organizations, educational institutions, and businesses that are offering large-scale online academic and training solutions include the following (*Forbes.com Best of the Web,* 2001):

Corpedia	http://www.corpedia.com
DigitalThink, Inc.	http://www.digitalthink.com/dtfs/index.html
ElementK	http://www.elementk.com
Kaplan College	http://www.kaplancollege.com
MindLeaders	http://www.mindleaders.com
SkillSoft	http://www.skillsoft.com
UNext	http://www.unext.com
Vcampus	http://www.vcampus.com/corpweb/index/index.cfm

These completely virtual universities require a dedicated electronics network infrastructure described by Boettcher and Kumar (2000) as the "Web campus infrastructure" or the "digital plant infrastructure." The digital plant infrastructure metaphor is based on the idea that large-scale online learning and training solutions are beginning to consolidate the physical spaces that we now recognize as the classroom, the library, faculty offices, department offices, and the student union into a virtual campus or a knowledge portal. Some CMSs (e.g., Virtual-U) are based on a virtual campus metaphor by design. In others (e.g., WebCT and Blackboard), campus portals and **learning objects technology** are being implemented to effectively address the need of large-scale online learning solutions. The technological and pedagogical evolution of CMSs is discussed in Chapter 8.

Several other frameworks have also been developed to convey delivery modes of online learning. For example, The Open University (2002) developed three broad streams for its e-learning courses: Web enhanced, Web focused, and Web intensive. The Web-enhanced delivery mode includes courses with basic e-services such as a course Web site, digital resources, and computer-conferencing capabilities. Students are not required to use these e-services to complete the course, but they can if they so choose. The Web-focused delivery mode requires students to use online information and communications technologies to complete some course activities. The Web-intensive delivery mode implies a fully online course in which all teaching and learning events are delivered online. The decision about the level and type of Internet or Web-based technology used in e-learning courses at The Open University is based on the degree to which these learning technologies enhance the students' learning experience.

Another framework that is media-function driven was suggested by Laurillard (1993). Laurillard classified online delivery media into four types: adaptive media; interactive media; **discursive,** or **conversational, media;** and reflective media. Under this classification, a tutorial that adapts its instruction according to a student's input is an example of adaptive media. A computer-based simulation is an example of interactive media. An online discussion facilitated through **threaded discussion forums** is an example of discursive, or conversational, media; and **online journaling** facilitated through the use of **Web logs** is an example of reflective media.

Bates (1997) classified WBI delivery modes by using three models to make analogies to traditional instructional strategies: the lecture model, the seminar model, and the problem-solving model. For example, posting lecture material to the Web would be similar to the lecture model, using computer-mediated communication technologies to initiate learner–learner and learner–instructor interactions would be similar to the seminar model, and implementing Web-based simulations and other immersive and virtual learning technologies would be similar to engaging students in problem-solving tasks in a classroom setting.

Summary

In summary, online learning delivery modes range from Web-supported or Web-enhanced instruction, in which a range of learning activities or course events are supported through the use of Internet and Web-based technologies, to fully online instruction, in which all learning activities and course events are supported through the use of these technologies. Online learning delivery modes can also be classified according to the type and functionality of the particular technology and the degree to which the use of a particular technology engages the student in meaningful action and interaction. As one moves along the continuum from Web-supported to fully online instruction and consider the different types and functions of the technologies used to deliver online learning, the notion of designing distributed course events discussed previously in this chapter becomes increasingly complex. This increasing complexity brings with it several pedagogical, technological, and institutional challenges and requires learners and instructors to acquire new competencies and skills to ensure successful learning. These challenges and competencies are discussed in Chapter 2.

Return for a final time to the three scenarios. Are they examples of the Web-supported, Web-enhanced, or Web-only mode?

CHAPTER SUMMARY

In this chapter, we discussed the characteristics of traditional learning environments and classic and current forms of distance learning environments, which resulted in a reconceptualization of the pedagogical construct of distance learning based on the principles of globalization and learning as a social process. Five specific attributes of distance learning were identified, and several pedagogical models or constructs that could be used interchangeably with the construct of distance learning were presented. These models included open, or flexible, learning; distributed learning; learning communities; communities of practice; and knowledge-building communities. Online learning was described as a derivative or subset of distance learning, possessing a sixth attribute: the use of Internet and Web-based technologies to support the teaching and learning process. A three-component model illustrating the relationship among the key components of online learning—identified as pedagogical models or constructs, instructional and learning strategies, and learning technologies—was presented. The model emphasized the iterative and transformative interaction among these three components and its impact on online learning. Several learning technologies and applications that support the delivery of online learning were identified and defined. These included knowledge networks, knowledge portals, asynchronous learning networks, the virtual classroom, telelearning, and Web-based instruction. Web-based instruction was described as a specific application of online learning in which Web-based authoring tools and course management systems are used to develop and deliver instruction. Last, we described the various delivery modes of online learning and Web-based instruction.

LEARNING ACTIVITIES

1. Develop a comprehensive list of the characteristics of traditional, or directed, learning environments. For example, include the learner's role, the instructor's role, and the types of interaction (e.g., learner–instructor, learner–learner) that occur and how these interactions are facilitated or initiated.
2. Describe the types of interaction that occur in distance learning environments, beginning with traditional distance learning (i.e., correspondence courses and independent study) and progressing to the current state of distance learning as defined in this chapter. Include examples of learning technologies that facilitate these interactions.
3. Research the theories of social constructivism and situated cognition. Develop a list of principles that convey how reality, knowledge, and learning are viewed according to these theories. Visit the Theory Into Practice (TIP) Database at the companion Web site to this book (http://www.prenhall.com/dabbagh).
4. Globalization and learning as a social process have inspired new ways of looking at distance education, which has led to pedagogical constructs such as open learning, distributed learning, and learning communities. Would this have been possible without the Internet? Why or why not? For example, compare the impact of television and radio on education with the impact of the Internet.
5. Research the pedagogical construct of communities of practice. Are all communities of practice sustained through the use of telecommunications technology? Why or why not? Find appropriate examples to support your answer.
6. Think of a context in which you designed, implemented, or experienced online learning, or find out how online learning is being implemented at your school or place of business. What pedagogical models or constructs are used? What types of learning technologies are used? Compare your findings with the attributes of online learning as defined in this chapter.
7. Consider the following scenario:

   High school juniors concentrating in business are required to take a course in investment strategies. Because not enough teachers are qualified to deliver a traditional classroom-based course to all interested students, the school plans to deliver most of the instruction through a Web-based delivery system and to enlist teachers as facilitators and coaches. The Web-based component of the course will introduce students to several fictional characters with different investment portfolios and financial goals. Web links to resources on stocks, bonds, mutual funds, and real estate will be embedded in each character's portfolio. Students will work in teams to explore these cases, with the goal of providing investment and financial planning advice to each character. Students may seek advice or guidance from their teachers through e-mail and online discussion forums. Each team will present its findings in class.

Questions

1. Is this an online learning environment?
2. Does it have the six attributes as defined in this chapter?
3. Which pedagogical model of distance learning does it most closely resemble?
4. Which learning technologies application or delivery model of online learning does it most closely resemble?
5. What type of delivery mode is being implemented?

RESOURCES

Explore additional resources at the companion Website (http://www.prenhall.com/dabbagh) to learn more about distance learning, online learning, and WBI.

REFERENCES

Allee, V. (2000). Knowledge networks and communities of practice. *OD Practitioner, 32*(4), 4–13.

Bannan-Ritland, B. (2004). Web-based instruction: An encyclopedia entry. In A. Kovalchick & K. Dawson (Eds.), *Educational technology: An encyclopedia* (Vol. 2, pp. 638–644). Santa Barbara, CA: ABC-CLIO.

Bates, A. W. (1997). *Restructuring the university for technological change.* Paper presented at The Carnegie Foundation for the Advancement of Teaching, Vancouver, British Columbia, Canada.

Boettcher, J. V., & Kumar, V. (2000). The other infrastructure: Distance education's digital plant. *Syllabus, 13*(10), 14–22.

Bronack, S. C., & Riedl, R. E. (1998, June). *Distributed learning environments: Pedagogy, implementation, and the early adopter.* Paper presented at the '98 World Conference on Educational Multimedia and Hypermedia & World Conference on Educational Telecommunications, Frieburg, Germany.

Brown, J. S., Collins, A., & Duguid, P. (1989). Situated cognition and the culture of learning. *Educational Researcher, 18*(1), 32–42.

The California State University Center for Distributed Learning. (2003). *Welcome to the CSU Center for Distributed Learning.* Retrieved July 15, 2003, from *http://www.cdl.edu*

Chambers, M. (1997). *Why the Web? Linkages.* Paper presented at The Potential of the Web, Institute for Distance Education, University of Maryland University College, Adelphi, MD.

Cognition and Technology Group at Vanderbilt (CTGV). (1992). Technology and the design of generative learning environments. In T. M. Duffy & D. Jonassen (Eds.), *Constructivism and the technology of instruction: A conversation* (pp. 77–90). Hillsdale, NJ: Erlbaum.

Collis, B. (1996). *Tele-learning in a digital world.* Boston, MA: International Thomson Computer Press.

Coming to terms: ALN. (2003). *Sloan-C View, 2*(4), 1, 3. Retrieved January 20, 2004, from *http://www.aln.org/publications/view/v2n4/cover2n4.htm*

Dabbagh, N. H. (1996). The effect of contextualizing instruction of quantitative subject matter in large introductory classes to students' most preferred and personally-relevant interests on knowledge acquisition and relevance (Doctoral dissertation, The Pennsylvania State University, 1996). *Dissertation Abstracts International, 57,* 08A.

Dabbagh, N. H. (2000). The challenges of interfacing between face-to-face and online instruction. *TechTrends, 44*(6), 37–42.

Dede, C. (2002, June). Interactive media in an interview with Chris Dede. *Syllabus, 16*(11), 12–14.

Duning, B., Van Kekerix, M., & Zabrowski, L. (1993). *Reaching learners through telecommunications*. San Francisco: Jossey-Bass.

Edwards, R. (1995). Different discourses, discourses of difference: Globalisation, distance education, and open learning. *Distance Education, 16*(2), 241–255.

Eisler, D. L. (2000). The portal's progress: A gateway for access, information, and learning communities. *Syllabus, 14*(2), 12–18.

Evans, T. (1995). Globalisation, post-Fordism and open and distance education. *Distance Education, 16*(2), 256–269.

Firdyiwek, Y. (1999). Web-based courseware tools: Where is the pedagogy? *Educational Technology, 39*(1), 29–34.

Forbes.com Best of the Web. (2001, February 26). Retrieved from *http://www.forbes.com/bow*

Galusha, J. M. (1997). Barriers to learning in distance education. *Interpersonal Computing and Technology Journal, 5*(3–4), 6–14.

Gandell, T., Weston, C., Finkelstein, A., & Winer, L. (2000). Appropriate use of the Web in teaching higher education. In B. L. Mann (Ed.), *Perspectives in Web course management* (pp. 61–68). Toronto: Canadian Scholar's Press.

Hannafin, K. M., & Mitzel, H. E. (1990). CBI authoring tools in postsecondary institutions: A review and critical examination. *Computers & Education, 14*(3), 197–204.

Hannafin, M. J., Hill, J. R., & Land, S. M. (1997). Student-centered learning and interactive multimedia: Status, issues, and implication. *Contemporary Education, 68*(2), 94–99.

Hanson, D., Maushak, N. J., Schlosser, C. A., Anderson, M. L., Sorensen, C., & Simonson, M. (1997). *Distance education: Review of the literature* (2nd ed.). Bloomington, IN: Association for Educational Communications and Technology.

Held, D., & McGrew, A. (n.d.). Globalization: Entry for *Oxford Companion to Politics*. In D. Held, A. McGrew, D. Goldblatt, & J. Perraton (Eds.), *Global transformations*. Retrieved January 23, 2004, from *http://www.polity.co.uk/global/globocp.htm*

Held, D., & McGrew, A. (2002). *Globalization/anti-globalization*. Cambridge, UK: Polity Press.

Hewitt, J., Brett, C., Scardamalia, M., Frecker, K., & Webb, J. (1995, April). *Supporting knowledge building through the synthesis of CSILE, FCL & Jasper*. Paper presented at Schools for Thought: Transforming Classrooms into Learning Communities, Symposium 29.57 & Poster Session 31.60. Symposium conducted and poster session presented at the annual meeting of the American Educational Research Association, San Francisco. Retrieved July 2, 2003, from *http://ikit.org*

Hiltz, S. R. (1990). Evaluating the virtual classroom. In L. Harasim (Ed.), *Online education: Perspectives on a new environment* (pp. 133–183). New York: Praeger.

Hudson, B. M., & Davis, R. G. (1980). *Knowledge networks for educational planning: Issues and strategies*. Paris: United Nations Educational, Scientific, and Cultural Organization.

Hutchins, E., & Hollan, J. (1999). *COGSCI: Distributed cognition syllabus*. Retrieved November 14, 1999, from *http://hci.ucsd.edu/131/syllabus/index.html*

Jones Knowledge. (2000, Fall). Distributed learning evolves to meet needs of lifelong learners. *E-Education Advisor: Education Edition, 1*(1), 1–15.

Kearsley, G. (2000). *Online education: Learning and teaching in cyberspace.* Ontario, Canada: Wadsworth/Thomas Learning.

Keegan, D. (1990). *Foundations of distance education.* New York: Routledge.

Kozma, R. B. (1994). A reply: Media and methods. *Educational Technology Research & Development, 42*(3), 11–14.

Laurillard, D. (1993). *Rethinking university teaching: A framework for the effective use of educational technology.* London: Routledge.

LeCourt, D. (1999). The ideological consequences of technology and education: The case for critical pedagogy. In M. Selinger & J. Pearson (Eds.), *Telematics in education: Trends and issues* (pp. 51–75). Kidlington, Oxford, UK: Pergamon.

Locatis, C., & Weisberg, M. (1997). Distributed learning and the Internet. *Contemporary Education, 68*(2), 100–103.

MacGregor, J., Smith, B. L., Tinto, V., & Levine, J. H. (1999, April 19). *Learning about learning communities: Taking student learning seriously.* Materials prepared for the National Resource Center for the First-Year Experience and Students in Transition Teleconference, Columbia, SC.

Maddux, C. D., Johnson, D., & Willis, J. W. (2001). *Educational computing: Learning with tomorrow's technologies* (3rd ed.). Needham Heights, MA: Allyn & Bacon.

Mayadas, A. F. (1999). *What is ALN?* Retrieved January 20, 2001, from *http://www.aln.org/alnWeb/aln.htm*

McMeen, G. R. (1985, October 17). *Designing and creating computer-assisted instruction.* Paper presented at the 12th annual conference of the Association for California College Tutorial and Learning Assistance, Sacramento. (ERIC Document Reproduction Service No. ED270077).

Moore, M. G. (1989, May). *Effects of distance learning: A summary of the literature.* University Park: Pennsylvania State University. (NTIS No. PB 90-125 238/XAB)

Moore, M. G. (1994). Autonomy and interdependence. *The American Journal of Distance Education, 8*(2), 1–5.

Moore, M. G., & Kearsley, G. (1995). *Distance education: A systems view.* Belmont, CA: Wadsworth.

Nardi, B. A. (1996). Studying context: A comparison of activity theory, situated action models, and distributed cognition. In B. A. Nardi (Ed.), *Context and consciousness: Activity theory and human–computer interaction* (pp. 69–102). Cambridge, MA: MIT Press.

Navarro, P., & Shoemaker, J. (2000). In M. G. Moore & G. T. Cozine (Eds.), *Web-based communications, The Internet and distance education* (pp. 1–15). University Park: The American Center for the Study of Distance Education, The Pennsylvania State University.

Oakley, B. (2000). *Introduction, learning effectiveness.* Paper presented at the 1999 Sloan Summer Workshop on Asynchronous Learning Networks, Nashville, TN.

The Open University, UK. (2002). *About The Open University.* Retrieved July 2, 2003, from *http://www.open.edu*

Pea, R. D. (1990, April). *Distributed intelligence and education.* Paper presented at the annual meeting of the American Educational Research Association, Boston.

Perkins, D. (1990, April). *Person plus: A distributed view of thinking and learning.* Paper presented at the annual meeting of the American Educational Research Association, Boston.

Picciano, A. G. (2001). *Distance learning: Making connections across virtual space and time.* Upper Saddle River, NJ: Merrill/Prentice Hall.

Riel, M., & Harasim, L. (1994). Research perspectives on network learning. *Journal of Machine-Mediated Learning, 4*(2–3), 91–114.

Rogers, Y. (1997, August). *A brief introduction to distributed cognition.* Retrieved November 8, 1999, from *http://www.cogs.susx.ac.uk/users/yvonner/dcog.html*

Rogoff, B. (1994). Developing understanding of the idea of communities of learners. *Mind, Culture, and Activity, 4,* 209–229.

Saettler, P. (1990). Cognitive science and educational technology: 1950–1980. In P. Saettler, *The evolution of American educational technology* (pp. 318–342). Englewood, CO: Libraries Unlimited.

Schlosser, L. A., & Simonson, M. (2003). *Distance education: Towards a definition and glossary of terms.* Retrieved from *http://www.aect.org/Intranet/Publications/Disted/Disted.asp*

Schrum, L. (1999). Trends in distance learning: Lessons to inform practice. *Educational Media & Technology Yearbook, 24,* 11–16.

Schrum, L., & Berenfeld, B. (1997). *Teaching and learning in the information age.* Boston: Allyn & Bacon.

Selinger, M., & Pearson, J. (Eds.). (1999). *Telematics in education: Trends and issues.* Kidlington, Oxford, UK: Pergamon.

Shrock, S. (1995). A brief history of instructional development. In G. J. Anglin (Ed.), *Instructional technology: Past, present, and future* (pp. 11–19). Englewood, CO: Libraries Unlimited.

Sims, R. (1995). *Interactivity: A forgotten art?* Retrieved November 5, 1999, from *http://itech1.coe.uga.edu/itforum/paper10/paper10.html*

Stevens, D. J. (1981). Computers, curriculum, and careful planning. *Educational Technology, 21*(11), 21–24.

Thach, E. C., & Murphy, K. L. (1995). Competencies for distance education professionals. *Educational Technology Research & Development, 43*(1), 57–79.

University of Guelph, Ontario, Canada. (2003). *About Office of Open Learning.* Retrieved July 2, 2003, from *http://www.open.uoguelph.ca/about/about.html*

Vedro, S. R. (1999). Toward the knowledge portal: Public broadcasting and university continuing education in the Internet age. *Technos, 8*(4), 1–5.

Walker, G. R., & Fox, M. A. (2000). *Globalization: An analytical framework* [Electronic version]. Retrieved from *http://www.law.indiana.edu/glsj/vol3/no2/walker.html#T1*

Wedemeyer, C. A. (1981). *Learning at the back door: Reflections on nontraditional learning in the lifespan.* Madison: University of Wisconsin Press.

Wenger, E. C., & Snyder, W. M. (2000, January/February). Communities of practice: The organizational frontier. *Harvard Business Review, 78*(1), 139–145.

Wilson, B., & Ryder, M. (1998). *Distributed learning communities: An alternative to designed instructional systems.* Retrieved from *http://www.cudenver.edu/~bwilson/dlc.html*

THE ROLES AND COMPETENCIES OF THE ONLINE LEARNER AND ONLINE INSTRUCTOR

After completing this chapter, you should understand the following:

- The differences between the classic distance learner and the emerging online learner

- The types of learning technologies that facilitate online learning and their application and use from the online learner's perspective

- The competencies and skills that lead to a successful online learner

- The differences between the traditional classroom instructor and the online instructor

- The competencies and skills that lead to a successful online instructor

- The technological, logistical, and implementation challenges facing the online instructor

- What the term *intellectual property* means and which considerations apply to instructors, developers, and learners when such property is used in electronic media and online learning

CONSIDER THE FOLLOWING THREE SCENARIOS:

The Working Professional: Beatrice is a 35-year-old single mother of two, working full time as a systems analyst for a financial investment company. She has been an employee at this company for 7 years. Beatrice's boss recently informed her that her salary would increase considerably if she earned a master's degree. Her boss also informed her that the company would subsidize a large part of her tuition. As a systems analyst, Beatrice is skilled at using information technologies. She is also comfortable with Internet and Web-based applications. She uses e-mail at work and home to communicate with her colleagues and friends and does most of her shopping, bill paying, and searching for information online. However, Beatrice is concerned that she will not have time to complete a master's degree. She has a full-time job and would like to spend her evenings and weekends at home with her children. Her friends at work inform her that she could pursue a master's degree almost completely online at some universities and recommend that she enroll in an online course to determine whether this mode of learning fits her needs. Beatrice begins searching for online degree programs in her area of interest.

The High School Student: Robert graduated from a rural high school where Internet connectivity was seldom available. Enrollment at his high school was about 1,800 students. The school had two computer labs with 24 computers each. The computers were old, and Internet access was extremely slow. In addition, the labs were reserved for information technology classes during the day, and students could use the labs only after school hours to do homework related to these classes and other classes that required papers to be typed on a word processor. Nevertheless, Robert had access to the Internet at home and frequently used e-mail and America Online's chat program to connect with his friends. In his freshman year at college, one of his instructors requires students to access all course material through a course management system. Students are also required to submit assignments by e-mail and to discuss course readings online in small groups in a discussion forum area. At first, Robert feels frustrated. He does not understand why the instructor requires the use of a course management system. His class meets three times a week in a classroom just as all his other classes do. Other instructors provide all course materials in class as handouts and do not require students to submit their assignments by e-mail or to participate in online discussions. However, as time passes, Robert begins appreciating the asynchronous mode of learning. He can complete his assignments late at night in his dorm room and e-mail them to his instructor when he is done. Robert also begins looking forward to the small-group online discussions. The class has an enrollment of 90 students and, coming from a small town, he does not know anyone. The online discussions give him the opportunity to interact with his classmates online. He enjoys reading and responding to multiple viewpoints on the issues discussed. Robert slowly begins to appreciate the richness of the learning environment and, as a result of interacting online with his peers, he begins to develop more meaningful relationships with his classmates. He also begins using e-mail regularly to communicate with his friends and instructors.

The Online Class: Twenty-two students who are enrolled in a graduate instructional technology program at a comprehensive university are nearing the end of their course work. They have one three-credit elective course remaining and a six-credit practicum requirement. The students have attended several classes together, and they all live in the same geographic area. The instructional technology program at this university does not typically offer courses online. However, one faculty member who wants to make the leap to online learning decides to offer an elective course titled "Instructional Strategies for the Web," using Blackboard, a course management system, as an online delivery platform. The instructor announces that students who want to sign up for this elective must have a reliable Internet connection, basic **HTML** skills, and a willingness to participate in course activities online and to interact with the instructor and peers at least four times a week for 3 to 4 hours each time. All 22 students sign up to take the course and successfully complete all requirements online.

As you read this chapter, think about these three scenarios. What are some factors that influence learners to participate in online learning activities or enroll in online courses? What are some factors that constrain learners from enrolling in online courses? What skills are necessary for engaging in a successful online learning experience? What are some of the pedagogical, logistical, and implementation challenges facing the online instructor and the online learner? What can online instructors do to sustain learner engagement?

In this chapter, we discuss the issues evoked by these questions. We also address the roles and competencies of the online learner and the online instructor, and the learning affordances and challenges inherent in online learning environments.

INTRODUCTION

In Chapter 1, we discussed three key components of online learning that work collectively to foster meaningful learning and interaction: **(a)** pedagogical models, **(b)** instructional and learning strategies, and **(c)** learning technologies. In this chapter, we focus on learning technologies and the challenges they pose for the learner, the instructor, and the learning institution. Specifically, we describe learning technologies from the perspective of their use and application in online learning and the roles and competencies they instantiate for the learner and the instructor. We also discuss institutional and administrative challenges associated with online learning, including **copyright** and **intellectual property** issues as they relate to electronic media and online courses.

THE ONLINE LEARNING ENVIRONMENT

To better describe the impact of learning technologies on the roles and competencies of the online learner and online instructor, we begin with a definition of a learning environment consistent with our pedagogical views on online learning as discussed in Chapter 1. This definition is based on constructivist learning principles, which emphasize the importance of meaningful and authentic activities that help learners build their own understanding of curricular phenomena (facts, concepts, and principles of learning domains) and develop critical thinking and problem-solving skills.

According to Wilson (1996), a constructivist learning environment is "a place where learners may work together and support each other as they use a variety of tools and information resources in their guided pursuit of learning goals and problem-solving skills" (p. 5). In mapping this constructivist interpretation of a learning environment to our definition of online learning (see Chapter 1), we can characterize the "place" where learning occurs as a virtual space (cyberspace), and the tools that learners (and instructors) use for gathering information, providing content and context, and interacting and collaborating as online learning technologies such as telecommunications technology, hypermedia technology, Web-based authoring tools, and course management systems (CMSs; defined later in this chapter).

The concept of a virtual learning space and its interdependence on Internet and Web-based technologies presents many challenges to learners, teachers, and learning institutions, which, if not properly addressed, could result in a learning experience that is frustrating and ineffective for all persons involved. We begin by describing the critical characteristics and skills that the online learner needs to have to address these challenges.

THE ONLINE LEARNER

The online learner is a key constituent of an online learning environment. Determining the online learner's characteristics and educational needs may not guarantee success in a distance education course or program (Galusha, 1997). However, doing so can significantly help administrators, teachers, and instructional designers understand who is likely to participate in online learning, which factors or motivators contribute to a successful learning experience in a virtual setting, and which potential barriers could deter some students from participating in or successfully completing an online course. Understanding the characteristics and perceived skills of the online learner and how these differ from those of the classic distance learner facilitates effective planning and development of online learning environments.

The Classic Distance Learner

Earlier profiles of the online learner can be traced to classic distance education settings (e.g., correspondence, or home, study), in which most learners were described as adults with occupational, social, and family commitments (Hanson et al., 1997). The National

Home Study Council (NHSC), founded in 1926, collected information about its students and created the following demographic profile for home study students (Lambert, 2000): "Average age is 34 years; 66% are male; 25% have a college degree; over 50% have had some college education; and over 75% are married" (p. 11). Home study students were also described as self-motivated, goal oriented, and disciplined self-starters (Lambert, 2000).

Purdy (2000) described the demographic profile of the classic distance education learner as follows: "Average age of 35; mostly women (or more women than men); most have had some college education but have not completed a college degree; full or part-time employed; mostly middle class" (p. 19). This profile was based on the use of tele-courses (courses delivered through television) as the main delivery medium for distance education. Purdy also described students as "very busy people . . . attracted to what seems like an efficient means to study" (p. 19), who have the goal of completing a degree for employment status or for personal enrichment. Beatrice, the systems analyst in The Working Professional scenario, fits this profile.

Dille and Mezack (1991) also studied the profile of students who enrolled in tele-courses, focusing on the student's **locus of control** (internal or external attribution of success and failure) and learning style (e.g., verbal, visual, or kinesthetic) as predictors of success among college distance education students. These researchers' findings revealed that locus of control is a significant predictor of success and persistence in distance education courses. For example, students with an internal locus of control (those who attribute success and failure on tasks to personal behaviors and efforts) were more likely to succeed (receive a grade of C or better) and persevere (complete a telecourse) when faced with the challenges of a telecourse than were students with an external locus of control (those who attribute success and failure on tasks to external or uncontrollable factors such as luck or task difficulty).

Several other studies were conducted in which researchers examined student attitudes, personality characteristics, study practices, course completion rates, and other academic, psychological, and social integration variables to identify barriers to persistence in distance education and determine predictors for successful course achievement (Bernt & Bugbee, 1993; Biner, Bink, Huffman, & Dean, 1995; Coggins, 1988; Fjortoft, 1995; Garland, 1993; Laube, 1992; Pugliese, 1994; Rekkedal, 1982; Stone, 1992). The results indicated that intrinsically motivated learners possessing a high internal locus of control, coupled with a positive attitude toward the instructor and a high expectation for grades and completion of a degree, were more likely to succeed in a distance education course. Therefore, a learner's academic self-concept is a key predictor for success in a distance education setting.

Interestingly, individual learning styles did not prove to be a significant predictor of success, the rationale being that distance education is inherently accommodating of various learning styles (Dille & Mezack, 1991). This finding is consistent with the pedagogical characteristics of technology-supported learning environments and in particular Web-based or online learning environments that emphasize interaction and collaboration. Such environments are multimodal (support audio, video, and text), provide individual and group interaction spaces in synchronous and asynchronous formats, support linear and nonlinear representation of content, and provide a variety of **learning tools** to cater to individual learning styles. In other words, "the Web affords the match we need between a medium and how a particular person learns" (Brown, 2000, p. 12).

The Changing Nature of the Distance Learner

The previously mentioned studies demonstrate that although distance learners share broad demographic and situational characteristics, no concrete evidence exists to indicate that this group is homogeneous or unchanging (Thompson, 1998). In fact, the current profile of the distance learner can be described as dynamic, responsive to rapid technological innovations and new learning paradigms, and progressively including a younger age bracket. Chances are that today's youth, who are increasingly growing up with computer games, search engines, America Online (AOL) chat, and other digital technologies, would welcome or be at ease with online learning activities such as downloading course syllabi and assignments from a course Web site, posting assignments to a course Web site, interacting with peers in virtual spaces on team projects, engaging in online discussions, researching term papers by using online resources, and developing Web sites and multimedia-based products to demonstrate learning. For example, in The High School Student scenario, Robert, although frustrated at first, adapted well to the use of online learning technologies because of prior experience with e-mail and chat programs.

Today's youth are also acquiring a new type of literacy known as *information navigation*, which is rapidly becoming a critical skill for successful online learning. Information navigation goes beyond text and image literacy, requiring learners to navigate "through confusing complex information spaces and feel comfortable doing so" (Brown, 2000, p. 14). Information navigation is facilitated through hypermedia, which is an inherent feature of the Web (and discussed at length in Chapter 8). Children's increasing competence in information navigation and other communications technologies, coupled with the flexibility that distributed learning provides to the adult population, may result in increased resistance to the delivery of distance education courses, or even face-to-face courses, by means of conventional or classic methods. Delivery models that make use of Internet and Web-based technologies (e.g., knowledge networks, asynchronous learning networks, and knowledge portals, as described in Chapter 1) are designed to effectively meet the needs of the changing distance learner and learners in general.

The distance learning population as a whole is also becoming more diverse, encompassing students from a variety of ethnic and educational backgrounds. Such diversity is largely the result of globalization (see Chapter 1). The globalization of distance education has enabled students from across the world to participate in online learning activities such as joining a moderated **Listservs,** participating in online seminars, and sharing information through knowledge portals. In addition, distance learners are becoming less location bound. Thompson (1998) elaborated on this point: "Increasingly, students in close proximity to traditional educational institutions are choosing distance study not because it is the only alternative, but rather because it is the preferred alternative" (p. 13). Negative past experiences with conventional educational methods and being time bound to on-campus instruction schedules are some of the reasons listed for the desire to be outside the educational mainstream (Eastmond, 1995; Willis, 1994).

The Emerging Online Learner

The concept of the independent, place-bound, adult, self-motivated, disciplined self-starter, and goal-oriented learner, which largely characterized the classic distance learner, is now being challenged with socially mediated online activities such as discussion forums, group contributions, shared resources, peer assessment, and group projects. Such activities deemphasize independent learning and emphasize social interaction and **collaborative learning.** According to Anderson and Garrison (1998), "The independence and isolation characteristic of the industrial era of distance education is being challenged by the collaborative approaches to learning made possible by learning networks" (p. 100). Therefore, online learners must be ready to share their work, interact within small and large groups in virtual settings, and collaborate on projects online or otherwise risk isolation in a community that is increasingly depending on connectivity and interaction. To do so effectively, online learners should be skilled at using online learning technologies such as telecommunications technology, hypermedia technology, and CMSs and should understand the potential of these new learning technologies in supporting interaction, **social negotiation,** and collaboration. Given this new context, what are the perceived characteristics of the emerging online learner?

Think about the first two scenarios presented at the beginning of the chapter. Does Beatrice seem to have the appropriate profile and skills to successfully engage in an online course? What about Robert? What additional information should we be seeking from these individuals to assess their potential for successfully engaging in online learning?

Powell (2000) described the online learner as someone who is self-directed, self-regulated, self-disciplined, responsible, independent, focused, not easily distracted, very comfortable with written communications, somewhat savvy with Web technologies, and proficient with computers. Powell's description retains many of the attributes of the classic distance learner, with the addition of comfort with written communications and fluency in the use of Web-based technologies. This description is consistent with recent research findings. For instance, Williams (2003) found that interpersonal- and communication-related skills (which include writing skills) dominated the top 10 general competencies across all roles in distance education programs supported by the Internet. In addition, Cheurprakobkit, Hale, and Olson (2002) reported that lack of knowledge and skill in the use of online learning technologies, particularly communication and collaborative technologies, could present barriers to learning for students in distance learning settings. Therefore, fluency in the use of online learning technologies is a critical competency for the online learner.

Not accounted for in Powell's description of the online learner is the importance of valuing or appreciating the learning affordances that online learning technologies present—primarily, interaction and collaboration. Some learners are inherently drawn to peer interaction or collaboration, whereas others need to understand the educational value of these learning activities. Being inherently drawn to interaction or collaboration can be characterized as an individual difference referred to in the literature as the *need for affiliation*. In online learning environments, the need for affiliation can be interpreted as the need to be connected or to belong to supportive groups (MacKeracher, 1996). A community of practice (CoP) is an example of how the need for affiliation can manifest in an online learning environment. Members of a CoP understand that a social mind is at work and that knowledge is shared intellectual capital. As discussed in Chapter 1, a CoP is a pedagogical model grounded in learning as a social process and is implemented in an online context through knowledge networks, asynchronous learning networks, and other Internet and Web-based collaborative and communication technologies. Although the online learner still needs to act competently on his or her own; have confidence in his or her knowledge, skills, and performance; and learn how to create and manage a personal presence, sensing or exhibiting a need for affiliation is key to the online learner's success. Therefore, online learners must understand and value the learning opportunities afforded by collaborative and communication technologies to be able to actively and constructively engage in learning.

Take a moment and revisit The High School Student scenario. At first, Robert did not value or appreciate online discussions. However, as he participated in these discussions, he began to understand the richness of the learning environment in terms of the multiple perspectives presented. Robert also began to feel a sense of belonging to a group of peers, which culminated in extending his communication beyond the scope of the course.

Another important characteristic of the online learner that carries forward from the profile of the classic distance learner is self-directed learning. Cheurprakobkit et al. (2002) reported that students in Web-based learning environments must possess "self" behaviors, such as self-discipline, self-monitoring, self-initiative, and self-management, which are components of self-regulated or self-directed learning. Self-directed learning can be described as the skill of "learning how to learn," or being metacognitively aware of your own learning (Olgren, 1998, p. 82). Given the absence of an instructor in the traditional sense in an online learning environment, learners' ability to monitor and regulate their own learning is critical. However, the degree of self-directed learning expected from an online learner is a function of the instructor's or course designer's pedagogy and the overall design of an online course.

Two primary schools of thought, or learning paradigms, relate to the overall instructional use of online courses: the objectivist and constructivist viewpoints (Bannan

& Milheim, 1997). Briefly, subscribers to the objectivist paradigm contend that knowledge or reality is external to the learner, or is mind independent. Therefore, knowledge can be transmitted or communicated to the student in concrete and objective terms, which results in the appropriate or correct way of knowing something. In contrast, subscribers to the constructivist philosophy contend that the learner builds, or constructs, an internal and personal representation of knowledge indexed by the learner's unique experiences, which results in knowledge that is usable and meaningful to the learner (Bednar, Cunningham, Duffy, & Perry, 1992). These two schools of thought about how learning occurs, knowledge is represented, and meaning is created have direct implications for how self-directed learning is viewed.

Under the objectivist paradigm, the learning environment is largely instructor led or program controlled (in the absence of an instructor), and to a large degree the learner is a passive recipient of information. Lessons, assignments, and activities are organized by the instructor or the instructional program and delivered to the student with a high degree of structure and guidance, which leaves little room for learner control, creativity, or ownership in the learning process. "Participation by the student is often prespecified by the instructor and designed to ensure mastery of particular content" (Bannan & Milheim, 1997, p. 382). In this context, self-directed learning as just defined is not supported or encouraged. Rather, the structuredness of the learning environment compensates for the lack of self-directed learning.

Under the constructivist paradigm, the learning environment is largely learner centered, providing multiple opportunities for the student to synthesize, organize, and restructure information, and to create and contribute resources to the virtual space of the course. Students can select and sequence educational activities as well as create their own learning opportunities to satisfy their learning needs (Hooper & Hannafin, 1991). With this understanding of the learner's role, self-directed learning is nurtured and supported, and self-directed learning skills are perceived as critical for steering the learner to take ownership of the learning process.

Our views on online learning, presented in Chapter 1, support the constructivist approach to learning. Therefore, online learners should possess self-directed learning skills or be encouraged and appropriately coached to acquire such skills so that they can actively engage in the learning process and shape their learning experience.

CHARACTERISTICS OF THE ONLINE LEARNER

On the basis of the preceding discussion, the following characteristics and skills are perceived to be critical to an online learner's success:

- Being fluent in the use of online learning technologies
- Exhibiting a need for affiliation
- Understanding and valuing interaction and collaborative learning
- Possessing an internal locus of control
- Having a strong academic self-concept
- Having experience in self-directed learning or the initiative to acquire such skills

To date, research has not converged on a typical or standardized profile of the online learner. Although some situational, affective, and demographic characteristics may cut across this learner population, what seems to be more constant is the changing nature of the online learner and the multiple learning styles and cultural differences represented in this student population. This finding is not surprising if we consider globalization as an enabling factor for this changing attribute. Globalization has stretched the scope of the classic distance learner from a homogeneous profile of mostly adult, mostly employed, place bound, independent, goal oriented, and intrinsically motivated, to one that is dynamic, tentative, and diverse. This new profile poses considerable implications for the design of online learning environments. Learning as a social process has also had an impact on the profile of the emerging online learner. Learners are increasingly discovering that "the Web is not only an informational and social resource but also a learning medium where understandings are socially constructed and shared" (Brown, 2000, p. 14).

To serve the needs of the dynamic, diverse, and emerging profile of the online learner and support shared knowledge construction, the online course instructor or developer should focus on designing and implementing distributed course events. As discussed in Chapter 1, *distributed* course events facilitate anytime, anywhere learning and are implemented through various online learning delivery models or applications, including asynchronous learning networks, knowledge networks, knowledge portals, virtual classrooms, and Web-based instruction (WBI). These applications are premised on the following Internet and Web-based technologies:

- Web-based hypermedia technologies
- Web-based multimedia technologies
- Asynchronous and synchronous communication tools
- Web-based publishing and authoring tools
- Presentation and visualization tools
- CMSs

Next, we describe each of these learning technologies and discuss their applications and uses from the online learner's perspective. Table 2.1 (pp. 41–42) provides an overview of these learning technologies, their level of difficulty, related skills, and examples of use.

Online Learning Technologies and Related Skills

Web-based hypermedia technologies The category of Web-based hypermedia technologies implies familiarity with the use of Web browsers, search engines, and information navigation and evaluation. Online learners must understand how to use a Web browser with all its attributes, which include being familiar with a **point-and-click interface,** understanding URL configurations, locating Web sites, bookmarking, saving or downloading HTML documents, navigating through Web links and information spaces, and understanding how search engines work and how to use them effectively to locate relevant information and critically evaluate the content of Web sites. Because information on the Internet is not subjected to the rigorous filtering by the publishing process as is scholarly information in libraries, the online learner should also acquire strategies

Table 2.1   Online Learning Technologies and Related Skills

CATEGORY	LEVEL OF DIFFICULTY	RELATED SKILLS	EXAMPLES OF USE
Web-based hypermedia technologies	Basic	Familiarity with use of browsers and search engines Ability to understand URL configurations, locate Web sites, navigate through hyperlinks, and evaluate Web content	Bookmark a URL for later use Save, download, or print an HTML document Search for information by using a search engine
Web-based multimedia technologies	Basic	Downloading and installing plug-ins to view multimedia files	Download and install Adobe Reader to view PDF files Download and install RealPlayer to view an AVI file (video)
Asynchronous and synchronous communication tools	Basic to complex	Ability to use tools that enable asynchronous and synchronous communication and collaborative and distributed learning activities	Send e-mails to the instructor (basic) Participate in an asynchronous discussion forum (intermediate) Construct a virtual room in a **MOO** or **MUD** and interact with other participants to accomplish a learning task (complex)
Web-based publishing and authoring tools	Basic to complex	Familiarity with HTML editors and other Web-based publishing tools and scripting languages Ability to upload HTML files to a designated Web site and link the files appropriately	Convert a Word document to an HTML file (basic) Create a Web site at which to share a collaborative project (intermediate) Create a Flash animation (complex)
Presentation and visualization tools	Basic to complex	Familiarity with media-creation tools such as PowerPoint, Adobe Photoshop, and concept-mapping software Ability to convert files created to a Web-based format	Convert a Word document to PDF (basic) Create a PowerPoint presentation and convert it to HTML (intermediate) Create a concept map by using Inspiration and export it to a gif file. (complex)

(continued)

Table 2.1   Online Learning Technologies and Related Skills (*continued*)

CATEGORY	LEVEL OF DIFFICULTY	RELATED SKILLS	EXAMPLES OF USE
Course management systems (CMSs)	Basic to complex	Skills range from familiarity with use of browsers and downloading files to use of asynchronous and synchronous communication tools, Web-based publishing tools, and presentation and visualization tools	Download course syllabus (basic) Use the e-mail feature of the CMS (basic) Upload an assignment to the student presentation area of the CMS (complex)

Note. PDF = portable document format; AVI = audio/video interleaved; MOO = multiuser domain—object oriented; MUD = multiuser domain.

for addressing the dynamic nature of Web sites and Internet documents (Cushing, 1998). The use of Web-based hypermedia technologies in online learning facilitates inquiry-based learning, self-directed learning, and authentic activity through the exploration of multiple resources and perspectives. Being proficient in the use of Web-based hypermedia technologies is a minimum requirement for successfully engaging in online learning.

Web-based multimedia technologies   The category of Web-based multimedia technologies implies familiarity with downloading and installing plug-ins (browser extensions that display multimedia content inside a Web page), which are needed to view video or audio files and various multimedia files, including graphics, animations, PowerPoint files, portable document format (PDF) files, and other file types developed by using multimedia and Web-based authoring tools such as Authorware and Flash. Web-based multimedia technologies allow learners to view learning content in multiple modalities; thus, these technologies accommodate different learning styles (e.g., visual vs. auditory). In addition, Web-based multimedia technologies facilitate the design of **authentic learning activities** (such as interactive courseware, simulations, and real-world problems), which help students interact with learning content, link content to everyday practice, and contextualize knowledge. However, online learners need not be skilled in authoring multimedia learning tasks. Instead, as a minimum requirement, online learners should become skilled in viewing different multimedia applications and file formats in a Web browser. The use of multimedia and Web-based authoring tools in designing online learning environments is discussed in detail in Chapters 8 and 9.

Asynchronous and synchronous communication tools   The category of asynchronous and synchronous communication tools implies familiarity with the use of e-mail, discussion forums, bulletin boards, newsgroups, chat programs, audio- and videoconferencing tools, electronic whiteboards, groupware and document-sharing tools, and multiuser shared virtual spaces (e.g., multiuser domains, or MUDs, and multiuser domains—object oriented, or MOOs, such as http://ti2.sri.com/tappedin and http://activeworlds.com). MUDs and MOOs are Internet-accessible text-based and object-based virtual environments well suited for creating CoPs and knowledge-building communities. Participants in MUD or MOO environments have the opportunity to create spaces (e.g., user-created rooms) and objects (e.g., icons and interactive graphics) online and to write code that increases the functionality of these spaces and objects and maximizes interaction and knowledge construction (TeleEducation NB, 2002).

These types of tools enable asynchronous and synchronous collaborative and distributed learning activities emphasizing learning as a social process and shared knowledge. The asynchronous mode allows users to interact in a delayed manner (users do not have to be online at the same time), whereas the synchronous mode requires users to be online at the same time to engage in a live discussion or planned activity. Bulletin boards, e-mails, and discussion forums are examples of **asynchronous communication tools,** whereas chat programs, audio- and videoconferencing, and electronic whiteboards are examples of synchronous communication tools. The use of asynchronous and synchronous communication tools in online learning facilitates interaction, collaboration, and problem-solving activities. This category of online learning technologies ranges from basic to complex. Online learners should become skilled in the use of basic asynchronous communication tools such as e-mail and discussion forums to successfully engage in online learning.

Web-based publishing and authoring tools   The category of Web-based publishing and authoring tools implies familiarity with HTML editors and Web publishing and authoring tools (e.g., Dreamweaver and FrontPage), **Java** scripting, and other **object-oriented** programming languages that facilitate the creation of simple Web pages to complex 3-D animations and virtual reality environments. In addition to developing Web-based products or artifacts, students should be able to upload such products to a designated Web site. Acquiring such skills facilitates learning in knowledge-building communities, shared **synthetic environments** (e.g., MUDs and MOOs), and asynchronous learning networks, which require learners to demonstrate their knowledge and understanding through the creation of Web sites, animations, and interactive modules. The use of Web-based publishing and authoring tools is not a requirement for engaging in online learning. However, the online learner should strive toward achieving the basic skill of developing a Web page to facilitate posting assignments online and sharing knowledge. More complex skills can be acquired as needed.

Presentation and visualization tools   The presentation and visualization tools category implies familiarity with media-creation tools such as PowerPoint, Adobe Photoshop, and Adobe Acrobat, which allow learners to synthesize content through the creation of multimedia presentations and products and to organize their learning by using concept-mapping software such as Inspiration, MindMapper, and MindManager.[1]

---

[1] Inspiration, MindMapper, and MindManager are computer-based visualization tools that allow users to create concept maps, semantic networks, outlines, graphic organizers, and other comprehension-monitoring activities. Concept maps are diagrams that represent concepts and relationships structurally.

The products resulting from the use of such tools can be exported to a format that is viewable in a Web browser. The use of **presentation and visualization tools** in online learning emphasizes thinking processes rather than mastery of discrete content outcomes and helps students deploy personal knowledge and use cognitive tools to augment their thinking. Online learners need not be familiar with the use of presentation and visualization tools, as described in this section, to successfully engage in online learning. However, as learners become more proficient in the use of the other categories of online learning technologies, presentation and visualization tools could prove highly effective in supporting self-directed learning.

Course management systems   CMSs are Web authoring tools that integrate technological and pedagogical features of the Internet and the Web into a single, template-based authoring system to facilitate the design, development, delivery, and management of Web-based courses and online delivery models such as WBI. Examples of CMSs include WebCT, Blackboard, Lotus LearningSpace, FirstClass, and WebMentor. Although CMSs are designed primarily to facilitate the online instructor's course administration and delivery tasks, they are becoming increasingly learner centered. Several learner tools are embedded in CMSs, which requires online learners to become familiar with their use. In Chapter 9, we discuss in detail CMSs and their implications for online learning.

Additional considerations   Simply being skilled in the use of online learning technologies does not guarantee meaningful interaction, collaboration, and knowledge building and sharing (Lindblom-Ylanne & Pihlajamaki, 2003). Rather, developing a sense of value and appreciation for interaction and collaboration and acquiring communication and interpersonal skills that promote collaborative learning are also needed to ensure a successful online learning experience. The absence or limited teacher presence in online learning environments has increased the need for collaboration and teamwork and has established collaborative learning as a core attribute that students are expected to develop (McLoughlin & Luca, 2002). In the next section, we discuss collaborative learning as an important competency for online learners.

Collaborative Learning

Collaborative learning can be defined as a collection of perspectives that emphasize the following (Spector, 1999, p. 4):

- Joint construction of knowledge (e.g., joint problem solving by mutual refinement)
- Joint negotiation of alternatives through argumentation, debate, and other means
- Student reliance on both other students and teachers as learning resources

These perspectives support learning as a social process, aligning with our conceptualization of online learning as defined in Chapter 1. Research reveals that collaborative learning increases student motivation and achievement, promotes greater use of higher level reasoning strategies and critical thinking, creates a sense of social cohesion, and creates a productive learning environment (Comeaux, Huber, Kasprzak, & Nixon, 1998). In online learning environments, collaborative learning is facilitated mainly through the use of asynchronous and synchronous communication tools. However, online learners should have or develop collaborative learning skills independent of these technologies. Such skills include the following:

Social Learning Skills: Social learning skills are skills that support decision making, communication, trust building, and conflict management, all of which are important components for effective collaboration. In addition, social learning skills are needed for individuals to assume leadership roles as well as other roles typically assigned in teamwork.

Discursive, or dialogic, skills: Discursive, or dialogic, skills include the ability to discuss issues (being discursive), share and debate ideas, negotiate meaning, be open to multiple perspectives, and have good articulation and listening skills.

Self- and Group Evaluation Skills: Self- and group evaluation skills include learning how to be individually accountable for (a) being active and engaged in group activity, (b) doing a fair share of the work, and (c) helping other group members to demonstrate competence and learning achievement (promotive interaction).

Reflection Skills: Reflection skills include the ability to apply frequent and substantive consideration and assessment of not only your personal learning process and products, but also the group's. Reflection is also a key component of self-directed learning.

Acquiring and demonstrating the skills just discussed ensures that online learning environments are truly collaborative and support joint construction of knowledge and joint negotiation of alternative perspectives. Acquiring these skills also ensures that students are actively engaged in group activities and are relying on their teachers and peers to reach a meaningful understanding of the concepts under study. So, how do students acquire these skills? The answer is through the design and implementation of appropriate instructional strategies and learning activities. Instructional strategies are a key component of the three-component model for online learning presented in Chapter 1 and are discussed in detail in Chapter 6.

An example of an instructional strategy that promotes collaborative learning can be found in The High School Student scenario. The small-group online discussions can be perceived as a distributed course event that fosters collaborative learning skills—particularly discursive and reflection skills. However, if all course events were delivered entirely online with no face-to-face meetings, Robert would probably need coaching in self-directed learning skills to complete all course requirements successfully. In contrast, Beatrice in The Working Professional scenario may be more qualified to manage and monitor her own learning given her context and experience.

The degree to which an online learner meaningfully engages in collaborative learning depends on the extent to which the learner perceives him- or herself to be self-directed. So, what does it mean to be a *self-directed* learner? Are the students in The Online Class scenario self-directed? In the next section, we discuss self-directed learning as an important competency for the online learner.

Self-Directed Learning

As defined previously in this chapter, self-directed learning can be described as the skill of "learning how to learn" or being metacognitively aware of your own learning. **Metacognition** involves three key components (Olgren, 1998, p. 82):

1. Awareness of how learning is being carried out
2. Knowledge about self, the learning task, and how you learn under different conditions
3. Control in terms of your ability and desire to plan and regulate the learning process

Learning with awareness, knowledge, and control requires learners to be skilled not only in time-management and orienting strategies that help them "prepare to learn," but also in cognitive learning strategies that help them meaningfully interact with content material. Time-management skills and orienting strategies have a direct impact on collaborative learning in terms of effectively and efficiently carrying out the responsibilities a learner has as an active and accountable group member. In contrast, although cognitive learning strategies have an impact on the quality of a learner's contributions to a group process, they are perceived to be most relevant to an individual's ability to reflect on, monitor, and assess his or her own learning during a learning task.

Cognitive strategies are how a learner manipulates and processes content. Weinstein and Mayer (1986) identified four types of cognitive learning strategies: (a) organizational strategies for basic learning tasks, (b) organizational strategies for complex learning tasks, (c) elaboration strategies for complex learning tasks, and (d) comprehension-monitoring skills. This classification suggests a relationship between the cognitive strategy and the learning task, which implies that different cognitive strategies are needed to support different learning tasks and that the more complex the learning task, the more engaging the strategy. Researchers have found, for example, that "learning for higher cognitive goals requires the student to both analyze (break down) and synthesize (put back together) information" (Olgren, 1998, p. 87). This destructuring and restructuring of content material requires a combination of several organizational and elaboration strategies. Examples of organizational strategies include "outlining, listing, classifying, ordering, diagramming, comparing and contrasting information," and examples of elaboration strategies include "paraphrasing, summarizing, visualizing, associating ideas with examples, **generative note taking,** creating analogies and metaphors, **role-playing,** reflecting, discussing, questioning, brainstorming, inferencing, and problem-solving" (Weinstein & Mayer, 1986, p. 317).

Given these examples, can you determine which categories of online learning technologies support each type of cognitive learning strategies? (See also learning Activity 4 at the end of this chapter.)

The six categories of online learning technologies described previously are increasingly supporting learners to regulate, monitor, and direct their own learning. For example, using specific features of CMSs, learners can annotate materials and create their own private and shared hypermedia links within the learning materials. In addition, learners can test the viability of their ideas, inferences, and interpretations of the learning content through the use of synchronous and asynchronous communication tools embedded in CMSs. More examples of learner tools in CMSs are provided in Chapter 9 and at companion Web site of this book (http://prenhall.com/dabbagh).

Summary

In summary, a successful online learner should have the following competencies:

- Skill in the basic use of online learning technologies
- A basic understanding and appreciation of collaborative learning and competencies in related skills
- Self-directed learning skills through the deployment of cognitive learning strategies

The students in The Online Class scenario can be perceived as having demonstrated these competencies. They all enrolled in the online course, given the stated prerequisite, and completed the course successfully. However, their success can also be attributed to the expertise of the online instructor, who was able to implement appropriate instructional strategies and provide the support and **scaffolding** needed to ensure success. In the next section, we discuss the characteristics and competencies of the online instructor.

CHARACTERISTICS OF THE ONLINE INSTRUCTOR

The success of any distance education effort rests squarely on the shoulders of the faculty (Willis, 2001). Willis listed special challenges confronting instructors teaching at a distance. For example, instructors must do the following:

- Develop an understanding of the characteristics and needs of distant students with little first-hand experience and limited, if any, face-to-face contact
- Adapt teaching styles, taking into consideration the needs and expectations of multiple, often diverse, audiences
- Develop a working understanding of **delivery technologies** while remaining focused on their teaching role
- Function effectively as a skilled facilitator as well as a content provider

With the shift to a social constructivist conceptualization of online learning and the learner assuming an active role in using online learning technologies to interact with peers and exercise awareness, knowledge, and control over his or her learning, the instructor's role is changing. Formerly an authoritative figure and bearer and transmitter of "correct" and expert knowledge, the instructor is now an adviser, a coach, a moderator, and a facilitator of learning. Therefore, the instructor's role in online learning environments must be reconceptualized so that it aligns with the principles of learning as a social process.

Thach and Murphy (1995) reviewed the distance education literature with the goal of identifying the competencies of distance education professionals in all roles. Seven competencies emerged that can be used as a framework for rethinking the teacher's role in online learning. In the following subsections, we describe each of these competencies and provide examples of how the online instructor can apply each competency in an online learning environment to foster meaningful action and interaction. Table 2.2 provides an overview of these competencies and their implications for the design of online learning activities.

Competencies of Distance Education Professionals Applied to Online Learning Contexts

Interpersonal communication and feedback   The interpersonal communication and feedback competency includes being able to communicate with students individually and/or in small groups and to understand the need for immediate responses such as praising students and providing individualized and guiding feedback to scaffold the learner in the online learning experience. Student expectations for fast responses increase in online learning environments (Burge, 1999). Teachers need strategies and support to cope with this expectation. One such strategy is to delegate learning to groups and thus implement the notion of distributed course events. Alternatively, instructors may create a class Listserv or a discussion area dedicated to addressing student concerns and questions and must check it frequently, providing appropriate and timely responses. The studies that Thach and Murphy (1995) reviewed showed that students responded positively to instructors who took the time to communicate with them individually, even though they were physically separated, and that program success and retention was greatly affected by the instructor's interpersonal and communication skills. Williams (2003) also found that interpersonal and communication skills were among the top 10 competencies in distance education. Asynchronous and synchronous learning technologies are instrumental in supporting these competencies.

Promotion of interaction   The competency of promoting interaction also relies heavily on the use of asynchronous and synchronous communication tools. However, the goal is to promote interaction and collaboration rather than timely responses to student concerns and feedback on assignments. For example, planning asynchronous online discussions based on the learning content, setting appropriate discussion

Table 2.2   Competencies of Online Instructors and Related Instructional Techniques

BROAD COMPETENCY	EXAMPLE OF IMPLEMENTATION
Interpersonal communication and feedback	Provide timely response to student questions by e-mail Provide timely feedback on student assignments by e-mail
Promotion of interaction	Facilitate a discussion forum, model appropriate discussion protocols, synthesize key points of discussion
Administrative and support service skills	Provide links from course Web site to institution's technical support services Provide e-mail addresses of technical support staff
Teamwork skills	Provide clear procedures for group activities (e.g., arrange students in small learning groups, provide a time line for completion of tasks, provide a group posting area for drafts, provide an evaluation rubric that includes peer assessment, and encourage students to support one another)
Knowledge of how to conduct a needs assessment	Provide links to online versions of questionnaires or inventories that assess students' technology skills, learning styles, prior knowledge and experience, etc. Use the results to determine the degree of structure and support you need to provide
Comprehension of new learning technologies and their impact on learners	Participate in an asynchronous discussion forum or an online community of practice to get a sense of what it means to engage in online discourse Reflect on your experience both as a learner and as an instructor
Development of a systems perspective of thinking	Examine your current face-to-face teaching practices and whether they apply to teaching online Examine the current research on online learning and which strategies apply to your context (see Chapter 3) Examine your institution's policies on distance education and online learning and the degree of technological and administrative support provided

protocols, and **modeling** to students how to engage in an asynchronous discussion and apply cognitive learning strategies to meaningfully synthesize the key points of a discussion is an effective strategy for promoting interaction in online learning. Recall that Robert's instructor in The High School Student scenario formed small-group discussion areas to promote interaction and collaboration. The instructor in The Online Class scenario also communicated to her students that interaction and collaboration are a major component of the online course. Protocols and rubrics for structuring asynchronous online discussions are provided in the Resources section for Chapter 7 at the companion Web site: http://www.prenhall.com/dabbagh.

Administrative and support service skills Administrative and support service skills can also be referred to as *managerial,* or *strategy planning, skills* (Williams, 2003). Online instructors must be prepared to assist students with administrative functions such as registration procedures (if this is a component of the online course) and provide technical support (or have a technical support mechanism in place for students to get help on technical issues). In addition, online instructors must provide clear expectations of what is required of students in terms of learning outcomes, assignments, the amount of time to be spent online and off-line, and any prerequisite skills needed. Beatrice, the systems analyst in The Working Professional scenario, would expect all these administrative and instructional elements to be clearly outlined at the beginning of an online course. Recall that Beatrice is a working mother of two whose goal is to complete a master's degree as efficiently as possible without having to leave her home. Therefore, she would need to know upfront what is expected in terms of time commitment, prerequisite skills, and where to get technical support. The instructor in The Online Class scenario included some of these requirements in the course announcement to apprise interested students of the prerequisites. Web-based hypermedia technologies can help online instructors operationalize these requirements. For example, online instructors can provide hypermedia links to technical support information and other resources that inform students of what is needed in terms of hardware, software, and prerequisite skills to successfully engage in an online course.

Teamwork skills In the study that Williams (2003) conducted, collaboration and teamwork skills were ranked first among general distance education competencies. In other studies (Thach & Murphy, 1995), researchers found that teamwork skills were necessary for two purposes: (a) for instructors to successfully interface with the technical and instructional support staff who are responsible for maintaining the servers and the software that delivers the online course, and (b) for instructors to promote teamwork, rather than competition, among students and thus enhance collegiality and learning as a social process. When online instructors promote teamwork, students learn how to value interaction and collaboration, which is a key characteristic of the successful online learner. Robert learned this in The High School Student scenario. The instructor was able to promote a collaborative atmosphere by assigning students to small learning groups and allowing them to discuss the learning content online, which fostered an appreciation for interaction and multiple viewpoints and understandings.

Knowledge of how to conduct a needs assessment Having knowledge of how to conduct a needs assessment is part and parcel of the need for online instructors and developers to have instructional design skills. Instructional design is a field of study in which instructional or learning systems are analyzed, designed, developed, implemented, and evaluated (see Chapter 4). The analysis phase of instructional design includes conducting a learner analysis to assess learning styles, degree of prior knowledge, experience in the use of online learning technologies, degree of collaborative learning skills, knowledge of time-management and orienting skills, and degree of self-directed learning. Several online surveys and inventories can facilitate such data collection (see the Resources section for this chapter at the companion Web site: http://www.prenhall.com/dabbagh). Having access to such information will ensure that online learners have the skills necessary to successfully engage in online learning. In addition, such information will inform the online instructor or developer about how to structure the course to provide appropriate learner support.

Comprehension of new learning technologies and their impact on learners Online instructors need to know the technology and appear competent in using it. We listed six categories of online learning technologies that online learners should strive to be competent in to engage in meaningful online learning. Online instructors need to be competent in the same technologies so that they can design, deliver, and facilitate meaningful learning events. Although not all six categories of online learning technologies are used in all online courses, the online instructor must be prepared to support students in the appropriate pedagogical use of the class of online learning technologies used in a specific course. For an online instructor to facilitate an online learning environment that models learning as a social process, he or she must be skilled in the use of at least three classes of online learning technologies: (a) Web-based hypermedia technologies, (b) asynchronous and synchronous communication tools, and (c) Web-based publishing tools. According to research, to become competent in the use of asynchronous and synchronous communication tools, instructors should participate in a collaborative online learning environment to get a sense of what it means to engage in online discourse and reflect on their practices both as learners and as instructors of others (Salmon, 2000). In addition, CMSs are now allowing instructors to design, deliver, and facilitate online learning by integrating all classes of online learning technologies into one application that is easy to use and supportive of first-time users (see Chapter 9).

Development of a systems perspective of thinking Developing a systems perspective of thinking requires online instructors to be skilled in strategically planning and envisioning (seeing the big picture) the design of an online learning environment to ensure that all necessary elements and activities have been incorporated and that online learners are effectively participating through the use of online learning technologies. This means that the online instructor needs to be aware of the technological, logistical, and administrative challenges associated with designing, delivering, and facilitating an online course. These challenges are discussed later in this chapter.

The Importance of Scaffolding as an Instructional Strategy

In addition to having the seven competencies just discussed, online instructors should be skilled in scaffolding learning to provide "timely guidance and help learners in the form of encouragement, questions, and materials that lead to thinking and problem-solving processes" (McLoughlin & Oliver, 1999, p. 43). Scaffolding involves supporting novice learners by limiting the complexities of the context and gradually removing these limits as learners gain the knowledge, skills, and confidence to cope with the full complexity of the context (Young, 1993). Skillful teachers in traditional learning environments can support students through a range of scaffolding strategies that can lead learners to "deeper engagement" in order to solve a problem or complete a task by themselves. Scaffolding in online learning environments should be aimed at promoting self-directed learning, self-awareness of learning processes and strategies (metacognition, or "learning how to learn," as described previously), and collaborative learning (Dabbagh, 2003). Such scaffolding is a challenge for online instructors because of the broad range of expertise and cultural differences typically represented in an online student population.

Online learning technologies—particularly asynchronous and synchronous communication tools—can help instructors apply scaffolding techniques in online learning. For example, online instructors can use synchronous tools such as the whiteboard to model thinking processes through the think-aloud technique. Electronic mail can be used to provide timely individual feedback to help sustain student engagement and motivation. Likewise, asynchronous discussion forums can be used to promote interaction and collaboration among students. In addition, online instructors can employ the full spectrum of scaffolding techniques through the use of CMSs and their features. Scaffolding and CMSs are discussed in more detail in Chapters 6 and 9.

Role reciprocity   Instructor scaffolding in online learning is needed to transform the group process into a meaningful learning experience. The instructor has the organizational task of creating meaningful learning experiences and assuming the supportive role of assisting students to engage in these experiences as a community of learners. Instructors need to create an atmosphere of trust and foster a give-and-take (social negotiation) approach to learning by being a participant, a corespondent, and a facilitator. The goal is to create a learning culture in which interaction, collaboration, and knowledge building are promoted among peers and in which the teacher's role is reciprocal, supportive, and communicative as it is responsive to learner needs (McLoughlin & Oliver, 1999). As the learning environment moves toward a collaborative and student-centered approach, teacher and student roles can be seen as increasingly reciprocal. Table 2.3[2] demonstrates how teacher and student roles are reciprocated.

The "right balance"   Scaffolding involves providing the appropriate amount of structure in a learning environment, keeping in mind that some learners may require little or no structure and others may require a lot of structure (Dabbagh, 2003). Too much scaffolding could result in dampening students' efforts to actively pursue their learning goals, which may cause them to lose their momentum or drive toward meaning-making and self-directed learning efforts. Too little scaffolding could result in the students' inability to successfully complete or perform certain tasks and instructional activities, which may lead to anxiety, frustration, and, finally, loss of motivation and attrition. Therefore, scaffolding is a delicate balancing act for online instructors that can be difficult to achieve without adequate support, training, and time. Students can help instructors find the right balance by fully participating, taking responsibility for identifying and asking for the level and type of scaffolding they need, and scaffolding others when possible. "With encouragement, students become skilled at seeking the type of scaffolding they require, and will also engage in peer scaffolding" (McLoughlin & Oliver, 1999, p. 44).

Table 2.3   Teacher–Student Roles in Traditional Versus Online Learning Environments

Type of Role	Teacher Role	Student Role	Learning Environment
Traditional role in face-to-face class	Manager, expert, disciplinarian, controller, dispenser of information, goal setter, timekeeper	Listener, receiver, novice, passive learner, reliant on instructor for assessment of learning	Objectivist, directed or teacher centered, much teacher scaffolding, use of supplantive strategies, highly structured
Supportive role in online learning	Resource, coparticipant, scaffolder, colearner, moderator, facilitator, coach, monitor, adviser	Problem solver, explorer, researcher, collaborator, goal setter, moderator, facilitator, scaffolder, participant	Constructivist, learner centered, emphasis on collaborative learning, use of generative learning strategies, less or adaptive teacher scaffolding, peer scaffolding

Note. Adapted from "Pedagogic Roles and Dynamics in Telematics Environments," by C. McLoughlin and R. Oliver, in *Telematics in Education: Trends and Issues* (p. 39), edited by M. Selinger and J. Pearson, 1999, Kidlington, Oxford, UK: Pergamon Press.

---

[2] This table is an adaptation of McLoughlin and Oliver's table (1999, p. 39) on contrasting roles and discourse in traditional versus information and communications technologies (ICT) classrooms. It was adapted to include the additional skills and characteristics of online teachers and learners discussed in this chapter.

Another process that could help teachers to find the "right balance" when they are scaffolding learners is conducting a **needs assessment**. As mentioned previously, conducting a needs assessment is an important competency for distance education professionals. By conducting a needs assessment, online instructors can determine the degree of scaffolding required on the basis of their learners' **cognitive characteristics.** For example, on one hand, a lesser amount of scaffolding is recommended when learners have much prior knowledge, have a wide range of cognitive strategies, are flexible and highly motivated, have low anxiety, and attribute success and failure on tasks to internal factors (internal locus of control). On the other hand, more scaffolding is recommended when learners have little prior knowledge, have few cognitive strategies, and have high anxiety, low motivation, and an external locus of control (Smith & Ragan, 1999).

Summary

In summary, the online instructor must be prepared to wear many hats and assume many roles. In an online learning environment that is premised on learning as a social process and experiencing an increasingly diverse and dynamic online learner population, the instructor's role needs to be reconceptualized from that of an expert, a main deliverer of knowledge, and an organizer of learning events to that of a resource, a scaffolder, a coparticipant, and a facilitator of learning. This transformation from a didactic role to a supportive role requires knowledge and skill in the competencies outlined previously. However, the online instructor faces many challenges that could present barriers to assuming these new roles. These challenges are discussed next.

CHALLENGES FACING THE ONLINE INSTRUCTOR

Although CMSs are allowing instructors to more easily design, deliver, and facilitate online learning because of their comprehensive and integrative nature, ease of use, and embedded user support systems, faculty and instructors using such tools for the first time are presented with several challenges, including pedagogical, technological, logistical, and implementation challenges. Pedagogical challenges are discussed in more detail in Chapters 4, 5, and 6. Several theoretical models and frameworks are presented, and their impact on the redesign of instruction for online delivery is discussed. In the next section of this chapter, we discuss the technological, logistical, and implementation challenges facing the online instructor, and the infrastructure needed to support the teacher and the learner in carrying out online learning activities.

Technological Challenges

Most online instructors assume that students who enroll in online courses understand how to use technology to support their learning. For example, one common assumption is that if students are familiar with the use of e-mail and class Listservs, they will easily adapt to actively engaging in other asynchronous learning tools such as threaded discussion forums (a type of online discussion format in which messages are grouped under threads). The fact is that, without proper instructional support and practice, many novice students will find posting messages to threaded discussions a daunting task, and the instructor will have to spend a considerable amount of time and effort communicating to students effective posting and reading techniques (Dabbagh, 2000).

Another technological challenge facing online instructors (and students) who use CMSs, for example, is uploading files and resources to the appropriate areas of the course Web site. Several steps are involved, and the procedure is not usually intuitive. Instructors and students who are skilled in the use of online learning technologies may have little problem with this task. However, without appropriate support and guidance, others may struggle endlessly. Such technological issues can interfere with the learning process, causing frustration for both the students and the instructor. Therefore, online instructors need to approach the implementation of a new learning technology by modeling its use to students and providing clear instructions on how it should be used in the context of the overall course structure and pedagogy.

The preceding examples can be characterized as software issues challenging the online instructor and the online learner. Other software issues include providing access to the appropriate class of technologies and applications that facilitate the learning activities of an online course and making sure that students have adequate online support to receive guidance in using these applications.

In addition, hardware issues challenge the online instructor. For example, instructors need to consider whether students are receiving appropriate guidance on how to set up hardware equipment and to ensure that hardware requirements for the course are clearly stated (Khan, 2001). Other hardware issues include bandwidth and speed of communication lines. "With a heavy reliance on a computer, modem, and network connection, access to hardware is a substantial issue" (Hill, 1997, p. 77). However, these issues are largely the institution's responsibility and not the instructor's. Institutions need to have an adequate technological infrastructure in place to support access to its servers and to Web-based courseware applications and online learning technologies. Institutional planning for a technological infrastructure is discussed in more detail in Chapter 9.

Logistical and Implementation Challenges

Instructors who have committed to the use of online learning technologies need administrative support to help them manage the logistical and implementation challenges of online learning. Many universities and organizations have initiated centers to support faculty in using innovative learning technologies, and the efficacy of these centers is instrumental to the success of online learning. The staff of administrative support centers for innovative learning technologies must keep abreast of faculty needs and provide instructional support through workshops, online tutorials, and help guides.

Most CMSs (e.g., WebCT and Blackboard) have extensive resources (some built into the tool) to support first-time users; however, faculty are often reluctant to rely on this type of guidance because it does not take into consideration the existing course format and pedagogy that faculty have been using in a traditional classroom environment. Instead, faculty find themselves spending double the time and effort in reorganizing their course materials to fit the new delivery medium, losing focus of the pedagogical implications of the technology. The transformation from face-to-face learning to online learning requires what Collis, Andernach, and van Diepen (1996) referred to as *pedagogical reengineering*, which is where support centers can help. Support centers should be staffed with instructional designers who are skilled at identifying the teaching needs of faculty and helping them integrate online learning technologies as effectively as possible by demonstrating the learning affordances that these technologies enable. In its report on the quality of online learning, the Institute for Higher Education Policy (2000) listed the following elements under what it calls *faculty support benchmarks*:

- Technical assistance in course development should be available to faculty;
- Faculty members should be assisted in the transition from classroom teaching to online instruction and are assessed during the process;

- Instructor training and assistance, including peer mentoring, should continue through the progression of the online course;
- Faculty members should be provided with written resources to deal with issues arising from student use of electronically-accessed data. (p. 3)

Having sufficient support at your institution will diminish the logistical and implementation challenges associated with making the leap to online learning. However, the implementation of online learning provokes changes in an institution's culture. The roles of instructors, learners, research assistants, libraries, administrators, and computer support personnel must shift to make these environments successful. In this chapter, we discussed how the roles of the online learner and the online instructor are shifting to promote successful engagement in online learning. It is beyond the scope of this book to discuss how the roles of other stakeholders in distance education and online learning should change. Suffice it to say that online learning "prompts a rethinking of the power relations between instructors, staff, students and administrators" (Besser & Bonn, 1997, p. 36).

Summary

Many of the technological, logistical, and implementation challenges just discussed can be addressed on a one-time start-up basis. However, issues of curricular support and instructional approaches need to be continually negotiated and reconceptualized as the technological infrastructure and educators' use of it changes. One important faculty support benchmark is the institution's preparedness to handle intellectual property and copyright as they relate to electronic media and online courses. In the last section of this chapter, we address this challenge.

INTELLECTUAL PROPERTY AND COPYRIGHT IN ONLINE LEARNING
CONSIDER THE FOLLOWING THREE SCENARIOS:

Beautiful Biology: You are taking your first steps toward putting your Introduction to Biology course materials online. You are a good writer, but you have no skills in graphic design. You would like your materials to look professional and appealing. You find some interesting graphics on someone's Web site. You decide to copy them and use them in your materials. You will reference the Web site from which you obtained them. Furthermore, when your students attend class sessions, they use an educational biology CD in their lab. The CD features a video file of wildlife unique to the Galapagos Islands. You would like to have your students review the video as a homework assignment. If you upload the video file, the students could easily use it. Are you doing anything wrong?

Newton's World: You are a physics instructor at a public institution. Your students always seem to have trouble understanding Newtonian physics. You develop an interactive microworld (computer simulation) to help them understand centrifugal force. It is a great success. You consider submitting the simulation to an educational publisher. The money you receive will help you pay for a course you would like to take so that you can make more sophisticated instructional interactions. Are you breaking the law?

Cartoon Character for Hire: You have just been engaged by an educational software developer to produce a CD that can be used to teach English as a second language to children. You would like to use some cartoon characters from popular TV shows to motivate the children. Should you discuss doing so with someone in the company's legal department?

These situations demonstrate examples of intellectual property, copyright, and plagiarism dilemmas facing instructors and developers in online learning. Think about them as you read the following general description of copyright and how it relates to online learning.

Intellectual Property, Copyright, and Plagiarism

Copyright law, especially that pertaining to technological uses of intellectual property, is changing rapidly. New legislation and legal cases have and will continue to amend or refine existing statutes. Furthermore, the law always lags behind technological innovations, uses of this technology, and the emergence of new stakeholders (both individuals and organizations) whose actions impinge on copyright issues. The companion Web site of this book (http://prenhall.com/dabbagh) contains additional background and topical information, as well as a list of resources and references, to help you explore copyright issues more fully. However, the information is only as current as its revision date. None of the information on the Web site or in this book is a substitute for professional legal expertise.

The terms *copyright* and *intellectual property* are often used interchangeably. Legally speaking, however, *intellectual property* is a broader term. Poltorak and Lerner (2002) discussed several distinctions that can be summarized as follows. *Intellectual property* refers to any class of item that meets one of the following criteria:

- An author's original creation expressed in any medium, including pictorially, lexically (textually), or recorded by digital or analog means
- A new invention that has utility
- A text and/or graphic that identifies a provider of services or goods

Each type of intellectual property is provided a specific legal protection that stipulates the conditions under which the work may be used. The legal protections for the first set of criteria fall under copyright law; the second set, patent agreements; and the third set, trademark or service mark statutes. In this section, we discuss only copyright because this law (the Copyright Act of 1976 and its amendments) governs most intellectual property used or developed in educational contexts. *Not "all things intellectual" are protected by law.* As Poltorak and Lerner (2002) observed, "Copyright protects only the expression of an idea, not the idea being expressed" (p. 30). For example, in the musical *West Side Story*, what is copyrighted is not the idea to portray the destructiveness of hate, but the expression of the idea in the musical score, the script, and the choreography.

Copyright law, Title 17 of the U.S. Legal Code, provides the creator of intellectual property (or the copyright owner) the exclusive right to use the work, including the right to deny or grant the use of the work (for free or in exchange for a payment) to anyone or any organization. Infringement, the unauthorized use of copyrighted work, is a violation of federal law. Infringement and plagiarism are two different misdeeds. The use of intellectual property without proper attribution is plagiarism, an ethical breach. By citing the author, an individual can avoid plagiarism. However, merely providing attribution does not relieve the user of responsibility for obtaining permission from the copyright holder and could be construed as infringement. The defense most often used against infringement asserts that the action falls under the protection of the **"fair use"** section.

Fair Use: Legal Versus Common Perspectives

The unauthorized use of intellectual property is becoming increasingly easy as technology makes it simpler to digitize, copy, and distribute text, images, audio, and video works with no loss of fidelity. What is becoming increasingly difficult for computer users is understanding which actions violate copyright law and which are protected under the same law as fair use. The perception of many computer users, especially those who use the Internet, is that anything posted publicly has no copyright protection and is fair game for copying. *This perception is incorrect.* In addition, not all electronic copying that can be done remotely and anonymously, and that does not involve monetary gain, can be justified as fair use. *Fair use* in the legal sense of the phrase does not exonerate all nonprofit uses of a work—even those that are strictly for educational purposes. The doctrine of fair use is articulated in Section 107 of the Copyright Act of 1976. It identifies four conditions (the *four-factor test*), all of which must be met for an unauthorized use of a work to be considered fair use:

1. The purpose and character of the use, including whether such use is of a commercial nature or is for nonprofit educational purposes
2. The nature of the copyrighted work
3. The amount and substantiality of the portion used in relation to the copyrighted work as a whole
4. The effect of the use on the potential market for, or value of, the copyrighted work

None of these conditions is straightforward. In an effort to help the average individual observe copyright restrictions appropriately, many organizations have developed guidelines that define fair use in terms of time and quantity limitations on the amount of materials used. These guidelines represent reasonable attempts to interpret the law in concrete terms. They focus on the third factor (quantity) in the four-factor fair use test. Although they can be helpful, as rules of thumb they are not "the law" verbatim.

Consider that this book contains many quotations. We (the authors) believe we made fair use of the materials, not simply because the quotations are so short (Factor 3) but because of the nature of the works quoted. We expect that these works will be discussed within the educational community and that they will be quoted as part of the discussions (Factor 2). Such activities will have no adverse impact on the market value of the work (Factor 4). Factor 4 is crucial to the test of fair use. The moment money enters the picture, the claim of fair use as a legal defense weakens considerably. Money can be a factor in even the most innocuous-looking circumstances. See the companion Web site (http://prenhall.com/dabbagh) for examples of significant court decisions in fair use cases.

Copyright law and fair use exemptions were developed before the advent of the Internet. Do the rules that apply to face-to-face classroom fair use map to the open **architecture** and ubiquitous nature of the Internet? Which considerations are important for the online instructor or course developer? Reexamine the Beautiful Biology scenario as you look at the role of fair use in online learning contexts.

Fair Use in Online Learning Contexts

Fair use, Section 107 of the Copyright Act, was originally written, as a guide for educators, to cover photocopying for classroom use. Section 110 of the law provided exemptions for educational uses of media such as audiotapes and videotapes. However, drafters of the exemption envisioned only certain types of educational contexts, such as face-to-face instruction or telecasts of live instruction to remote sites. Nothing in the law provided for the type of learning environment afforded through the Internet. The Technology, Education, and Copyright Harmonization (TEACH) Act of 2002 was written as a response to this need. It amends Section 110 of the law to provide for the transmission of copyrighted **digital media** (e.g., digital reproductions of literary works and "reasonable portions" of performances such as dramas) over the Internet as part of an instructional course offered by a nonprofit educational organization. The provisions of the TEACH Act require that the media be "displayed" as part of a class "session" within the scope of regular "mediated instructional activities." Copyrighted materials must be made available only to students enrolled in the course and must be accessible by these students for only a limited time. The TEACH Act stipulates that reasonable precautions should be taken to prevent students from downloading and saving copyrighted materials. If media have embedded copyright protection, this protection may not be removed or circumvented.

Some online learning technologies discussed previously in this chapter have direct relevance to the TEACH Act. CMSs are clearly important to ensuring compliance with the TEACH Act. Instructors can control who accesses instructional materials, including copyrighted works, by enrolling only registered students. Courses can be password protected, and course sections can be "closed" at the end of a semester. So, if our biology instructor includes the copyrighted media in a course delivered through a CMS, he or she would have potentially satisfied the criterion that media are limited to enrolled students. In addition, by taking advantage of fair use and the provisions of the TEACH Act, institutions can avoid incurring substantial expenses for licensing fees. Carnevale (2003) presented the following situations, which existed before the TEACH Act was passed:

> Avoiding royalties is a big attraction, especially for colleges that have been paying to use copyrighted materials online. For example, Bellevue Community College, near Seattle, pays $50 to $100 for each article from *National Geographic* that it posts online; Eastern University, near Philadelphia, pays about $5 each for articles from *Fortune Magazine*. The fees add up: Copyright works for its online courses cost University of Maryland University College about $200,000 a year, which it would not have to pay under the TEACH Act. (p. 29)

The TEACH Act could help these institutions save money and justify the expenses of purchasing and maintaining a CMS to support online learning. However, some experts wonder whether CMSs have all the safeguards necessary to satisfy the TEACH Act. Others believe that the newest versions of well-known CMSs have adequate protections, even for the thorniest requirement, to prevent unauthorized duplication of copyrighted material. Talab (2003) wrote:

> Reasonably effective technological measures would indicate that the institution or body had made all reasonable efforts to use software and hardware that would prevent unauthorized duplication. RealNetworks, Quicktime and most other streaming audio or video products that are a part of Blackboard, WebCT, etc., that are recently updated have these security controls. (p. 5)

The adequacy of these protections may ultimately be decided in the courts. In the meantime, CMS providers will continue to enhance their copyright protection features to attract the educational market.

One additional facet of the TEACH Act is its departure from the tradition of placing the responsibility for decisions of fair use exclusively on the educator. In a report on the TEACH Act for the American Association of Librarians, Crews (2002) noted the following:

> Many provisions focus entirely on the behavior of educational institutions, rather than the actions of instructors. Consequently, the institution must impose restrictions on access, develop new policy, and disseminate copyright information. (p. 3)

Such provisions would involve the participation of the administration, the legal and policy-making parties, and the technical personnel in the management of copyright. In fact, educational institutions are taking a more active role in defining and communicating guidelines for educators, staff, and students about copyright and other aspects of responsible use of technology for education and research. Only a rare organization does not have a published set of guidelines, checklists, and policies, and, increasingly often, procedures for dealing with infractions. Refer to the companion Web site (http://www.prenhall.com/dabbagh) for examples of organizational policy statements on copyright.

Application of Copyright Law in Different Contexts

The educator As an educator, you must consider a complex set of copyright issues. First, you should know the law and your institution's policy as they apply to you and your activities. Encouraged by the TEACH Act, educational institutions are developing guidelines for the use of copyrighted multimedia in courses developed for online learning and for protecting materials their employees develop. An institution may also publish policies describing the circumstances under which individuals may claim ownership of work developed while they are working at the institution. If your organization has a copyright office, a library, or a technology support group, these administrative units may provide information on copyright guidelines. Second, if you are involved in research, you may need to consider whether you own the copyrights to the outputs of your research. Your funding source, either from the private (for-profit) sector or from public (nonprofit) sources, may affect the status and ownership of your work. Last, you should also know how copyright law applies to your students and their work.

The student Students who use copyrighted materials for a project connected to their coursework are not exempt from intellectual property law. However, because student projects have limited circulation and probably would not impinge on the owner's market, fair use generally applies. Note that students' works that are published on the Internet (as opposed to posted within a controlled environment, such as a CMS) may not be eligible for fair use exceptions. For example, the companion Web site for this book features Web prototypes developed by students as class projects. The projects were posted in a CMS that had a section allocated only to members of their class. To use these student-developed works, we (the authors) had to obtain the students' permission. If a student used copyrighted materials in his or her project, we either removed them or sought permission for their use. Although the students might have made fair use of copyrighted materials for a project, using these materials as part of a textbook or an educational product without proper consent would not be considered fair use.

Institutional guidelines for students are important. They may be published within the same policies that apply to educators and staff, or they may be contained in other sources, such as a student handbook or a "responsible use of computing" policy. They may also be referred to as "acceptable use" or "appropriate use." The library, the technology support group, or the registrar's office (at a college or university) may be able to help you locate such guidelines. If your organization's Web site has a search engine, you can search for "intellectual property" or "copyright" using that feature.

The instructional developer The statement was made previously that the moment money enters the picture, fair use and other defenses available under copyright law are no longer applicable. This is the case if you work for a for-profit organization. For example, consider the Cartoon Character for Hire scenario. If you want to use Mickey Mouse in your educational CD to teach English, what do you as an online developer need to do? The for-profit situation can be something of a roller coaster. The downside of the situation is that permission must be obtained for every piece of intellectual property incorporated into your educational product. This sometimes daunting task is often handled by staff whose job is to do just that. These permissions most often come with fees and licensing agreements. The upside is that the course (in this case the CD) can be copyrighted. It can be sold, and fees can be charged for even a partial use of it. However, you still do not own the copyrighted material within the course, even though it is "housed" in your work. Another downside is that if you produced the course as an employee in fulfillment of your regular employment, you probably do not own any of your work (Poltorak & Lerner, 2002). You cannot sell it or take it with you if you get another job. However, prior to the start of the work, you may be able to execute an agreement with your organization to retain your ownership rights.

The online instructor The situation just described could also be true if you are an online instructor at a public institution. For example, what should the instructor do to market the Newton's microworld software described in the Newton's World scenario? You must not make assumptions if you plan to claim ownership and charge fees for an instructional product that you developed. The physics instructor needs to be aware of any institutional policies about works developed for classes taught at the institution. An institution may have reason to claim monetary and control rights to such work. For instance, it may have bought the instructor special software or provided technical assistance during the development phase of this instructional product. If the physics instructor used no institutional resources to develop the simulation, he or she could more easily make the case for ownership and market rights if an agreement had been in place prior to the start of the work.

Summary

The goal of protection of intellectual property, which is to allow the creator of a work to enjoy the fruits of his or her labor in the market, seems to be straightforward. However, its expression in copyright law is anything but straightforward. The details of the application of the law have been left to the courts to decide on the basis of individual merits in individual cases. As online learning grows in popularity, the number of court cases defending fair use will increase as institutions begin to test the limits of the TEACH Act. As an online instructor, developer, or learner, you will need to stay informed about changes in the law, its interpretation, and your organization's policies as they affect your roles and responsibilities.

CHAPTER SUMMARY

In this chapter, we discussed the characteristics of the online learner and the online instructor and their changing roles in online learning. The profile of the classic distance learner was described on the basis of earlier research findings. We determined that the current online learner does not fit a typical or standard profile and that the only constant in this emerging population is its changing dynamic. Specific skills and competencies of the online learner and the online instructor were presented on the basis of the principles of globalization and learning as a social process. Three competencies, or skills, were identified as critical for an online learner to be successful: (a) being proficient in the use of online learning technologies, (b) valuing interaction and collaboration, and (c) acquiring self-directed learning skills. Six broad categories of online learning technologies were identified and described from the perspective of their use by the online learner. These are Web-based hypermedia technologies, Web-based multimedia technologies, asynchronous and synchronous communication tools, Web-based publishing and authoring tools, presentation and visualization tools, and course management systems (CMSs). Seven competencies were identified for the online instructor: (a) interpersonal communication and feedback, (b) promotion of interaction, (c) administrative and support service skills, (d) teamwork skills, (e) knowledge of how to conduct a needs assessment, (f) comprehension of new learning technologies and their impact on learners, and (g) development of a systems perspective of thinking. In addition, scaffolding was described as an important instructional strategy in online learning. Also discussed were the technological, logistical, implementation, and administrative, or institutional, challenges facing the online instructor and the online learner. Last, intellectual property and copyright were discussed as they relate to electronic media and online learning environments.

LEARNING ACTIVITIES

1. Develop a checklist outlining the characteristics and competencies of the online learner as described in this chapter. On a scale of 1–5, rate yourself on each competency to determine whether you would qualify as a successful online learner. Identify the competencies in which you think you are lacking and what you might do to develop these competencies.
2. Develop a checklist outlining the competencies of the online instructor as described in this chapter. On a scale of 1–5, rate yourself on each competency to determine whether you would qualify as a successful online instructor. Identify the competencies in which you think you are lacking and what you might do to develop these competencies.
3. Visit the companion Web site (http://www.prenhall.com/dabbagh) and take the pretest "Is Online Learning for Me?" Share the results with a classmate. On the basis of your reading of this chapter, what would you add to this survey to make it more comprehensive?
4. Using the six categories of online learning technologies presented in this chapter and the four classes of cognitive learning strategies identified by Weinstein and Mayer (1986), develop a table that maps the technologies to the strategies. Break down the technologies and strategies into their constituents as you develop this chart.

5. Return to the three scenarios described at the beginning of the chapter. Do you think working professionals and graduate students are better positioned to engage in online learning than undergraduate students are? Why or why not? Reexamine the discussion of the classic distance learner, the changing nature of the distance learner, and the emerging online learner to support your answer. Conduct a small survey at your organization to validate your answer.

6. Research your organization's technological infrastructure and administrative support potential. Determine to what degree your organization can support online learning. Share your findings with your classmates.

7. Return to the three scenarios described at the beginning of the intellectual property discussion. On the basis of your reading of this section, what conclusions can you make about the legality of each case? What other kinds of information might you need to know? Where do you think you might find it? Make a list of assumptions, knowns, unknowns, and potential sources of information.

8. Visit the companion Web site (http://www.prenhall.com/dabbagh) and research the list you made in the previous activity. How good were your assumptions and conclusions? Find additional sources of information to answer your "unknowns." You may not be able to reach a definitive "finding" without making many assumptions. Share your findings with your classmates.

9. Research your company or your college or university's policies on intellectual property. Record where you found the information and whom you would contact for clarification.

10. Develop your own case study on intellectual property and copyright or select a court case from the companion Web site. Identify how your organization might solve it. Challenge others to resolve the issue from their organization's perspectives.

RESOURCES

Explore additional resources at the companion Website (http://www/prenhall.com/dabbagh) to learn more learning technologies, learning styles, and barriers to distance learning.

REFERENCES

Anderson, T. D., & Garrison, D. R. (1998). Learning in a networked world: New roles and responsibilities. In C. C. Gibson (Ed.), *Distance learners in higher education* (pp. 97–112). Madison, WI: Atwood.

Bannan, B., & Milheim, W. D. (1997). Existing Web-based instruction courses and their design. In B. H. Khan (Ed.), *Web-based instruction* (pp. 381–388). Englewood Cliffs, NJ: Educational Technology Publications.

Bednar, A. K., Cunningham, D., Duffy, T. M., & Perry, J. D. (1992). Theory into practice: How do we link? In T. M. Duffy & D. H. Jonassen (Eds.), *Constructivism and the technology of instruction: A conversation* (pp. 17–34). Hillsdale, NJ: Erlbaum.

Bernt, F. L., & Bugbee, A. C. (1993). Study practices and attitudes related to academic success in a distance learning programme. *Distance Education, 14*(1), 97–112.

Besser, H., & Bonn, M. (1997). Interactive distance-independent education: Challenges to traditional academic roles. *Journal of Education for Library and Information Science, 38*(1), 35–42.

Biner, P. M., Bink, M. L., Huffman, M. L., & Dean, R. S. (1995). Personality characteristics differentiating and predicting the achievement of televised-course students and traditional-course students. *The American Journal of Distance Education, 9*(2), 46-60.

Brown, J. S. (2000). *Growing up digital: How the Web changes work, education, and the ways people learn* [Electronic version]. Retrieved from *http://www.johnseelybrown.com/ Growing_up_digital.pdf*

Burge, E. J. (1999, April). *Keeping our balance in times of techno-turbulence.* Notes for a colloquium in honor of Helen Hugenor Lyman, School of Information and Library Studies, State University of New York–Buffalo. (ERIC Document Reproduction Service No. ED429170)

Carnevale, D. (2003). Slow start for long-awaited easing of copyright restriction. *The Chronicle of Higher Education, 49*(29), A29–A31.

Cheurprakobkit, S., Hale, D. F., & Olson, J. N. (2002). Technicians' perceptions about Web-based courses: The University of Texas system experience. *The American Journal of Distance Education, 16*(4), 245–258.

Coggins, C. C. (1988). Preferred learning styles and their impact on completion of external degree programs. *The American Journal of Distance Education, 2*(1), 25–37.

Collis, B., Andernach, T., & van Diepen, N. (1996). The Web as process tool and product environment for group-based project work in higher education. In *Proceedings of WebNet 96— World Conference of the Web Society, San Francisco, California, October 15–19, 1996.* Norfolk, VA: Association for the Advancement of Computing in Education.

Comeaux, P., Huber, R., Kasprzak, J., & Nixon, M. A. (1998, November). *Collaborative learning in Web-based instruction.* Paper presented at the 3rd WebNet 98 World Conference on the WWW, Internet, and Intranet, Orlando, FL.

Crews, K. D. (2002). *New copyright law for distance education: The meaning and importance of the TEACH Act.* Retrieved June 2, 2003, from Indiana University–Purdue University, Indianapolis, Copyright Management Center Web site: *http://www.copyright.iupui.edu/ teach_summary.htm*

Cushing, B. E. (1998). Critical Internet resource evaluation skills for adult learners in online learning environments. *Journal of Instruction Delivery Systems, 12*(4), 9–12.

Dabbagh, N. (2000). The challenges of interfacing between face-to-face and online instruction. *TechTrends, 44*(6), 37–42.

Dabbagh, N. (2003). Scaffolding: An important teacher competency in online learning. *TechTrends, 47*(2), 39–44.

Dille, B., & Mezack, M. (1991). Identifying predictors of high risk among community college telecourse students. *The American Journal of Distance Education, 2*(1), 25–37.

Eastmond, D. V. (1995). *Alone but together: Adult distance study through computer conferencing.* Cresskill, NJ: Hampton Press.

Fjortoft, N. F. (1995). *Predicting persistence in distance learning programs.* Paper presented at the Mid-Western Educational Research Meeting, Chicago. (ERIC Document Reproduction Service No. ED387620)

Galusha, J. M. (1997). Barriers to learning in distance education. *Interpersonal Computing and Technology Journal, 5*(3/4), 6–14.

Garland, M. R. (1993). Student perceptions of the situational, institutional, dispositional, and epistemological barriers to persistence. *Distance Education, 14*(2), 181–198.

Hanson, D., Maushak, N. J., Schlosser, C. A., Anderson, M. L., Sorensen, C., & Simonson, M. (1997). *Distance education: Review of the literature* (2nd ed.). Bloomington, IN: Association for Educational Communications and Technology.

Hill, J. R. (1997). Distance learning environments via the World Wide Web. In B. H. Khan (Ed.), *Web-based instruction* (pp. 75–80). Englewood Cliffs, NJ: Educational Technology Publications.

Hooper, S., & Hannafin, M. J. (1991). The effects of group composition on achievement, interaction, and learning efficiency during computer-based cooperative instruction. *Educational Technology Research & Development, 39*(3), 27–40.

The Institute for Higher Education Policy. (2000, April). *Quality on the line: Benchmarks for success in Internet-based distance education.* Retrieved from *http://www.ihep.com/Pubs/PDF/Qualiy.pdf*

Khan, B. H. (2001). A framework for Web-based learning. In B. H. Khan (Ed.), *Web-based training* (pp. 75–98). Englewood Cliffs, NJ: Educational Technology Publications.

Lambert, M. P. (2000). The home study inheritance. In M. G. Moore & N. Shin (Eds.), *Speaking personally about distance education: Foundations of contemporary practice* (pp. 7–11). University Park: The American Center for the Study of Distance Education, The Pennsylvania State University.

Laube, M. R. (1992). Academic and social integration variables and secondary student persistence in distance education. *Research in Distance Education, 4*(1), 2–5.

Lindblom-Ylanne, S., & Pihlajamaki, H. (2003). Can a collaborative network environment enhance essay-writing processes? *British Journal of Educational Technology, 34*(1), 17–30.

MacKeracher, D. (1996). *Making sense of adult learning.* Toronto, Canada: Culture Concepts.

McLoughlin, C., & Luca, J. (2002). A learner-centered approach to developing team skills through Web-based learning and assessment. British Journal of Educational Technology, *33*(5), 571–582.

McLoughlin, C., & Oliver, R. (1999). Pedagogic roles and dynamics in telematics environments. In M. Selinger & J. Pearson (Eds.), *Telematics in education: Trends and issues* (pp. 32–50). Kidlington, Oxford, UK: Pergamon Press.

Olgren, C. H. (1998). Improving learning outcomes: The effects of learning strategies and motivation. In C. C. Gibson (Ed.), *Distance learners in higher education* (pp. 77–96). Madison, WI: Atwood.

Poltorak, A. I., & Lerner, P. J. (2002). *Essentials of intellectual property.* New York: Wiley.

Powell, G. C. (2000). Are You Ready for WBT? Paper posted to Instructional Technology Forum electronic mailing list, archived at *http://it.coe.uga.edu/itforum/paper39/paper39.html*

Pugliese, R. R. (1994). Telecourse persistence and psychological variables. *The American Journal of Distance Education, 8*(3), 22–39.

Purdy, L. N. (2000). Telecourses in the community college. In M. G. Moore & N. Shin (Eds.), *Speaking personally about distance education: Foundations of contemporary practice* (pp. 7–11). University Park: The American Center for the Study of Distance Education, The Pennsylvania State University.

Rekkedal, T. (1982). The drop-out problem and what to do about it. In J. S. Daniel, S. A. Stroud, & J. R. Thompson (Eds.), *Learning at a distance: A world perspective* (pp. 118–121). Edmonton, Canada: Athabasca University. (ERIC Document Reproduction Service No. ED222635).

Salmon, G. (2000). *E-moderating: The key to teaching and learning online.* London: Kegan Page.

Smith, P., & Ragan, T. (1999). *Instructional design.* Upper Saddle River, NJ: Prentice Hall.

Spector, J. M. (1999). *Teachers as designers of collaborative distance learning.* Paper presented at SITE 99: 10th Society for Information Technology & Teacher Education International Conference, San Antonio, TX. (ERIC Document Reproduction Service No. ED432259)

Stone, T. E. (1992). A new look at the role of locus of control in completion rates in distance education. *Research in Distance Education, 4*(2), 6–9.

Talab, R. (2003). An initial look at the TEACH Act. *TechTrends,* 47(2), 4–6.

TeleEducation NB. (2002). *New media survey.* Retrieved February 13, 2004, from *http://teleeducation.nb.ca/content/web-guides/english/NewMediaSurvey/index.htm*

Thach, E. C., & Murphy, K. L. (1995). Competencies for distance education professionals. *Educational Technology Research & Development, 43*(1), 57–79.

Thompson, M. M. (1998). Distance learners in higher education. In C. C. Gibson (Ed.), *Distance learners in higher education* (pp. 9–24). Madison, WI: Atwood.

Weinstein, C. E., & Mayer, R. E. (1986). The teaching of learning strategies. In M. C. Wittrock (Ed.), *Handbook of research on teaching* (3rd ed.; pp. 315–325). New York: Macmillan.

Williams, P. E. (2003). Roles and competencies of distance education programs in higher education institutions. *The American Journal of Distance Education, 17*(1), 45–57.

Willis, B. (1994). *Distance education: Strategies and tools.* Englewood Cliffs, NJ: Educational Technology Publications.

Willis, B. (2001). *Distance education at a glance.* Retrieved June 7, 2001, from *http://www.uidaho.edu/eo/distglan.html*

Wilson, B. (1996). What is a constructivist learning environment? In B. G. Wilson (Ed.), *Constructivist learning environments: Case studies in instructional design* (pp. 3–8). Englewood Cliffs, NJ: Educational Technology Publications.

Young, M. F. (1993). Instructional design for situated learning. *Educational Technology Research & Development, 41*(1), 43–58.

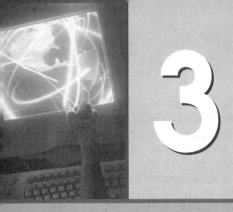

3

RESEARCH ON ONLINE LEARNING

After completing this chapter, you should understand the following:

- The types of research related to online learning

- The prominent categories of online learning research, such as asynchronous learning, synchronous learning, interactivity, online learning communities, hypertext and hypermedia, Web-based instruction, student perceptions of online learning, and faculty and instructor perspectives on online learning

- The prominent topics and constructs in each presented category of research

- The instructional strategies and activities suggested by online learning research

- The applicability of research results to the practice of online learning

- The current state and focus of much of the research on online learning

CONSIDER THE FOLLOWING SCENARIO:

Clay and Marta work for the training department of a major government agency. Their responsibilities include designing, developing, and administering the in-house training, policies, and procedures related to online learning or e-learning, initiatives. Recently, Clay and Marta teamed up to present a business case for the development and implementation of a customized **learning management system (LMS)** for their agency and its bureaus. They defined an LMS to their supervisors as "a software application or Web-based technology used to plan, implement, store and assess learning activities." Clay and Marta thoroughly explored the need for this technology by reviewing their experiences with online training, interviewing agency employees, reviewing the latest reports on the use of LMSs, and examining other agency e-learning activities. Afterward, they drafted a formal report and presentation that described the need for and benefits of a comprehensive, automated LMS. The analysis and documentation of the need for a customized system that could assess, identify, develop, implement, and evaluate online learning sold the agency's leadership. Clay and Marta gained approval to supervise the design, development, and implementation of the LMS and to outsource the programming to a multimedia development firm. Working closely with the contractors, Clay and Marta then developed an LMS that includes asynchronous and synchronous communication, online communities, evaluation tools, authoring capabilities, and Web-based courses that can incorporate a range of instructional methodologies. Now that the LMS infrastructure is in place, Clay and Marta find themselves in a position to guide the implementation and use of the system in their agency. Although both are experienced in developing and conducting online training, there is a current trend and emphasis on accountability in government activities, so the two trainers want to base their guidance for online course development and teaching on scientifically based practices. Marta wonders aloud what research exists related to teaching and learning online because the field is so new. She tells Clay that she is not a researcher and does not think they will find anything useful or practical to help their efforts. Clay is currently enrolled in a graduate program in instructional technology and offers to locate and review with Marta the research that is available on online learning to guide online instructors who will design courses and instructional activities for the LMS.

Have you ever wondered what is actually known about online learning? What are some categories of research in this area? What can be learned from the research on designing and developing online learning, or e-learning? What types of studies are conducted in online learning research? What do the research results suggest for designing specific instructional strategies in an online context?

In this chapter, we address the preceding questions by discussing eight prominent categories of online learning research and present their findings and implications for the design of online learning. Instructional strategies gleaned from the research studies are also presented to assist you in linking the research to the practice of designing online learning environments.

INTRODUCTION

Although you should be respectful of the fact that [research] results do not always transfer perfectly from one setting to another, there is surely no better place to start inventing a better mousetrap than with the plans for one that actually worked **(Locke, Silverman, & Spirduso, 1998, p. 20)**.

We begin this chapter with two simple questions: What do we really "know" about online learning, or what does the research tell us? and What are the recommended or suggested instructional strategies or activities that someone charged with designing online instruction can glean from the research base? With the proliferation of technological tools and techniques surrounding online learning environments since the 1990s, what we can say we know from research on the impact and use of online learning systems is relatively little. The field of online learning (and educational research in general) is beset with criticisms of the research efforts conducted thus far, and reading the research is often an exercise in patience because of the need to weed through the various approaches and results. Reading research is also often associated with negative perceptions such as conflicting results and trivial topics. However, one useful point to remember is that the essence of the research process is to weave together small bits of insight into a larger fabric of understanding (Locke et al., 1998).

Although negative perceptions and criticisms abound, research is still the best evidence on which educators can base their practice and advance their knowledge of a field. Synthesizing and building on others' progress provides an integrated view of what is known about online learning and can prevent the repetition of mistakes. Although online learning is still in its infancy, overall, the fabric of knowledge of the field is expanding as researchers attempt various methodologies and more sophisticated techniques to test their theories and assumptions. Most important, reviewing research related to online learning can provide valuable guidance for practitioners who are implementing online materials without many existing outstanding models. The best place to begin is by attempting to determine from the research literature which online learning methods have worked or not worked. If practitioners can critically review insights gleaned from the research base, perhaps they can build a "better mousetrap" and collectively work toward improving future online learning and research methods.

In this chapter, we attempted to collect, categorize, and synthesize some of the most current studies that represent the diversity of methods and approaches to online learning research as well as synthesize the results for practical application. Although not exhaustive, this synthesis is based on systematically collecting studies from more than 15 published or online educational technology and distance education journals from 1995 to 2003, categorizing the studies into prominent themes, and selecting several studies in each category that are representative of the divergent methods and prominent categories in the research base. If you look across categories and studies, some trends are prominent. For example, much of the research is descriptive of particular learning contexts rather than experimental (i.e., including random assignments of participants, controlled variables, and comparisons of learning situations). In this chapter, we attempted to select examples of the most rigorous studies while providing an overview of a variety of research methods. The studies occurred most often in a higher education context because online learning and research occur mostly at colleges and universities. However, we also tried to include studies related to corporate or K–12 school contexts when possible. We attempted, for each category, to not only report the research findings, but also synthesize these results into suggested instructional strategies and activities that individuals involved in designing online learning environments can use (see associated tables providing additional details on these studies at the companion Web site: http://www.prenhall.com/dabbagh). We hope that this effort can inform others of the current direction of research on online learning and provide an overview of the nature of this research during the last several years. We also hope to provide insight into future research methods and the practice of designing and developing more powerful online learning environments with the capabilities of course management systems (CMSs).

Marta turns to Clay and asks, "Now that we have the capability for agency trainers to develop their own online courses in the LMS, I am being asked all kinds of questions about how to construct and facilitate online discussions." Clay stops what he is doing and asks what types of questions Marta is being asked. Marta says she just returned from a meeting with some of these trainers, and many of the questions were related to the more commonly used asynchronous discussion features of online courses. The questions are as follows: (a) What exactly is the role of the instructor or moderator? (b) What kinds of questions should I pose to facilitate discussions and should I place a limit on the length of the responses? (c) How formal or informal should online discussions be, and how do I promote a positive environment online? (d) Should I encourage or discourage the discussion of interpersonal issues in online discussions? (e) What if participants in the discussion do not participate or argue? How can I use asynchronous discussions to promote groups to work together? Clay says "Wow, these are good questions. Let's see if we can find out some answers so that you can recommend some strategies to them." Marta looks relieved, and she and Clay begin to weed through the research literature that they have just begun to collect and categorize, looking specifically for studies related to asynchronous communication.

RESEARCH ON ASYNCHRONOUS COMMUNICATION TOOLS

Much of the short history of research related to online learning, or e-learning, is in the context of using asynchronous tools such as e-mail, Listservs, and computer conferencing environments for instruction and training. These tools initially emerged as separate components and were later integrated into online course management systems (see Chapter 9 for a thorough discussion of CMS) along with synchronous tools and other functions. Examining the past research is useful because the techniques and strategies found in previous studies may offer recommendations that are applicable to the functionality of current online systems and tools. A review of the research issues and variables associated with asynchronous delivery reveals that constructs such as the participation rate, communication patterns, social exchange, participant roles, and structure of instructional activities are prevalent in past studies. These issues provide a picture of the current state and focus of the research.

Quality and Complexity of Asynchronous Communication

Tracking patterns of communication and participation in asynchronous and synchronous learning environments is a common approach in studies on online learning. Several research techniques are applied. For example, *descriptive techniques* involve tracking use and providing automated logs of the users' activity. More in-depth **content analysis techniques** involve examining the symbols of communication (characters, words, paragraphs, etc.) in an attempt to infer meaning from the context of the study. For example, Hara, Bonk, and Angeli (2000) used content analysis to investigate the cognitive processing of and interaction among 20 graduate students in an online educational psychology course in which FirstClass software was used. These researchers examined the participation rate, type of interaction, social cues, and cognitive and metacognitive skills that emerged during 4 weeks of the course. They found that the participants' communication patterns became more complex and interactive with time but also depended on the quality of the initial questions posed. This finding is strikingly similar to Beaudin's (1999) recommendation of placing great importance on carefully designed questions. This recommendation was based on the ratings of 135 experienced online instructors, who rated common techniques used to keep learners on topic during online discussions.

As the course progressed, Hara et al. (2000) found that students increasingly referred to other students' online comments, and the communication progressively became less formal. More than half the messages in the course represented an in-depth level of processing; most (70%) reflected a cognitively elaborate level evidenced by students' linking facts and ideas, offering new elements of information, and making judgments supported by examples or justifications. Hara et al. concluded that longer messages seemed to include additional support for students' conclusions because such messages incorporated the readings, made comparisons, and integrated personal experiences. In contrast, in another study, Warren and Rada (1999) found that the length of messaging alone did not ensure the quality of online comments. Requirements were established for the length of homework messages (150 characters minimum) and comments (no less than 40 characters) that rated other students' work. However, mandating the length of the messages did not increase the quality of student postings. These results seem to suggest that instructors who design online learning environments should emphasize the quality of initial questioning and the cognitive level of responses in online asynchronous discussions, rather than the length of messaging, to promote quality responses in asynchronous learning environments.

Patterns and Amount of Participation ... lationship
to Students' Roles in Asynchronous Dis

In other studies on asynchronous communication, de ... or's contributing more than 50% of the messages at the beginning of ... ents did not synthesize the online discussion to the level expected ... n examining the students' roles and the nature and amount of particip ... ed that students primarily acted in three roles: contributors to the disc ... o other students, or wanderers. (*Wanderers* were defined as persons wl ... nnect topics but did add to the discussion by initiating cognitive confl ... that urged readers to think about issues.) Interestingly, students did ... iscussion around the introductory questions and ignored the closing ... ivity, or wrapper. On the basis of these descriptive results, Zhu recommended that instructors implement student roles such as facilitator and mentor in online discussions and closely monitor these roles. She also suggested pairing more advanced students, as mentors, with novice-level students to promote richer discussions. These suggestions align with the competencies for online learners detailed in Chapter 2 that promote leadership and other social roles related to collaborative learning skills necessary for successful online learning experiences.

Interpersonal Communication Patterns
in Asynchronous Courses

Interpersonal communication, or social exchange, is another factor of interest evident in research studies on asynchronous discussions. Because online learning environments lack the natural social cues of face-to-face interaction, researchers initially thought that these environments might not promote high levels of interpersonal exchange among learners. However, McDonald and Campbell Gibson (1998) found that the patterns of social exchange among graduate students interacting in an electronic computer conferencing discussion progress through stages of group development (inclusion, control, and affection) similar to those of students interacting in face-to-face groups. On the basis of this study, the researchers suggested that interpersonal issues are crucial at the beginning of the course, and online instructors need to model openness, warmth, and expressions of feelings and self-disclosure to help create a trusting learning environment when asynchronous communication is used. These results provide an empirical basis for the required interpersonal competencies for distance education professionals detailed in Chapter 2.

Expertise, Attitudes, and Classroom Activity Structures

Clay-Warner and Marsh (2000) found that student openness to using computer-mediated communication tools increased with the number of previous classes in which these tools were used. In another study, Fishman (2000) found that the higher the confidence level of teachers in the K–12 school environment in which asynchronous tools were used, the more students used these tools. Similar to the Hara et al. (2000) study, a study by Fishman (2000) revealed that high school students' use and perception of value of these asynchronous learning activities depended on the quality of the initial instructional task. The use of asynchronous tools was also heavily influenced by the school calendar, so the constraints of the K–12 setting should be considered when these tools are implemented in such classes. Collectively, these studies indicate that with increased student experience and instructor confidence with asynchronous computer-mediated communication, students are more open and use these tools more often. However, the instructional task and the constraints of the specific setting need to be considered. (The importance of instructor competence with technology and instructional design was also addressed in Chapter 2.) In addition, according to these results, instructor attention to promoting positive interpersonal communication patterns, such as acceptance and warmth, within online discussions helps establish a supportive, trusting online learning environment.

Online Social Interchange, Discord, and Knowledge Construction

To determine whether asynchronous learning environments promote more than social interchange in the work environment, Kanuka and Anderson (1998) surveyed 25 workplace managers across Canada who participated in a 3-week computer conference. The participants thought that the online forum successfully provided opportunities for reflection and exposure to multiple perspectives. However, less agreement occurred among participants about using computer conferencing to construct new knowledge about the topic area. Most of the discussion at this conference involved lower level sharing or comparing information rather than higher levels of knowledge construction such as negotiating, testing, or applying new ideas. When inconsistencies or conflicts arose, conference participants often ignored them. However, as with Zhu's (1998a) student role of the wanderer, occasional instances of inconsistency or contradiction seemed to promote new perspectives or provide evidence of knowledge construction. Interestingly, Kanuka and Anderson (1998) concluded that **social discord** may be a catalyst to learners' creating new knowledge in online settings. These findings may support the use of instructional strategies that promote debate or take advantage of inconsistencies or contradictions that may arise in online asynchronous discussions as teachable moments. (see Chapter 6 for specific online instructional strategies).

Given the research results just described, how would you structure online asynchronous discussions? Which factors would be important to consider in facilitating and moderating online discussions? What would you recommend Clay and Marta do to address the trainers' questions?

Suggested Instructional Strategies and Activities

The previously mentioned studies incorporated, or their results suggested, the following instructional strategies and activities related to the integration and use of asynchronous communication tools in online learning contexts (for additional information on these research studies and their findings, visit the companion Web site at http://www.prenhall.com/dabbagh):

Instructional Strategies and Activities Suggested in Hara et al. (2000)

- Acknowledge the crucial role of the moderator in determining and encouraging the depth of dialogue.
- Provide frequent feedback, templates, and examples to stimulate student ideas and prevent anxiety.
- Provide metacomments or weaving statements that summarize the discussion.
- Promote student ownership and dialogue by using strategies such as starter–wrapper.
- Use asynchronous tools such as issue-based forums or debates and comment labeling for deeper discussions.
- Use synchronous chat tools for building rapport, brainstorming ideas, and communicating with guest experts.

Instructional Strategies and Activities Suggested in Zhu (1998a)

- Monitor, implement, and revise student roles in conferencing.
- Require instructor approval for introductory and synthesis comments.
- Recruit other students for facilitator and mentoring roles each week.
- Pair advanced students, as mentors, with novices.
- Promote issue-based introductory questions, allowing students to develop their own ideas and thoughts.

Instructional Strategies and Activities Suggested in McDonald and Campbell Gibson (1998)

- Consider using asynchronous computer conferencing for group activities and group development.
- Be aware that interpersonal issues are important at the beginning of a course.
- Model openness and expressions of feelings, self-disclosure, and solidarity, and demonstrate affection, acceptance, and warmth in asynchronous environments to create an environment of trust.

Instructional Strategies and Activities Suggested in Fishman (2000)

- Student use of computer-mediated communication tools is influenced by classroom structure or the way activities are constructed.
- Students are more likely to use asynchronous tools that their teachers know how to use.
- Instructors need to anticipate school calendar influences on patterns of computer-mediated communication use (e.g., start and end of quarters, before Christmas break).

- The structure of the academic task developed by the teacher drives the use and value of computer-mediated communication in the classroom.
- Teachers need support in both professional development and technology to increase their confidence and ability to teach with these tools.

Instructional Strategies and Activities Suggested in
Kanuka and Anderson (1998)

- Forums devoted to professional activities may require the participation of an expert on or an instructor of the subject matter to promote a higher level of sharing among participants.
- A cognitive process involving social interchange and some social discord may occur in computer conferencing environments.
- Asynchronous forums can provide reflection and exposure to **multiple perspectives** but may not promote application of new knowledge.
- The instructor should promote issue-based introductory questions, allowing students to develop their own ideas and thoughts.

On the basis of their exploration into the research literature, Marta and Clay feel more confident about providing sound recommendations to the agency's trainers. They put together an online performance support aid for the trainers, detailing the recommendations and strategies gleaned from the research. Clay says to Marta, "Since we have provided recommendations for asynchronous communication, we should provide similar guidelines for the synchronous capabilities of the LMS." Marta agrees but also raises the issue that in online courses, the synchronous features of chat rooms and audio and video **Webcasting** seem not to be used as often as the asynchronous discussions. Clay replies that perhaps this is because instructors or trainers are less familiar with these capabilities and have fewer strategies for implementing them. "If we provide the trainers with some information on what to expect in using synchronous communications and how to best support their participants, the trainers might take better advantage of these features," he says. Marta laughs, "Well, we can just bring in my teenage son to train the trainers because he is a professional at using instant messaging!" Clay laughs and says that he is sure Marta's son could introduce the trainers to the communication conventions used in synchronous text messaging for entertainment but they also need to determine how it should be used for instruction and training.

RESEARCH ON SYNCHRONOUS COMMUNICATION TOOLS

Research related to synchronous communication is not as prevalent as studies involving asynchronous communication. However, studies in this area are beginning to emerge that address the nature of communication, the differences between asynchronous and synchronous discussion, and the distinctive instructional features and characteristics of synchronous communication.

Learner-Centered Synchronous Courses

Chou (2001) examined the use of various types of synchronous communication in an online course covering theories and applications of computer-mediated communication. In an extensive **formative evaluation** of the course, she found that the quality of synchronous, or chat, discussions greatly improved with the implementation of guidelines and small-group activities. As many researchers of asynchronous tools found, Chou found that with prior knowledge of the use of the synchronous tools, students seemed to demonstrate an increased level of analysis and integration of concepts into their daily lives. These findings also support the idea that technological fluency is an important prerequisite skill of the online learner described in Chapter 2. Interestingly, the students who participated in this study initially complained about the authoring system used (WebCT), but at the end of the course rated the system very high compared with their ratings of other synchronous tools. This result may indicate that a learning curve is present when teachers are introducing new technology-based systems, and instructors need to account for the time needed for learners to adopt new systems. In Chou's study, the systems that received the students' highest ratings for **social presence** also received high ratings for communication and interface. This finding may mean that the systems that are perceived to best support social interaction by online learners using synchronous discussion may also provide more intuitive communication mechanisms and interface elements.

Communication Conventions in Instructional Synchronous Chats

Murphy and Collins (1998) examined the need for and characterization of communication conventions used by graduate students engaged in a *single* synchronous chat session in a course on distance learning. These researchers determined that students implemented the following communication mechanisms, in order of frequency. The students demonstrated shared meaning or interest in discussion topics by exchanging facts and helpful hints. Key words or personal name descriptors were often used at the beginning of a line to indicate who or what the discussion was directed toward. Students used shorthand for common phrases and created a sense of social presence by referring to one another by name and sharing personal experiences. Participants also exhibited playfulness and humor and used nonverbal cues, including underlining, punctuation marks, and capital letters to express nonverbal communication. In the chat session, questions and directions to others provided clarification of meaning and demonstrated status by directing the group activities. Students also used not only ellipses, to indicate a continuation of a thought from one line of input to another, but also emoticons, such as smiley faces, which attempt to express emotions in the online context.

Other results of this study are as follows: The students elicited a significant amount of the conversation (71.2%), compared with the instructor (28.8%). Students were well aware of their need to use particular communication conventions. They suggested using key words to clarify communication and used metaphors to create shared meanings, often elaborating on and explaining new words to reduce potential misunderstandings. Challenges perceived by students included the nonnative English speakers' struggle with the rapid flow of text and the students with slow typing skills, who experienced frustration in the communication. Students also used self-disclosure to help create a sense of personal presence and a safe learning environment.

Prior to implementing an online course involving synchronous chat, designers and developers can increase their awareness and understanding of the potential communication protocols that students may use in synchronous communication by examining this type of research. Such prior knowledge can greatly increase the success of the online instruction design and development.

Combined Synchronous and Asynchronous Communication

Sotillo (2000) investigated the functions and complexity of the language used in both synchronous and asynchronous communication in an attempt to determine the most appropriate use for each type of communication. Using **discourse** analysis, Sotillo analyzed the complexity of writing of 25 undergraduate English-as-a-Second-Language (ESL) students in two writing classes at four intervals during a semester. She determined that the categories of behavior in electronic discourse—such as requests, responses, apologies, greetings, complaints, and reprimands—represented the range of functions of communication or discourse. *Complexity* was defined as the students' ability to produce writing that shows how ideas and large chunks of information are represented with the use of subordination and embedded subordinate clauses. In comparing the same groups' synchronous and asynchronous communication, Sotillo found that these two modes of computer-mediated communication elicit different forms of discourse or communication. Synchronous sessions included such types of discourse as greetings, imperatives, requests for clarification, and information, whereas asynchronous sessions elicited topic-initiation moves, student-generated questions, and student responses to the instructor or comments on postings by the instructor or other students.

Similar to Murphy and Collins (1998), Sotillo (2000) reported that in synchronous communication, students initiated most communication moves (78%), whereas instructor-initiated moves accounted for a much smaller amount of the communication (22%). Overall, the study showed that asynchronous discussions were more constrained than synchronous discussions were and provided a form of communication akin to the more linear question–response–evaluation nature of the face-to-face classroom. Asynchronous discussions were also found to be longer and more complex and had more accurate spelling and punctuation. In contrast, the synchronous discourse focused on communicating meaning and disregarded writing accuracy. Drawing on similarities to other studies involving synchronous communication, Sotillo concluded that synchronous discussions are highly interactive and demonstrate a high level of student control. These results may be interpreted to direct developers of online learning materials to integrate asynchronous elements when the instructional objective requires lengthier, more complex language and would benefit from a direct response from the student to teacher requests. Synchronous elements have specialized features that may be highly beneficial in less constrained situations and permit students a high level of fluency and control in the usage of language conventions and writing online. According to this research, synchronous tools provide an opportunity to increase interaction in an online course. However, instructors should consider the use of small groups, specific guidance, and student-initiated topics and discussion.

> *What should Clay and Marta include in an online job aid for instructors who want to incorporate synchronous communication tools into their teaching? Given the preceding research results, what are some specific guidelines for online learning developers to follow, and what should they avoid when they are implementing synchronous online chat sessions?*

Suggested Instructional Strategies and Activities

The previously mentioned studies incorporated, or their results suggested, the following instructional strategies and activities related to the integration and use of synchronous communication tools in online learning contexts (for additional information on these research studies and their findings, visit the companion Web site at http://www.prenhall.com/dabbagh):

Instructional Strategies and Activities Suggested in Chou (2001)

- Instructors should provide continuous guidance and support; be responsive; provide individual, one-to-one coaching; demonstrate concern for student progress; clarify instruction at all times; demonstrate a positive attitude and good rapport with students; be accessible; and provide immediate feedback and explanations of class policy and criteria.
- Guidelines and small groups are needed for online chat sessions.
- Teachers must provide time for students' adoption of a new instructional system.

Instructional Strategies and Activities Suggested in Murphy and Collins (1998)

- Encourage clear communication when you are providing guidance for online chats, recommending techniques such as providing key word descriptions or referents to topics discussed or referring to others by name or nickname.
- Encourage the use of metaphors and explanations to create shared understandings and prevent misunderstandings.
- Provide a safe and trusting learning environment in which appropriate levels of disclosure can occur.
- Recognize that nonnative English speakers and slow typists may face increased challenges in synchronous environments.

Instructional Strategies and Activities Suggested in Sotillo (2000)

- Expect a decrease of teacher control in synchronous communication.
- Use synchronous communication to encourage language fluency and student-initiated discussions on varied topics.

- Recognize that asynchronous communication provides opportunities for lengthier, more complex discussions with more accurate spelling and punctuation.
- Use asynchronous communication when requiring students to respond to teacher questions, or promote discussion based on students' personal experiences.

Marta says to Clay, "Ok. Now we have some solid recommendations for asynchronous and synchronous discussions to share with the trainers. However, the studies we reviewed so far did not give us clear suggestions for increasing interactivity. As online instructors, we are all striving to make our courses more interactive. Everyone defines it differently; so, what exactly is interactivity and how can we encourage it?" Clay replies that interactivity is an amorphous concept, but researchers must define terms related to their studies so he and Marta should be able to shed some light on this term by looking at the literature and seeing how the researchers define their terms. He turns to the pile of studies, smiles at Marta, and says, "Your turn . . ."

RESEARCH ON INTERACTIVITY

Many studies related to online learning focus on examining the construct of interactivity. These research studies often incorporate both asynchronous and synchronous communication and attempt to provide insight into the nature of the interaction that occurs among students or between students and instructors online. *Interactivity* is a notoriously difficult term to define. In fact, entire issues of academic journals, conference presentations, and articles are devoted to determining its functional definition (Hirumi, 2002; Soo & Bonk, 1998). The research reveals multiple definitions of *interactivity* from which scientifically based recommendations for designing online learning environments can be gleaned (Bannan-Ritland, 2002).

Types of Interactions in Asynchronous and Synchronous Communication

Pena-Shaff, Martin, and Gay (2001) conducted a study in which they examined interactivity as the participation, flow of interaction, and character of dialogue in an online course. These researchers defined *interactivity* as asking or answering questions, supporting or clarifying ideas, and building consensus and social interaction. The study revealed that most (69%) of the messages in the asynchronous environment were noninteractive (did not answer or refer to other messages or persons) and were primarily task-related, self-reflective, and subjective monologues. In contrast, synchronous messages were perceived to be more interactive but much less task oriented and reflective. Overall, in both forms of communication, messages that contained opinions, personal experiences, or evaluations of the topic at hand (or another topic) were found to vary from interactive to noninteractive in this study. Messages that contained questions or answers, provided support or clarification, and demonstrated social interaction or consensus building were found to be highly interactive.

Conclusions from the Pena-Shaff et al. (2001) study are that asynchronous systems are appropriate for interactive activities such as self-questioning and rationalization related to specific tasks, whereas synchronous chat activities are more appropriate for social, brainstorming-type interactions but not for building arguments and consensus. These findings are somewhat similar to Sotillo's (2000) recommendations to implement asynchronous elements when more direct, complex communication is desired and to capitalize on the attributes of synchronous communication when student-directed, social, and fluent communication is desired.

Factors Influencing Interaction in Online Courses

Vrasidas and McIsaac (1999) attempted to define a conceptual framework of interactivity in an online course and found that multiple factors influence interaction. Their definition of *interactivity* involved the "reciprocal actions of two or more actors within a given context" (p. 25). This definition provides insight into how instructors should structure an online course to attempt to influence the amount and nature of interaction. Required activities demonstrated more interactivity in how often each student communicated with the instructor and other students. However, demanding workloads were detrimental to online interaction. Student perceptions in this study indicated that they thought the asynchronous discussions were repetitive of the numerous written assignments and did not add value to the learning experience. Caution should be taken not to duplicate written work in paper-based and online activities in a course (Dabbagh 2000). Asynchronous discussions need to provide a venue for instructional activities that address objectives different from those of traditional face-to-face assignments. A smaller class size, an adequate amount of feedback, and prior experience in online environments were found to support interaction. These results provide basic considerations that online instructors should incorporate into any course that uses a Web-based component.

Marta sips her coffee and says to Clay, "Well, we must be doing our homework because I am beginning to see some overlap in the results of the studies examining asynchronous and synchronous communication and the studies involving interaction!" Clay replies, "See, Marta, we will make you a researcher yet!" "Not so fast," Marta tells Clay. "Something is still bothering me about this issue of interactivity: How can we sell the trainers on promoting interactivity—what is the benefit for them and the participants?" "Another good question," says Clay, as he silently points to the pile of articles.

Student and Teacher Perceptions of Interaction in Online Courses

Instructors' and students' perceptions of the nature of interactivity in online courses were also examined in a study by McIsaac, Blocher, Mahes, and Vrasidas (1999). These researchers defined *interactivity* as the amount of teacher and student participation as well as their respective purposes and goals for this participation. Interestingly, instructors perceived their interaction with students in an online course to be of higher quality than that in traditional face-to-face courses. The researchers concluded that students have specific goals for each interaction in an online course, including getting help with or sharing information related to the course content, getting help with the technology, submitting homework, and participating in discussions to exchange ideas or for socializing. Although the demand on the instructor to provide frequent and quality feedback in an online course is high, instructors who teach in these environments believe they are better able to serve their students and individually and collectively interact with them. Students assume much of the responsibility in learning as well—by initiating interaction with one another and the instructor. In Chapter 2, we detailed the specific competencies and responsibilities of the online instructor and learner that directly relate to these research results.

Characteristics of Conference Interactions

In another study, Tsui and Ki (1996) examined the interchange between students and the instructor in an e-learning context for 16 months. These researchers' definition of *interactivity* focused on the amount and directionality of online messages. The results of this study revealed an explicit pattern of communication: The student posts questions, the instructor provides responses, then the student acknowledges the responses and shares ideas with others. This research showed that specific directional communication patterns exist between instructor and students and among peers, as well as evidence of increasing numbers of messages with time. Results such as these seem to indicate that online instructors should anticipate certain communication patterns and allow students to become comfortable interacting in the course environment before expecting interaction to increase.

Given the preceding research results, what are some of the ways online instructors can promote interactivity? What is the overlap in results that Marta was referring to?

Suggested Instructional Strategies and Activities

The previously mentioned studies incorporated, or their results suggested, the following instructional strategies and activities related to the integration and use of interactivity in online learning contexts (for additional information on these research studies and their findings, visit the companion Web site at http://www.prenhall.com/dabbagh):

Instructional Strategies and Activities Suggested in Pena-Shaff et al. (2001)

- Asynchronous conferencing is best used for reflective activities, including self-questioning and rationalization.

- Synchronous activities are appropriate for social, brainstorming communication but not for building arguments and consensus.

Instructional Strategies and Activities Suggested in Vrasidas and McIsaac (1999)

- Instructors must consider the online course workload and structure of the course and be careful not to duplicate assignments in face-to-face and asynchronous components of the course.
- Face-to-face meetings may reduce the need for online social interaction.
- Class size and adequate feedback mechanisms are important considerations in an online course.
- Prior experience, practice, and explanations of online communication conventions are important to prevent users from feeling overwhelmed and intimidated.

Instructional Strategies and Activities Suggested in McIsaac et al. (1999)

- E-learning courses can benefit independent, motivated learners; individuals who want an alternative to face-to-face instruction; and previously underserved populations.
- Instructors should add credibility as coach or facilitator rather than imposing views in online courses.
- Instructors need to create an environment in which learners can feel socially present, providing face-to-face opportunities before meeting online.
- Group activities increase interactivity and need to be deliberately designed.
- Instructors must incorporate significant, personalized feedback to prevent student feelings of isolation.

Instructional Strategies and Activities Suggested in Tsui and Ki (1996)

- Expect the following pattern of interaction: Participants ask questions, the instructor responds, and students acknowledge the response and share ideas.
- Expect peer communication and initiation of questions by participants to increase with time in an online environment.

Clay states, "It looks as if we can emphasize to the trainers, on the basis of the results of these studies, that online learning provides a context for satisfying, high-quality interaction that allows instructors to interact with participants individually and in groups." He goes on to say, "Speaking of groups, I was stopped in the hall yesterday by a manager at the agency who wants to use the LMS to share ideas and promote team building among the dispersed work groups he is directing." Clay explains that this manager is hesitant to try the LMS for something that is not strictly instructional. Marta replies that in her reading she has located some studies that address developing online learning communities, gestures to the article pile, and says, "Ok, Clay, get to it!"

RESEARCH ON ONLINE LEARNING COMMUNITIES

The formation and characteristics of online learning communities is another research area in which researchers examine the collective effort and achievement of groups operating in an online context who use different means of communication that often rely on both asynchronous and synchronous tools. Online learning communities have been defined as groups that work together to achieve joint learning tasks (Harasim, Hiltz, Teles, & Turoff, 1997). Research is beginning to emerge supporting the idea that students co-construct a sense of community online by promoting a social context of rapport, collegiality, and shared meanings.

Interpersonal Involvement Strategies and Community Development

Simich-Dudgeon (1999) found that students used interpersonal involvement strategies through written online text, such as imagery, repetition, dialogue, metaphors, and irony, to engage and interact with other students in asynchronous computer conferencing. The students worked cooperatively to create a supportive community and establish shared meaning of content through their online text communication.

In an online environment, a sense of community is promoted through strong interpersonal ties that provide support for learning and prevent feelings of isolation. Viewing a *community* as what people do together rather than as a geographic location where tasks are accomplished is the focus for integration of virtual online communities into the educational process. Haythornthwaite, Kazmer, Robins, & Shoemaker (2000) investigated students' perceptions of the characteristics of community, as well as who and what contribute to a sense of community, in a graduate library education program experience. The program consisted of an initial 2-week face-to-face experience and relied primarily on online communication throughout the remainder of the courses required for the master's degree. These researchers found that students perceived an initial community building through their shared history and experience with the face-to-face component of the course that carried over and was maintained throughout the program by online communication.

With the common goal of completing the program and entering the profession of library education, students in this online course provided one another with social and emotional support as well as multiple resources, which created a safe, reciprocal, and trusting learning environment. However, a few students who failed to make social or educational community connections were distressed and could not overcome a sense of isolation resulting from a lack of face-to-face contact with the instructor and other students. Likewise, a lack of cues in the online environment and reduced amounts of positive and negative feedback on their contributions created a sense of insecurity in some students about the appropriateness of their contributions. Establishing strong personal ties and social support with other students and/or the instructor helped to stave off feelings of insecurity and isolation and enhanced the benefits of the educational experience.

In this study, students perceived maintaining a community through online interaction as requiring more effort than in traditional face-to-face communities. As students engage with other students and faculty, they move from isolation to full membership in the community. The students reported that disengaging or "fading back" from online communication was fairly easy to do and that regular synchronous communication (chat whispering, real-time lecturing, whiteboard use) prevented fading back and feelings of isolation, and contributed to maintaining community. Haythornthwaite et al.'s (2000) study underscored the importance of providing enhanced social interaction through a range of computer-mediated communication technologies as a way to promote a sense of community that can provide an enhanced and effective collaborative educational experience for all participants. Instructors must take an active role in establishing a trusting, safe, and supportive environment. They can do so by providing frequent feedback, creating opportunities for social exchange, and maintaining awareness of disengagement so that individuals are encouraged to contribute to the community and help create a positive educational experience for all. Specific instructional strategies used to promote this type of engagement are presented in Chapters 6 and 9.

Classroom Community Building

Rovai (2001) distinguished between task-driven and socioemotional interaction as well as between differences in gender communication patterns in building a sense of community in online contexts. As Haythornthwaite et al. (2000) found, Rovai (2001) found that **socioemotional communication** in an online context was key to establishing community in a 5-week graduate course. The focus of this research extended to identifying differences in communication patterns exhibited by males and females. In the socioemotional discourse, females posted more messages overall and used significantly more *connected* voice patterns, which included references to family, self, others' families, praise, encouragement, and support. In socioemotional types of messages, males posted significantly more *independent* voice messages, which were more impersonal, assertive, authoritative in tone, and less likely to permit alternative viewpoints. In addition, at the end of the experience, females rated the course higher for having a feeling of community and made more positive comments about the course, whereas males made most of the critical comments. These results behoove online instructors not only to encourage socioemotional communication to promote a sense of community, but also to be sensitive to different communication patterns and to use strategies that provide all learners with opportunities for expression.

Clay comes into the office, looking frustrated. "Ok. I shared with the manager the research-based recommendations we found so far about how to promote a sense of community, and he tried to implement them. Trouble is, his group is now sharing much more personal information online, and he is not sure he is comfortable with this or that it supports his goals of building a cohesive team across departments." Marta indicates that she has struggled with this issue in her online experiences and believes that, especially when participants cannot interact regularly in face-to-face contexts, promoting the sharing of interpersonal information online is important to building a cohesive group. Clay is not sure that he should recommend this practice. Marta suggests, "Some articles are still left to review on this topic. Let's see if the research agrees with my intuition or not."

Collaboration in Online Learning

From a more qualitative perspective, Barab, Thomas, and Merrill's (2001) study further supports the notion that the online context can support learners engaged in deep and meaningful interpersonal interaction. In an adult learning online course, these researchers examined online transcripts, course products, and assignments, and interviewed the graduate-level course participants. The researchers found that this particular course afforded freedom and flexibility in the design of course activities and encouraged openness and personal sharing among participants. This environment was accomplished through activities such as posting autobiographies, creating individual learning plans, and integrating personal perspectives into assignments. Overall, the most meaningful learning for students seemed to occur when they shared personal experiences related to course content. As in the previous studies we reviewed in this section, Barab et al.'s work provided evidence that the online context can promote and sustain deep, meaningful, interpersonal exchanges that can support learning. An important conclusion in this study was that instructors need to place as much emphasis on establishing the appropriate instructional climate as on providing appropriate content, particularly when they want to reap the meaningful educational benefits of attempting to create an online learning community.

Does the research seem to agree with Marta's position? What can be done to facilitate involvement and community building in online environments?

Suggested Instructional Strategies and Activities

The previously mentioned studies incorporated, or their results suggested, the following instructional strategies and activities related to the integration of online communities (for additional information on these research studies and their findings, visit the companion Web site at http://www.prenhall.com/dabbagh):

Instructional Strategies and Activities Suggested in Simich-Dudgeon (1999)

- Create awareness that students and instructors work collaboratively to promote shared meaning and to create a supportive learning community.
- Consider encouraging the use of interpersonal involvement strategies such as personal stories, metaphors, and irony.
- Encourage students to use personalized greetings to promote a sense of community.

Instructional Strategies and Activities Suggested in Haythornthwaite et al. (2000)

- Promote initial and sustained bonding through group interaction by multiple means of communication (including both face-to-face and online public and private communication) related to work and social activities.
- Establish a regular schedule to provide opportunities for patterns of work and social exchange.
- Provide opportunities for both public and private synchronous interaction to facilitate community building.
- Monitor and support continued interaction and participation. Stay aware of students who "fade back," and attempt to draw them into both social and educational interaction to facilitate community.
- Provide students with initial feedback on appropriate communication.

Instructional Strategies and Activities Suggested in Rovai (2001)

- Attempt to create a sense of community by designing for and supporting student interaction and involvement.
- Build community by encouraging socioemotional communication as well as educational task-driven interactions.
- Be sensitive to differences in communication patterns and adapt your teaching to facilitate interaction while not silencing any members of the group.
- Consider incorporating a rubric to promote discussion standards to encourage uniform contributions.

Instructional Strategies and Activities Suggested in Barab et al. (2001)

- Significant portions of online courses may involve interpersonal issues, depending on the course content.
- Online courses can promote the sharing of personal experiences, integration of content that is personally meaningful, and establishment of a sense of community.
- Instructors should consider explicitly designing a course with the purpose of establishing an online community.
- Instructors should emphasize course climate as well as course content to encourage the emergence of an online community.
- Instructors need to consider asynchronous communication methods for promoting the reflective thought necessary to create personally meaningful experiences online.

Clay concedes to Marta that the research has supported her instincts to promote social interaction online. He also indicates that the manager was reassured that some socializing and sharing of personal information among his distributed work teams does not detract from the learning or business focus but may even help to promote it by creating a trusting and collaborative work environment. The manager likes the suggestion to create areas in his online community for both public and private communication. Marta replies, "You know, Clay, we have been gleaning suggestions from the research on broad topics like interactivity and community building, but we have not covered the basics of navigating information and organizing content online. We need to provide our trainers with some information about how to organize and present their information and links when they are developing online instruction." She looks at Clay and says, "I know, I know, the pile is over there. . . ."

RESEARCH ON HYPERTEXT AND HYPERMEDIA

Hypertext stores and interconnects information on the Web, allowing learners to determine what is critical to review and in what sequence. *Hypermedia systems* contribute multimodal information to a hypertext network, linking audio, video, or graphical information to search capabilities. Both systems contain attributes of links and *nodes* (or chunks) of information that interconnect and provide a network that users can navigate in different ways. Patterns of learner navigation and their influence on learning is a primary area of investigation in many studies related to the use of hypermedia and hypertext systems.

Cognitive Load, Learning, and Hypertext

Niederhauser, Reynolds, Salmen, and Skolmoski (2000) conducted a study in which undergraduate students were provided with opportunities to freely investigate hypertext information presented hierarchically and exploration was permitted laterally across topics or vertically by exploring more details about a specific topic. These researchers examined the resulting influences on learning. They found that the students who moved systematically through each branch vertically, reading all content contained in a particular branch before embarking on the next branch, learned more than students who navigated the topics laterally, or in a crisscross manner, comparing and contrasting information across topics.

Although the results of this study suggest that navigating through hypertext information in a crisscross manner is not conducive to learning, other researchers have indicated that such a system requires additional structured support for learners. One prominent research effort in which the researchers explored these types of supports related to hypertext systems involving **cognitive flexibility theory**. One tenet of this theory is that the unique characteristics of hypertext that allow learners to traverse digital content may promote deeper cognitive processing of the information. Cognitive flexibility theory involves using multiple ways to represent knowledge by linking concepts in cases and capitalizing on interconnecting themes by using hypertext to assist learners in actively constructing knowledge when they are dealing with complex content (Jacobson, Maouri, Mishra, & Kolar, 1996). Jacobson et al. (1996) conducted a study in which they examined the differences in providing students with varying amounts of guidance (through enhanced modeling and scaffolding strategies) and learner control in a **cognitive flexibility hypertext (CFH)** system. These researchers also examined students' attitudes and beliefs about learning and related the information to their performance on several knowledge-synthesis and problem-solving tests. The results revealed that the more complex beliefs students had about learning, the higher their scores on knowledge-synthesis tests. These researchers also found that merely providing the opportunity to navigate through case-based information by using hypertext is insufficient to support learning. Encouraging deeper learning requires additional structural guidance, such as modeling and scaffolding, so that the learner can attend to the more abstract connections in order to learn from theme-based hypertext systems.

Prior Knowledge, Goal Strength, and Hypertext

Additional research shows that the influence of learners' prior knowledge and goals is important to consider when instructors use hypertext for learning. Last, O'Donnell, and Kelly (2001) investigated students' intentions, goals, and path through a hierarchically presented hypertext system of content related to educational measurement. Students who had prior knowledge of the content area and strong academic goals related to exploring the content for answers to specific questions easily navigated the content, located relevant information, and filled in their knowledge gaps. In contrast, students with little prior knowledge were generally unsuccessful at locating answers, demonstrated higher anxiety levels, and desired additional navigational aids such as content maps or records of nodes visited. Students with little prior knowledge who participated in the weak academic goal task of generally exploring material relied on their own inefficient knowledge of the material to go through the system and were much less effective at learning. The results of this study indicate that learners' level of prior knowledge and goals can influence the effectiveness of their navigational strategies for obtaining specific information for learning.

Hypermedia, Links, and Nodes

In contrast to studies on hypertext learning environments, studies involving hypermedia provide an investigation into the learning effects of software that can incorporate digital text, graphics, audio, and video connected through hyperlinks and navigated by using graphical icons or search strategies (Gayeski, 1993). These features, although permitting easily accessible information in multiple modes, may also create a complex navigational system that can cause disorientation in learning. Zhu (1998b) found that the fewer nodes (or chunks of information) and the fewer links provided on each screen, the more improved were students' learning and location of information. In addition, the fewer links and nodes, the better were students' attitudes toward the hypermedia program. These results suggest that designers of hypermedia systems should be cautious when they are providing multiple screens of information with many links because doing so may prove detrimental to learning and induce cognitive overload and disorientation.

Hypermedia and Learning Styles

Researchers have also attempted to establish a relationship between hypermedia systems and learners' cognitive styles. Ford and Chen (2000) conducted a study in which graduate students used a hypermedia system that taught them how to construct a Web page. Afterward, the students' patterns of navigation, learning, and interaction were compared with their established cognitive styles of field independence or dependence. These researchers found no learning differences between learners with different cognitive styles. However, they did find significant differences in the navigational patterns. Learners characterized as **field independent** (more analytic, preferring to structure their learning) used specific hypermedia features such as maps, the index, and back and forward buttons, and examined more detailed information than did the learners who were characterized as **field dependent** (process information more globally). In addition, learners with more prior knowledge of Web construction and the use of computers and the Internet spent more time in the detailed levels of the hypermedia system than did students with less prior knowledge. This study indicates a potential relationship between cognitive styles and navigational patterns among learners using a hypermedia system for learning.

Given these research results, how would you structure the content of an online instructional or training module? What features might you include for field-dependent and field-independent learners?

These studies demonstrate important factors related to hypertext and hypermedia elements of online courses. Such factors include patterns of navigation, learner guidance, learner intention and learning style, and the number of links or nodes in hypermedia or hypertext presentations.

Suggested Instructional Strategies and Activities

The previously mentioned studies incorporated, or their results suggested, the following instructional strategies and activities related to the integration and use of hypertext and hypermedia in online learning contexts (for additional information on these research studies and their findings, visit the companion Web site at http://www.prenhall.com/dabbagh):

*Instructional Strategies and Activities Suggested
in Niederhauser et al. (2000)*

- Consider **cognitive load** issues when developing hypertext-based materials.
- Consider presenting information in a sequential, left-to-right, top-to-bottom manner to reduce students' cognitive load.

Instructional Strategies and Activities Suggested in Jacobson et al. (1996)

- Students need explicit scaffolding and modeling in case-based thematic hypertext environments.

- Providing flexible access and user control is not sufficient and may encourage more surface processing of content.
- Students require additional support that provides guidance on structural features of cases that contain abstract themes.
- Instructors should be aware that students' beliefs about learning affect their performance with thematic case-based hypertext materials.

Instructional Strategies and Activities Suggested in Last et al. (2001)

- Consider student goals and levels of prior knowledge when developing hypertext learning tasks.
- Provide alternative navigational paths and aids in hypertext systems to assist students with less prior knowledge of the content.
- Be cautious when assigning students with less prior knowledge to demanding tasks in a hypertext environment.
- Provide opportunities for students to impose their own structure on information.

Instructional Strategies and Activities Suggested in Zhu (1998b)

- Instructors should use fewer links in hypermedia programs designed for learning or should provide filters for multiple links.
- A relationship between the number of links and nodes and disorientation may exist when hypermedia systems are used for learning and locating information.
- Presenting simple information in smaller nodes may aid students' recall of information.
- Moving back and forth between links and main nodes of information may cause disruption in the reading process and affect learning.

Instructional Strategies and Activities Suggested in Ford and Chen (2000)

- Instructors should be aware that a relationship may exist between cognitive style and navigational pattern in hypermedia systems.
- Learners with more prior knowledge seem to spend more time in detailed levels of hypermedia systems.
- Learners who are more analytic, preferring to structure their own learning, which demonstrates field independence, may use specific hypermedia features (such as maps, an index, back and forward buttons) and examine detail more than students who process information more globally and are considered field dependent do.

Marta and Clay are spinning after receiving an e-mail from their boss, the director of training, indicating that the undersecretary of their government agency wants to know if any research exists to support the effectiveness of online or Web-based instruction. Marta says to Clay, "You know—after reading all this research, I am beginning to understand why proving the overall effectiveness of online instruction and training is so difficult." Clay responds, "Yeah, there are so many variables, and it is difficult to control all of them to attribute learning differences to one thing or to directly translate findings in one situation to another." Marta muses that the undersecretary probably wants a simple answer—that the technology systems improve learning—but they are discovering that the issue is much more complex. Clay wonders if they can craft their response to focus on the suggested instructional strategies, such as collaborative interaction, that have been shown through research to support learning in some online contexts, or if they can highlight embedded supports in online learning systems, including self-assessment features such as quizzes or summaries, and match these supports with individual learning styles that have also been linked to differences in learning. Marta wishes more studies existed that could provide additional evidence to present to the undersecretary, but she reminds herself that the field of online learning is still young and more studies are conducted every year. Marta says, "You know, another problem is that most of the research has been conducted in higher education, not training contexts, which makes sense since professors are typically the ones who conduct studies. But, wouldn't it be great if more online learning developers in government, corporate, and K–12 contexts would evaluate their online strategies and materials so that we would have more results to rely on and a better basis for what works?" Clay nods in agreement and thinks about investigating how to evaluate his next online course. Marta turns back to Clay and says, "Let's focus on what we know the research says and provide that to the undersecretary. We'd better get to work!"

RESEARCH ON WEB-BASED INSTRUCTION

Assessing the learning impact of courses delivered through the World Wide Web is extremely difficult because of the multiple variables present in educational situations. Heines (2000) stated the following after examining student performance and attitudes before and after the implementation of a course Web site:

> It is virtually impossible to prove conclusively that students learn better as a result of any application of technology due to the large number of uncontrolled variables in such studies, not to mention the numerous extraneous conditions that influence results. (p. 73)

However, Heines's research did show that students believed the presence of course materials on a Web site had a significant impact on their ability to keep up with the course. The students in this study also expressed their desire for other professors to maintain course Web sites. Using a probability-of-success technique, Heines effected a significant change in the percentage of students achieving grades of B or C or better across 10 semesters for one computer science course and across 5 semesters for another course. These results, although dramatic, cannot be attributed solely to the introduction of the course Web site. However, the results are bolstered by the fact that the same professor taught at least one section prior to and after the introduction of one of the course Web sites. This study demonstrates the difficulty of attributing an increase in student performance solely to the introduction of a course Web site.

Focusing on the instructional methodology, or instructional strategy, in Web-based courses as the variable of interest has produced some useful research. For example, incorporating specific instructional strategies such as collaborative learning in Web-based instruction has been shown to improve students' performance in problem solving. Uribe, Klein, and Sullivan (2003) investigated how individuals and collaborative groups with one higher ability participant and one lower ability participant performed on a problem-solving scenario when they were engaged in an online course using Blackboard. The study showed that participants working in pairs scored significantly higher than those working individually on the problem scenario. Those who worked in groups also spent significantly more time on task than those who worked alone. In general, the participants preferred working collaboratively, although some who worked in pairs believed they did not have enough time and thought communicating through text in Blackboard was more difficult than communicating in a face-to-face environment. This study also provides support for an orientation toward collaborative learning and specific skills in social learning, sharing through dialogue, and self- and group evaluation skills, which were discussed in Chapter 2 as important skills to cultivate in online learning contexts. In other studies, reviewed subsequently, researchers attempted to demonstrate differences in student performance after implementing different instructional strategies in Web course environments and examined individual differences that exist for learners in these instructional contexts.

Structured Support in Web-Based Instruction

Collis, Winnips, and Moonen (2000) investigated providing students with structured support (required online and face-to-face communication, discussion, summarization, material selection, and regular feedback) and learner choice of the use of these same supports in a Web-based learning context. Their results indicated that although students in the structured support group spent twice as much time in the online course, no significant differences in learning the course material were found on multiple-choice tests. Instructors spent a significant amount of time on the course in both cases, compared with the amount of time students spent. The results of this study raise questions related to the value of providing additional instructor time and support with no benefit of increased student learning. However, these researchers pointed out that skills such as teamwork may have been gained in addition to knowledge of content, but these skills are difficult to measure. The conclusions of this study are that structured support may be important for some students to persist in Web courses and may have intangible benefits as well as qualify as good teaching.

Individual Learning Differences and Web-Based Learning Environments

An individual's emotions, intentions, and goals may also affect his or her learning in Web-based environments. Martinez and Bunderson (2000) explored individual learning differences in a Web-based environment, taking into account learners' emotions, intentions, and social processes that may affect learning. In the study, learners were classified by their particular **learning orientation,** which described a range of characteristics related to the individual's ability to take control, set goals, attain standards, manage resources, solve problems, and take risks. The students were described as *intentional learners* (e.g., set and accomplish personal short- and long-term goals; commit great effort to gaining knowledge; etc.), *performing learners* (e.g., set and achieve short-term, task-oriented goals; selectively commit effort to assimilate knowledge; etc.), *conforming learners* (e.g., follow and try to accomplish simplistic task-oriented goals; commit careful, measured effort to meet learning requirements; etc.), and *resistant learners* (e.g., accept lower standards, have fewer academic goals, avoid learning, etc.).

The participants were then randomly assigned to interact with eight Web-based lessons and assessments that incorporated the learning orientation factors just described plus a training session on intentional learning, a program that included only the learning orientation factors, or a program with identical content that did not incorporate the learning orientations or training. At the conclusion of the study, the effect of the different Web-based learning environments on individual learning orientations was examined. The researchers found that the learners who participated in the Web-based program that matched their learning orientation scored higher (not significantly) than did the students who interacted with the parts of the program that did not match their particular orientation. The group that experienced the additional strategies and training on intentional learning also scored higher (not significantly). The study also showed that the students who participated in the programs matched to their learning orientations experienced more satisfaction and believed they learned more. This study provides some evidence that matching learners' particular learning styles, instead of providing a one-size-fits-all approach to instruction, may have benefits for Web-based instruction.

Use and Effects of Web-Based Instruction

Few studies exist that specifically address Web-based instruction using particular CMSs, and many theorists bemoan the lack of pedagogical features to support constructivist learning in these tools (Marra & Jonassen, 2001). One study incorporating CMSs was conducted by Lu, Zhu, and Stokes (2000). In this study, the researchers examined the relationships among students' prior knowledge, behavior in an online course context, and grades on a final exam in a physics course delivered by using specific components of WebCT. This study revealed that the students who reported that they surfed the Web frequently did less well on the final exam than those who surfed occasionally or not at all. The study also revealed that the incorporation of self-tests, quizzes, and summaries into the Web-based instruction correlated with improved student performance on the final exam. These results suggest that online instructors should discourage non-content-related Web surfing in online courses and should build in additional content-related resources such as self-tests and summaries to improve student performance.

What do these studies indicate about effective instructional strategies in Web-based courses? What evidence would you provide to the agency's undersecretary as a synthesis of the research results on the effectiveness of Web-based courses or online training?

Suggested Instructional Strategies and Activities

The previously mentioned studies incorporated, or their results suggested, the following instructional strategies and activities related to Web-based instruction (for additional information on these research studies and their findings, visit the companion Web site at http://www.prenhall.com/dabbagh):

Instructional Strategies and Activities Suggested in Heines (2000)

- Students respond positively to particular course Web sites.
- Creation and careful maintenance of a course Web site can be worth extra time and effort.
- Web-based courses may be one important factor related to the increased probability of students' success in particular courses with large enrollments. However, caution should be taken in interpreting these results because of numerous possible educational variables.

Instructional Strategies and Activities Suggested in Collis et al. (2000)

- Although only suggestive, the results of Collis et al.'s study indicate that students may respond well to a structured approach but may not do as well when left to their own structuring and decision making with regard to studying in Web-based courses.
- Redesigning or designing a Web-based course and responding to students is time intensive for the instructor.
- The payoff for more communication, discussion, self-selection of materials, summarization, and feedback may not be necessary or better for student learning.
- Providing structured support in the form of required discussion, collaboration, summarization, and feedback prompts students to spend more time on the course but may not influence achievement.

Instructional Strategies and Activities Suggested in Martinez and Bunderson (2000)

- Evidence suggests that recognizing and adapting to learning orientations in advance is useful in guiding the design of instructional learning environments.
- Determining learner profiles can assist developers in designing and matching learning environments to learners for the greatest success.

Instructional Strategies and Activities Suggested in Lu et al. (2000)

- Full-time students may be more focused on content than part-time students who enjoy exploring Web features may be.

- Instructors should encourage a focus on core content and discourage Web surfing for unrelated content in online courses.
- Instructors need to promote the use of self-tests, quizzes, and summaries in content-based Web courses.

"Whew, I am glad that is over," says Clay, after sending the agency's undersecretary a carefully crafted e-mail synthesizing the research results he and Marta found on Web-based instruction. Marta says, "Don't speak too soon because here is her reply." Marta and Clay read the undersecretary's response. The undersecretary now wants more answers. She is asking, "How do learners react to online instruction? Why would they want to participate in online instruction or training? What can we do to create and promote an effective and positive learning environment?" Marta yells, "Aha! There is a lot more research on student perceptions of Web-based instruction that we can synthesize for her! The only problem is that some of it compares students' impressions of face-to-face instruction with Web-based instruction. This is really difficult to do since you are comparing two different forms of delivering instruction. But I know there are studies in that pile that can provide some answers for her!" Clay glances over and says, "I am glad you are now so enthusiastic about the research because here we go again!"

RESEARCH ON STUDENTS' PERCEPTIONS OF WEB-BASED INSTRUCTION

Research that attempts to compare media delivery formats such as Web-based and face-to-face instruction is problematic because of the confusion between the instructional method or strategy (sequencing lessons, examples, tests, etc.) used and the delivery mechanism (book, computers, teachers, etc.; Clark, 2000). This type of research is mainly related to evaluating student experiences and perceptions of Web-based and online instruction (and is discussed further in Chapter 7). Clark (2000) stated that when you are conducting research related to distance education and online learning, you must establish baseline information about the conditions that will be replaced by distance education or online learning programs, the reactions of the individuals involved, and ways to evaluate achievement or learning outcomes. In the studies discussed next, researchers examined student experiences and perceptions of online learning.

Students' and Tutors' Experiences and Learning Outcomes of Internet-Based and More Conventionally Delivered Distance Education Courses

A study by Carswell, Thomas, Petre, Price, and Richards (2000) provides an example of research in which students' perceptions of online learning were examined. The study involved students in an online environment and students enrolled in traditional courses at The Open University in the United Kingdom. These researchers attempted to combat the problems of media delivery comparison studies by providing instructional methods (content, tutors, resources, and materials) that matched as closely as possible and then examining any differences in the experiences of students who used the Internet as their learning environment and those who participated in conventional course methods. At The Open University, conventional courses follow a correspondence course model, including printed text, audiotape and videotape, CD-ROMs that rely on the traditional mail system, and participation in local tutorials and self-help groups. In contrast, the Internet students capitalize on e-mail, computer conferencing, and Web forms to communicate about and submit course assignments.

Carswell and colleagues (2000) initially established existing baseline differences between the Internet group and the conventional instruction group by collecting detailed data on background experience with computers, prior knowledge of course content, and learning style. The two groups were determined to be similar across personal attributes and learning outcomes. Additional results revealed that students perceived the use of the Internet as a convenient delivery mechanism that increased interaction with other students and with tutors and provided a more rapid turnaround time for feedback on assignments. These students also thought that the use of the Internet in instruction provided learning opportunities beyond the content, including sharing issues with other students and increasing their Internet skills.

Consistency, Contact, and Communication in the Virtual Classroom

Online survey methods to collect data are prominent in studies related to student perceptions of Web-based courses. Swan et al. (2000) studied 1,108 students' perceptions of their learning, interaction with instructors and peers, and satisfaction in 73 online courses at the State University of New York (SUNY), using an online survey. The results provided valuable insights for online instructors and designers, including interesting relationships among student perceptions and course attributes. The researchers found that students elected to participate in an online course primarily because of scheduling conflicts and family responsibilities rather than geographic reasons. The study revealed that the online courses were generally small. Most courses at SUNY had fewer than 20 students enrolled in them. Interaction with the instructor was found to be the most influential factor in students' perception of the learning experience. Students who perceived high levels of online interaction with their instructor rated their satisfaction and learning in the course high. Students who thought they actively participated in the course also reported the highest levels of satisfaction and learning. These results place grave importance on interaction between the online instructor and the student and directly align with the recommendations and competencies discussed in Chapter 2.

Swan et al.'s (2000) study also revealed interesting and applicable results related to student perceptions and course design features. Most of the courses contained few external links and did not capitalize on creating links within the course. Most of the courses also had weekly assignments and based between 10 and 50% of the grade on online discussion participation. Interestingly, the greater the percentage of the grade based on discussion contributions in a particular course, the higher students rated their satisfaction, level of interaction, and learning. In contrast, the higher the percentage of the grade placed on cooperative work, the less the students believed they learned, although this result might be a function of poor pedagogical design of the collaborative activities. In addition, the fewer instructional modules in an online course and the more consistent the format of the modules, the more students thought they learned. These results have implications for the appropriate design of online courseware, including the consideration of small numbers of students when possible, the provision of high levels of instructor and peer interaction, the value of emphasizing participation in online discussion through grading, and the need to strive for consistency and redundancy in the design of individual instructional modules.

Students' Frustration with a Web-Based Distance Education Course

Another valuable research direction related to student perspectives on the online learning environment involves their frustrations and the types of supports needed to provide a meaningful learning experience in Web-based instruction. Hara and Kling (1999) conducted an informative case study providing an in-depth view of frustrations students experienced in a specific Web-based course. Although these results are not directly generalizable to other courses, they do raise common issues related to student frustration with online courses. In this particular Web course, students experienced frustration primarily related to technological issues, an inadequate amount and the untimeliness of instructor feedback, and ambiguous instructions related to course assignments. In addition, students experienced anxiety related to falling behind in reading messages and difficulty with dealing with information overload and with spending more time than anticipated online. For some students, the lack of the instructor's physical presence seemed to promote a feeling of insecurity in their level of progress in the course, and these concerns, along with the other frustrations, were not always communicated to the instructor. Hara and Kling's study draws attention to challenges in the online learning environment that are supported by other literature. Web-based instructors need to pay strict attention to providing adequate technological support for online students and need to ensure that they plan for a high level of feedback in their communication with students. Also, attempting to limit the amount of reading of online messages (such as the use of small-group communication and reporting to the larger group), providing clear directions and instructions, and finding ways to monitor and inform students of their progress in the course at multiple points would assist instructors in preventing student frustration. These results and those of other studies formed the basis for the online instructor competencies described in Chapter 2.

> *How would you summarize the reactions and experiences of online students in the studies reported? What recommendations would you make to online instructors on the basis of these results?*

These studies demonstrate the importance of considering student perceptions, experiences, and frustration levels in online courses.

Suggested Instructional Strategies and Activities

The previously mentioned studies incorporated, or their results suggested, the following instructional strategies and activities related to improving students' perceptions of Web-based instruction (for additional information on these research studies and their findings, visit the companion Web site at http://www.prenhall.com/dabbagh):

Instructional Strategies and Activities Suggested in Carswell et al. (2000)

- Instructors should provide instruction using the Internet to support a faster response, interaction, and feedback to students.
- Instructors should expect an increase in communication between the instructor and individual students in an Internet-based course.
- Internet courses can extend learning beyond course material by providing opportunities for sharing problems related to content and increasing online expertise.

Instructional Strategies and Activities Suggested in Swan et al. (2000)

- Smaller classes of 11 to 20 students may be optimal to support interaction in online courses.
- Interaction with instructors is critical to the success of online courses.
- Interaction with peers is also important to consider during course design.
- Creating active learning opportunities, reducing the number of outside links, and basing a greater percentage of grades on online discussion participation may affect students' perception of courses.
- Fewer modules that are consistent in design may influence students' perception of their learning.

Instructional Strategies and Activities Suggested in Hara and Kling (1999)

- Technology support needs to be provided for online learning contexts.
- Instructors should consider increasing the frequency and timeliness of feedback in a Web-based course to prevent student frustration.
- Students' computer competence and prerequisite skills should be adequately assessed before the start of an online course.

- Instructors of Web-based courses should take care not to overwhelm students with too many online messages.
- Online directions and instructions need to be clear.

After reporting the results of the research on students' perceptions of and experiences in Web-based instruction to the undersecretary, Marta and Clay are ready to give the research pile a rest. Their boss, the director of training, comes into their office and says, "You two have learned a lot about online learning and have helped the agency's case by basing our online activities on current research. After seeing your response to the undersecretary about online learners, I was wondering what we might be able to find out about the online instructor's perspectives?" Clay thinks for a moment and replies, "You know, Chuck, this is a research area in which multiple studies have been conducted related to university faculty but not much has been reported by the government and corporate sectors." Chuck responds that he thinks the agency could still learn something from higher education's experience; after all, many of the online tools originated in higher education, and university faculty were some of the first online instructors. "Ok," Clay says, "We will try to find out what research is out there, and I might even use this information to write a report for one of my classes." Clay thinks his professor will be interested because she incorporates online instruction into her teaching.

RESEARCH ON FACULTY AND INSTRUCTOR PERSPECTIVES ON WEB-BASED INSTRUCTION

Most research related to faculty, instructor, and designer perspectives on Web-based instruction focuses on providing descriptions of the higher education faculty population, faculty opinions and perspectives on this medium for teaching and learning, and success factors and barriers for faculty participation in online instruction. The National Education Association (NEA, 2000) conducted a survey among its members and described the perspectives of faculty who teach distance learning courses and those who teach traditional courses. The results of the study revealed that 1 in 10 of the NEA faculty teach a distance learning course, which was defined as more than half the instruction delivered online and instructor and students in different locations. Faculty who taught distance learning courses had a more positive view of this form of teaching than did instructors who did not teach online. Technical support was the most crucial factor for promoting positive feelings about online teaching among faculty who taught distance learning courses. This fact points to a primary consideration for higher education institutions that are launching a distance learning effort. This research underscores the importance of a solid technological infrastructure and support for online learners (discussed in Chapters 2 and 9) in preventing frustration and ensuring a successful online learning experience.

Additional results of the NEA study reveal that a faculty member often functions as both the designer of content and the manager of information in his or her distance learning courses, and more than half of all faculty members spend more time per week preparing and delivering these courses than doing so for their traditional courses. However, most faculty who teach distance learning courses are not compensated for this additional time. Interviewed faculty believed that distance learning courses present an enhanced method of providing students with (a) access to information, (b) high-quality course material, (c) assistance in mastering the subject matter, (d) improved assessment of course effectiveness, and (e) accommodation for different learning styles.

Motivating and Inhibiting Factors for Faculty Participation in Distance Learning

In other studies, researchers examined the factors that motivate or inhibit faculty participation in Web-based learning. Schifter (2000) examined these factors in a large northeastern institution in the United States. She surveyed 263 faculty members who did and did not participate in distance learning, plus 11 administrators, to determine their top five motivating and inhibiting factors for participating in distance education. She then compared the results of these three groups. Schifter found that all three groups agreed that a high motivating factor (in the top three) for incorporating distance or online learning into courses was a personal motivation to use technology. The faculty who did not currently participate in online learning and the administrators also rated the intellectual challenge involved in distance learning as a strong motivator. The differences in study ratings are often most interesting; in this case, both groups of faculty members (participating and nonparticipating in distance learning) rated monetary support, reduced teaching load, and credit toward promotion and tenure much lower than administrators did. This result indicates that monetary and other rewards are not the reason faculty members embark on using distance or Web-based learning in their courses.

The faculty participants in distance learning rated the opportunity to use their personal research as a teaching tool in their online courses high as a motivating factor. Nonparticipating faculty rated support from colleagues and career exploration as motivating factors for using distance learning methods lower than participating faculty and administrators did. These results may indicate that instructors who use distance learning methods value the research opportunities, support from colleagues, and expanding career options related to online learning.

As the results of studies related to student preferences in online learning indicate, the primary factor that also inhibits faculty use of distance learning methods is a lack of institutional technical support. All three groups agreed that this lack of support was the top reason why faculty choose not to use distance learning methods. All three groups at this institution also agreed that an increasing faculty workload and lack of release time were inhibiting factors. Administrators agreed with participating faculty that a lack of grant money was a strong inhibitor against participating in distance learning methods. These factors point to important considerations for supporting faculty currently teaching online and faculty who may decide to teach in this manner, as well as how administrators could best support and not inhibit their efforts.

On the basis of these results, what would motivate or demotivate instructors to incorporate Web-based instruction into their teaching or training? Why do you think some instructors are willing to spend more time developing and implementing online instruction when they are not directly compensated for it?

Suggested Instructional Strategies and Activities

The previously mentioned research studies incorporated, or their results suggested, the following instructional strategies and activities related to improving instructors' perceptions of Web-based instruction (for additional information on these research studies and their findings, visit the companion Web site at http://www.prenhall.com/dabbagh):

Instructional Strategies and Activities Suggested in NEA (2000)

- Providing technical support and gaining experience teaching online are important factors to consider to promote faculty's positive feelings toward Web-based instruction.
- Providing training for faculty is important so that they can function adequately as course designers and managers.
- Compensation should be considered for the extra faculty time spent preparing and delivering online courses.
- Online courses should be considered when faculty goals include providing high-quality course material, assisting students in mastering subject matter, assessing course effectiveness, and addressing student learning styles.

Instructional Strategies and Activities Suggested in Schifter (2000)

- Capitalize on intrinsic factors such as personal interest in and the intellectual challenge of technology to motivate faculty to use distance learning methods in their courses.
- Provide adequate institutional support and an adequate technological infrastructure for online courses.
- Provide support with regard to workload, release time, and grant opportunities as a means to encourage faculty to use distance learning methods in courses.

Clay and Marta deliver their final research report on faculty perspectives to the director of training. Marta says, "You know, Clay, you were right; the research on online learning has a lot to offer in steering us in the right direction for developing courses for the LMS." "Not only that," Clay says, "It also gives us strategies for promoting interactivity, a sense of community, and positive learner and instructor attitudes in online contexts." Marta comments that research is extremely useful after all and she is surprised at the range of categories of studies. Marta tells Clay she has an idea. Why don't they conduct their own study as they develop and implement their next online course? Clay smiles and says he cannot believe that she has become a researcher and throws a small pile of studies into the air.

CHAPTER SUMMARY

In this chapter, we focused on presenting specific examples of research related to various categories of studies on online learning. Studies from eight categories of research were presented: (a) asynchronous communication tools, (b) synchronous communication tools, (c) interactivity, (d) online communities, (e) hypertext and hypermedia, (f) Web-based instruction, (g) student perceptions of Web-based instruction, and (h) faculty and instructor perspectives on Web-based instruction. Although the chapter did not provide an exhaustive review of the literature, it did provide an overview of some current research in the field and a synthesis of specific results for application and consideration in designing, developing, and supporting online learning environments. These results are particularly useful to consider when instructors are implementing a systematic process for developing online learning. Exploration into strategies suggested by research results—as well as practice—becomes the foundation for creating effective online learning and is presented as part of a systematic process for designing and developing online course materials in Chapter 4.

LEARNING ACTIVITIES

1. Using the detailed research results located in the Resources section for this chapter (Chapter 3) at the companion Web site (http://www.prenhall.com/dabbagh) and the suggested instructional strategies and activities provided in this chapter, create a list of recommendations for online instructors who want to incorporate asynchronous communication tools into their online courses. Select a particular Web CMS and adapt the research-based recommendations to the features of the online tool to provide specific guidance for online instructors who use this tool.

2. Using the detailed research results located in the Resources section for this chapter (Chapter 3) at the companion Web site (http://www.prenhall.com/dabbagh) and the suggested instructional strategies and activities provided in this chapter, determine when synchronous communication would *not* be appropriate to use. Create a mock presentation that synthesizes the detailed results of this body of research and communicates to online instructors what to avoid when they are using synchronous tools.

3. Write a paragraph describing how you define *interactivity* on the basis of your experiences. Compare your definition with others' definitions reported in the research in this chapter.

4. Using the detailed research results located in the Resources section for this chapter (Chapter 3) at the companion Web site (http://www.prenhall.com/dabbagh) and the suggested instructional strategies and activities provided in this chapter, determine the similarities and differences in the conclusions and suggested instructional strategies of these studies for asynchronous communication, synchronous communication, and interactivity.

5. Identify an online community related to your work or personal interests and observe the interaction that occurs. Document your observations and compare what you observed with the detailed research results presented in the Resources section for this chapter at the companion Web site and in the suggested instructional strategies and activities. Can you suggest some additional, creative ways to try to promote a sense of community online?

6. Given the research presented on hypertext and hypermedia, review the content structure and navigation of an instructional lesson on the Web to determine how it might be improved. Does the site demonstrate hierarchical or vertical navigation in presenting information to the learner? Could the instructional content be presented in smaller chunks of information and through fewer links? How could participants or learners structure the information or their learning process?

7. Write an executive summary of the research results presented in the Web-based instruction section of this chapter. In the summary, emphasize the researchers' findings or claims, then provide evidence for these claims based on the details of the study found at the companion Web site.

8. List some of the most important considerations for promoting a positive learning experience and preventing student frustration with Web-based instruction. Refer to the results of the studies cited in the Research on Students' Perceptions of Web-Based Instruction section of this chapter.

9. If you know people who teach online or incorporate online learning into their instruction or training, survey them to find out what motivates them to use online learning methods. What barriers or obstacles do they face in designing or implementing online learning? Synthesize the results to present to someone else.

RESOURCES

Explore additional resources at the companion Web site (http://www.prenhall.com/dabbagh) to learn more about the research on online learning.

REFERENCES

Bannan-Ritland, B. (2002). Computer-mediated communication, eLearning and interactivity: A review of the research. *The Quarterly Review of Distance Education, 3*(2), 161–179.

Barab, S. A., Thomas, M. K., & Merrill, H. (2001). Online learning: From information dissemination to fostering collaboration. *Journal of Interactive Learning Research, 12*(1), 105–143.

Beaudin, B. P. (1999, November). Keeping online asynchronous discussion on topic. *Journal of Asynchronous Learning Networks, 3*(2), 41–53. Retrieved from *http://www.sloan-c.org/publications/jaln/v3n2/index.asp*

Carswell, L., Thomas, P., Petre, M., Price, B., & Richards, M. (2000). Distance education via the Internet: The student experience. *British Journal of Educational Technology, 31*(1), 29–46.

Chou, C. C. (2001). Formative evaluation of synchronous CMC systems for a learner-centered online course. *Journal of Interactive Learning Research, 12*(3/4), 173–192.

Clark, R. E. (2000). Evaluating distance education. *The Quarterly Review of Distance Education, 1*(1), 3–16.

Clay-Warner, J., & Marsh, K. (2000). Implementing computer-mediated communication in the college classroom. *Journal of Educational Computing Research, 23*(3), 257–274.

Collis, B., Winnips, K., & Moonen, J. (2000). Structured support versus learner choice via the World Wide Web: Where is the payoff? *Journal of Interactive Learning Research, 11*(2), 131–162.

Dabbagh, N. (2000). The challenges of interfacing between face-to-face and online instruction. *Techtrends, 44*(6) pp. 37–42.

Fishman, B. (2000). How activity fosters CMC tool use in classrooms: Reinventing innovations in local contexts. *Journal of Interactive Learning, 11*(1), 3–27.

Ford, N., & Chen, S. Y. (2000). Individual differences, hypermedia navigation and learning: An empirical study. *Journal of Educational Multimedia and Hypermedia, 9*(4), 281–311.

Gayeski, D. (1993). *Multimedia for learning: Development, application, evaluation.* Upper Saddle River, NJ: Educational Technology Publications.

Hara, N., Bonk, C. J., & Angeli, C. (2000). Content analysis of online discussion in an applied educational psychology course. *Instructional Science, 28*(2), 115–152.

Hara, N., & Kling, R. (1999, December). Students' frustrations with a Web-based distance education course. *First Monday, 4*(12). Retrieved from *http://www.firstmonday.dk/issues/issue4_12/hara/index.html*

Harasim, L., Hiltz, S. R., Teles, I., & Turoff, M. (1997). *Learning networks: A field guide to teaching and learning online.* Cambridge: MIT Press.

Haythornthwaite, C., Kazmer, M. M., Robins, J., Shoemaker, S. (2000, September). Community development among distance learners: Temporal and technological dimensions. *Journal of Computer-Mediated Communication, 6*(1). Retrieved from *http://www.ascusc.org/jcmc/vol6/issue1/haythornthwaite.html*

Heines, J. (2000). Evaluating the effect of a course Web site on student performance. *Journal of Computing in Higher Education, 12*(1), 57–83.

Hirumi, A. (2002). A framework for analyzing, designing and sequencing planned eLearning interactions. *The Quarterly Review of Distance Education, 3*(2), 141–160.

Jacobson, M., Maouri, C., Mishra, P., & Kolar, C. (1996). Learning with hypertext learning environments: Theory, design and research. *Journal of Educational Multimedia and Hypermedia, 5*(3/4), 239–281.

Kanuka, H., & Anderson, T. (1998). Online social interchange, discord and knowledge construction. *Journal of Distance Education, 13*(1), 57–74.

Last, D. A., O'Donnell, A. M., & Kelly, A. E. (2001). The effects of prior knowledge and goal strength on the use of hypertext. *Journal of Educational Multimedia and Hypermedia, 10*(1), 3–25.

Locke, L. F., Silverman, S. J., & Spirduso, W. W. (1998). *Reading and understanding research*. Thousand Oaks, CA: Sage.

Lu, A. X., Zhu, J. J., & Stokes, M. (2000). The use and effects of Web-based instruction: Evidence from a single source study. *Journal of Interactive Learning Research, 11*(2), 197–218.

Marra, R. M., & Jonassen, D. H. (2001). Limitations of online courses for supporting constructivist learning. *The Quarterly Review of Distance Education, 2*(4), 303–317.

Martinez, M., & Bunderson, C. V. (2000). Building interactive World Wide Web (WWW) learning environments to match and support individual learning differences. *Journal of Interactive Learning Research, 11*(2), 163–195.

McDonald, J., & Campbell Gibson, C. (1998). Interpersonal dynamics and group development in computer conference. *The American Journal of Distance Education, 12*(1), 7–25.

McIsaac, M. S., Blocher, J. M., Mahes, V., & Vrasidas, C. (1999). Student and teacher perceptions of interaction in online computer-mediated communication. *Educational Media International, 36*(2), 121–131.

Murphy, K. L., & Collins, M. P. (1998). Development of communication conventions in instructional electronic chats. *Journal of Distance Education, 12*(1/2), 177–200.

National Education Association (NEA). (2000). *A survey of traditional and distance learning higher education members*. Washington, DC: Author.

Niederhauser, D. S., Reynolds, R. E., Salmen, D. J., & Skolmoski, P. (2000). The influence of cognitive load on learning from hypertext. *Journal of Educational Computing Research, 23*(3), 37–255.

Pena-Shaff, J., Martin, W., & Gay, G. (2001). An epistemological framework for analyzing student interactions in computer-mediated communication environments. *Journal of Interactive Learning Research, 12*(1), 41–68.

Rovai, A. P. (2001). Building classroom community at a distance: A case study. *Educational Technology Research & Development, 49*(4), 33–48.

Schifter, C. C. (2000, June). Faculty participation in asynchronous learning networks: A case study of motivating and inhibiting factors. *Journal of Asynchronous Learning Networks, 4*(1), 15–22. Retrieved from *http://www.sloan-c.org/publications/jaln/v4n1/index.asp*

Simich-Dudgeon, C. (1999). *Interpersonal involvement strategies in online textual conversations: A case study of a learning community*. (ERIC Document Reproduction Service No. ED435169)

Soo, K., & Bonk, C. (1998, June 20–25). *Interaction: What does it mean in online distance education?* Paper presented at the ED-MEDIA/ED-TELECOM 98 World Conference on Educational Multimedia and Hypermedia & World Conference on Educational Telecommunications, Freiburg, Germany.

Sotillo, S. M. (2000). Discourse functions and syntactic complexity in asynchronous communication. *Language Learning & Technology, 4*(1), 82–119.

Swan, K., Shea, P., & Fredericksen, E., Pickett, A., Pelz, W., & Maher, G. (2000). Building knowledge building communities: Consistency, contact and communication in the virtual classroom. *Journal of Educational Computing Research, 23*(4), 359–383.

Tsui, A., & Ki, W. W. (1996). An analysis of conference interactions on TeleNex—A computer network for ESL teachers. *Educational Technology Research & Development, 44*(4), 23–44.

Uribe, D., Klein, J. D., & Sullivan, H. (2003). The effect of computer-mediated collaborative learning on solving ill-defined problems. *Educational Technology Research & Development, 51*(1), 5–19.

Vrasidas, C., & McIsaac, M. S. (1999). Factors influencing interaction in an online course. *The American Journal of Distance Education, 13*(3), 22–36.

Warren, K. J., & Rada, R. (1999). Manifestations of quality learning in computer-mediated university courses. *Interactive Learning Environments, 7*(1), 57–80.

Zhu, E. (1998a). Hypermedia interface design: The effects of number of links and granularity of nodes. *Journal of Educational Multimedia and Hypermedia, 8*(3), 331–358.

Zhu, E. (1998b). Learning and mentoring: Electronic discussion in a distance learning course. In C. J. Bonk & K. S. King (Eds.), *Electronic collaborators: Learner-centered technologies for literacy, apprenticeship, and discourse* (pp. 233–260). Mahwah, NJ: Erlbaum.

4

INTEGRATIVE LEARNING DESIGN FRAMEWORK FOR ONLINE LEARNING ENVIRONMENTS

After completing this chapter, you should understand the following:

- A systematic and flexible process for designing and developing online learning—the Integrative Learning Design Framework (ILDF)

- How the ILDF and the Three-Component Online Learning Model intersect to form the ILDF for Online Learning

- The phases and components of the ILDF for Online Learning

- Activities and methods related to the exploration phase

- Activities and methods related to the enactment phase

- Activities and methods related to the evaluation phase

CONSIDER THE FOLLOWING THREE SCENARIOS:

A Teacher's Journey to Mars: Anya teaches 11th-grade science. She has been interested in space exploration and astronomy since she was a child and loves sharing her interest with her students. After teaching the 11th-grade science curriculum at her school for 4 years and seeing students who are not interested in learning science, she strongly desires to find a way to engage their interest. Anya's school district is partnering with a local university on a federal grant to pilot a program to develop and implement online courses in certain secondary subject areas. In her teaching, Anya has used the Internet on a limited basis, but she has no idea how to design, develop, or evaluate an online course. She has much to offer with regard to her knowledge of what works for her students in the science classroom and has found some incredibly useful online materials related to a National Aeronautics and Space Administration (NASA)–supported educational Web site involving students in the exploration of the planet Mars. The only problem is that she does not know how to begin to integrate these materials with her teaching to create an engaging and effective online learning experience for her students.

A Professor's Online Community for Teachers: Dr. Priscilla Norton has been teaching and training teachers to successfully integrate technology in the K–12 classroom for many years. In those years, she has carefully observed and analyzed what works and does not work in the complex environment of schools. Dr. Norton also has advanced knowledge of teaching and learning theories. Her knowledge of working with teachers and theory-based approaches poses a problem for her as she examines some of the emerging online materials produced for teachers. In her assessment, she finds that the current design of online learning experiences does not match her criteria for engaging experiences and sound theoretically based instructional design. Given this finding, Dr. Norton sets out to develop her own online learning environment that will support teachers in their integration of technology into their classrooms. Her model is based on a mentoring model in which teacher–experts (mentors) will support teacher–mentees by guiding them to appropriately integrate technology into their teaching. Aligning her own perspective on learning with what she knows works with this audience and this context, Dr. Norton strives to develop a powerful system based on how teachers learn from one another. What she does not have is a systematic process that matches and can capitalize on how she views learning in this context to help her produce an effective online community for teachers.

The Blended Learning Objects Training Approach: The managers of a major parent corporation that encompasses many companies in multiple fields decide to commit to a training approach that capitalizes on blended learning. The managers' definition of the term *blended learning* is "to provide training to employees that involves many forms of instructional delivery, such as instructor led; paper based; real-world scenarios; mentoring; online learning materials; and modular, digital learning objects accessed through the company's learning management system." Although the managers believe in this training approach, they do not have evidence that it works for their employees, nor can much evidence be found in the literature about the viability of a blended learning approach. The managers decide to embark on a rigorous evaluation of their blended learning approach, but to do this, they realize that they need to carefully design the training context and the learning activities and then determine appropriate ways to evaluate them. The managers realize this effort will require many resources and much thought for it to succeed.

Where and how would you begin to design and develop online learning? What process might you follow? How would you advise the people represented in each of these scenarios as to what process they should follow? As you read through the chapter, consider these situations and how they intersect with the systematic process for online learning design and development we present.

In this chapter, we introduce and provide a detailed overview of the **Integrative Learning Design Framework (ILDF) for Online Learning**. This framework provides a systematic approach for the design and development of online learning environments.

INTRODUCTION: DESIGN AND DEVELOPMENT OF ONLINE LEARNING

Instructional design and development has been characterized as a complex problem-solving task (Bannan-Ritland, 2001; Dabbagh, Jonassen, Yueh, & Samouilova, 2000). The design process is one of the most difficult kinds of problem solving because in most situations no clear, predetermined solution or goal and no direct solution path exist, and information from multiple sources must be integrated (Jonassen, 2000). This characterization is especially true of online learning design because many online instructors serve as the designer and developer and need to determine what is to be learned, implement effective instructional strategies capitalizing on available technological features, and evaluate the effectiveness of the online instruction or training. Knowledge of pedagogical models, delivery methods, and competencies needed by instructors and learners, as well as an awareness of research outcomes and effective instructional strategies (as detailed in Chapters 1 through 3), are important to consider during the design and development of online learning. How does an online instructor or developer incorporate all this information into an effective online course? How does he or she best approach the design and development of online learning? To most effectively navigate the complex decision making and multiple sources of information involved in the design and development process, the online learning developer must adopt a systematic process or an organized approach that helps him or her consider the many variables in an instructional or training situation. The process of design and development for online learning needs to adhere to sound principles of course design but also include consideration of the unique attributes of online learning. In addition, the design and development process should be sufficiently flexible to address the multiple settings or contexts in which this form of instruction is used. The process of design and development of online learning also needs to include careful consideration of the global and social attributes involved in the design of effective and successful online learning.

In this chapter, we introduce a systematic yet flexible process for designing and developing online learning that grows out of our experience in creating different types of online learning environments, including Web-based instruction, virtual classrooms, online learning communities, and electronic performance support systems. These different forms of online learning environments were designed and developed by using a process adapted from traditional instructional systems design that we call the *Integrative Learning Design Framework (ILDF) for Online Learning*. The ILDF for Online Learning provides a systematic, iterative approach for designing online learning materials and activities that incorporate the three key components of online learning described in Chapter 1: (a) pedagogical models, (b) instructional strategies, and (c) learning technologies. The ILDF is based on the integration of multiple perspectives on the design and development process from the fields of instructional design, product design, and **usage-centered design**, as well as research and evaluation processes that can be incorporated into the activity of online learning design (Bannan-Ritland, 2003). We present the ILDF for Online Learning in progressively more detail throughout the chapter to provide you with a comprehensive and flexible model that can be applied in multiple design settings. To explain the need for this new model, we first discuss current perspectives on online learning design and development.

THE STATE OF ONLINE LEARNING DESIGN AND DEVELOPMENT

Online instruction and training has been criticized for presenting stale, unengaging instruction with limited interaction, which results in a high dropout, or attrition, rate ("E-Defining Education," 2002). The creation process for online course content is often perceived to be the direct transfer or copying of traditional curricular material to the Web with little or no modification. Educational journals report that many online courses resemble the "text-and-talk format" found in most classrooms and focus primarily on delivering information rather than on engaging students ("E-Defining Education," 2002, p. 38). Online course delivery and management systems have also been criticized for their limited support of meaningful learning and knowledge construction (Marra & Jonassen, 2001). Although effective and engaging online courseware does exist, the common public perception of this instructional format is that online learning is often not appropriate, interesting, or engaging.

Many online curricular delivery products, such as course management and learning management systems (see Chapters 8 and 9), are flooding the commercial market. The targets for these products are schools, universities, and corporate training departments. The products range in quality and delivery formats, although many systems permit the custom design and development of online learning materials and courses. A poll of 219 eLearning Guild members—representing an online community of designers, developers, and managers of e-learning, or online instruction, in primarily corporate but some academic settings—indicates that most online courseware (64.38%) is developed by in-house staff, followed by online courseware developed equally by in-house staff and outsourced contractors (11.42%; The eLearning Guild, 2003). A smaller percentage uses off-the-shelf, or commercial, courses (8.22%) or buys off-the-shelf commercial courseware and customizes it (4.11%). Because most online learning courses or materials are custom developed by corporate trainers, university professors, or others, familiarity with learning processes, effective instructional strategies, and a systematic process of design development and evaluation may make the difference between success and failure in online learning.

The investment of time and effort in designing and developing successful online learning is significant, whether undertaken by an individual or by a team. Also significant is the time that a student invests in online learning. This investment of time should be a rewarding and engaging experience for both instructors and students, rather than a frustrating and limiting experience. Systematic consideration of the multiple factors that affect sound instructional design is crucial for improving the effectiveness and quality of online materials at the start of the process (as well as in all phases) and can save time and prevent problems in the long term. Implementing a process that emphasizes iterative cycles for continual improvement is one of the best ways to improve the effectiveness of online instruction and increase the developer's knowledge of what works. The purpose of the ILDF for Online Learning is to provide a systematic framework for development of online learning materials that is based on pedagogy and iterative evaluation rather than on the developer's whims. This framework presents a flexible process that can be adapted to multiple settings—including school-based, corporate, academic, military, and nonprofit organization contexts—in which formal or informal methods of design and development may be used. Our goal for this chapter is to provide a general guide of the broad phases of the framework and to then present the more detailed stages and methods included in each phase that can be tailored to specific settings.

The ILDF for Online Learning draws heavily from the iterative nature of traditional systematic processes in the field of instructional design. Traditional instructional system design models that include analysis, design, development, implementation, and evaluation stages have been applied to the development of many types of learning materials, including online learning. These models have been found to be difficult to apply in practice in both corporate and school-based settings (Moallem, 1998; Tessmer & Wedman, 1992). Critics argue that current instructional design models are too linear or require a rigid, step-by-step process that is too formal and inflexible and dictates that an instructional designer strictly follow all the steps (Zemke & Rossett, 2002). Given the variation of online learning settings, technological tools, and content, as well as the high-level problem solving required of the developer of online materials, a rigid, inflexible process can add to the design and development complexity. So that this complexity can be reduced, online developers need more flexible, interactive, and adaptable processes in which the social and cultural contexts of learning that are not emphasized in traditional instructional design models are specifically considered (Moallem, 1998; Zemke & Rossett, 2002). Our purpose in presenting the ILDF for Online Learning is to provide a flexible, adaptable process of design and development that emphasizes the specific social and cultural contexts of learning and design. In addition, the ILDF for Online Learning encourages the developer to base his or her design decisions on constructivist learning models (see Chapter 5) that can engage participants and promote meaningful learning through a systematic, iterative development process.

Although the ILDF for Online Learning focuses primarily on constructivist learning models, the broad phases included in the model (i.e., exploration, enactment, and evaluation) are based on time-tested processes from behaviorist models of instructional design that rely on systematic and iterative design methods. Therefore, the overarching process of the ILDF for Online Learning could conceivably be used in design and development efforts that focus on pedagogical approaches other than constructivist theory. This framework differs from other models mainly in the view of design as a creative, complex process that can facilitate change and is based in great part on human judgment (Nelson, 1994) and consideration of the social and global aspects inherent in instructional design (Moallem, 1998). Consideration of the judgment, expertise, and prior knowledge of individuals who develop online instruction about teaching and learning is crucial in the systematic process and typically ignored in other models. In addition, considering the social and cultural context of design, as well as the learning issues, can promote more efficient and effective online learning design from the start and throughout the process. The main reason we selected this framework as opposed to other models is that it better aligns with a constructivist view of online learning design. Cennamo, Abell, and Chung (1996) stated that constructivist principles should be used for the design and development of instruction that embeds this philosophy of learning. Although we strive to incorporate this philosophy in the ILDF for Online Learning, we believe the overarching systematic process of this framework can also be applied to design and development efforts that adhere to different pedagogical perspectives.

THE ILDF FOR ONLINE LEARNING

All good instructors rely on their intuitive and explicit knowledge of learners, settings, content, and activities, which has been acquired through their multiple experiences in teaching or training. In traditional instructional systems design models, the teacher's, trainer's, professor's, or instructional designer's beliefs, insights, or intuitive understandings about teaching and learning are not typically considered. In contrast, the ILDF for Online Learning attempts to tap the online learning developer's intuitive understandings and beliefs about learning and learners, as well as his or her explicit knowledge from deliberately gathered information, to create successful online learning. Even if the developer is new to online learning materials design and development, he or she usually has a wealth of knowledge about learners and content that can be applied to online learning design. The core idea of the ILDF for Online Learning is to make explicit what the online developer knows and believes about teaching and learning in order to transfer this valuable information to online teaching and learning. In addition, the framework presents a menu of formal or informal methods for gathering useful information that, when combined with the developer's insights and intuitive understandings in a systematic design process, can produce effective online instruction or training. The ILDF for Online Learning also promotes the idea that following a systematic, explicit process provides the developer with a knowledge-building opportunity to learn more about his or her learners, instructional settings, pedagogical approaches, and design effectiveness. Viewed in this manner, the ILDF for Online Learning is a systematic and iterative constructivist-based design process that can be used not only to develop meaningful instruction, but also to prompt a learning process for the developer as he or she expands his or her understanding of the instructional or training situation.

The ILDF for Online Learning has been used in multiple online learning design contexts, including the development of online university courses with common authoring tools, online learning communities, and electronic performance support systems (Bannan-Ritland, 2001; Bannan-Ritland, Egerton, Page, & Behrmann, 2000; Jeffs, Behrmann, & Bannan-Ritland, 2004). The framework is applicable for developing formal custom software or for using common Web-based authoring tools and course management systems to design a single course. Persons involved in designing and developing online learning can select from a menu of formal or informal activities in each phase in the ILDF for Online Learning, determining what is most applicable to their situation. Both the informal and the formal activities associated with each phase of the development of online learning materials and associated learning activities are presented later in this chapter. First, the overarching iterative, systematic process of online learning development is presented.

The three phases of the systematic development of online learning are as follows (see Figure 4.1):

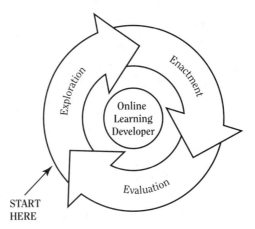

Figure 4.1   Systematic Process of Online Learning Development

1. **Exploration phase:** Investigating and documenting relevant information related to the instructional or training setting, including individual and collective beliefs on learning and information solicited from others involved in the instruction or training situation, to inform the design
2. **Enactment phase:** Mapping information gathered in the exploration phase about learning processes, content, and context to existing pedagogical models, with consideration of the characteristics of the selected model, to identify and implement effective instructional strategies online
3. **Evaluation phase:** Determining the purpose, desired results, and methods of evaluation of an online learning design, incorporating formative evaluation and revision cycles that result in effective implementation and informative results

The Developer's Role

Figure 4.1 illustrates the overarching iterative process of design and development of online learning. Note that the online learning developer is placed at the center of the systematic process. We prefer the term *online learning developer* rather than *designer, instructional designer, developer, instructor,* and so forth because we believe that professionals in many contexts participate in or contribute to the design and development of online learning, and many do not have specialized training in the instructional design field. Therefore, the online learning developer could be a teacher, a trainer, a professor, a graduate student, an instructional designer, a multimedia developer, a programmer, or any combination of these people and others in a team-based or an individual effort. The online learning developer may design, develop, and facilitate the course or may participate in the design and development of a course for someone else to facilitate. Typically, in many school-based and higher education settings, the online learning developer is also the course facilitator and subject matter expert. In training settings, the online learning developer may work with a team comprising subject matter experts and programmers for customized online development projects. Despite the role(s) the online learning developer assumes, he or she has a central part to play in the design and development process that requires exploring his or her perspective and experience related to teaching and learning, as well as others' perspectives related to the particular instructional or training setting, and enacting these ideas into a feasible design.

Placing the online learning developer at the center of the iterative process represented in Figure 4.1 was a deliberate decision because the knowledge gained by the developer in exploring perspectives on learning, enacting specific instructional strategies, and learning from the results can promote the development of effective instruction. Through this systematic implementation, the developer's knowledge of what works also increases.

Intersection with the Three-Component Online Learning Model

We presented the three phases of systematic development of online learning (i.e., exploration, enactment, and evaluation) and the central role of the online learning developer.

However, all the elements of the framework are not yet in place. In Chapter 1, we introduced a three-component model of online learning that comprised (a) pedagogical models or views of teaching and learning, (b) instructional strategies and activities that embody particular views of teaching and learning, and (c) learning technologies that embody specific features for implementing the selected instructional strategies. Each of these components must be considered when an online learning developer designs or develops instruction that is grounded in theories of teaching and learning, regardless of pedagogical orientation (Hannafin, Hannafin, Land, & Oliver, 1997). The problems of presenting unengaging and stale online learning instruction may occur when these three key components are not considered in the design and development process. Therefore, the overarching systematic process of design and development represented in Figure 4.1 intersects with the Three-Component Online Learning Model to promote the design of instruction and training that is grounded in theories of teaching and learning. Figure 4.2 represents the merging of this process and model to yield the ILDF for Online Learning.

Each component of the ILDF for Online Learning is necessary to guide the online learning developer in the **exploration,** enactment, and evaluation of online courses or materials. The three components are the eventual products of the broad phases of the framework. The ILDF for Online Learning begins with exploration of the instructional

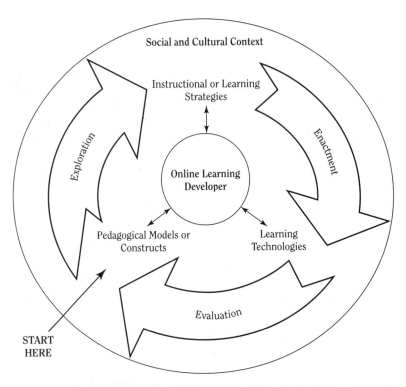

Figure 4.2   Integrative Learning Design Framework for Online Learning

or training context ar   g and learning as a way for the
online learning devel   al models or approaches. Next,
the developer examin   gical models so that he or she
can select appropriate instructional strategies that can then be enacted with specific
learning technologies. Evaluation of the enacted design can then reinform what is
known about the pedagogical models. In this manner, considering each component in
the iterative design process encourages the online learning developer to iteratively explore,
enact, and evaluate pedagogical models, instructional strategies, and technologies.

One of the most interesting elements of the framework is the interaction, represented by the double-headed arrows, between the developer in the center and the three
components (pedagogical models, instructional strategies, and learning technologies).
This representation depicts the interactive and ongoing, implicit and/or explicit interaction between the online learning developer's knowledge and experience and the selection of appropriate models, strategies, and learning technologies in the iterative design
process. The developer's knowledge and experience interacts with his or her attempt to
explore new models, enact new strategies, implement them through available technologies, and continually evaluate the results to validate or inform his or her methods of
online learning development. This process builds the online learning developer's knowledge base about the teaching and learning process in the specific social and cultural
context that incorporates online learning.

The Importance of the Social and Cultural Context

The process of online learning design and development occurs in a specific context of
learning in which particular tools, philosophies, and personnel are available (or unavail-
able) to the developer. The social and cultural context of design and development of
online learning is represented by the circle that encompasses all the elements of the
framework shown in Figure 4.2 In Chapter 1, we emphasized the view that learning is a
social process embedded in a social and cultural setting that represents a constructivist
perspective on learning. The design and development process can be viewed similarly.
Designing and developing instruction involves a collaborative, problem-solving process
that engages the developer in analyzing information about the learners, setting, strategies, and content. The design and development of instructional or training materials is
not conducted in isolation; rather, it involves implicit or explicit interaction with others.

*Look back to the first scenario presented at the beginning of this chapter. Who
else might be involved in Anya's efforts to develop the online science course experiences? Should she consult individuals involved in the grant from the local university or her school administrators for guidance or advice? What about her colleagues or the instructional technology resource person at her school? Should
she involve her students in her efforts to design this new part of the curriculum
or look back at their work to determine which online activities might work for
them?*

When creating instruction or training online, the developer typically interacts explicitly or implicitly within not only a community of learners, colleagues, and specialists, but also situational constraints. Consideration of these perspectives can be crucial to the successful design and development of online learning experiences. In addition, the online learning developer interacts with others in a specific organizational culture with inherent politics, social processes, and access to particular technological tools. These affordances or constraints can often drive the design and development process. For example, a corporate trainer involved in online learning development may be limited by the skills of the programmer on the team or the available technological tools in the design of training. Similarly, the professor is constrained by the features of the only course management system that the university supports. Teachers are often limited by a lack of resources and strict policies in curricula and grading. The online learning developer may also be limited by the policies or perspectives on learning that exist in the organization. Many teachers must conform their lessons to specific learning standards established by school administrators and government officials. Identifying and working within the specific constraints and affordances of the social and cultural contexts surrounding the design process is important for producing online learning experiences that will be accepted and used.

The online developer relies on not only individual expertise, but also the knowledge and input from learners, colleagues, technology experts, and many others, to create a successful online course. The information sources may differ among school-based, higher education, and training settings. However, the systematic process of gathering, analyzing, integrating, and applying information from many sources is similar. The specific resources and technologies available to the online developer in specific social and cultural settings, as stated previously, play a significant role in the design and development of online instruction. For example, teachers may have limited access to resources, so they often take advantage of their more experienced colleagues' creativity and rely on available online technologies to create classroom-specific solutions when integrating online learning into their teaching. In higher education, professors may access multimedia and instructional design specialists and university-based technology training programs and explore literature on integrating technology into their subject matter in order to design or redesign existing instruction for online delivery. The corporate online developer is usually provided with multiple resources in the form of content specialists and programmers necessary to produce broad-scale, cost-effective, and efficient training solutions but still requires some type of systematic process. Each of these groups of online learning developers relies on what the context affords in order to design and develop effective online learning.

The ILDF for Online Learning deliberately frames the systematic process of design and development in the social and cultural context. The importance of considering the specific situational affordances and constraints in the design process of online learning cannot be overstated. The specific contexts of both learning *and* design need to be considered when the developer is designing and developing online learning. The technological, political, or pedagogical constraints often dictate what is possible in designing online instruction. This fact is particularly true for online learning because the resources that this form of instruction requires (e.g., appropriate technological infra-structure, student training and technical support, instructor support), the buy-in from stakeholders (e.g., school and university administrations, corporate management), and increased knowledge of effective online instructional strategies can greatly affect a developer's efforts. One purpose of the framework is to promote the learning process of the online learning developer through exploring new pedagogical models and instruc-tional strategies that can be applied to online learning. Exploring multiple perspectives on learning, enacting these perspectives through specific instructional strategies that take advantage of the features of the technological tools available, and systematically eval-uating the results is the essence of the ILDF for Online Learning. These activities can be accomplished either formally or informally, which is discussed in the next subsection.

Formal and Informal Processes of the ILDF for Online Learning

The complex, problem-solving task of design requires the developer to consider all the factors just detailed to develop effective instruction or training. However, the methods the online learning developer uses for exploring, enacting, and evaluating pedagogical models, instructional strategies, and technologies, as well as the methods he or she uses for considering the social and cultural context, may vary. Many different methods, rep-resenting formal or informal approaches, can be used for systematically examining and gathering information in the design and development process. For example, in the exploration phase, a school teacher like Anya (see the first scenario at the beginning of this chapter) might informally examine her insights into her students' abilities and their interaction with the content that she teaches before she designs an online learning expe-rience for them. She might also have informal conversations with her colleagues and school administrators to collect information about the viability of implementing online learning in her school. She will consider the state learning standards related to the con-tent she plans to cover. Her knowledge and beliefs about learning processes, online instructional strategies, and technologies will inform her design of these new experi-ences for her students. A teacher's methods of information gathering or data collection may be more informal and implicit but can represent a systematic approach to collecting and examining relevant information for the effective design of the online instruction.

In contrast, in the third scenario presented at the beginning of this chapter (The Blended Learning Objects Training Approach), a new manager charged with organizing the blended learning evaluation may use both formal and informal methods in the exploration phase. He might first informally gather information through conversations with employees and from existing literature about the organizational culture and phi-losophy on learning, about the skills of his colleagues and subordinates in conducting blended learning experiences, and about the available software tools involved. He might also conduct a formal needs analysis, using survey methods to explore in more detail the employees' experiences with a blended learning approach, and use the results as baseline data for constructing the learning experiences in the evaluation. He might collect information about how others across the corporation are implementing blended learning and read articles in trade magazines that describe this training approach. All this information is integrated to identify and operationalize the corporation's pedagogical approach specific to its social and cultural context, which can then be evaluated. The methods or techniques for gathering the information and the persons involved may vary, but both the teacher and the manager are systematically (or thoroughly and regularly) collecting data to inform their design or enactment of specific pedagogical approaches and eventually their evaluation methods.

Using a more formal method for gathering information in the exploration phase to inform the design, an academic researcher, such as Dr. Norton in the second chapter opening scenario, might first conduct a literature review to examine the research and pedagogical models used in online learning. After considering these pedagogical approaches and evaluation methods, she might use a precourse questionnaire to gather specific information about her students prior to the design and implementation of her online course. Peled and Rashty (1999) used this formal data-gathering approach to examine information about the characteristics of students in and their expectations of an online political science class. This information might have been combined with other research results and used to inform the initial design of the course or might have been compared with data from a postcourse student survey in the evaluation phase to inform the next semester's iteration or revised design. Peled and Rashty capitalized on several methods at different points in the design process, including pre- and postcourse surveys. This research study represents a more formal and systematic process that informs the design and revision of online learning materials. The demands of the academic social and cultural context helped to dictate the selection of methods in this online design, development, and evaluation effort.

Regardless of the formality or informality of the methods used and the nature of the specific social and cultural context, in all these examples, a thorough, regular, methodological, systematic, and iterative design process was used. The ILDF for Online Learning places the responsibility for the selection of appropriate methods and techniques in each phase on the developer and his or her judgment and perception of the requirements of the social and cultural context. In this chapter, suggestions for both formal and informal methods for each phase of the framework are presented after the description of the phase. The flexibility of this approach allows for a systematic, iterative process in which both the implicit and the explicit knowledge of the developer is considered and the developer is allowed to determine data-gathering and analysis techniques according to the specific social and cultural context of the design.

Summary

The ILDF for Online Learning incorporates not only elements that are designed to promote the systematic development of effective online learning materials grounded in learning theory, but also consideration of the specific social and cultural context to increase the online learning developer's knowledge of the effectiveness of his or her designs. The design process is a complex problem-solving process that can be implemented in a flexible manner by using multiple methods at varying levels of formality. The methods or techniques that inform the stages of each phase of the ILDF for Online Learning are described further and illustrated in the remainder of this chapter as well as in Chapters 5 through 7. In Chapters 5 and 6, we describe in detail the pedagogical models and instructional strategies that are considered in the enactment phase, and in Chapter 7, we describe the evaluation phase. In summary, the following points are the major principles of the ILDF approach to the design and development of online learning:

- With the ILDF for Online Learning, we attempt to combine the best of systematic instructional design models with consideration of a teacher's, an instructor's, or a trainer's valuable knowledge, experience, and learning related to the specific context, content, learners, strategies, and technologies.
- The ILDF for Online Learning values the developer's internal processing, judgment, decision making, and experience, incorporating the flexible implementation of formal or informal methods to systematically implement the broad phases of exploration, enactment, and evaluation.
- The social and cultural context of the instruction greatly influences this systematic process because knowledge of design and development is contextually bound and socially situated.

PHASES, ACTIVITIES, AND METHODS OF THE ILDF FOR ONLINE LEARNING

The Exploration Phase

Exploration involves not only investigation and analysis of several sources of information—including learners, stakeholders, clients, and colleagues—but also self-examination by the online learning developer, for the purposes of designing and developing effective online instruction or training. The best methods of investigation and analysis involve some type of documentation. The exploration phase of the ILDF for Online Learning directs the developer to investigate and document his or her perspectives on teaching and learning and to analyze the instructional or training context. This framework also directs the developers to gather and study information on other perspectives related to the audience, setting, content, and outcomes. This phase results in an increased understanding of teaching, learning, and contextual issues that is then used to identify an appropriate and specific pedagogical approach. Specific activities in the exploration phase include the following:

- Explicitly document insights and findings from the gathered information.
- Gather information about the instructional or training context.
- Examine individual perspectives on the learning process.
- Incorporate published perspectives on the learning process.
- Solicit perspectives and existing information on the learning process, content, and online delivery method.

Explicitly document insights and findings from the gathered information
Documenting insights and information related to teaching and learning in the class-room and online can provide an important window for reflection and analysis and allow some of the implicit nature of this complex activity to become explicit. For the online learning developer, finding some way to document personal understandings, beliefs, and insights into the students and content can create a valuable source of information to use in investigating and analyzing different approaches for teaching online. These rich reflections can help the developer to begin to transform what he or she knows about learning, learners, and the context for online delivery. Collis (1997) termed this process of transforming an instructor's knowledge of general teaching and learning for online delivery **"pedagogical reengineering."** The online context requires a reconsideration of traditional methods of teaching for the developer to take advantage of the unique attributes of online tools and teaching approaches. Documentation of and reflection on techniques, beliefs, and learning processes assists the developer in considering new ways to present content and engage students in online learning. A method for documentation should be selected prior to gathering information so that the online learning developer has an established method for keeping track of incoming data or information.

Documenting these reflections need not be a time-consuming exercise because many creative and informal methods of collecting impressions, insights, and gathered information can be used to systematically improve instruction—such as using a tape recorder or recording brief notes in a lesson plan book or PalmPilot (see Table 4.1). One design team used a project Web site and Web-based portfolios as its form of documentation in the exploration phase. This documentation contained (a) team meeting notes, (b) a record of impressions of interaction with the client, (c) a listing of individual and collective perspectives on applicable learning theories, (d) notes on target audience members' understanding of the instructional task, and (e) written reflections on data from usability tests of the previous prototype (Bannan-Ritland, 2001). The developer should use the method that he or she is most comfortable with as long as it permits the explicit documentation of insights and reflections on teaching and learning processes, and of solicited information, which will enlighten the decision making in systematic online design and development.

More formal methods of documenting information on and insights into learning and the instructional context are required when developers are involved in corporate reporting, qualitative research, or the initial phases of action-based or design-based research efforts (see Table 4.1). These methods can also be used in the ILDF for Online Learning because more formal documentation activities in the exploration phase provide a high level of detailed information on the online learning setting and learners that can be used to inform the design. Corporate reports or requests for proposals (RFPs) in obtaining grants can be used to create a case for the design and development of an online project in the exploration phase. These documents often contain a persuasive account of the organizational beliefs and philosophies, as well as details about the learning requirements and context of the potential online instruction (Kapp, 2003). The research process promotes an inherent documentation process that can greatly inform the design and provide baseline information for later evaluation. These formal methods

Table 4.1   Exploration

INFORMAL METHODS	FORMAL METHODS
Explicitly document insights and findings from the gathered information: • Notebook entries • PalmPilot digital notes • Audiotape recordings • Lesson plan reflections • Web site housing impressions, data, beliefs	**Explicitly document insights and findings from the gathered information:** • Formal corporate report • Request for proposal (RFP) • Qualitative research proposal • Action research plan • Design-based research plan
Gather information about the instructional or training context: • Conversations • Examination of relevant documentation • Informal interviews • Informal surveys • Discussions with stakeholders • Observations • Expert opinions	**Gather information about the instructional or training context:** • Performance analysis • Examination of relevant documentation • Needs assessment • Qualitative analysis • Surveys • Focus groups • Observations • Expert panel
Examine individual perspectives on the learning process: • Individual reflection • Individual articulation • Group discussion	**Examine individual perspectives on the learning process:** • Theoretical conjectures • Learning circles • Design document or rationale
Incorporate published perspectives on the learning process: • Examination of magazines and journals • Review of online course or lesson examples	**Incorporate published perspectives on the learning process:** • Literature review • Benchmarking • Competitive research
Solicit perspectives and existing information on the learning process, content, and online delivery method: • Conversations • Examination of relevant documentation • Informal interviews • Informal surveys • Discussions with colleagues and stakeholders • Observations • Expert opinions	**Solicit perspectives and existing information on the learning process, content, and online delivery method:** • Profiles, role models, or personae • Contextual analysis • Qualitative analysis • Surveys • Focus groups • Observations • Expert panel

require an orientation in writing corporate reports, writing RFPs, or training in research techniques but can provide valuable, in-depth information related to the systematic design and development of online learning (see the companion Web site—http://prenhall.com/dabbagh—for recommended readings on these subjects). Design-based research is an emerging methodology that holds great promise for integrating knowledge gained from design activities with rigorous research methods to inform what is known about teaching and learning (see Kelly, 2003).

Explicitly documenting the insights and gathered information (described in the next subsection), whether informally or formally, provides a systematic means for comparing, contrasting, and integrating multiple sources of information that informs the design. This activity is the first and most important of the exploration phase and is encouraged throughout the entire cycle of the ILDF for Online Learning.

Think about the first scenario. How might Anya document her reflections, ideas, and gathered information? What about the second scenario involving Dr. Norton and her graduate students? Which documentation process might work for her and her development team to house and share the information they will collect in the exploration phase? Individuals involved in the corporate effort of evaluating the blended learning approach will need to present their plan to their bosses. Which methods of documentation might make sense for them to use to collectively report their learning design for the evaluation and to analyze the data they will gather?

Gather information about the instructional or training context The political, social, cultural, financial, and other contextual influences inherent in any organization can contribute to the success or failure of online instruction or training. For example, to design a new online lesson, a teacher like Anya, teaching in the United States, would likely consult the existing curriculum and state and national standards related to the subject area. She might also think about her school's mission, her principal's goals, her colleagues' teaching approaches in the same subject area, her students' performance and feelings about the existing instruction, parents' expectations, the school's budget for new technologies, and the school district's criteria for minimum competencies. Considering and integrating these discrete bits of information is often an intuitive and implicit thinking process for teachers (Moallem, 1998). Information on these issues and gaining buy-in and support from the organization (i.e., school or university administration or corporate management) are often crucial for successful implementation of online learning initiatives. In the process of online learning design in any context, these influential factors should be made explicit as part of gathering information about the context for consideration and analysis. Doing so ensures that important factors are taken into account to inform the design and development process and so that the developer can work toward ensuring the success of online learning.

Considering and working within the factors that can constrain or promote the success of online instruction is important in the design process. The process for identifying and explicitly examining these factors can be conducted informally or formally (see Table 4.1). The deliberate gathering of information about the instructional or training context can take place through informal conversations, interviews, surveys, observations, or discussions with project stakeholders, as well as through examination of relevant literature that helps to describe the context. The most important factor is that available information that might affect the success or failure of an online learning design be considered before the intensive design effort so that significant time can be saved and potential problems avoided. For example, prior to designing an online course that taught troubleshooting skills to operators of technical equipment in a pharmaceutical firm, the developers had initial conversations and informal discussions with many of the operators to identify the major problems that required troubleshooting. The printed manuals for the equipment were examined for details on the successful operation of this equipment. An informal survey and ranking of the major problems was conducted at a meeting of all floor operators so that the developers could confirm the initial information gathered in discussions and assess the reception of such training. In addition, discussions with the supervisors and technical trainers who were the stakeholders of the project most interested in the successful design and development of this online training revealed that one operator on the floor who was about to retire was one of the best troubleshooters of this equipment. Arrangements were made for the developers to observe him in action for a few weeks, to document problems that occurred and his solutions, and to encourage him to explicitly talk through his troubleshooting process.

All this information was gathered, documented, and synthesized informally, but systematically, in the exploration phase. In the following enactment phase, the integrated information was considered during selection of the most appropriate design and instructional strategies for the online training on troubleshooting skills. The exploration resulted in an interactive course that presented a troubleshooting process that could be applied to scenarios based around the core problems identified in the company. If the corporate training developers had not investigated the various sources of information available in the pharmaceutical company, they would have put significant time and effort into producing online training that may have been inappropriate and not valued by the target audience. By taking a small amount of time upfront to investigate different information sources in the training context, the developers greatly increased the possibility of producing online training that was necessary, usable, and valued by their target audience.

Rossett (1999) described a formal process of gathering information about the instruction or training context: performance analysis that takes advantage of both informal and formal information gathering but presents a rigorous approach to clearly exploring and defining an instructional or a training problem. Clearly defining the instructional or training problem can provide justification for time-intensive online learning design and development. For example, gathering information from employees about their inability to schedule a full day for required training on quality control and their willingness to participate during smaller time segments of their choosing could help to justify online delivery of this information and instructional strategies delivered by asynchronous technologies rather than classroom-based or synchronous methods. To define a performance problem in a training or an education context, Rossett advocated that information, or data, be gathered that includes both human sources of information (e.g., students, alumni, experts, colleagues, managers, supervisors, customers) and inanimate sources of information (e.g., grades, assignments, course materials, articles, interviews, policies, records, products, reports). Interpreting the term *data* broadly, she suggested that the developer needs to access multiple sources of information on the problem and select the sources wisely to try to gain the most valuable information that can provide insight into the educational or training problem quickly and efficiently and can later inform the design.

The integration of these data can help developers to clarify and define an organization's or individual's goals related to proposed online instruction. Considering information related to the context or setting of online learning can reveal valuable information that can prevent later problems. For example, when one professor designed his first online course, which was to be delivered in the upcoming semester, he required all his students to participate in whole-class online discussions. Later, this professor discovered that 30 students were enrolled in the course, yet he maintained his original course design. The result of the online course design was student frustration that negatively affected learning because of the numerous messages resulting from the exchange of 30 people in an online discussion. Had the professor taken some time to investigate and integrate the available contextual information about his course, or had he communicated with colleagues more experienced in online methods, he might have prevented the negative consequences. The enrollment information and/or conversations with individuals who had used online learning in the past might have prompted him to consider implementing smaller discussion groups that would write summaries of their discussions and report them to the whole class. This instructional strategy would have been more manageable and more successful.

As mentioned previously, integrating available information and perspectives can reveal important constraints and affordances of the instruction or training context that can affect the success or failure of online instruction or training. This information can be gathered informally by relying on conversations, discussions, informal surveys, interviews, or observations. Formal methods can also be implemented, including research processes that incorporate observations, surveys, talk-aloud protocols, focus groups, or expert panels that might be used in formal needs analysis or other research efforts in the exploration phase. With these formal methods, developers can thoroughly investigate, document, and analyze baseline conditions that can greatly inform the design and production of online instruction or training. For example, to inform the design of an online technology system that supported children with disabilities in the reading process, qualitative and quantitative data were gathered from parents, children with disabilities, a review of related software programs, surveys, questionnaires, reading and writing samples, and documented reactions to a simulation of computer-based instructional activities that would be included in the design of the online system (Bannan-Ritland, 2003; Jeffs et al., 2004). The integration and synthesis of contextual data, whether conducted informally or formally, provides valuable information that can inform the design and allow selection of appropriate instructional strategies in the following enactment phase. Explicitly documenting information at all phases in the ILDF for Online Learning prompts consideration of the influential factors that can encourage or prevent success in online instruction or training.

What are the political, social, cultural, financial, technical, and other contextual factors that Dr. Norton (in the second scenario at the beginning of the chapter) might need to consider during development of her online learning course? To whom might she talk to gather important contextual information related to offering an online course through the university to train teachers to integrate technology into their classrooms? Which informal methods of information gathering might she use? Does she need to use any formal methods to gather information about the instructional context? Why or why not?

Examine individual perspectives on the learning process   Not explicitly considered in many instructional design models, the developer's beliefs, knowledge, and practical experience are considered of equal importance to gathered and published perspectives in the ILDF for Online Learning. The developer's prior knowledge of instruction or training is particularly important in the problem-solving process of online learning design and development because most instructors, professors, teachers, or trainers move to online technologies after having significant initial experience in face-to-face classrooms. So, naturally these individuals should capitalize on their implicit and explicit knowledge of learners, learning processes, content, and context and apply it to online methods of instruction. Leveraging this valuable experience and knowledge is as important for online learning as it is in other types of instruction. Much of the decision making in classroom-based and online learning curriculum design involves similar processes: assessing the students' knowledge level, considering the complexity of the content, presenting instructional strategies appropriate for the students' developmental level and for specific content, and so forth—regardless of the delivery method.

Weimer (2002) wrote about transforming college teaching toward a more learner-centered approach and stated that higher education faculty members typically move through developmental stages related to their reflection on students and learning. This finding may be true of online learning developers as well. Weimer cited work by Biggs (1999) that suggested that instructors move through three typical stages: (a) focusing on student abilities and differences; (b) focusing on delivering instructional strategies, or the "how-to" of teaching; and (c) focusing on what students do, which emphasizes what it means to understand concepts and principles in the content area of the discipline. Reflection on and analysis of these issues moves teachers through this developmental progression to more learner-centered and constructivist forms of teaching (Biggs, 1999; Brookfield, 1995). The ILDF for Online Learning supports this perspective for online learning by encouraging the developer to reflect on and analyze what he or she knows about students, instructional strategies, and the activities students can do that promotes engagement and understanding of the content or training delivered. This reflection and analysis process can provide a sound basis for transferring this knowledge to the online context by applying this knowledge to the specific technical attributes of online delivery tools. Many learner-centered instructional strategies used in the face-to-face classroom—including discussions, debates, round-robins, role-playing, collaborative learning, guest speakers, and others elaborated on in Chapters 5 and 6—can be transformed for the online context. Explicit examination of current and past teaching practices, experiences, beliefs, and learning processes, as well as the students' developmental level, the content complexity, and appropriate instructional strategies, can greatly inform the design of effective online learning.

Exploration, reflection, and analysis of instructional experiences can also yield valuable insights into the design process. A team of graduate students in instructional design were charged with designing and developing a Web-based system to help children with learning disabilities learn to read. While brainstorming about how learning occurs in this context, one team member who was also a parent of a child with a disability shared an insight based on her experience. Her child did not learn how to read by himself, but through intimate and sustained interaction, with her as a facilitator and coach. This insight led to a total shift in the design of the Web-based system from a tutorial-based format in which the child worked alone with the computer to a collaborative Web-based system that supported parent and child as they worked together on reading tasks (Bannan-Ritland et al., 2000). Many theorists and researchers in education are beginning to recognize that teachers' beliefs, insights, and knowledge have traditionally been undervalued in research, professional development, and other change efforts such as technological development and implementation (van Driel, Beijaard, & Verloop, 2001). This undervaluing is true of the instructional design field as well and in corporate and higher education contexts in which new technological tools are often mandated by management for use in training development without consideration of the employees' or the end users' perspectives on and experience with strategies and approaches that might work best in the specific context.

Part of the instructional design process is to document the **instructional problem**, goal, objectives, learner characteristics, instructional strategies, delivery mechanism, and evaluation processes in a thorough design document for presentation to clients. Typically, individual teachers, trainers, or professors are not required to produce a rationale for their beliefs and/or decision making in the classroom or for online learning. However, documenting or articulating pragmatic knowledge and beliefs about learners, learning processes, technology, and the instructional or training environment from a developer's perspective can generate new ideas and transform existing knowledge into effective online learning design and development. This process of reflection and analysis does not have to be conducted individually. One form of articulating and reflecting on practical experience and insights into learning is in a group. For example, a group of teachers in a Midwestern high school wanted to explore online learning for their classes. They decided to create a "learning circle," in which they met weekly to discuss how each of them might incorporate online learning methods into their individual teaching. The teachers articulated their current goals, understanding of learners, instructional strategies, evaluation methods, and available technologies. Their discussions provided a forum for expression of their individual perspectives, practical knowledge, and beliefs and capitalized on this information to then translate their knowledge so that they could design effective online lessons.

Another more formal method for reflecting on, analyzing, and documenting perspectives on the teaching and learning process is *theoretical conjecture,* or making an inference about how teaching and learning should happen in a particular content area, such as mathematics (Confrey & Lachance, 2000). Theoretical conjectures result from the researcher's perspectives on learning (informed by literature), practical knowledge of the classroom, and direct experience with learners. For example, related to the second scenario presented at the beginning of the chapter, Dr. Norton (2003) produced the following theoretical conjecture, which represented her perspective on learning, to describe what an alternative e-learning system should include:

> This learning system should situate learning in the problems derived from the context to which the content of learning pertains, build bridges between knowledge and action/learning and practice and maximize the resources and expertise of both the instructional design and expert practitioner. (p. 3)

The online developer's explicit beliefs, inferences, and practical experiences can not only shed light on the selection of instructional strategies that align with the developer's perspectives on teaching and learning, but also inform the selection of instructional strategies that can be considered for online learning delivery.

Revisit the third scenario, which involves the corporation and its blended learning approach with learning objects and other training methods. On the basis of the corporation's decision to incorporate a blended learning approach, what do you suppose management's beliefs about learning might be? How should the corporation articulate its perspective on the learning processes involved in blended learning and to whom might it need to articulate this information? How would doing so enhance the credibility of the corporation's blended learning training approach?

Incorporate published perspectives on the learning process   Taking the time to investigate published perspectives on how learning occurs related to the specific content and audience in face-to-face classrooms as well as in the online learning context can greatly benefit design efforts. More informal sources—such as magazines, trade journals (or journals devoted to teaching or training practice), and the Web—provide published perspectives that can inform the online learning design. In addition, more formal published resources include academic and research journals. The articles and examples in such journals can provide some insights into learning processes that can be applied to the design and development of effective online learning. For example, an entire special issue of the trade journal *Education Week* (No. 35, May 9, 2002) was devoted to highlighting how virtual schools and online learning are transforming teaching and learning ("E-Defining Education," 2002). In the articles, the authors described the broad benefits of online learning, the specific challenges facing practitioners of online learning in K–12 and higher education contexts, and examples of how educators are using these online teaching methods.

Academic journals, which include more formal research and conceptual articles, can also shed light on learning issues that can inform online design. For example,

Schwier (2001) investigated what is known about interpersonal communication and contrasted it with communication in an online virtual learning community. The processes of reflection, interaction, and engagement were discussed as important learning processes in virtual communities and as products of effective communication. Schwier presented 10 elements of community that provide excellent guidance for designing an online community based on the learning and communication processes that may occur in that context. For example, Schwier described *historicity* as an element that promotes stronger community ties when individuals share history and culture, as opposed to communities that are based on general and abstract ideas, which can promote a weak sense of community. For instance, one online developer was interested in designing an online community for fourth-grade science teachers who use inquiry-based methods in their teaching. Reading through Schwier's description of the historicity element made her realize that fostering online discussion around teachers' shared histories, their experiences, and their backgrounds, rather than initially presenting an abstract theoretical paper for discussion, may better promote the formation of an online community among this group.

Similarly, an instructional designer working for a defense contracting firm that integrates online learning created a knowledge management system that embodies Schwier's idea of autonomy. *Autonomy* is striving to "respect and protect individual identity" in an online community; interaction is based on "influence among participants rather than power relationships" (Schwier, 2001, p. 14). After examining this idea, the developer included in the knowledge management system individual profiles and areas of expertise that are shared across the company to encourage spontaneous online communities to form around core issues important to the company, with interaction based on current problems of interest rather than traditional supervisor–employee power relationships. These examples briefly illustrate how published resources can inform and enlighten developers' efforts to design online learning experiences. Published information can assist online learning developers in weeding through the complex issues and prompt new design ideas. Intersected with the developer's knowledge, published perspectives on learning processes can provide a sound foundation for effective design that is based on how people learn and communicate.

More formal approaches also exist for considering published perspectives on learning and the online context, including conducting a comprehensive literature review common to the research process. If time is available, formally reviewing and synthesizing the literature can provide a solid, informed background for design and thereby help to ensure success because the design will be based on a comprehensive understanding of what is known about learning. Academic literature is only one source of published perspectives that are applicable to online learning design. Many examples of online learning courses and environments are published on the Web—some freely accessible and others requiring permission to be reviewed. These examples provide another form of published material to investigate to provide insight into your designs.

One method that can be used to formally investigate or compare existing online learning examples is called *benchmarking*. Benchmarking is a process involving the evaluation of products or best practices, the results of which can then be compared with the executed design and development of an existing product. Reviewing and comparing other published examples of online learning systems can greatly inform an individual's personal design. An approach similar to benchmarking is *competitive research,* which involves profiling and comparing the competitors' products to inform in-progress design and development. According to Kuniavsky (2003), competitive research involves (a) identifying the competition, (b) profiling the competitors' products for key attributes that make them competitive, (c) comparing the competitors' products with one another (and with your product), (d) using the comparison to create "actionable intelligence" (p. 421). Creating actionable intelligence is the overall goal of the exploration phase: to analyze all the information gathered and make it useful enough to inform your online learning design. These two formal evaluation approaches can be used at many points in the design and development cycle, but they can be particularly useful as part of the initial exploration phase to then inform the enactment phase.

Examining and comparing other published examples of online learning, as well as examining the literature for insights into learning processes and online technology, can provide solid direction for a design based on a clear picture of what has worked and not worked in other situations. Visit the companion Web site—http://www.prenhall.com/ dabbagh—for specific references that provide additional details on implementing these formal methods.

Refer to the scenarios at the beginning of this chapter and think about the published sources you are aware of that Anya might consult to inform her design. Where might Dr. Norton look for resources with which she can conduct a formal literature review on online learning for teachers? What about the corporation implementing blended learning: How might the manager capitalize on benchmarking or competitive research to inform his design and evaluation efforts?

Solicit perspectives and existing information on the learning process, content, and online delivery method To this point in the exploration phase, the online developer has gathered and documented information about the instructional or training context and has examined personal and published perspectives on learning. The developer must also solicit from others specific information related to the learning process, content, and delivery method so that he or she can proceed into the enactment phase with the most information possible to create an effective design. Involving the learners (students, employees, trainees, etc.), stakeholders, colleagues, experts, and others in your information gathering provides multiple perspectives to consider in the design of online learning materials. Each documented perspective can have much to offer beginning or existing designs.

Examining the target audiences' perspectives related to the specific content and online learning is a natural place to begin to solicit information to inform the design. Learners' or employees' knowledge, attitudes, and preferences can direct the online developer to particular instructional strategies or assist him or her in avoiding significant mistakes. Multiple methods are available for investigating learning processes and related information, including both formal and informal approaches. Informal conversations and experiences with target audience members, as well as access to materials such as previous tests, assignments, and work products or processes, can greatly inform the design of online learning. For example, an experienced teacher naturally integrates information from daily observations of his or her students in the classroom and evidence from their work on assignments and tests into the teaching approach. He or she can also directly solicit and gauge their interest in future activities through classroom discussions and individual conversations with students. Not typically thought of as data, this information and the teacher's knowledge of his or her students' abilities, accomplishments, and preferences can provide a rich source of information for considering different instructional strategies to implement online. Similarly, a professor in higher education can base his or her online learning design on knowledge of previous students' responses to particular activities as well as on assessment of student performance on previous assignments and tests. The corporate trainer typically implements some form of evaluation for training sessions and can review this information to look for clues about what may most engage employee participants. Trainers who have direct access to employees can also conduct informal conversations, interviews, or surveys with accessible employees to collect information related to the potential content, design, and online delivery method.

A more formal method of soliciting information about the users or target audience for online design is creating a profile of who will use your learning environment to provide a focal point for design ensuring consideration of the audience's needs. This method is used in software design and is referred to as *profiles* (Kuniavsky, 2003), *role models* (Constantine & Lockwood, 1999), or *personas* (Cooper, 1999). These profiles are based on the developer's direct experience with the target audience. Relevant audience characteristics are compiled into a fictitious description of a person who will use the online learning design. These personas, or profiles, allow the developer to describe the representative audience and continually view the evolving design through the eyes of the learner or audience. This audience representation or role modeling is included as part of a software design and development process originated by Constantine and Lockwood (1999) called *usage-centered design*. The creation of role models, profiles, or personae in the exploration phase provides a more formal but easy way to help ensure that your online learning design meets learners' needs. For example, following is a role model, persona, or profile representing a compilation of characteristics from direct experience with and solicited information from several teachers. It was used to focus the design of an online learning community for teachers and professionals in the special education community in Virginia (by Claudette Allen, Cindy Johannessen, Deena Mansoor, Shawn Miller, Robert Moss, Rob Parrott, Trista Schoonmaker, and Lisa Stedge):

Mary-Beth, a Caucasian 29-year-old, has been working for 5 years as a special education teacher in Northern Virginia. She specializes in children with learning disabilities at an elementary school. Typically, she works as a self-contained teacher with the same eight or nine students all day. The students range from learning disabled to emotionally disturbed. An occupational therapist joins her in the classroom twice a week, for an hour each time. They work with the children to develop fine and gross motor skills, visual tracking abilities, and so forth. Often, she has extra duties such as writing and updating individual education plans (IEPs), testing, having playground duty, and attending staff meetings. These extra duties pull her away from her already time-consuming schedule and her limited planning time. She enjoys her job even though it proves to be extremely stressful and she often feels burned out. Her comfort level on a computer is average, but she does not have time to learn new programs to aid her in her job. She is married but has not had time for children yet. Financially, she and her spouse have enough money to pay the bills but do not have a lot of extra resources. To earn extra money, she tutors after school. Her commute can be as long as 1 hour one way.

Similar information could be compiled into fictitious role models, personas, or profiles based on the developer's experience with K–12 school or university students or corporate employees. The purpose of these profiles is to solicit useful information about the audience of online learning to help focus the developer on learner needs and requirements and guide design in the following enactment phase. The profiles provide a context for considering the target audience's learning process, reaction to content, and preferences for online learning delivery formats. Drafting a profile, persona, or role model emphasizes the learner's requirements for the online design rather than the developer's needs and desires.

Understanding learners' experiences and perspectives provides a wealth of information for design. Intersecting the learners' perspectives with other stakeholders' and experts' views of what works online related to the specific content and the online context can also help to ensure success. Soliciting information from experienced colleagues or experts who have developed and conducted online courses is one of the best ways to informally explore and gather information to guide your design and prevent problems. Faculty support organizations in universities often promote sharing of online learning courses among experienced online instructors. Furthermore, many teachers have access to a technology specialist who may be able to provide some guidance on using the Web for instruction. Corporate conferences and presentations on online learning are common places for developers to explore and solicit collegial and expert perspectives on what works in similar online learning designs.

Other formal methods, including focus groups, expert panels, and qualitative interviews, can also be used to solicit information from learners, stakeholders, or experts. Observations of work processes can provide another rich form of information exploration and gathering to inform the content of your design. For example, while developing an online learning module for training nurses in postpartum assessment of mothers, a development team videotaped an experienced nurse–practitioner performing the assessment and then asked her to talk the team through her process while watching the video. This experience was a rich source of information on the assessment approach and the content required in the training and prompted design ideas about how to structure or deliver this information online.

Kuniavsky (2003) recommended a technique called *contextual analysis*, which consists of an in-depth study of a few individuals to provide a better understanding of work practices that can then inform online product design. According to Kuniavsky, contextual analysis includes examining learners' demographic profile, Web use, regular tasks, tool use, and problem-solving approaches. This method promotes the consideration and analysis of learners' existing knowledge (of content and process) and use of technology and other tools. This information can then be considered during the design of online instruction or training. Such information is crucial to developing an appropriate online learning environment.

Whether using a formal or an informal approach to directly solicit information related to the learning processes, content, and online delivery media, the online learning developer can gain significant information that, when synthesized, results in targeted, appropriate, and effective online learning.

Summary   The exploration phase provides an opportunity for the developer to investigate different facets of the instructional or training problem, incorporate multiple perspectives, and produce usable information or data that can result in effective online learning. Selecting from the formal or informal methods presented in Table 4.1 or a combination of them provides a flexible process of exploring and integrating the many perspectives and sources of information in the complex activity of instructional design. Through interaction with the learners, stakeholders, clients, and others, the online learning developer integrates these perspectives to produce usable and effective instruction or training. Table 4.2 provides some activities and guiding questions for you to use so that you can begin to apply these methods to your own online learning exploration.

In summary, the exploration phase provides the online learning developer with valuable information from multiple perspectives (including his or hers) and multiple sources that are integrated and analyzed to determine possible online design directions that can be pursued in the enactment phase. In the enactment phase, the developer will consider this information and select a pedagogical grounding or model that fits his or her perspective on learning and the situational constraints. The developer will then investigate the pedagogical model to identify specific **instructional characteristics** and strategies that align with this perspective on learning and to determine how these strategies can be implemented by using the specific technological attributes of the online learning medium. The enactment phase is described in the next subsection.

The Enactment Phase

The enactment phase involves generating instructional strategies that are congruent with theories of learning and the instructional or training context. These strategies are then enacted (or acted out) through available technological features in the most engaging way possible for the learner. The information gathered and analyzed in the exploration phase directs the developer toward particular pedagogical models or theories that can then suggest specific instructional strategies that can be fully implemented in online learning. The developer's beliefs and gathered information on learning processes, content, and context are integrated and reflected on to provide a direction for considering various pedagogical perspectives. Once a particular perspective on learning is determined to be congruent with the developer's perspectives, specific instructional strategies can be

Table 4.2 Activities and Prompting Questions for the Exploration Phase

---

Explicitly document insights and findings from the gathered information.
- What form of documentation are you planning to use to create a way to revisit your thinking, insights, and gathered information related to your online learning design?
- Do you need to formally document what you learn and your reflections through a corporate report, an RFP, or a design document, or can documentation be done more informally?
- Will you use methods such as note taking, journaling, reflections, Web sites, or learning circles?
- Will you articulate or document your insights individually or collaboratively? If so, plan how to maintain the information so that you can revisit it periodically throughout the ILDF cycle.

Gather information about the instructional or training context.
- What are the specific organizational, social, cultural, and financial factors that exist for the online learning context that can impact your online learning design?
- How will you deliberately gather information about the instructional or training context?
- What sources of information might you use to clearly identify the instructional or performance problem that online learning might help to solve?

Examine individual perspectives on the learning process.
- What are your beliefs and philosophies about teaching this content? Be sure to document your understanding of how learning occurs in your context through a theoretical conjecture or statement.
- What knowledge do you have about the learners, content, and context of instruction or training that you can potentially apply to the online environment?
- What instructional strategies have worked with your learners in a face-to-face environment? Do you have any initial ideas about how you might apply these ideas by using online learning technologies?
- How can you synthesize and communicate, to yourself and others, your perspective on and knowledge of the learning process involved in your targeted instruction or training?

Incorporate published perspectives on the learning process.
- Do any resources exist that can provide models, suggestions, or strategies for designing and developing online learning for your subject matter?
- Have you examined print and online resources related to online learning in general? related to your field and/or industry?
- Analyze the online strategies of the online course examples you locate. Are they potentially useful for your project?
- How do your beliefs and knowledge intersect with published literature and/or online course examples? Are there differences or similarities in what you think may work for your learners? Are there design ideas that may work with your learners?

Solicit perspectives and existing information on the learning process, content, and online delivery method.
- What sources of information can provide information on your understanding of the learning process, content, and online context?
- How would you describe or characterize the learners who will be involved in your course? Consider writing one or more profiles, role models, or persona based on your direct experience with the learners to provide a focus for your design efforts in the enactment phase.
- Consider the learners' current knowledge level, preferences, or attitudes toward the subject matter and online learning. Are there any past assignments, work products, or evaluations you can review to add to your knowledge about what may work for this particular audience?

(Continued)

Table 4.2   Activities and Prompting Questions for the Exploration Phase (*Continued*)

- Select appropriate informal or formal methods of exploration on the basis of your context to gather and document the information solicited from learners, stakeholders, colleagues, and/or experts. How does this information intersect, overlap, or differ?
- Synthesize the solicited information with your beliefs and published perspectives. Which potential strategies, activities, or directions for online learning design might you consider in the enactment phase? Document this information for later review.

Note. RFP = request for proposal; ILDF = Integrative Learning Design Framework.

considered. This process ensures that the design and development of online learning materials is grounded in theories of teaching and learning rather than merely the developer's whims. Given a range of instructional strategies for each pedagogical model, there are many ways to implement these strategies by using existing technological tools and many creative approaches to consider during the design of online learning. Specific examples of pedagogical models and instructional strategies are described in Chapters 5 and 6 and provided at the companion Web site (http:// www.prenhall.com/dabbagh). In essence, the phases of the ILDF for Online Learning are connected through information gathered in the exploration phase, which is then synthesized into specific instructional strategies appropriate for the audience, content, curriculum, and context and aligned with learning theory in the enactment phase. These strategies are then enacted or embodied in the online learning technological delivery system, which can be evaluated in the next and final phase. Specific activities in the enactment phase include the following:

- Map information gathered in the exploration phase to pedagogical models.
- Consider the instructional characteristics of the selected pedagogical models.
- Select specific instructional strategies that align with the selected pedagogical models.
- Enact the instructional strategies by using the features of technological delivery systems.

Map information gathered in the exploration phase to pedagogical models
The enactment phase of the ILDF for Online Learning connects exploration into the developer's and others' insights about learning and the learning context with established pedagogical models (or models that encompass the art and science of teaching). The overall purpose of the enactment phase is for the developer to meld what he or she knows about the learners, the content, and the social and cultural context of instruction or training into a theoretically grounded approach to online design and development. After examining their own and others' insights, online learning developers review the characteristics of established learning theories and select appropriate instructional strategies. These strategies are the activities that the learner will engage in during the online instruction. Designing powerful instructional strategies in the online context involves basing the activities on how people learn and creatively implementing engaging instructional strategies through the available features of technology (see Table 4.3).

Table 4.3 Enactment

INFORMAL METHODS	FORMAL METHODS
Map information gathered in the exploration phase to pedagogical models.	**Map information gathered in the exploration phase to pedagogical models.**
• Review documented beliefs, experiences with learners, and contextual information.	• Review documented beliefs, experiences with learners, and contextual information.
• Articulate or discuss beliefs about learning in relation to the pedagogical models.	• Document reflections on or beliefs about learning in relation to the pedagogical models with qualitative research memos or theoretical conjectures.
• Select and justify pedagogical models that most closely map to your personal beliefs or understanding of how learning occurs in the specific online learning context.	• Select and justify pedagogical models that most closely map to your personal beliefs or understanding of how learning occurs in the specific online learning context.
Consider the instructional characteristics of the selected pedagogical models.	**Consider the instructional characteristics of the selected pedagogical models.**
• Review online or classroom-based examples of the selected pedagogical models.	• Review academic articles describing classroom-based or online examples of the pedagogical models.
• Identify and describe the instructional characteristics of the models (see Chapter 5).	• Examine federally funded technology-based research for implementation of the selected pedagogical models.
	• Identify and describe the instructional characteristics of the models (see Chapter 5).
Select specific instructional strategies that align with the selected pedagogical models.	**Select specific instructional strategies that align with the selected pedagogical models.**
• Operationally define the instructional strategies of the selected models for the specific context and learners.	• Operationally define the instructional strategies of the selected models for the specific context and learners.
• Consider the instructional strategies described in Chapter 6.	• Consider the instructional strategies described in Chapter 6.
• Create a table mapping the instructional characteristics of the selected models to instructional strategies that may work in the specific instructional or training context.	• Document how you choose to implement the instructional characteristics of the selected models for your context and your learners for an academic paper or a journal article.
Enact the instructional strategies by using the features of technological delivery systems.	**Enact the instructional strategies by using the features of technological delivery systems.**
• Examine the features of online systems for implementation of the selected instructional strategies.	• Compare and contrast online learning systems for implementation of the selected instructional strategies.
• Create a table aligning the instructional characteristics of a pedagogical model and the selected instructional strategies and brainstorm about the technological features that will directly support the strategies (see Chapter 6).	• Produce an online prototype or storyboard materials representing the instructional strategies and test them with learners for their reaction.
• Implement the strategies by using features of the online learning tool.	• Implement the strategies by using features of the online learning tool.

The enactment phase of the ILDF for Online Learning ensures congruence between models of learning, instructional strategies, and technological features, which provides the best chance for substantive learning to occur and leads to more powerful instruction or training using online learning technology.

One logical question to ask to begin the enactment phase is this: On the basis of your experiences in the classroom and/or online, how do you think learning happens? The online learning developer should have had the opportunity in the exploration phase to think about his or her knowledge of learning processes in the context of experiences with learners and should have some idea of his or her individual beliefs and philosophies. The assumptions that are made about learning are the foundation for how all instructors enact strategies and activities in teaching and training. These assumptions must be explicitly examined so that instructors have some idea about why they engage learners in specific activities in the classroom, corporate boardroom, or virtual environment. As Weimer (2002) indicated, the progression of thinking by the teacher, instructor, or trainer from the "how-to" of teaching, or the pragmatic delivery of information, to focusing on what students do and what it means to understand is what moves instructors to create more powerful, learner-centered experiences. Helping students, employees, or other learners understand content, learn processes, or engage in high-level problem solving requires a clear understanding of how learning may occur and implementation of strategies that align with these foundational assumptions.

Many established perspectives on how learning occurs can provide insights into the selection of applicable or appropriate instructional strategies for online learning. The important point is that each pedagogical model presents a different view of teaching and learning and incorporates different assumptions. These different perspectives on learning are described in detail in Chapter 5. In the enactment phase, the online learning developer examines his or her assumptions about learning, which are based on individual (or collective, if a team environment) knowledge and experiences, and aligns his or her beliefs with an established pedagogical model.

For example, in the second scenario presented at the beginning of this chapter, A Professor's Online Community for Teachers, Dr. Norton was not satisfied with existing models of online learning. Norton (2003) closely examined her beliefs and assumptions about how learning occurs so that she could design and develop an online learning system for teachers. She found the more traditional models of teaching and learning inadequate for supporting teachers and students involved in online instruction. On the basis of her knowledge of learning and her direct experiences with teachers and their students, Norton articulated her beliefs (in this case, through a formal academic paper, but this could be accomplished more informally) in her exploration phase and mapped them to a situated cognition or **situated learning** pedagogical model. In this model, learning is described as the individual's engagement in social interactions, in cultural perspectives, and with artifacts in the work of a community. Norton integrated her beliefs about learning with this perspective when she described the design of a community of practice learning system for teachers in the following way:

All members of a community of practice (i.e. social studies teachers or elementary teachers or technology-integrating teachers) including novitiates become learners and teachers simultaneously. Each member seeks to contribute to the "work" of the community collaborating with and assisting fellow members. Those with expertise serve as mentors and a support system for novice learners who simultaneously contribute to the community in increasingly sophisticated ways while learning. Solving shared problems is the goal, learning is an embedded activity and natural outcome of participation in the community of practice. Success is judged by increasing facility at developing solutions to shared problems and advances in meeting goals. (p. 4)

Note the absence of any discussion on learning technologies at this point. This formal statement explicitly describes her understanding and assumptions of the learning processes that need to occur in the online learning environment she is designing. This statement will form the basis for the specific instructional strategies she selects and the technological attributes that seem most appropriate for enacting this perspective. This statement could also serve as her theoretical conjecture (discussed in the exploration phase) that provides explicit communication about how she believes teaching and learning occur in a specific context (in this case, teacher learning and professional development). The statement could also serve as a reflective memo in a qualitative research study that documents the personal perspective on learning that she brings to a design or a research effort (Maxwell, 1996). Norton (2003) has mapped her beliefs, her experiences, and what she knows about the teaching and learning context to an applicable pedagogical model and is now in a position to consider the specific instructional characteristics of this model and then select instructional strategies for her online system.

Consider the instructional characteristics of the selected pedagogical models In the enactment phase, the online learning developer needs to closely examine the instructional characteristics of the pedagogical models that align with his or her thinking and experience with learners to determine what might work online. This process facilitates the transference of theoretical ideas to the practice of designing online learning. In Norton's (2003) formal example, situated learning was the pedagogical model or theoretical grounding that she selected. Some of the characteristics that describe this perspective on learning include the following four:

1. Promoting authentic learning through meaningful and purposeful activities that represent real-life practices and contexts
2. Providing opportunities to seek information in a problem context or scenario
3. Promoting collaborative learning and opportunities for learners to internalize, self-monitor, and self-correct with support
4. Promoting transfer to real-life problem solving through authentic experiences

These characteristics provide the backdrop to implementing the specific instructional strategies that may work for her learners online. Norton reviewed similar characteristics by concluding that her "community of practice builds on the fact that knowledge and understanding are socially constructed through talk, activity, and interaction around meaningful problems and tools" (p. 4). The specific instructional strategies that she implemented are described in the next stage of the enactment phase; however, consideration of instructional characteristics of pedagogical models can also be accomplished in other ways.

Clearly, Norton reviewed the literature on the pedagogical model of situated learning and thought deeply about how to meld the characteristics of this model with her personal perspectives to determine what is valuable for teacher learning in her setting. This approach is one way to glean important characteristics of these models to consider for implementation through instructional strategies online.

In another example of the benefit of reviewing the literature for characteristics of these models as a foundation for design, graduate students at the Pennsylvania State University examined the literature for the instructional characteristics of a pedagogical model called *cognitive flexibility hypertext*. This theoretical perspective advocates learner investigation of complex content through hearing, seeing, and creating multiple representations of and perspectives on what is to be learned. After reviewing these characteristics (described further in Chapter 5), the graduate students created a simple Web site that embodies this pedagogical model by allowing investigation of the complex issue of reintroducing the wolf into the southwestern United States. This Web site provides a powerful instructional activity in which students involved in the College of Earth and Mineral Sciences can hear and see multiple perspectives on the issue and articulate their own positions (see http://www.ems.psu.edu/Wolf/AIFF/WolfTop.html). More important, the design of this site is grounded in the characteristics of an established view of teaching and learning.

An informal method of considering instructional characteristics of pedagogical models can be implemented by reviewing online examples, such as the Web site on the reintroduction of the wolf, to see how others have enacted theoretical ideas and approaches. For example, a simple Web search using terms related to another pedagogical model—**cognitive apprenticeship**—revealed several sources of information, including papers describing the instructional characteristics of this model and papers that discuss online examples of implementing this theory. This particular search revealed a paper by Wang and Bonk (2001) describing in detail an example of implementing a cognitive apprenticeship approach in developing a groupware-based learning environment. This paper included screen shots that show the implementation of the instructional characteristics of this pedagogical model or approach in an online instructional context. Reviewing theory-based examples of online learning is an excellent way to generate design ideas or ways to enact particular theories of learning in an online context. Basing your online learning design on existing theoretical approaches significantly improves the credibility and learning potential of your online instruction or training.

More formal approaches for considering instructional characteristics of various pedagogical models might involve examining online and classroom-based learning examples that align with a specific approach and are created through federally funded grant project development. Organizations such as the Department of Education and the National Science Foundation provide descriptions of and access to funded online learning projects or lesson clearinghouses that are available and freely accessible. Searching these resources for specific theory-based examples of online learning and classroom materials can provide excellent examples of a specific enacted theory. For example, a Department of Education–funded initiative called *The Gateway to Educational Materials (GEM)* is a consortium effort to provide educators with quick and easy access to thousands of educational resources found on various federal, state, university, nonprofit, and commercial Internet sites (see http://www.thegateway.org/welcome.html). A search of this site for a pedagogical model called **problem-based learning (PBL)** yielded 24 examples of online and classroom-based activities that are based on this instructional approach. Examination of one resource from this search, called the *NASA SCIence Files,* revealed an interesting example of PBL. This NASA-supported, award-winning site provides multiple examples of the implementation of PBL with online resources, video segments, teacher guides, and Web activities. Although designed to integrate classroom-based and online learning activities that encompass the PBL approach, the site can provide rich models for other developers to examine to consider how they might implement this theoretical approach online.

Select specific instructional strategies that align with the selected pedagogical models   After examining the instructional characteristics of a selected pedagogical model or approach (discussed in detail in Chapter 5), the online developer selects specific instructional strategies to enact by using online learning technologies. *Instructional strategies* are the planned activities, techniques, or processes implemented by the instructor to engage learners and induce learning. Each pedagogical model has instructional characteristics that provide guidance for determining key instructional strategies or activities that align with the model or perspective on learning. In Chapter 6, we provide detailed descriptions of the instructional strategies supported by constructivist models, such as authentic learning, problem solving, exploration, hypothesis generation, role-playing, articulation, reflection, collaboration, multiple perspectives, modeling and **explaining**, **coaching**, scaffolding, and self-directed learning. More important, also in Chapter 6, a strong connection is made between these instructional strategies and how common features of online learning technologies can support the enactment of these strategies.

In the scenario involving Dr. Norton, she closely examined and articulated the instructional characteristics of a situated learning pedagogical model and then needed to translate these ideas to the online context through selected instructional strategies. She and her graduate students subsequently created an online community of practice learning system (COPLS) for teachers that incorporated instructional strategies such as articulation, collaboration, and modeling, among others. The design of this community of practice provided teachers with a representative problem related to integrating technology in the classroom that served as the basis for teacher and expert–mentor communication and interaction. Norton (2003) described her instructional strategies in terms of six major subsystems:

1. **A Community of Practice:** Shared intentional activity with learning occurring through "the interaction of the learner, resources, and mentor" (p. 4).
2. **Learners:** "One member of a community of practice participates with another more skilled or expert [member]" (p. 4).

3. **Instructional Resources:** Resources "created, gathered and organized to be used by the learner and the expert mentor to provide structure and guidance for the interactions of the learner and expert mentor" (p. 5).
4. **Expert Mentor:** "Expert mentors are assigned to learners as models and coaches for appropriate instructional periods from a single representative problem through a set sequence of problems" (p. 5).
5. **Representative Problems:** Problems that "provide a shared learning activity that structures the learner's interactions with the instructional resources and provides a common focus for the interactions of the learner and expert mentor" (p. 5).
6. **Performances of Understanding:** "The visible outcome of the interaction of the learner with the instructional resources, the representative problem and the expert mentor" (p. 5).

These subsystems, or major elements, formally articulate Norton's instructional strategies or activities that align with the development of an online community of practice grounded in situated learning theory. Her description of the instructional strategies operationally defined the instructional characteristics of the situated learning model for her learners and context. Instructional strategies were enacted in this system to promote learners' articulation of their knowledge through the online activities and communication with their mentors. The collaboration between the teacher and the mentor, as an instructional strategy, provided an opportunity to share different viewpoints and ideas focused on a specific problem-solving activity. Modeling was provided by the multiple online instructional resources available to the learner and additional modeling and coaching provided to the teacher by the expert–mentor. These instructional strategies provided learners with theoretically based activities delivered through appropriately selected technological delivery mechanisms.

A similar but less formal approach was taken to identify instructional strategies for an online instructional design course developed for graduate students. The online learning developer, who was also the course instructor, based her decision making primarily on an informal exploration phase in which she reviewed both literature on online learning and her experiences with instructional technology graduate students in the face-to-face version of the course. She mapped the gathered information and her beliefs about how learning occurred in that course to the pedagogical model of PBL. For more information on how this process can be operationalized or enacted, review Table 6.1. The online learning developer then operationally defined these characteristics as specific instructional strategies related to her context of teaching and her students. When developing online instruction or training, other instructors or trainers could apply a similar informal process to mapping established characteristics of pedagogical models to instructional strategies and generate powerful activities based on how people learn. In the next stage of the enactment phase, we discuss how features of technological tools can enable these instructional strategies.

Enact the instructional strategies by using the features of technological delivery systems Translating instructional strategies for the online context, or enacting theories of learning online, is one of the most creative activities related to the

ILDF for Online Learning. Whether developing a custom-designed technological solution or using a course management system to create online learning environments, the developer needs to consider which technology-based features can best support the selected instructional strategies and learning online. In Chapter 5, we provide detailed descriptions of the specific learning technologies associated with various pedagogical models, and in Chapter 6, we provide guidance on promoting instructional strategies aligned with a particular approach by using technological features. Following through on the Dr. Norton scenario, we next examine how she and her team enacted their selected instructional strategies by capitalizing on particular features of online learning technologies.

Dr. Norton formally enacted the instructional strategies related to her community of practice primarily by using Web-based learning technologies. To determine the most appropriate learning technologies, she compared and contrasted other online systems and reviewed online examples of the instructional strategies she planned to use. To promote the interaction between and among the learner, resources, and mentor, Norton (2003) implemented a comprehensive Web site that housed the instructional resources and provided multiple methods of presentation, including Web-based, print-based, video, audio, and performance support materials. To enact the instructional strategy of involving teachers with other, more skilled members of the community, expert–mentors interacted with the teachers, using various online communication tools such as e-mail and asynchronous, synchronous, and videoconferencing tools, among others. The online communication tools promoted the articulation of teachers' knowledge and explanations of their understanding and facilitated clarification of the instructional tasks.

The representative problem posed in the online community of practice was delivered by means of Web pages, video, and/or, e-mail so that the teachers could interact with and seek any additional clarification or guidance from their mentor. The collaboration between the teacher and the expert–mentor provided an opportunity for them to share different viewpoints and ideas focused on a commonly shared problem-solving activity. The available online instructional resources also provided additional modeling and scaffolding of the required tasks. The mentors implemented and provided the teachers with additional modeling and coaching strategies by means of e-mail and asynchronous and synchronous discussion tools. The performances of understanding, or "the visible outcome of the interaction of the learner with the instructional resources, the representative problem and the expert mentor" (Norton, 2003, p. 6), were published online, in many instances through Web-page project development. Although other instructional delivery mechanisms were also included in the community of practice, much of the instructional experience relied on online learning technology features. This formal approach to the enactment phase highlights the use of technologies based on features that support the selected instructional strategies.

Similarly, the professor who developed the online graduate course on instructional design processes informally reviewed her instructional strategies to select the most appropriate learning technology features to support the strategies. Selecting a blended delivery approach, the instructor used WebCT, an existing course management system, to support the small-group design activities, applying instructional design processes in a problem-based approach, and to supplement her face-to-face class sessions. In the WebCT environment, she assembled resources supporting students in their application of instructional design processes and content resources related to the authentic instructional design problem. The instructor created separate discussion forums in which each group of four to five students could discuss, develop, and track its progress on the project. The instructor also facilitated interaction between the students and the client or subject matter expert by providing collaborative access to the discussion forums and e-mail contact information. Students identified, located, and shared resources related to their projects and design processes online with the whole class and within their small groups. The final deliverable product was an online prototype instructional design solution with an accompanying design document that provided a rationale to the client for the design decisions. These final deliverable products were posted in the WebCT class forum for comment by other students, the professor, and the client or subject matter expert. This problem-based learning experience was facilitated through the asynchronous, synchronous, and shared document capabilities of the WebCT course management system.

Technologies provide a vehicle for delivering powerful instruction. However, the features and attributes of available technology require alignment with the selected instructional strategies to provide maximum support for learners. Only after identifying appropriate instructional strategies based on perspectives on learning can the developer then creatively capitalize on specific technological features. The ILDF for Online Learning promotes both the thorough examination of the learning processes and context and the selection of instructional strategies grounded in theories of learning as a foundation for the creative use and implementation of available technological features. Adhering to this process ensures the design, development, and implementation of theoretically based online instruction. The framework also promotes creative problem solving involving the use of learning technologies in new and creative ways to support learning processes rather than for their own sake. Table 4.4 includes guiding questions for you to use so that you can begin to apply these methods to your online learning context and enact instructional strategies with technological features appropriate for your learners.

Summary   The enactment phase allows the online learning developer to align his or her perspectives with established views of learning by guiding him or her to review the instructional characteristics of these models and to select powerful instructional strategies that can be implemented with the available technological features. This process approach places on the developer the responsibility for the important problem solving and decision making related to determining the most appropriate instructional strategies for a specific context and specific learners. In Chapters 5 and 6, we provide detailed guidance for making these decisions by presenting several pedagogical models, instructional characteristics, and instructional strategies from which the developer can select. Technological features are aligned with these strategies in Chapter 6 to further support the developer's decision making. After implementing powerful instructional strategies

Table 4.4 Activities and Prompting Questions for the Enactment Phase

---

Map information gathered in the exploration phase to pedagogical models.
- How do you think learning occurs in your setting?
- What did you learn from the exploration phase about the learners, content, and context and how does it affect your thinking about the design of your online instruction or training?
- Which pedagogical models are most closely aligned with your beliefs and understanding of learning processes?

Consider the instructional characteristics of the selected pedagogical models.
- Can you identify the instructional characteristics of the models you selected?
- Can you describe the necessary instructional characteristics of these models through other online or classroom-based examples?
- What instructional characteristics seem most appropriate for and applicable to your learners and setting?

Select specific instructional strategies that align with the selected pedagogical models.
- How can you transform or operationalize the instructional characteristics of your selected pedagogical models into powerful instructional strategies specific for your learners and context?
- Are the instructional strategies you selected congruent or aligned with the characteristics and perspectives of the pedagogical approach you want to implement?

Enact the instructional strategies by using the features of technological delivery systems.
- What technological system are you using or designing? Can you determine the available features and attributes of the system? If not, document which features and attributes you would like in the potential technological delivery system.
- Which technological features might best support the instructional strategies you selected?
- Are you limited in the technological features available to you for implementing your instructional strategies? If so, can you creatively use the features you do have to deliver your instructional strategies?
- Can you identify any examples of these instructional strategies in other online learning development?
- How can you capitalize on the affordances and features of the technological delivery system to create powerful, engaging instructional experiences for your learners?

---

through technological features, the online learning developer must find ways to evaluate the results of his or her efforts. The evaluation phase of the ILDF for Online Learning is discussed in the next subsection.

The Evaluation Phase

The evaluation phase of the ILDF for Online Learning presents specific decision-making challenges to online learning developers so that they can clearly determine what they want or need to evaluate in the online context. The determination of which processes to select and how to best incorporate evaluation is often a function of the demands of the sociocultural context. A teacher may use drastically different methods than those used by a corporate trainer, who may use different methods than those used by a university professor, when they are selecting evaluation processes based on the context of their work. Clearly, many formal and informal ways are available to evaluate instruction or training, and the online setting provides some unique features that can be used for specific evaluation purposes. However, the most important determination for the developer to make in the evaluation phase is an assessment of the evaluation requirements of the sociocultural context and then an informed selection of evaluation measures that reflect these needs or goals. Other processes such as formative evaluation and revision of instructional or training materials should be incorporated in any iterative online learning development.

The evaluation phase yields rich information on the value and effectiveness of the efforts made in the exploration and enactment phases. Only through evaluation of our attempts at online learning design can we improve our processes and practices. Specific activities in the evaluation phase include the following:

- Clearly determine the purpose, desired results, and methods of evaluation of online learning.
- Formatively evaluate the design and development prior to launching the online course.
- Revise the online materials according to the results of the formative evaluation.
- Implement the online learning experience and evaluate the results according to the identified goals.

Clearly determine the purpose, desired results, and methods of evaluation of online learning   Determining the purpose, desired results, and methods of an evaluation effort in online learning requires careful, systematic thought and analysis. Whether the online learning developer is a teacher, a corporate trainer, or a university professor, determining which elements to evaluate in online learning is a challenging task. A guiding framework can help the developer to systematically determine the overall purpose, desired results, and appropriate methods for evaluation of online learning. The ILDF for Online Learning has integrated a systematic approach originally presented by Barksdale and Lund (2001) in their book *Rapid Evaluation*. Their approach, along with formative evaluation and revision processes, was adapted (and is further detailed in Chapter 7) to facilitate evaluation of online learning. Distinguishing between formal and informal methods of evaluation is more difficult in that the logical process used in both cases should be the same (as reflected in Table 4.5). Clark and Mayer (2003) classified the types of research or evaluation that primarily have conclusions based on feedback from and observation of students as *informal* and other evaluation efforts that involve comparing randomly assigned participants to groups and comparisons of a specific outcome measure as *controlled,* or perhaps more *formal*, studies. In the ILDF for Online Learning, differences in formal and informal evaluation approaches are determined by the developers' goals and purposes and the social and cultural context. Evaluation efforts can reflect formal research processes involving controlled studies or in-depth qualitative investigations (e.g., demonstrated by the studies outlined in Chapter 3) or the more informal evaluation efforts that do not involve control groups and randomization of subjects

Table 4.5   Evaluation

Informal Methods	Formal Methods
Clearly determine the purpose, desired results, and methods of evaluation of online learning.	**Clearly determine the purpose, desired results, and methods of evaluation of online learning.**
• Determine the need for evaluation.	• Determine the need for evaluation.
• Determine the purpose of evaluation.	• Determine the purpose of evaluation.
• Write an evaluation strategy statement.	• Write an evaluation strategy statement.
• Determine the objectives of the evaluation strategy.	• Determine the objectives of the evaluation strategy.
• Consider the social and cultural factors related to the evaluation.	• Consider the social and cultural factors related to the evaluation.
• Determine the desired results of the evaluation strategy.	• Determine the desired results of the evaluation strategy.
• Conduct multilevel, or balanced evaluation using Kirkpatrick's levels of evaluation.	• Conduct multilevel, or balanced, evaluation using Kirkpatrick's levels of evaluation.
• Determine the levels of formality or informality of the evaluation methods.	• Determine the levels of formality or informality of the evaluation methods.
• Select evaluation methods congruent with the learning activities.	• Select evaluation methods congruent with the learning activities.
• Determine applicable measurement approaches.	• Determine applicable measurement approaches.
Formatively evaluate the design and development prior to launching the online course.	**Formatively evaluate the design and development prior to launching the online course.**
• Expert review	• Expert review
• One-to-one evaluation	• One-to-one evaluation
• Small-group evaluation	• Small-group evaluation
• Field-test evaluation	• Field-test evaluation
• Usability testing	• Usability testing
Revise the online materials according to the results of the formative evaluation.	**Revise the online materials according to the results of the formative evaluation.**
• Review and prioritize the results from formative evaluation testing.	• Review and prioritize the results from formative evaluation testing.
• Target the problem areas in design.	• Target the problem areas in design.
• Generate design solutions to the targeted problem areas.	• Generate design solutions to the targeted problem areas.
• Implement redesign or revisions.	• Implement redesign or revisions.
Implement the online learning experience and evaluate the results according to the identified goals.	**Implement the online learning experience and evaluate the results according to the identified goals.**
• Consider formative and summative evaluation methods related to the specific goals.	• Consider formative and summative evaluation methods related to the specific goals.
• Determine a systematic evaluation approach.	• Determine a systematic evaluation approach.
• Implement the online learning experience.	• Implement the online learning experience.
• Evaluate the results in a manner aligned with the evaluation goals.	• Evaluate the results in a manner aligned with the evaluation goals.
• Report the results to the field.	• Report the results to the field.

and focus more on feedback from learners or instructors in real-world online settings (highlighted in Chapter 7).

Essentially, the evaluation phase begins with the online learning developer's outlining the overall needs for and purposes of the evaluation and writing an evaluation strategy statement. The evaluation strategy statement serves as an anchor for determining the specific objectives or tasks that need to be accomplished to conduct the evaluation. The ILDF for Online Learning also explicitly requires the developer to consider the sociocultural context when he or she is determining evaluation methods because many online learning situations require different types of evaluation, depending on the developer's needs and context. Determining the desired results of the evaluation strategy, or what the developer hopes to learn or gain from the evaluation, is important to consider and helps the developer to identify specific methods for eliciting this information. Finally, determining the appropriate levels of evaluation (according to Kirkpatrick, 1998) assists the developer in selecting specific methods. Online learning developers also need to ensure that the evaluation methods selected are congruent with the online learning activities so that the evaluation yields useful and meaningful results. The evaluation phase of the ILDF for Online Learning promotes the appropriate selection of measurement approaches (e.g., tests, surveys, etc.) by first requiring the developer to determine the needs, purposes, strategy, and methods.

To illustrate this process, we examine two case studies, one involving a more formal evaluation approach and the other a less formal approach. These published cases illustrate only two ways to conduct evaluations of the many factors that could be examined in online learning. In Chapter 7, we present the process of the evaluation phase in more detail. First, to provide an overview of the evaluation phase, we further describe The Blended Learning Objects Training Approach scenario presented at the beginning of this chapter. Second, we present a case study based on a less formal evaluation of adult learners in an online graduate program. These cases describe the implementation of the stages of the evaluation phase of the ILDF for Online Learning.

The Thomson Corporation, a leading global provider of integrated information solutions to business and professional customers (described in the third scenario at the beginning of this chapter), embarked on a formal evaluation effort related to online learning (NETg, 2003). As a parent company to many e-learning initiatives and companies in multiple fields, the Thomson Corporation adopted a "blended learning" approach to delivering online instruction and training that incorporates a combination of types of media and support mechanisms. The blended learning approach incorporates training elements such as instructor-based, self-directed classroom scenarios; computer software and training resources; learning object modules; online mentoring; frequently asked questions (FAQs); and relevant Web sites. Given that little knowledge and evidence of the value of blended learning approaches exist, the company managers wanted to determine whether and which blended learning approaches involving different combinations of these learning support mechanisms were effective. The stated evaluation need of this company communicated the desire to determine whether a particular approach to online learning (in this case, blended learning as defined by their representation of it) was warranted. Barksdale and Lund (2001) advocate asking questions related to whether a particular online (or training) approach is warranted to determine the need for online evaluation. (See Chapter 7 for additional prompting questions to consider when you are determining the need for online learning evaluation.)

In a less formal evaluation of adult learners in a higher education online cohort program, Conrad (2002) defined the need for her study to be determining how the first class in an online course should be structured. The need for this evaluation effort was based on documented confusion by online students as to when and how an online course needs to be introduced and a lack of information related to the instructors' and students' roles at the beginning of such a course. The need for evaluation expressed by Conrad attempts to answer the question What additional elements may need to be included to enhance the online experience? Although she conducted this evaluation during the course, Conrad analyzed the data for the purposes of applying the findings to another course. Conrad surmised that the results might also be considered by other online learning developers in their designs.

In both the corporate and the higher education examples, the developers provided more detail when stating the purpose of their evaluation efforts. Barksdale and Lund (2001) advocated writing an evaluation strategy statement to define the purpose of the evaluation. The researchers who conducted the Thomson study (NETg, 2003) stated the following evaluation strategy: to determine "whether or not these approaches truly deliver measurable impact in on-the-job business productivity" (p. 2). In contrast, Conrad's (2002) purpose was stated less formally: "to increase our understanding of learner's perceptions about how the first "class" in an online course *should* be and to further understand how learners' experiences in the first class contribute to their sense of well-being" (p. 205). Both examples indicate efforts to find ways to conduct these evaluations by determining or developing tools and processes to measure on-the-job performance and examine learners' experiences online.

The social and cultural contexts of these two evaluation efforts differed dramatically and influenced the type of evaluation methods that could be used. In the Thomson study report (NETg, 2003), the researchers described a clear focus on integrating real-world tasks, the use of workplace software tools, and determination of business results as an outcome of the evaluation. These issues align with the organizational objectives, values, and culture typical of the corporate context. In contrast, the Conrad (2002) evaluation effort focused on student-centered experiences, self-reported feelings and engagement, and a focus on the outcome of improving students' experiences in online courses. These issues seem to reflect the general goals of higher education. In each context, the social and cultural factors shaped the evaluation efforts.

Determining who will be affected and the desired outcome or results focuses the evaluation effort. The Thomson study (NETg, 2003) involved 200 employees at all organizational levels across a wide range of industries with the intended result of creating a positive impact on job performance through the use of the blended training system. It was important to the individuals who conducted this study that the results reflect a broad range of contexts that might benefit from the blended training and that the evaluation results indicate whether job performance increased. For the Conrad (2002) study, the sample size was small (only 28 students in a new online graduate program), and the study was focused on providing online instructors with guidance about how and when to present themselves and the content of the course to learners. This evaluation was not conducted with the purpose of generalizing the results to other situations by using statistical methods. However, the researcher did have the goal of presenting insights and conclusions that might be applicable and considered by developers of other online programs and by instructors.

The next part of determining the purpose, desired results, and methods of evaluation involves outlining the specific levels of evaluation, or "balancing" the evaluation, to ensure consideration of the customer's or learner's view, the organization's view, and evidence of learning and/or performance. Identifying the multiple levels of evaluation has been championed by Kirkpatrick (1998) and provides a way for online learning developers to think about evaluating the online context in multiple ways to yield rich information and results. Kirkpatrick's levels of evaluation included (a) learners' reactions to instruction or training (Level 1); (b) the extent to which learners change attitudes, gain knowledge, or increase skill (Level 2); (c) how learners change their behavior as a result of instruction or training (Level 3); and (d) results that have occurred at the organizational level as a result of the instruction or training. Many informal evaluation efforts in online learning never exceed Level 1. Evaluations that yield the most useful results seem to integrate a multilevel, multimethod approach in attempting to evaluate the impact of online learning. For example, the Thomson study (NETg, 2003) was structured to evaluate the impact of the blended learning strategy on multiple levels, including the participants' reaction to the learning system (Level 1), their learning of the instructional content (Level 2), and the accuracy of their performance (Level 3). The multiple levels examined enriched the results from the study to provide several conclusions and directions for the field and the company.

In contrast to the Thomson (NETg, 2003) investigation, the Conrad (2002) study relied only on evaluating student experiences and expectations (Level 1). Although this evaluation was less comprehensive and perhaps less formal, it still revealed interesting insights and considerations for the design of online learning.

Determining the level of formality or informality required of the evaluation effort is important to consider so that appropriate methods for the context can be selected. A rigorous and comprehensive evaluation of the value of the blended learning approach was warranted for the Thomson Corporation to best market its instructional approach. One goal of the evaluation effort by Conrad was that the findings might inform similar situations, but the evaluation seemed to be conducted primarily to inform the efforts of that particular online program. Evaluation efforts take on different meanings in different contexts. For example, in the school-based setting, teachers' evaluation efforts can be focused on improving their practice through action research and may involve less formal research designs yet still incorporate systematic evaluation processes (Arhar, Holly, & Kasten, 2001). Considering the contextual requirements to determine the formality or informality of the methods provides the online learning developer with guidance for selecting appropriate measurement approaches.

Aligning the evaluation method or measurement approach with the learning activities of the online instruction or training ensures that the developer is obtaining meaningful results from the evaluation and prompts the consideration of creative online data-gathering methods. For example, in the Thomson case, the evaluators decided to conduct a formal study that included assigning participants, on the basis of their characteristics, to particular forms of blended training in Microsoft Excel. The instructional experiences of the five groups varied. The first group received training with multiple elements and supports, including self-directed classroom scenario exercises, a classroom instructor, text and other resources providing introductory concepts and techniques, the Microsoft Excel application, NETg Microsoft Excel Learning Objects, online mentors, FAQs, and relevant Web sites. The second group received the same elements except for the classroom instruction, and the third group did not have access to the instructor or text resources. The fourth group used primarily an e-learning approach, with only the NETg learning objects reflecting the same objectives and learning activities. The fifth group served as a control and did not receive any training. The instructional elements or strategies that the participants interacted with were specifically structured to yield any differences among groups. As a common approach to a formal, quantitative evaluation effort, the learning activities closely aligned with the evaluation methods. The methods selected to evaluate the differences among these groups incorporated the goals of the evaluation and a multilevel, multimethod approach. The specific evaluation methods used in the Thomson study included the following:

- Proficiency ratings and satisfaction with Microsoft Excel (Level 1—reaction)
- Postassessment (Level 2—learning)
- Performing real-world Excel tasks (Level 3—behavior)

Other data were collected prior to the study, involving supervisor proficiency ratings, demographic questionnaires, self-ratings of Excel proficiency, and a learner profile inventory. Qualitative data were also collected through observations during the training sessions, discussion, and written comments. Looking closely at the selection of methods, you can see how the information from this evaluation will show the differences among groups with regard to their reactions to the learning materials, how well they learned, and how well they performed the task. The selection of methods informed how they would measure the results. The report was unclear as to whether the data were collected online or in the training classroom. However, you can easily see how some of this information might be collected through an online learning management system with database and survey capabilities. The measurement approaches were aligned with the preceding methods and included the following:

- Demographic questionnaires
- A learner profile inventory
- Tracking of accuracy related to improvement of performance, including time on task
- Number of times mentors were accessed
- Number of questions asked
- Satisfaction surveys
- Supervisor proficiency ratings
- Self-ratings of Excel proficiency
- Posttest assessment

The Thomson report (NETg, 2003) represents a highly formal approach to evaluation but provides an excellent example of a multimethod, multilevel evaluation that clearly determined the purpose, desired results, and appropriate methods for this particular context. The evaluation yielded some interesting results in that the three blended learning groups (first, second, and third groups described previously) that used the self-directed classroom scenario exercises significantly outperformed the e-learning and control groups (fourth and fifth groups described previously). The blended learning groups required significantly less time to complete the real-world tasks than did the e-learning group. The e-learning group performed significantly better on the real-world task than did the control group. No differences were found among the groups that received the blended approach with regard to performance and time on task. Although many of the original data are not reported, the results seem to indicate that some value can be found in using a blended learning approach when a teacher is integrating self-directed classroom scenario exercises and other online and classroom-based activities.

The Thomson Corporation evaluation involved more than 200 participants, many companies, and a significant number of personnel. Not all evaluation efforts need to be this complex. However, all evaluation efforts should progress through a similar systematic process of determining the purpose, results, and methods. Conrad (2002) accomplished this process in a less formal manner. To evaluate students' experiences in and expectations of (Level 1) their first course, Conrad relied primarily on these three methods:

1. Surveys asking students to describe some of their experiences from their first online class
2. Open-ended questions to examine their perception of instructors' roles in establishing procedure and mood for the learning experience
3. Provide adjectives to describe their feelings during the first class. (p. 206)

The evaluative report did not clarify whether these data were collected online and at what point they were collected. We assumed that, given the nature of the online graduate program, data may have been collected online at the conclusion of the first course for some of the participants. These methods seem congruent with the learning activities related to a retrospective analysis of the students' feelings about their participation in the online course. The measurement approaches used also seemed to align with the preceding three methods and to reflect a more qualitative-like analysis in finding meaning or patterns in the responses. The terms used to describe the students' feelings prior to the course were also reported, with the number of times particular adjectives appeared. This evaluation yielded some interesting results related to adult learners in an online graduate program in that it showed that the learners in this study wanted access to the online course materials well in advance of the course start date so that they could preview the course and gather information and study the requirements. The participants in this study were not concerned as much about social interaction prior to the start of the course but did want some evidence of the instructor's presence, such as a welcome message when they chose to enter the course site.

The participants' perception was that their engagement with the course began when they first accessed the course materials rather than when they began interacting with others.

These insights may provide guidance for online learning developers and reflect a systematic evaluation effort related to a specific course experience. Although the results of this evaluation are not as broad ranging or generalizable as those of the Thomson study, Conrad's efforts to systematically evaluate a specific online learning issue contributes to developers' learning about what might work in this new instructional medium. All systematic evaluation efforts in online learning should be valued and encouraged so that developers can use the rich information gained to improve on their practice and create effective and engaging online learning experiences. Many additional examples of formal evaluation approaches were described in Chapter 3, and many other examples of more informal evaluation approaches are described in Chapter 7.

Given the details of the Thomson Corporation's and Conrad's evaluation efforts, compare and contrast the methods they used in each stage and think about why they selected these methods. Compare these researchers' needs, purposes, evaluation strategy statements, and social and cultural factors. How might Conrad have implemented a more formal evaluation effort, and how could the Thomson Corporation have implemented a less formal study?

Formatively evaluate the design and development prior to launching the online course   Evaluation efforts such as those described previously in this chapter are typically perceived as *summative,* or occurring when all the learning materials have been produced and finalized. Another type of evaluation involves determining the strengths and weaknesses of learning materials while they are being developed. This type is termed *formative evaluation* and may involve many methods and approaches. All online learning development efforts should include some type of formative evaluation. In an iterative design and development effort, the formative evaluation process determines the specific strengths and weaknesses of a design so that any problems can be corrected. This process of iterative design, evaluation, and revision gives credibility to the ILDF for Online learning and other systematic instructional design approaches. In its absence, online learning developers may never know whether what they have designed is appropriate for their learners.

Formative evaluation processes typically include a progression from testing the online learning materials in smaller, contrived settings with just one learner, to small groups with more realistic settings, then, finally, to larger groups reflecting the context in which the instruction or training will be delivered. Formative evaluation methods may also include reviews of the online materials by experts who critique the design. These formative evaluation methods can take place at multiple points in the design and development cycle. In the ILDF for Online Learning, formative evaluation can begin as early as when the need and purpose of the project are determined in the exploration phase. Involving experts at this point in the framework to review the stated purpose of the project and determine whether it is aligned with the online learning developer's assessment of the context, learners, and learning process can provide additional credibility to the design direction. In the enactment phase, many types of formative evaluation can be implemented, including review of early design ideas with one or more learners and stakeholders. After the design ideas are more fully developed or enacted, small-group evaluations can take place in which the developer tries out the learning environment with several learners to collect data across several authentic perspectives. Finally, in the evaluation phase, the online materials may be mature enough to be tested in realistic-like conditions with a large group characteristic of the targeted learners.

Another type of evaluation related to formative evaluation is usability testing. Usability testing attempts to capitalize on the user's perspective to inform the effective design of online learning or software environments. Focused on improving the operation and performance of online software, usability testing involves engaging users in actual tasks with the software to determine any problems with the interface design, the functionality, or the accomplishment of tasks. Many specific methodologies (or ways to carry out evaluations) are associated with usability testing, including focus groups, surveys, walk-throughs, tests, and expert reviews. These methods are structured to collect data that can then be analyzed to improve the usability of the online system. With multiple possible methods, the online learning developer can select what is most appropriate for his or her needs and context. The important point is to implement some type of formative evaluation to provide useful information to improve online learning designs. Additional methods and examples of formative evaluation are described in Chapter 7.

Revise the online materials according to the results of the formative evaluation After the online learning design undergoes formative evaluation, the results of the evaluation dictate the revisions or changes that need to be made. The results of a formative evaluation or a usability test are usually informative and reveal issues that the online learning developer may have overlooked or taken for granted. For example, while evaluating an online learning community for teachers and educators, one design team found that the learners or users could not progress past the log-in page because they could not determine whether and when they had logged in. As a result of this finding, the entrance page of the Web site was redesigned to more clearly identify the log-in requirement and to provide an automatic acknowledgment to the user through a dialogue box after log-in. The designers' familiarity with the Web site resulted in their overlooking this simple but important design element. The problem was revealed by early formative evaluation testing and corrected through a revised design. Prioritizing the most critical elements for revision is a function of analyzing the results of formative evaluation for targeted areas of revision and redesign. Informally, the online learning developer can simply try out materials with one or more learners to gain insights into how he or she might revise the materials to make them more effective. These evaluation processes need not be complex or complicated. However, the more effort put into formatively evaluating online learning materials, the better the resulting design.

Implement the online learning experience and evaluate the results according to the identified goals The Thomson evaluation study (NETg, 2003) demonstrates the implementation of a comprehensive research effort involving quantitative and qualitative analysis. Designing and implementing this type of evaluation is demanding and time consuming. However, the results yield rich insights for practitioners in the field of online learning and in this case provided evidence for the use of a blended learning approach and scenario-based examples and facilitated an increased level of job perform-ance. The results aligned with the corporation's original goals of determining whether a blended learning approach provided a measurable impact on the job. The Conrad (2002) evaluation, although less formal and involving only 28 students in one online course, fulfilled the stated evaluation purpose to better understand learners' experiences and provide insight into learners' perceptions of which elements are needed to ensure a successful first online course. Both sets of online learning developers clearly determined their evaluation methods, yet implemented them in different ways according to their goals. The evaluation phase of the ILDF for Online Learning is structured to provide guidance for online learning developers to implement evaluations that meet their spe-cific needs, purposes, and goals.

Summary   The purposes and goals of evaluation for online learning developers may vary across contexts, which may result in different methods and approaches. However, all forms of evaluation can provide useful information. The ILDF for Online Learning reinforces a systematic process that integrates multiple perspectives to inform the design and the enactment of theoretically based instructional strategies to produce the most effective online instruction or training. The online learning developer uses his or her best decision-making and problem-solving strategies to consider all the complex fac-tors involved in the instructional or training setting. The process of evaluation (either formative or summative) provides the developer with increased knowledge about the effectiveness of his or her design. Through evaluation, the developer can assess whether the creative act of design has satisfied learners, induced learning, promoted behavioral change, or made a difference in the organization. Given the multiple ways available to evaluate an online learning environment, the developer should select methods appro-priate for his or her goals and assessment of the instructional and development context. Although the ways to implement these methods vary considerably, the overall systematic process is similar. Table 4.6 presents activities and prompting questions for you to use to begin to apply the evaluation phase in your online learning context.

The power of online learning technologies also affords interesting forms of data col-lection in evaluation efforts, including the following:

- Preservation of asynchronous text-based online discussions
- Capture of synchronous text discussions
- Computer logs of learner actions
- Statistics on learner use of online tools and elements
- Online surveys and questionnaires
- Reflective online journaling or logs preserving the learners' reflections
- Online observations of course activities
- Online focus group interaction
- Online tests

Table 4.6   Activities and Prompting Questions for the Evaluation Phase

---

Clearly determine the purpose, desired results, and methods of evaluation of online learning.
- What is your need, purpose, and evaluation strategy?
- What are the specific tasks and objectives related to your evaluation strategy that need to be accomplished for you to implement your evaluation?
- How do the social and cultural factors specific to your context affect the type of evaluation you need to conduct?
- What results do you expect from this evaluation? What do you hope to find out or support?
- How can you implement multiple levels in your evaluation strategy?
- How formal or informal do the methods that you will use need to be? Do you need to implement a formal quantitative study, or can you informally evaluate what is happening in your online learning context?
- Do your selected evaluation methods map to the learning activities or strategies embedded in your online learning environment?
- Which measurement approaches or tools seem most applicable? Can you implement any of them in the online context?

Formatively evaluate the design and development prior to launching the online course.
- How will you formatively evaluate your online learning design? Which methods might you use?
- When will you implement formative evaluation methods? In which phase of the Integrative Learning Design Framework (ILDF) for Online Learning does it seem most appropriate for you to gather information for revision of the materials?

Revise the online materials according to the results of the formative evaluation.
- How will you prioritize the results from your formative evaluation?
- Which areas of your design seem to be the most crucial to revise?
- Do you need to totally redesign some parts of your online learning design?

Implement the online learning experience and evaluate the results according to the identified goals.
- With many available methods of formative and summative evaluation, which do you think are most applicable to your online learning context, goals, and purpose?
- What is your systematic evaluation plan approach?
- How will you evaluate your results?
- How will share your results?

- Learner-produced products and assignments posted online
- Online portfolios
- Online interviews

   These online data collection capabilities should be aligned with a clear evaluation purpose, desired results, and determined methods to produce the most valuable results. Online capabilities for data collection can be used for both formative and **summative evaluation** efforts and in formal as well as informal evaluation efforts. Many of these data collection procedures are used in the evaluation efforts described in Chapter 7 to illustrate how online learning experiences were implemented and then evaluated according to the developer's specific goals. With the inherent data collection capabilities of the online learning context and an informed understanding of a flexible and systematic process of design and development that incorporates both formal and informal methods, we hope that more online learning developers will embrace evaluation to provide additional information to the field. With more systematic exploration, enactment, and evaluation of online learning designs, the field will grow and developers will learn to provide improved learning experiences for all learners.

CHAPTER SUMMARY

In this chapter, we presented an overview of the phases of the Integrative Learning Design Framework (ILDF) for Online Learning. First, the nature and current state of online learning design and development was presented, then the ILDF for Online Learning was described as an alternative systematic process for designing and developing online instruction or training. The role of the online learning developer and his or her knowledge, experience, and central position in developing effective online instruction by using this systematic approach were discussed. The intersection of the three phases of the ILDF with the Three-Component Online Learning Model was highlighted to encompass the comprehensive approach of the ILDF for Online Learning to develop instruction and training grounded in theories of learning. The importance of the social and cultural context was discussed in relation to the framework as an important consideration typically ignored in other instructional design and development models. The consideration of the social and cultural context in online learning design prompts the flexible use of the processes and methods used by the developer and was presented next. Finally, the phases of exploration, enactment, and evaluation were described, along with the specific stages and formal and informal methods appropriate for each phase. Examples illustrating each phase and stage were provided, and the chapter concluded with the call for more systematic development of online learning to improve the field of practice and research.

LEARNING ACTIVITIES

1. For each phase of the ILDF for Online Learning, map the elements of Tables 4.1, 4.3, and 4.5 to a selected scenario (Anya, Priscilla, or the training corporation). You might want to create a new table that maps the scenarios across three columns and the stages of the ILDF for Online Learning across the rows. What activities and methods do you already have information about that were reported in the chapter? After you determine the available information, imagine how the rest of the phases, activities, and methods might be implemented in one of these online learning situations and present it to your colleagues.
2. In the preceding activity, did you use formal or informal methods when applying them to one of the scenarios? State your rationale for the methods you selected for each phase for the three scenarios.

3. Begin documenting your own online learning design and development effort using the activities and prompting questions for each phase of the ILD Framework for Online Learning (found in Tables 4.2, 4.4, and 4.6). Plan to document and share your insights and findings through discussions, reflections, or a published article.
4. Compare the ILDF for Online Learning with other instructional design and development models. What are the differences and similarities? Share with your colleagues what you think makes an approach to online learning development systematic.

RESOURCES

Explore additional resources at the companion Web site (http://www.prenhall.com/dabbagh) to learn more about the ILDF for Online Learning.

REFERENCES

Arhar, J. M., Holly, M. L., & Kasten, W. C. (2001). *Action research for teachers: Traveling the yellow brick road*. Upper Saddle River, NJ: Merrill/Prentice Hall.

Bannan-Ritland, B. (2001). Teaching instructional design: An action learning approach. *Performance Improvement Quarterly, 14*(2), 37–52.

Bannan-Ritland, B. (2003). The role of design in research: The integrative learning design framework. *Educational Researcher, 32*(1), 21–24.

Bannan-Ritland, B., Egerton, E., Page, J., & Behrmann, M. (2000). Literacy explorer: A support tool for novice reading facilitators. *Performance Improvement Journal, 39*(6), 47–54.

Barksdale, S., & Lund, T. (2001). *Rapid evaluation*. Alexandria, VA: American Society for Training and Development.

Biggs, J. (1999). *Teaching for quality learning at university: What the student does*. Bristol, PA: Open University Press.

Brookfield, S. D. (1995). *Becoming a critically reflective teacher*. San Francisco: Jossey-Bass.

Cennamo, K., Abell, S., & Chung, M. (1996). A "layers of negotiation" model for designing constructivist learning materials. *Educational Technology, 36*(4), 39–48.

Clark, R. C., & Mayer, R. E. (2003). *E-learning and the science of instruction*. San Francisco: Jossey-Bass/Pfeiffer.

Collis, B. (1997). Pedagogical reengineering: A pedagogical approach to course enrichment and redesign with the World Wide Web. *Educational Technology Review, 8*, 11–15.

Confrey, J., & Lachance, A. (2000). Transformative teaching experiments through conjecture-driven research design. In A. Kelly & R. A. Lesh (Eds.), *Handbook of research design in mathematics and science education* (pp. 231–265). Mahwah, NJ: Erlbaum.

Conrad, D. L. (2002). Engagement, excitement, anxiety and fear: Learners' experiences of starting an online course. *The American Journal of Distance Education, 16*(4), 205–226.

Constantine, L. L., & Lockwood, L. A. D. (1999). *Software for use: A practical guide to the models and methods of usage-centered design.* Reading, MA: Addison-Wesley.

Cooper, A. (1999). *The inmates are running the asylum.* Indianapolis, IN: Sams.

Dabbagh, N., Jonassen, D. H., Yueh, H.-P., & Samouilova, M. (2000). Assessing a problem-based learning approach in an introductory instructional design course: A case study. *Performance Improvement Quarterly, 13*(3), 60–83.

E-defining education: How virtual schools and online instruction are transforming teaching and learning. (2002). *Education Week, 21*(35).

The eLearning Guild. (2003, January). *The source of e-learning poll.* Retrieved February 2004 from *http://www.elearningguild.com/pbuild/linkbuilder.cfm?selection=fol.28*

Hannafin, M., Hannafin, K. M., Land, S., & Oliver, K. (1997). Grounded practice and the design of constructivist learning environments. *Educational Technology Research & Development, 45*(3), 101–117.

Jeffs, T., Behrmann, M., & Bannan-Ritland, B. (2004). Assistive technology and literacy difficulties: What parents and children have to say. *Journal of Special Education Technology, 19.*

Jonassen, D. H. (2000). Toward a design theory of problem solving. *Educational Technology Research & Development, 48*(4), 63–85.

Kapp, K. M. (2003). *Winning e-learning proposals.* Boca Raton, FL: J. Ross

Kelly, A. E. (2003). Research as design. *Educational Researcher, 32*(1), 3–4.

Kirkpatrick, D. L. (1998). *Evaluating training programs: The four levels* (2nd ed.). San Francisco: Berrett-Koehler.

Kuniavsky, M. (2003). *Observing the user experience: A practitioner's guide to user research.* San Francisco: Morgan Kauffman.

Marra, R. M., & Jonassen, D. H. (2001). Limitations of online courses supporting constructive learning. *The Quarterly Review of Distance Education, 2*(4), 303–317.

Maxwell, J. (1996). *Qualitative research design: An interactive approach* (Vol. 41, Applied Social Research Method Series). Thousand Oaks, CA: Sage.

Moallem, M. (1998). An expert teacher's thinking and teaching and instructional design models and principles: An ethnographic study. *Educational Technology Research & Development, 46*(2), 37–64.

Nelson, H. G. (1994). The necessity of being "un-disciplined" and "out of control": Design action and systems thinking. *Performance Improvement Quarterly, 7*(3), 22–29.

NETg. (2003). *Thomson Job Impact Study: Final results: The next generation of corporate learning: Achieving the right blend.* Retrieved from *http://www.netg.com/Upload/uk_Thomson JobImpactStydy.pdf*

Norton, P. (2003). COPLS: An alternative to traditional online course management tools. In C. Crawford, N. Davis, J. Price, R. Weber, & D. Willis (Eds.), *Technology and teacher education annual, 2003.* Charlottesville, VA: Association for the Advancement of Computing in Education (AACE).

Peled, A., & Rashty, D. (1999). Logging for success: Advancing the use of the WWW logs to improve computer mediated distance learning. *Journal of Educational Computing Research, 21*(4), 413–431.

Rossett, A. (1999). *First things fast: A handbook for performance analysis.* San Francisco: Jossey-Bass.

Schwier, R. A. (2001). Catalysts, emphases and elements of virtual learning communities: Implications for research and practice. *Quarterly Review of Distance Education, 2*(1), 5–18.

Tessmer, M., & Wedman, J. (1992, April). *The practice of instructional design: A survey of what designers do, don't do, and why they don't do it.* Paper presented at the annual meeting of the American Educational Research Association, San Francisco. (ERIC Document Reproduction Service No. ED404712)

van Driel, J. H., Beijaard, D., & Verloop, N. (2001). Professional development and reform in science education: The role of teachers' practical knowledge. *Journal of Research in Science Teaching, 38*(2), 137–158.

Wang, F.-K., & Bonk, C. J. (2001). A design framework for electronic cognitive apprenticeship. *Journal of Asynchronous Learning Networks, 5*(2), 131–151. Retrieved from *http://www. sloan-c.org/publications/jaln/v5n2/pdf/v5n2_wang.pdf*

Weimer, M. (2002). *Learner-centered teaching: Five key changes to practice.* San Francisco: Jossey-Bass.

Zemke, R., & Rossett, A. (2002). A hard look at ISD. *Training, 39*(2), 26–34.

CONSTRUCTIVIST-BASED PEDAGOGICAL MODELS: PRINCIPLES, CHARACTERISTICS, AND ONLINE APPLICATION

5

After completing this chapter, you should understand the following:

- The relationship among knowledge acquisition models, pedagogical models, and learning theory

- The implications of knowledge acquisition models for epistemological beliefs, learning theory, and instruction

- The various pedagogical models that are grounded in situated cognition and constructivism and their instructional characteristics

- The instructional and technological implications of classifying constructivist-based pedagogical models into exploratory, dialogic, and integrational learning environments

- The application of constructivist-based pedagogical models in online learning

CONSIDER THE FOLLOWING THREE SCENARIOS:

Paradise Found, by Sue Sarber: During the first half of the 20th century, U.S. armed forces used Kahoolawe, an island in the Hawaiian chain, as a target for gunnery and bombing practice. After World War II, it was returned to the stewardship of the state of Hawaii. As a middle school teacher, you think this scenario would provide an excellent opportunity for your students to understand the interdependencies of ecology and human activity. By assuming the responsibility the government had, "to restore the island of Kahoolawe for use by the Hawaiian people," students will enhance their skills in several domains, including science, community planning, team building, and problem management. Extensive data on the Web and in various media are available for students to use; however, there is no one correct or ideal solution. You decide to implement this scenario in your classroom as follows.

Students will be grouped into multidisciplinary teams. Each team member will have a different role and responsibility and may collaborate with members of other teams charged with a similar role. Team members will research, problem solve, collaborate, and develop a comprehensive island restoration plan. Each team will present its conclusions and justify its findings. Restoration plans must include provisions for infrastructure, human services, business enterprises, and ecological sanctuaries. To ensure students can effectively transfer their skills to new contexts, you will "move the exercise" into a different geographic location—either to Prince William Sound, Alaska, after the Exxon Valdez oil spill, or to the overlogged tropical forests of Costa Rica.

Take It to a Higher Level, by Hasan Altalib: RecoPort provides training for employees at financial institutions. One of its most popular programs is called "Take It to a Higher Level." The program is designed for employees who have worked as assistant planners at a financial institution, including brokerage and insurance companies. The goal of the program is to familiarize assistant planners with the skills that seasoned financial planners use when they are preparing an investment portfolio. A seasoned financial planner will have a variety of "soft" skills, such as communicating, planning, and consensus building. The seasoned planner will be able to thoroughly research a wide array of companies and identify the best performers. He or she will be able to interpret relevant tax laws, fee structures, and risk factors when analyzing a business or a mix of financial products.

Trainees are introduced to each case through transcripts of actual client–planner interviews. They are given access to a large sample of company and industry data. They are to develop a research plan and identify relevant data sources to assist them in making appropriate investment recommendations to their client. They will do their research and analysis individually; however, they will rely on members of their "financial team" to critique their analysis. Accomplished financial planners are available throughout the program to scaffold and mentor students. Each learner (trainee) will present his or her recommendations to a panel of expert financial planners who will provide feedback on the quality of the research, the validity of the analysis, and the depth of the student's communication and planning skills.

Watchers on the Web, by Susan Akers: The New Millennium Institute at a prestigious university is expanding its Society and Technology curriculum to include a course called "Privacy in the Digital Age." The course will address the balance between personal privacy and freedom of speech, and national security by examining the government's responses to the terrorist attacks of September 11, 2001. Some citizens have applauded the government's efforts; others have worried about abuses of power and potential weakening of First and Fourth Amendment rights.

The Privacy in the Digital Age course must develop a student's ability to assess and weigh potential security benefits against the possible infringement of citizens' rights in a democracy and to apply these judgments to a variety of complex situations related to Internet and computer use. Students will study a range of cases, including those pertaining to the USA Patriot Act, the Cyber Security Enhancement Act, the Department of Homeland Security, and electronic surveillance technologies such as Carnivore. Students will examine the cases from several perspectives, judging their relevance to legal, political, constitutional, ethical, practical, technological, or cultural considerations. The course will provide the students with an increased ability to apply a variety of concepts to a complex scenario in a consistent and reflective manner.

Take a moment to reflect on these scenarios. What do they have in common? Examine the learning content described in these scenarios and the perceived learning outcomes. Following are five questions to guide your thoughts:

1. Is the learning content ill defined (i.e., open ended, subject to multiple interpretations, crossing multiple subject domains, complex, authentic) or well defined (i.e., has finite and predictable solutions, depicts an identifiable subject domain or principle)?
2. Does the learning content contain multiple perspectives?
3. Does each scenario, problem, or instructional challenge have a single correct solution or multiple viable solutions and solution paths?
4. Is the learning outcome at the declarative level? the procedural level? the analysis, synthesis, or evaluation level?
5. Does the learning outcome require students to generate hypotheses, frame problems, and identify action plans?

In addition to the preceding questions, think about the following issues:

- How can we use online learning technologies to support the delivery and implementation of these scenarios?
- Do any of the pedagogical models or online learning delivery applications discussed in Chapter 1 apply to these instructional contexts? (You may want to revisit Chapter 1 to refresh your memory.)

In this chapter, we discuss the principles and characteristics of pedagogical models that support the type of content and learning outcomes depicted in the three preceding scenarios and provide a method for recognizing appropriate models for specific instructional contexts. We also discuss the learning technologies that support the implementation of such models in online learning.

INTRODUCTION

In Chapter 1, we defined *online learning* as "an open and distributed learning environment that uses pedagogical tools, enabled by Internet and Web-based technologies, to facilitate learning and knowledge building through meaningful action and interaction." We also introduced a three-component model for online learning consisting of (a) pedagogical models, (b) instructional strategies, and (c) learning technologies (or pedagogical tools), and we emphasized the importance of the interaction among these three components to promoting meaningful online learning. This interaction, or mapping of pedagogical models to instructional strategies and learning technologies, occurs in the enactment phase of the Integrative Learning Design Framework (ILDF) for Online Learning discussed in Chapter 4. The enactment phase includes the following four design methods, or steps, that the online developer should consider when he or she is designing online learning environments:

1. Map information gathered in the exploration phase to pedagogical models.
2. Consider the instructional characteristics of the selected pedagogical models.
3. Select specific instructional strategies that align with the selected pedagogical models.
4. Enact the instructional strategies by using the features of technological delivery systems.

Formal and informal activities for operationalizing these methods were provided in Chapter 4. In this chapter, we further elaborate on these tactics and provide a theory-based approach for mapping personal beliefs and other information gathered in the exploration phase of the ILDF for Online Learning (see Chapter 4) to grounded pedagogical models. We then focus on constructivist-based pedagogical models, their instructional characteristics, and associated learning technologies and theoretical constructs. In Chapter 6, we focus specifically on the third and fourth steps of the enactment phase of the ILDF for Online Learning: selecting specific instructional strategies that align with the selected pedagogical models and enacting these strategies by using online learning technologies.

WHAT ARE PEDAGOGICAL MODELS?

Pedagogical models can be described as views about teaching and learning. Pedagogical models are cognitive models or theoretical constructs derived from learning theory that enable the implementation of specific instructional and learning strategies. In other words, they are the mechanism by which theory is linked to practice. To help you better understand pedagogical models, we first examine some "metaphors of the mind" (Duffy

& Cunningham, 1996), or **knowledge acquisition and representation models**, that have framed current understanding about how people learn and how knowledge is constructed, stored, and later retrieved for use. Understanding knowledge acquisition models is fundamental to understanding teaching or pedagogical models because pedagogical models are, in essence, derived from knowledge acquisition models, which form the basis for learning theory. Next, we briefly discuss three knowledge acquisition models that have had an impact on theories of learning and instruction.

Knowledge Acquisition Models

Information processing model (or "mind as a computer" metaphor) **Information processing theory**, in which "the human learner is conceived to be a processor of information in much the same way a computer is" (M. P. Driscoll, 1994, p. 68), has led to a knowledge acquisition model known as **cognitive information processing (CIP).** In the CIP model, the mind is portrayed as having a structure consisting of components for processing information (e.g., sensory registers, short-term memory, long-term memory) and procedures for using these components (e.g., storing, retrieving, transforming, using). Implicit in this knowledge acquisition model is the principle that information undergoes a series of transformations in the mind in a serial manner until it can be permanently stored in long-term memory in packets of knowledge that have a fixed structure. Resulting from this view of CIP is the specification of instructional and learning strategies that assist the learner in processing information in discrete and linear events that align with internal cognitive processes such as selective attention, **encoding**, retention, and retrieval. Additional implications for instruction include providing for organized instruction, arranging for extensive and variable practice, and enhancing learners' self-control of information processing (M. P. Driscoll, 2000). One inherent presumption in this cognitive view of information processing is a separation of processes and knowledge. Another implication is that instructional strategies are (or should be) independent of the knowledge being taught and that different learning outcomes require different cognitive processes and hence different instructional strategies.

Parallel distributed processing model (or "mind as a brain" metaphor)   An alternative view of CIP is the **parallel distributed processing (PDP) model.** In the PDP model, long-term memory is perceived as a dynamic structure (or network) that represents knowledge in patterns or connections with multiple pathways instead of fixed schemata such as concept nodes and propositions (M. P. Driscoll, 2000; Duffy & Cunningham, 1996). Information processing is understood to be a process of activating these patterns, in parallel, to accommodate new information by strengthening the knowledge structure pattern that is most relevant to the learner's goals at the time of learning. Therefore, knowledge (or cognition) is thought to be "stretched over" or distributed across the whole network structure of long-term memory (much like a neural network, hence the "mind as a brain" analogy) and not residing in fixed loci in the brain (Salomon, 1993). Thus, one fundamental distinction between PDP and CIP knowledge acquisition models is that knowledge is stored in an active connectionist representation in PDP, versus a static and localized representation in CIP, and that information processing occurs in parallel (in PDP) instead of serially (in CIP), so that knowledge patterns are activated simultaneously and adjusted as a function of new information to resolve cognitive dissonance.

Situated cognition model (or "mind as a rhizome" metaphor)   The situated cognition model resembles the PDP model but has additional characteristics that distinguish it from both PDP and CIP. These characteristics are (a) the concept that knowledge extends beyond the individual, and (b) an emphasis on perception (how individuals perceive the situation or the environment) rather than on memory (how individuals retrieve knowledge). Nardi (1996) explained that situated, or distributed, cognition is concerned with knowledge representations inside and outside the mind and the transformations these structures undergo. As discussed in Chapter 1, situated cognition implies that rather than being thought of as an isolated event that occurs inside an individual's head, cognition should be viewed as a distributed phenomenon that is more global—that goes beyond the boundaries of a person to include the environment, artifacts, social interactions, and culture (Hutchins & Hollan, 1999; Rogers, 1997). The idea that cognition or intelligence is distributed suggests that learning spaces are becoming more dynamic and complex and that individuals learn from activity and the tools supporting such activity to extend their cognitive potential (Oubenaissa, Giardina, & Bhattacharya, 2002).

So where does the "mind as a rhizome" metaphor fit in? A rhizome is a "root crop, a prostate or underground system of stems, roots, and fibers whose fruits are tubers, bulbs, and leaves" (Duffy & Cunningham, 1996, p. 177). For example, a tulip is a rhizome. The root of the tulip generates shoots, which lead to new roots and new crops, which creates a self-organizing system that is constantly evolving and changing. The metaphor of "mind as a rhizome" rejects any fixed cognitive structure or static loci of schemata, which suggests that knowledge representations are dynamic—constantly evolving and changing—and subject to infinite juxtapositions, just as a rhizome is. This metaphor also suggests that knowledge resides in an open, global, and infinite network of interactions and activities mediated through symbols and tools (e.g., language, pictures). Therefore, the "mind as a rhizome" metaphor is not intended to describe how knowledge is represented in a single mind, but rather how knowledge is distributed across multiple minds and the interactions or activities that connect these minds through the use of tools and symbols forming sociocultural and other contexts.

Take a moment and think about which knowledge acquisition models are most closely aligned with your beliefs about teaching and learning and what you know about the instruction or training context. Remember that for your particular online learning design situation, the exploration phase of the ILDF for Online Learning provides a variety of techniques to assist you in reflecting on your teaching and learning beliefs (see Chapter 4).

Implications for Instruction

The situated cognition model is consistent with the epistemological assumptions of **constructivism**, which stipulate that meaning is a function of how the individual creates meaning from his or her experiences and actions (Jonassen, 1991). In constructivist theory, the learner is viewed as an active participant in the instructional experience, developing knowledge through a process of perception and meaning making. Situations, activities, and social interactions are constantly challenging the learner's understandings, which results in new meanings. Therefore, the context or the activity, which frames the knowledge, is as important to the learner as the knowledge itself. Knowledge or cognition in the constructivist view is perceived to be indexed or linked to the experiences in which it was learned, which results in multiple representations and infinite juxtapositions. Rather than acquiring concepts as abstract, self-contained entities, a person acquires useful knowledge through understanding of how knowledge is used by a group of practitioners or members of a community.

The epistemological assumptions of constructivism are in contrast with the epistemological assumptions of **objectivism**. In the objectivist view, knowledge is portrayed as an entity that exists independently of the individual and the instructional or learning context, so that knowledge is separate from the individual's experience. According to objectivist epistemology, the learner is a passive recipient of information and the producer of predetermined knowledge deemed correct or appropriate by experts. In contrast, constructivism requires the learner to manipulate, interpret, organize, or, in some active manner, make sense of his or her environment. The learner creates meaning by generating associations between and among elements in the instructional environment and his or her knowledge base.

Along the continuum from objectivism to constructivism lie several learning theories and knowledge acquisition models such as behaviorism; Ausubel's assimilation theory, or meaningful reception learning (MRL); and **schema theory**, among others. Behaviorism aligns most closely with the epistemological assumptions of objectivism, and situated cognition aligns most closely with the epistemological assumptions of constructivism. Table 5.1 provides an overview of these learning theories, their epistemological orientations, and their implications for learning and instruction. For more information on learning theories and models, visit the Theory Into Practice database at the companion Web site for this book: http://www.prenhall.com/dabbagh.

The result of the situated cognition and constructivist views of learning is the specification of pedagogical models and strategies that allocate control of the instruction sequence to the learner (Coleman, Perry, & Schwen, 1997) and empower the learner to create, elaborate on, or otherwise construct representations of individual meaning (Hannafin, 1992). Examples of pedagogical models that exemplify these characteristics include situated learning, or **anchored instruction**; problem-based learning; cognitive apprenticeships; cognitive flexibility hypertexts; communities of practice, or learning communities; computer-supported intentional learning environments; microworlds; simulations; and virtual learning environments (see Table 5.1). In the next section, we define each of these constructivist-based pedagogical models

Table 5.1 Learning Theories and Their Implications for Instruction

LEARNING THEORY	DEFINITION OF LEARNING	EPISTEMOLOGICAL ORIENTATION[a]	PROCESSES THROUGH WHICH KNOWLEDGE IS ACQUIRED	LEARNER'S ROLE	INSTRUCTOR'S ROLE	IMPLICATIONS FOR INSTRUCTION
Behaviorism	A Stimulus response that begins and ends in the environment that is external to the learner	Objectivism	Shaping, chaining, and fading	To be a passive recipient of information; to respond to a stimulus	To provide a stimulus and reinforcement; to be a transmitter of knowledge	Use principles of reinforcement to strengthen or weaken existing behaviors. Use shaping, chaining, and fading to teach new behaviors.
Cognitive information processing (CIP)	Cognitive operations that help the learner encode information into long-term memory, and to retrieve information in response to external cues	Objectivism	Memory processes (e.g., sensory input, pattern recognition, rehearsal, chunking, encoding, retrieval)	To use learning strategies to facilitate encoding	To support the learner's use of learning strategies	Provide organized instruction. Arrange extensive and variable practice. Enhance the learners' self-control of information processing. Use **Gagné's "events of instruction."**
Meaningful reception learning (MRL)	The activation of prior knowledge so that the learner can assimilate new knowledge with existing knowledge to provide meaning	Cognitivism	Derivative and correlative subsumption; **superordinate** and **combinatorial learning**	To activate prior knowledge	To help the learner activate prior knowledge	Activate the learners' prior knowledge. Use analogies and metaphors. Use advance organizers (comparative and expository). Make instructional materials meaningful.

Learning theory	Description	Paradigm	Learning process	Learner's role	Teacher's role	Instructional implications
Schema theory	The activation and reconstruction of a relevant schema for understanding new knowledge based the on learner's perception of the context	Cognitivism	Accretion, tuning, restructuring	To actively organize past experience to interpret new content	To identify misconceptions in the learner's schema; to provide opportunities for restructuring	Identify learner's existing mental models. Track development of learners' mental models. Provide conceptual models to make instructional materials meaningful.
Situated cognition	The construction of meaning from activity and experience	Constructivism	Mediated forms of interaction and enculturation into a CoP	To actively negotiate personal perception with the external world; to be a primary meaning maker; to take ownership of the learning process	To be a facilitator, guide, coach, and mentor; to create scaffolds for learning; to create a resource-rich learning environment	Provide open-ended learning environments that support multiple perspectives, discovery learning, inquiry-based learning, experiential learning, social interactions, role-playing, debates, and authentic contexts. Examples include the following: situated learning, or anchored instruction; PBL; cognitive apprenticeships; CFHs; CoPs, or learning communities; CSILEs; microworlds; simulations; and VLEs.

Note. CoP = community of practice; PBL = problem-based learning; CFHs = cognitive flexibility hypertexts; CSILEs = computer-supported international learning environments; VLEs = virtual learning environments. [a]In the objectivist view, reality is independent from and outside the knower; knowledge is equated with truth. In the cognitivist view, knowledge should reflect reality to the extent possible; however, what works is often accepted as viable. In the constructivist view, truth is viable; therefore, knowledge depends on the knower's frame of reference.

and their instructional characteristics and discuss their application or enactment in online learning.

CONSTRUCTIVIST-BASED PEDAGOGICAL MODELS

Situated Learning, or Anchored Instruction

Situated learning is a pedagogical model that promotes authentic learning activities to ensure that learning is situated in contexts that reflect the way the knowledge will be useful in real-life situations (Collins, 1991). Situated learning environments provide instruction through the exploration of authentic scenarios, cases, or problems. These authentic situations provide opportunities for meaningful and purposeful activities that cut across several content domains and skill sets. Rich media (graphics, video, and audio) are often used to contextualize the scenarios and embed relevant resources and data. In situated learning, students experience the complexity and ambiguity of the real world. They learn from confusion, noise, and interaction. More important, students work in groups to solve the case or problem at hand, and they reflect on their solutions and learning activities with the teacher's help. The teacher scaffolds the learning environment by providing structured collaborative activities, learning resources, and instructional support. In summary, situated learning is based on four major beliefs: (a) Learning arises from the actions of everyday situations, (b) knowledge is gained in context and transfers to similar situations, (c) learning is acquired through social interaction, and (d) learning is not separable from the world of action (Stein, 1998). Following are the instructional characteristics of situated learning.

Situated Learning

- Promotes authentic learning through coherent, meaningful, and purposeful activities that represent ordinary practices in real-life situations and contexts
- Provides opportunities for learners to internalize learning and develop self-monitoring and self-correcting skills
- Supports exploration and interaction within a real-world context
- Supports inter- and multidisciplinary learning (several content domain skills are embedded in the learning context; the scenario is purposefully interdisciplinary)
- Promotes role-playing activities
- Allows learners to seek information through embedded data (data are embedded in the problem context or scenario)
- Promotes articulation, reflection, and critical thinking skills (e.g., decision making and problem solving)
- Promotes collaborative learning (students work in groups to solve the problem through social negotiation; collaboration is not just a division of labor)
- Promotes transfer to real-life problem solving by allowing students to index their learning through authentic experiences (students acquire knowledge as well as a sense of when and how to use it)

Keeping the preceding instructional characteristics in mind, look at the first scenario, Paradise Found, provided at the beginning of this chapter. Which characteristics of situated learning does it support? Which characteristics seem to be emphasized most in this scenario?

First, in Paradise Found, several learning domains are supported: science, ecology, geography, history, community planning, team building, and problem management. Therefore, the multidisciplinary characteristic is evident. Second, the problem or scenario is ill structured (does not have one correct solution or solution path), involves the real world, is meaningful, and is purposeful. Students will assume the role the government had in addressing this issue. Therefore, authenticity is supported, as well as role-playing in the broad sense. Third, extensive media resources are available to be explored, which supports the embedded data characteristics. Fourth, students will be working in teams to research the issues and provide restoration plans, which supports the collaborative learning characteristic. Last, several new contexts for the transfer of learning are available in which students may apply their acquired knowledge and skills.

Problem-Based Learning

Problem-based learning (PBL) is a pedagogical model that engages the learner in a complex problem-solving activity in which the problem drives all learning and no formal prior learning is assumed. In PBL, instruction begins with a problem to be solved rather than content to be mastered (Barrows, 1985). Students are introduced to a real-world problem that is complex and has multiple solutions and solution paths (is ill structured) and are provided with an iterative heuristic problem-solving model (a reasoning process) that supports reasoning, problem-solving, and critical thinking skills. Students, in groups of four to six, take ownership of the problem and construct their own understanding of the situation by formulating the problem space (identifying what the problem is), identifying learning needs, determining a plan of action, and eventually finding a viable and cogent solution (Grabowski, Koszalka, & McCarthy, 1998). Tutors or teachers are assigned to each group and act as mentors and coaches by facilitating the problem-solving process and providing appropriate resources. The major goals of PBL are to help students develop collaborative learning skills, reasoning skills, interpersonal and communication skills, and self-directed learning strategies (Barrows, 1985). Following are the instructional characteristics of PBL.

Problem-Based Learning

- Promotes ownership of the learning process (the problem context motivates students to "own" the problem; students must define the problem)
- Assumes no formal prior knowledge in the content area(s) for which the problem is intended

- Promotes a student-centered, group learning environment
- Promotes self-directed learning (students have to set their own learning goals and choose strategies for achieving these goals)
- Promotes authentic learning through real-world problems that are ill structured (do not have one solution or solution path)
- Emphasizes problem solving as the primary learning goal by allowing the problem to serve as the center for instruction
- Promotes self-reflection as the primary assessment tool
- Allows students to generate hypotheses, set their learning goals, apply their own learning strategies, and solve the problem through searching for and identifying relevant resources
- Allows learners to integrate, use, and reuse newly learned information in context
- Supports recursive, iterative cycling through a reasoning process until a hypothesis is reached (provides scaffolding for learning a reasoning process)
- Promotes facilitation and scaffolding through instructor guidance (the instructor serves as a tutor and coach)

Look at the Paradise Found scenario once again. Could it have been designed as a PBL environment? Or is it best suited as a situated learning model?

The argument could go both ways. Paradise Found has most of the instructional characteristics for PBL. However, depending on how the teacher plans on implementing the activities in the middle school classroom, self-directed learning, which is a major goal of PBL, may be compromised. The teacher may need to provide extensive scaffolding to ensure that students are staying on task, particularly because one teacher is assisting all groups simultaneously. In addition, in PBL, the instructor assumes the students have no formal prior knowledge in the content area for which the problem is intended. In the middle school context, students would have had several years of directed instruction in history, geography, and science. This assumption is not necessarily a deterrent, but in PBL the goal is to provide as many opportunities as possible for students to construct their own understanding of the knowledge domain within the context of the problem prior to the interference of directed instruction. In addition, the problem in PBL is not intended as a culminating or summative activity that synthesizes knowledge after instruction has occurred but rather as an advance organizer that frames all new learning. Last, the scenario does not clarify whether the emphasis is on a problem-solving, heuristic reasoning process, which is a fundamental principle of PBL. Therefore, the decision about which model is appropriate may rest on the degree and type of scaffolding envisioned and the learners' knowledge and skills in managing their own learning. (*Note:* The student who developed this scenario and its design solution used a hybrid of situated learning and PBL models. See the companion Web site for this book— http://www.prenhall.com/dabbagh—for details on how this scenario was implemented by using Web-based technologies.)

Cognitive Apprenticeship

The cognitive apprenticeship model is similar to the anchored instruction model in that learning is situated in a real-world context and learners are encouraged to engage in meaningful and purposeful activities. The difference is that in a cognitive apprenticeship, learners are invited into the actual practices of a knowledge domain and are asked to perform these practices as an apprentice or intern. Students interact with experts, who model and explain their actions and decisions. **Cognitive apprenticeship** is "the showing and telling characteristic of apprenticeship" (Collins, 1991, p. 124). Experts model and explain which strategies are being used to solve problems in their knowledge domain. Cognitive apprenticeships incorporate strategies similar to those typically adopted in traditional apprenticeships—such as authentic learning, modeling, coaching, and **fading**—but they differ in that they emphasize cognitive skills and technology-enabled reflection, articulation, and exploration (Collins, 1991). Following are the instructional characteristics of cognitive apprenticeships following.

Cognitive Apprenticeships

- Promote mentoring and coaching (a mentoring and coaching relationship exists between the novice learner and the expert practitioner)
- Support modeling and explaining expert performance (the teacher models the activity by making tacit knowledge explicit through think-aloud procedures and worked examples)
- Focus on performance mastery within the context of the knowledge domain
- Support increasing complexity (the task is first embedded in a familiar activity, then complexity is added progressively with gradual fading of support)
- Encourage collaborative learning such as collective problem solving, developing teamwork skills, experiencing multiple roles, and confronting misconceptions
- Support learning strategies such as articulation of understanding and reflection on performance
- Promote the enculturation of students into authentic practices through activity and social interaction (apprentice-type learning; introducing students into the community of practice)

Keeping the preceding instructional characteristics in mind, look at the second scenario provided at the beginning of this chapter—Take It to A Higher Level. Does this scenario seem to fit the instructional characteristics of the cognitive apprenticeship model? If so, how?

Clear evidence exists that the trainees at RecoPort are apprentices. They are assistant planners (novices) working with seasoned planners (experts) to learn how to prepare an investment portfolio. Accomplished financial planners are available throughout the program to coach and mentor students. The transcripts provided to the assistant planners serve as a vehicle for modeling best practices. In addition, the assistant planners will work with a "real" client portfolio and make recommendations based on research, analysis, and interaction within a financial team. Therefore, the assistant planners are enculturated into the authentic practices of the financial community through activity and social interaction. Last, the assistant planners' recommendations are judged by a team of experts instead of a single teacher or authority. This type of appraisal is reflective of authentic assessment practices or assessment in situ, which is a characteristic of constructivist-based pedagogical models.

Cognitive Flexibility Hypertexts

A cognitive flexibility hypertext (CFH) is a pedagogical model based on the principles of cognitive flexibility theory, a constructivist-like theory that emphasizes real-world complexity and the ill-structuredness of knowledge. Cognitive flexibility "involves the *selective* use of knowledge to *adaptively fit* to decision making in a particular situation" (Fitzgerald & Semrau, 1996, p. 2). Avoiding reductive bias (simplification) and representing a knowledge domain in its full complexity maximizes the potential for adaptive, or flexible, knowledge assembly. Ill-structured problems, in which concepts may apply to one case but not to all cases of the same nominal type, are perceived to be appropriate representations of knowledge domains to help learners achieve cognitive flexibility. A CFH supports exploration of a complex and ill-structured (ill-defined) knowledge domain through multiple representations of the content, which promotes flexible knowledge acquisition that transfers to real-world contexts (Spiro, Feltovich, Jacobson, & Coulson, 1992). A CFH is, in essence, a hypermedia learning environment that provides users with several nonlinear paths of traversing content through the use of cases, themes, and multiple perspectives. The World Wide Web is an ideal medium for designing a CFH because of its hyperlinking ability and access to widespread resources that add richness to content. Following are the instructional characteristics of CFHs.

Cognitive Flexibility Hypertexts

- Promote active learning by providing the student with multiple perspectives to explore and comment on
- Support nonlinear case-based learning through hypermedia technology to stress the interrelated, weblike nature of knowledge
- Provide cognitive flexibility by allowing students to revisit the same material at different times, in rearranged contexts, for different purposes, and from different conceptual perspectives
- Promote theme-based learning (cases can be traversed through themes that are interplayed or articulated differently from each perspective on the issue at stake)
- Provide learning of complex content and concepts (advanced knowledge acquisition; complexity is not compromised but rather emphasized)
- Promote flexible and reflexive knowledge acquisition that transfers to real-world problem solving in multiple contexts

- Emphasize multiple representations of content, which encourages restructuring of student knowledge by allowing students the opportunity to develop their own meaningful and personal representations of the content domain
- Link abstract concepts to case examples

Look at the third scenario, Watchers on the Web, provided at the beginning of this chapter. Do you think this scenario has the instructional characteristics of CFHs? Why or why not?

First, in Watchers on the Web, the leading cue is the use of multiple cases. The scenario implies that there are multiple perspectives on the issue of privacy in the digital age and that the learning environment will expose students to these perspectives through a variety of cases. Students will be asked to evaluate these cases by judging their relevance to legal, political, constitutional, ethical, practical, technological, or cultural considerations. This requirement supports the presence of themes connecting the different perspectives of a complex and ill-structured issue, which is a fundamental principle of a CFH. In addition, the scenario implies that students may explore the different cases individually, constructing their own understanding and ultimately articulating their own views on the issue. Therefore, collaboration, or teamwork, is not an implicit requirement of this learning environment, but, at the same time, it is not necessarily precluded. Students can explore the cases on their own, weighing and assessing potential security benefits against the possible infringement of citizens' rights in a democracy, and then work in groups to apply these judgments to a variety of complex situations related to Internet and computer use.

Communities of Practice, or Learning Communities

As defined in Chapter 1, communities of practice (CoPs) are formed when members of a community are united by a common purpose and engage in mutual activities, mediating common values, interests, and goals (Schrum & Berenfeld, 1997, p. 64). When the common purpose is learning, CoPs are known as *learning communities* and can be described as "shared environments that permit sustained exploration by students and teachers and enable them to understand the kinds of problems and opportunities that experts in various areas encounter and the knowledge that these experts use as tools" (Cognition and Technology Group at Vanderbilt, 1992, p. 79). In online learning environments, CoPs include learners and instructors who interact with one another and other experts by means of online learning technologies to build a reciprocal interchange of ideas, data, and opinions. *Transformative* styles of communication are characteristic, which means that the contributor, the participator, and the lurker (receiver) are changed (transformed from novice to expert) as they share in the goal of learning and knowledge generation and application (Wilson & Cole, 1991). The purpose of a CoP is to develop members' abilities and skills and to build and exchange knowledge in a relevant and meaningful context and a supportive learning environment. Following are the instructional characteristics of CoPs.

- Control of learning is distributed among the participants in the community and is not in the hands of a single instructor or expert.
- Participants are committed to the generation and sharing of new knowledge.
- Learning activities are flexible and negotiated.
- The participants exhibit high levels of dialogue, interaction, collaboration, and social negotiation.
- A shared goal, problem, or project binds the participants and provides a common focus and an incentive to work together as a community.
- Diversity, multiple perspectives, and epistemic issues are appreciated.
- Traditional disciplinary and conceptual boundaries are crossed.
- Innovation and creativity are encouraged and supported.

Following is a scenario that aligns with the CoP pedagogical model and its instructional characteristics.

Engaging in Cultural Inquiry,[1] (by Kristin Percy-Calaff)

Introduction

A national professional teaching society estimates that more than half the public schools in America are wrestling with cultural diversity issues and learning needs stemming from differences in students' educational and ethnic backgrounds. Some diversity issues come from the fact that the families of many school-aged children emigrated from foreign countries and do not speak English. Other issues arise because American families are more mobile than they were 25 years ago. Many students spend only 1 or 2 years in the same school system. When they arrive at a new school, they have differing academic backgrounds and expectations.

Teachers need to be able to analyze student problems and identify whether they are developmental issues, cultural differences, or learning disabilities. Perhaps the "difficulties" are the result of the teacher's overly narrow expectations. Educators must be able to locate resources and use these resources to flexibly solve problems that interfere with their students' learning.

This year's public school educational conference will address this issue; the theme is "Cultural Inquiry and Effective Education (CIEE)." The goal of the CIEE conference is "to support teachers working in culturally diverse classrooms so that they might provide effective educational opportunities for all students." The conference will be divided into tracks geared to four audiences: teachers in K–7, teachers in 8–12, school administrators, and technology support professionals. Presenters and participants will be encouraged to collaborate and

---

Note. [1]Some ideas in this scenario are adapted from the Cultural Inquiry Process (http://classweb.gmu.edu/cip/).

share their experiences, and to recommend resources and methods for supporting culturally diverse classrooms. As the conference organizer, you want this event to lay the groundwork for a teacher support base for cultural issues.

Learning Outcomes
The task force will be charged with designing an environment that will enable teachers to do the following:

- Identify appropriate cultural approaches, knowledge domains, and intervention strategies used in different educational situations
- Develop a research plan and identify relevant resources, including other teachers, to solve a culturally based educational problem
- Decide how and when resources should be used to support decisions, methods, and information given in a situation
- Envision alternative ways of viewing educational processes
- Provide experiential guidance to instructors who are unfamiliar with the cultures of the students they are encountering
- Identify strategies to improve educational practice
- Reflect on strategy outcomes and refine their solutions for future practice

Study the preceding scenario and identify which instructional characteristics of a CoP are applicable or evident and why. Add your own characteristics as you see fit. Think about how a CoP differs from other pedagogical models discussed so far in this chapter.

Computer-Supported Intentional Learning Environments

A **computer-supported intentional learning environment (CSILE)** is a collaborative learning computer application with more than 10 years of research and development behind it (M. P. Driscoll, 2000). A CSILE is a networked, computer-supported instructional model that supports **generative learning** (construction of knowledge) through collaborative interactions. Generative learning is based on the same principles as those of constructivism and enables learners to create or construct meaning through generative associations between and among elements (objects and artifacts) in the instructional environment and the learner's knowledge base through scaffolding. To scaffold the learner in creating these generative associations, a CSILE provides a common database in which files from several media elements can be stored, retrieved, and linked. Through its networking and articulation tools, a CSILE enables students to build knowledge representations comprising text, pictures, audio, and video, and to make these knowledge representations accessible to other students through a communal database. This structure allows all the students to share information, provide comments, answer questions, and refine and organize their knowledge (Scardamalia & Bereiter, 1994). A major goal of the CSILE is to build a collaborative learning environment in which learners study authentic problems, communicate their ideas, participate in group dialogues and decision making, record the rationales for their choices, and identify their goals and specify a time frame in which to achieve them (Dede, 1996; Scardamalia & Bereiter, 1994). Following are the instructional characteristics of CSILEs.

Computer-Supported Intentional Learning Environments

- Provide a group-oriented knowledge-building environment in which the learner is responsibile for learning
- Foster student control of learning by helping students activate their own learning strategies and decide how to represent knowledge and what to share with others
- Support intentional learning: "Students are not only responsible for putting knowledge into the system, they are also responsible for evaluating it, interrelating it, labeling and sorting it, and performing periodic reorganization to enhance the quality of the community knowledge base." (Scardamalia, Bereiter, McLean, Swallow, & Woodruff, 1989, p. 63)
- Support multiple representations of knowledge through the use of media
- Promote peer mentoring through social negotiation, articulation of ideas, reflection, discussion, and shared understanding
- Allow students to share in problem solving by working as a team and setting goals
- Promote individual learning styles
- Build a collective database of students' thoughts, ideas, and understanding
- Support self-regulated learning

Following is a scenario that aligns with the CSILE pedagogical model and its instructional characteristics. Study the scenario and identify which of the preceding characteristics it exemplifies. Add your own characteristics as you see fit. See the companion Web site for this book (URL) to see how this scenario was implemented by using Web-based technologies.

Building Culture Quilts: Cross-Cultural Knowledge Networks, (by Zeena Altalib, Margie Joyce, Nechele Hill, and Paula Richardson)

Introduction
The XXX County population has been growing steadily for the past decade. Many of the new residents are immigrants coming from many different countries and cultures. Many of the county's middle schools are experiencing increases in disciplinary problems, especially when students of different ethnic backgrounds, religions, or races must interact.

An educational task team studying the disciplinary problems recommended that, instead of studying culture and geography in the traditional instructor-led format, seventh- and eighth-grade students should be encouraged to collaborate and generate their own questions and solutions during their study of other cultures. In lieu of taking tests and writing papers, students would build an electronic knowledge base incorporating everyone's work. Students would be able to use online references and multimedia to learn about cultures from Latin America, Africa, the Middle East, Europe, Asia, and North America. They would then use electronic knowledge-builder tools to verbally or visually represent their ideas and questions. Learners would also be encouraged to share personal observations and to interact and comment on those of other students within the growing database. The instructor would monitor the knowledge-building process and intervene only if necessary. Making students partners in the learning process and co-owners of the product reduces competition between students and establishes a nonthreatening learning environment in which to communicate cultural differences.

Learning Outcomes

The learning environment is designed to enable learners to do the following:

- Exhibit increased tolerance for peoples of a different race, sex, or ethnic origin
- Compare and contrast cultural characteristics of different groups of people
- Appreciate the importance of cultural awareness in dealing with others
- Describe technological advances that have led to increasing interaction among regions
- Have better interpersonal cross-cultural communication skills
- Feel more comfortable with and better equipped for collaborating with their peers
- Identify general types of issues that members of other cultures experience when they are a cultural minority
- Describe some of the challenges people face when they are moving to a new location with a different culture
- Understand some of the apprehensions natives of a particular culture feel when members of another culture move "into the neighborhood"

Microworlds, Simulations, and Virtual Learning Environments

Microworlds are computer-generated exploratory and experiential learning environments in which students test "What do you think will happen if?" questions in "constrained problem spaces that resemble existing problems in the real world" (Jonassen, 1996, p. 237). Learners generate hypotheses as they use their knowledge and skill to guess what will happen, try out these guesses, and reformulate them on the basis of the results of their actions within the microworld. Microworlds provide the learner with the observation and manipulation tools necessary to engage, experience, explore, and test. In addition, a microworld is structured to match the user's cognitive level so that it is appropriate for the user's needs and experience level (Rieber, 1992). Next, we present the instructional characteristics of microworlds, followed by an illustrative scenario. We then discuss simulations and virtual learning environments and their instructional characteristics.

Microworlds

- Promote exploratory and experiential learning
- Promote a controlled real-world environment in which hypotheses can be tested and speculation can occur with the goal of solving the problem
- Resemble existing problems in the real world, which encourages rich, meaningful learning and enables students to explore the ideas being learned
- Compress time and space so that multiple hypotheses may be tested in a short time frame
- Embody the simplest model of a domain that is deemed accurate and appropriate by an expert
- Support an initial entry point congruent with the learner's cognitive abilities
- Support incremental acquisition of complex skills
- Include a wide variety of versatile tools that learners may use to interact with and manipulate environmental and social parameters (direct engagement)
- Balance deductive (from general to specific) and inductive (constructing the whole from its components) learning
- Emphasize the utility of errors
- Encourage incidental learning
- Promote **hypothesis generation** and higher order thinking
- Provide students with a path from the known to the unknown
- Provide simple ideas and methods that are grounded in a visual reality
- Support just-in-time informative feedback

The following scenario is illustrative of a microworld. Study the scenario and identify its instructional characteristics. Compare these characteristics with the characteristics of previously discussed models. The actual microworld may be found at the companion Web site for this book (http://www.prenhall.com/dabbagh). See the learning activities at the end of this chapter for additional examples.

Vis-Ability: A Sculpture Quest Microworld (by Jacqueline Austin)

Introduction

A sculptor's goal is to creatively express his or her vision in three dimensions. However, the ultimate success of failure of the work also depends on the sculptor's ability to envision the many practical variables that influence the final outcome. Fine arts students in the studios at L'Ecole usually discover this the hard way. For instance, a student often finds out only after the final casting or sculpture that his or her selection of materials does not support the design model. Works of art are not exempt from the laws of physics, installation parameters, budgets, material availability, or applicability.

Currently, students have no reliable methods for analyzing the feasibility of their constructions. How can they predict whether a 3-D object of significant scale can stand erect, hang, or fly, or whether a 100-foot-by-100-foot-by-1-inch curvilinear shape can be constructed from Styrofoam with no visible means of support? Furthermore, fine arts students usually fail to calculate whether an installation can be accomplished within the given budget. To eliminate the trial-and-error approach students often use in the design process, L'Ecole is investing in a technology-based environment to assist students with creative and practical planning issues. The system will help students visualize their concept in thee dimensions and make decisions that determine "if" and "how" the piece can exist in the real world. Students can manipulate design aspects within the system and see the effects of their decisions on the end product. By understanding the many facets of a sculptor's work, the students can ensure that their creative visions will take shape.

Learning Outcomes
Learners will be able to do the following:

- Predict real-world structural integrity of prototypes
- Analyze the physical properties and integrity of materials used in their sculptures
- Judge the applicability of various materials to a particular project
- Develop abstract mental models of the relationship between art concepts and materials or media
- Organize and balance a multiplicity of artistic considerations such as scale, texture, and surface
- Follow a sound decision-making process during the design stage
- Use problem-solving skills to address potential production and design problems
- Analyze the spatial impacts and limitations of installation
- Select the best tools for sculpting particular materials
- Determine realistic budgets for individual pieces

Simulations are similar to microworlds in that they are experiential and exploratory and model the simplified essence of reality. However, they go beyond microworlds to provide "elaborate synthetic environments with immersion interfaces that place students inside alternate virtual worlds" (Dede, 1996, p. 14). For example, Virtual University (http://www.virtual-v.org; Penrod & Perry, 2003) is a computer-based simulation that provides an opportunity for graduate students and administrators to confront the complicated dilemmas encountered by college and university leaders. The simulation emulates physical spaces, offices, and everyday tasks, immersing students in a realistic scenario or dilemma with time constraints and impending executive evaluation and consequences. Therefore, simulations are more realistic than microworlds are and could fulfill some of the limitations of microworlds, such as the constrained and circumscribed nature of problems often portrayed in microworlds.

Another powerful learning model that builds on the principles of microworlds and simulations is **virtual learning environments** (VLEs). VLEs are computer-generated learning environments that rely heavily on high-end computer graphics and 3-D modeling to immerse learners in a real-world experience by mimicking the experience virtually.

Sometimes, these virtual worlds border on the fantasy and surreal. For an example of a 3-D VLE, visit the companion Web site at http://www.prenhall.com/dabbagh and look for the Project ScienceSpace link.

Not all virtual learning environments are 3-D. According to Follows (1999), engaging and exciting learning environments can be created two-dimensionally by using prerecorded videos, graphics, and animation embedded in an exploratory program. For example, "Thirst for Knowledge," created at Acadia University, is a VLE that simulates the Quaker Oats Company workplace. Students are assigned the VLE midway through a course in introductory marketing, and their objective is to evaluate the market potential of new Gatorade products. Students typically spend 16 hours "going to work for Quaker Oats." While working in this virtual office world, students walk through the building, attend meetings, read reports, receive e-mail, answer the telephone, and use a computer to query a database. At the end of the VLE, students write a report recommending a specific course of action, which is then discussed in class during an instructor-led debriefing session. Following are the instructional characteristics of simulations and VLE.

Simulations and VLEs

- Support learning by doing. For example, in virtual reality environments "learners can immerse themselves in distributed, synthetic environments, becoming **avatars** (assuming synthetic roles) who vicariously collaborate and learn by doing" (Dede, 1996, p. 14).
- Support self-regulated learning. Learners identify their own goals and directions.
- Promote authentic learning experiences. For example, virtual reality environments model the complexities and uncertainty of working in the real world (Follows, 1999).
- Support learner-centeredness or learner control. Learners control, explore, interact with, and construct their own knowledge.
- Support problem-solving activities. Learners are involved in high-level, ill-structured problem solving.
- Accommodate a wide range of student learning styles, abilities, and strategies, which enhances the learning outcomes compared with those of more traditional forms of teaching.
- Support personalized or individualized learning experiences.

In addition, in networked VLEs, known as *shared synthetic environments*, learners communicate on different levels (i.e., one to one, one to many, synchronously and asynchronously), interacting, collaborating, and exchanging information from multiple perspectives. Such environments support learning as a social process.

Summary

Take a moment and consider all the pedagogical models just discussed. Which pedagogical models most closely align with your understanding of the learning processes involved? Which instructional characteristics seem feasible and appropriate with regard to your beliefs and the learning situation that you might be considering?

Each pedagogical model discussed previously has specific instructional characteristics, but they all collectively subscribe to the epistemological assumptions of constructivism and situated cognition. In general, all the models subscribe to the following five main instructional conditions or design principles (M. P. Driscoll, 2000):

1. Embed learning in complex, realistic, and relevant contexts.
2. Provide for social negotiation as an integral part of learning.
3. Support multiple perspectives and the use of multiple modes of representation.
4. Encourage ownership in learning.
5. Nurture self-awareness of the knowledge construction process. (p. 382)

These design principles align with the five questions presented at the beginning of this chapter. We restate these questions next and ask that you keep these questions in mind when you are examining your own learning context.

1. Is the learning content ill defined (i.e., open ended, subject to multiple interpretations, crossing multiple subject domains, complex, authentic) or well defined (i.e., has finite and predictable solutions, depicts an identifiable subject domain or principle)?
2. Does the learning content contain multiple perspectives?
3. Does each scenario, problem, or instructional challenge have a single correct solution or multiple viable solutions and solution paths?
4. Is the learning outcome at the declarative level? the procedural level? the analysis, synthesis, or evaluation level?
5. Does the learning outcome require students to generate hypotheses, frame problems, and identify action plans?

Having established the specific and general instructional characteristics of constructivist-based pedagogical models, we now provide a general framework or structure to facilitate the implementation of such models in online learning.

EXPLORATORY, DIALOGIC, AND INTEGRATIONAL LEARNING ENVIRONMENTS AND ASSOCIATED LEARNING TECHNOLOGIES AND THEORETICAL CONSTRUCTS

To help you establish a meaningful structure for further understanding the pedagogical models discussed in the previous section and their application in online learning, we classified these models, according to their instructional characteristics, into three categories, or types, of learning environments: exploratory, dialogic (**collaborative or conversational**), and **integrational.** Each category is further described in the following subsections. Table 5.2 provides an overview of these categories, related pedagogical models, and associated learning technologies and theoretical constructs. Table 5.2 can be used as a scaffold for thinking about the types of learning technologies that support the implementation of constructivist-

Table 5.2 Exploratory, Dialogic, and Integrational Learning Environments and Associated Learning Technologies and Theoretical Constructs

PEDAGOGICAL MODELS AND APPLICATIONS	ASSOCIATED LEARNING TECHNOLOGIES	ASSOCIATED THEORETICAL CONSTRUCTS
EXPLORATORY		
Microworlds Simulations Virtual learning environments Cognitive flexibility hypertexts Cognitive apprenticeships Situated learning Case-based learning Problem-based learning WebQuests	Hypertext and hypermedia Graphics Animation Direct manipulation interface Digital video and audio Authoring tools Search engines Self-contained instructional modules Plug-ins	Learner control Interactivity Authentic activity Contextualized learning Guided learning by doing Experiential learning Inquiry-based learning Action learning Cognitive flexibility Thematic-based learning Self-directed learning Generative learning Discovery learning
DIALOGIC		
Asynchronous learning networks Knowledge networks Communities of practice Learning communities Knowledge-building communities Virtual classrooms Shared synthetic environments Computer-supported intentional learning environments Telelearning	E-mail Bulletin boards, discussion forums, and Listservs Computer conferencing Video teleconferencing Document-sharing technologies Groupware Virtual chat Internet Relay Chat (IRC) Multiuser domains—object oriented Multiuser domains	Computer-mediated communication Collaborative learning Distributed learning Self-directed learning Generative learning Cyberspace cultures Anthropomorphosis or avatar Open or flexible, learning
INTEGRATIONAL		
Online learning E-learning Web-based instruction Web-based courseware Knowledge portals	Web-based course authoring tools Course management systems Learning objects Object-oriented technology Self-contained interactive modules Database technologies Dynamic Web pages	Computer-mediated communication Interactivity Collaborative learning Embedded authentic activities Learner control Distributed learning Self-directed learning Open, or flexible, learning Generative learning

based pedagogical models in online learning and the theoretical constructs instantiated. However, pedagogical models are operationalized or enacted through instructional strategies, which are subsequently enacted or implemented through the use of online learning technologies and delivery models. These processes constitute the third and fourth steps of the enactment phase of the ILDF for Online Learning and are discussed in Chapter 6.

Exploratory Learning Environments

Exploratory, or experiential, learning environments are based on the theoretical construct of discovery learning, or **inquiry-based learning,** in which learners are provided with a scientific-like inquiry or an authentic problem in a given content area. Learners are then asked to generate a hypothesis, gather relevant information using a variety of resources, and provide solutions, action plans, recommendations, and interpretations of the situations. Several of the pedagogical models discussed in this chapter are examples of exploratory, or experiential, learning environments: microworlds, simulations, VLEs, CFHs, cognitive apprenticeships, situated learning, and PBL. If you look at the instructional characteristics of these models, you will find that exploratory-type activities are promoted in each. The exploratory, or experiential, mode of learning is provided within online learning or Web-based instruction through the use of several online learning technologies, including hypermedia, animation, graphics, digital audio and video, plug-ins, **self-contained instructional modules** developed by using a variety of authoring tools, search engines, and **direct manipulation interfaces.** We briefly define each of these technologies next. See also Chapter 2 for a review of Web-based hypermedia and multimedia technologies.

Hypermedia   Derived from the term *hypertext*, *hypermedia* uses computer-addressable files that embed hyperlinks to multimedia information and/or objects. Hypermedia links (hyperlinks) are usually contained in Web documents and in instructional products generated through the use of authoring tools, and they include text, graphic images, video, audio, and animation displays. "In simplest terms, it [hypermedia] is a product that connects media (text, audio, graphics, video, and animation) in a non-linear manner" (M. M. Driscoll, 1998, p. 135). Hypermedia is a powerful tool for online learning, Web-based training, and other computer-based instructional applications, offering learners the opportunity to control the pace, sequence, and depth of content in a computer environment. Hypermedia allows the user to explore text in the order that makes the most sense to the individual (Jonassen, 1988). CFHs are premised on this learning technology.

Animation   Animation can be used to simulate software, describe physical processes, or simply gain students' attention (B. Hall, 1997). It can be as simple as an animated GIF (graphic interchange format) or as complex as an advanced Macromedia Flash movie. Some animation software, such as 3D Studio MAX, creates 3-D animations useful for developing more realistic simulations such as VLEs, which were discussed previously.

Graphics   Graphics can be in the form of static images, animated graphic files, or video files. They can be displayed anywhere on a page of instruction or represented as hyperlinks.

According to B. Hall (1997), "The ability to display graphics as well as text is one of the most powerful functions of the Web" (p. 34). One of the best examples of good use of graphics in technology-based learning is the "virtual museum," in which artifacts are displayed on a Web page with accompanying text about the artifacts. Graphics on the Web can be used to create authentic contexts and scenarios as required in situated learning models.

Digital audio and video As technology advances, digital audio and video are being used more widely as delivery media for instruction, particularly in hypermedia and exploratory environments. *Digital audio* is used in technology-based instruction as short alert sounds, narrative voice-overs, synthesized music, and more (B. Hall, 1997). Synthesized sounds are generated with a variety of sound studio applications, whereas voice recordings and real-world sounds must be captured by using audio recorders and editors that capture input through an external microphone. To be used in a computer-based instructional application, the audio must be converted to an acceptable digital format. The types of audio files most commonly used include AIFF (Apple Instrument File Format), MIDI (musical instrument digital interface), MPEG (a name for the industry group, different from the video file format), RealAudio, and wave. Digital audio is often used along with animation or video. Digital audio and video can be used to support the design of CFH, situated learning, and cognitive apprenticeship models by providing realistic contexts and multiple perspectives.

To use *digital video* in a computer-based or Web-based instructional application, you must convert it from its original analog source to a digital computer file. The types of video files most commonly used include AVI (audio/video interleaved), QuickTime, and MPEG (Motion Picture Experts Group). Various software studio applications are available for editing and converting video.

Digital audio and video are most often delivered over the Internet by means of streaming technology. With streaming media, the Web user does not have to wait for an entire large file to download before hearing the sound or seeing the movie. Rather, the sound or pictures are delivered over the Internet in a continuous fashion using data packets (*Streaming Media,* 2002).

Plug-ins Plug-ins are "small programs that are installed on your computer and aid your Web browser to do special things" (R. Hall, 2001, p. 56). They allow different types of animation, audio, and video files to be played within the Web browser. Along with a Web browser application, plug-ins translate the different kinds of files for viewing in the browser window (B. Hall, 1997). For example, a Macromedia Authorware file requires a special plug-in from Macromedia called *Shockwave* before it can be viewed on the Web. Although some plug-ins come bundled with a browser application, such as Netscape Navigator or Microsoft Internet Explorer, often they must be downloaded from a Web site and installed. These tasks sometimes pose a problem for end users, depending on technical or policy-based restrictions imposed by their institutions. Thus, the need to download and install plug-ins must be considered during the design of Web-based training and online learning.

Self-contained instructional modules Self-contained instructional modules can be described as modular instruction (previously known as *computer-based instruction*). The use of such modules is a "trend that reflects the need for efficiency in training"

(Moore & Lockee, 2001, p. 272). Self-contained instructional modules are the result of **"chunking"** content to support a limited set of very specific learning outcomes. In essence, learners access information as needed rather than using a larger, more comprehensive instructional program. Self-contained instructional modules can be generated as Web-based, requiring the use of plug-ins, or stand-alone applications, such as training distributed through a CD-ROM. From a technical aspect, delivering such self-contained modules through a CD-ROM offers a bandwidth advantage. Self-contained instructional modules can be created by using several authoring tools with varying degrees of complexity. Authoring applications allow the developer to define inter-activity and combine various types of media such as text, graphics, animation, audio, and video (see Chapter 8 for a comprehensive discussion on authoring tools).

Search engines   A search engine is "a software application that locates words, phrases, and files on a Web site" (M. M. Driscoll, 1998, p. 274). The front end of a search engine is a Web site that has a place for the user to type in "key words" and then returns "hits," which are occurrences of these key words. Behind the Web site is "a very sophisticated database that uses software robots that travel the Web, looking at Web sites" (R. Hall, 2001, p. 57). Google, Ask Jeeves, and WebCrawler are examples of search engines. Search engines can be used to support exploratory activities in various instructional contexts.

Direct manipulation interfaces   An interface is "the screen through which the learner and the computer communicate and access, transfer, add, and exchange information" (M. M. Driscoll, 1998, p. 272). *Direct manipulation* refers to a principle for designing user interfaces that calls for continuous representation of the objects of interest. Objects may be manipulated "through physically obvious and intuitively natural means" such as labeled button presses and other "rapid, reversible, incremental actions" (*Software Systems and Their Development*, 2002). An instructional screen with a drag-and-drop-type activity in which the learner can use the mouse to move objects to new locations is an example of a direct manipulation interface. Direct manipulation interfaces are appropriate for the design of microworlds, simulations, VLEs, and CSILEs.

How to choose among learning technologies   When an online learning developer is designing online learning based on exploratory pedagogical models, the decision about which learning technologies or combination of learning technologies to use will ultimately rest on the developer's expertise, the available resources and technologies, the audience characteristics, and the instructional characteristics of the pedagogical model implemented. One online learning activity popular with K–12 teachers that supports many of the instructional characteristics of exploratory learning models is a WebQuest. A **WebQuest** is an inquiry-oriented activity in which most or all of the information used by learners is drawn from the Web. WebQuests are designed to use learners' time to help them focus on using information rather than looking for it, and to support learners' thinking at the levels of analysis, synthesis and evaluation. (The WebQuest Page, 1997).

   An example of a WebQuest aimed at teaching science concepts for fifth graders is presented next. Examples of more specific instructional strategies and activities that support **exploratory learning environments** in online learning are presented in Chapter 6.

Cell WebQuest, (by Lisa Prillaman)

Introduction

What are you made of? You could say atoms or elements. That would be correct, but rocks, people, desks, and boxes are made of atoms and elements, too. What makes you different from those things? Perhaps the better question is What are you made of that makes you alive? The simplest answer is that you and each and every other living thing are made of cells. However, each living thing is made of millions of cells and many different types of cells. The differences between cells make each living thing unique.

Task

Today, astronomers confirmed that a meteorite that fell to Earth last week is from the planet Mars. Even more interesting, they discovered several specimens they believe might point to life on Mars. You and your team of scientists have been asked to evaluate the specimens, believed to be cells. Lab employees have supplied you with slides of the specimens and other materials you will need for your investigation.

As the most-sought-out team of scientists, you must develop hypotheses based on any information you already know and, identify the specimens and the implications they hold for life on Mars. You must be able to support your findings and decisions with factual information. You will present your findings to the National Aeronautics and Space Administration (NASA) and must provide scientific models and/or visuals to explain the process leading you to your conclusions.

You should follow several steps as you seek to solve the problem. Before beginning, you may want to go to the Evaluation page to see the expectations of individuals and groups during the project. Keep all your information and products in your Cell WebQuest folder.

- Identify roles: Your group is made up of a research biologist, a horticulturalist, and a cell biologist. To learn more about your specific viewpoint on biology, click on the folder below. You may also use books and the online encyclopedia to find more information about your role. Discuss and record your ideas about why you, in your role, would be interested in finding out more about the "meteorite cells."
- Biology-Related Careers (http://www.aibs.org/careers/)
- Examine the available specimens and develop a hypothesis you would like to investigate based on what you already know about cells. Write down your hypothesis and develop a list of questions you need to answer to solve your problem.
- Use the resources available on the Resources page to find out more information about the type of cells, their organelles, and the similarities and differences in cell types.
- In your search of these Web sites and books, your team will create a concept map like those completed in other science lessons to show relationships between the information you discover. You should use Inspiration to create your concept map. This map may be a part of your presentation if you think it will help support your

conclusions. Please save and then print this concept map at the end of each session and label it according to the date.

- After you think your group has gathered enough information to make your conclusion, you should begin developing a presentation that you will give to share your findings. You may choose to do this in the form of a video or a live press conference, a Web page, a newspaper article, posters, or another form you have obtained approval for from your teacher.

Reflect on the preceding example. Which learning technologies are used to implement this WebQuest? Which theoretical constructs apply? Which instructional characteristics are relevant? Consult Table 5.2 and the instructional characteristics of exploratory pedagogical models (listed in the Constructivist-Based Pedagogical Models section of this chapter) to assist you in developing your answers.

Dialogic Learning Environments

Dialogic learning environments emphasize social interaction through dialogue and conversation. The idea is to assist learners in constructing new knowledge primarily through dialogue as a form of interaction. Internet and Web-based technologies provide various mechanisms for supporting dialogue related to both informal and formal learning situations. For example a Web-based group forum (discussion board) can support a formal conversational exchange that occurs in support of specific instructional objectives or an informal conversational exchange based on content interest. Both these conversational exchanges foster a sense of community and belongingness. Learning communities, knowledge-building communities (CSILEs), and CoPs are examples of dialogic learning environments. If you look at the instructional characteristics of these models, you will find that dialogic-type activities such as articulation, reflection, collaboration, and social negotiation are emphasized. Exploratory pedagogical models such as situated learning and cognitive apprenticeships can also be classified as dialogic learning environments because collaboration through social interaction is a fundamental instructional characteristic of these models. Learning technologies that support the implementation of dialogic learning environments include asynchronous and synchronous tools, such as electronic mail (e-mail), bulletin boards or discussion forums, computer conferencing, groupware, **document sharing,** Listservs, **Internet relay chat (IRC),** videoconferencing, and virtual chat. We briefly define each of these learning technologies next. See also Chapter 2 for a review of asynchronous and synchronous communication tools.

Electronic mail Electronic mail (e-mail) "uses the Internet to send and receive text, graphics, sounds, and other attachments on a personal basis" (R. Hall, 2001, p. 53). It allows learners to send messages to the instructor or one another over the Internet or intranet (M. M. Driscoll, 1998). Because learners are typically familiar with e-mail and need little instruction, it is easy to implement. There are several educational uses for e-mail. A more complex example of e-mail interaction is asking an expert to reply to a question and sharing the response with the class. E-mail is an asynchronous technology or tool.

Bulletin boards or discussion forums   Bulletin boards or discussion forums are a Web service that provides people with a virtual way to connect and read or "post" messages, similar to a cork bulletin board you might find on a wall. Bulletin board systems let subscribers carry on discussions, upload and download files, and make announcements (M. M. Driscoll, 1998). Such systems may also be referred to as *threaded discussions*, *forums*, or *notes conferences*. In an educational environment, students can "post and answer questions, debate ideas, and read about topics of interest" (Romiszowski, 1997). Conversation threads remain on the forum, which allows students to follow the conversation and respond at any time.

Computer conferencing   Computer conferencing, sometimes referred to as *online conferencing*, involves interactive dialogue over the Web. This activity is often asynchronous and text based. Usually, an instructor posts a topic or question(s) for discussion to a conference and students visit the course Web pages and add to the discussion or respond to the question(s). Students respond at any time of the day or night and as frequently as the instructor permits. Special conferencing software is required and is available for purchase through commercial packages (R. Hall, 2001).

Groupware   Any type of software designed for groups and for communication is considered groupware. It is technologically designed to facilitate the work of groups (Brink, 1998). "This technology may be used to communicate, cooperate, coordinate, solve problems, compete, or negotiate" (Brink, 1998, para. 1). Traditional technologies, like the telephone, may be classified as groupware when they are used for conference calls, for example. However, the term is primarily used to describe modern technologies that use computer networks, such as e-mail, Listservs, videophones, or chat. Groupware technologies can be either asynchronous or synchronous. Groupware applications provide multiple users with the opportunity to access, share, and work on the same documents and files (R. Hall, 2001). CSILEs are an example of groupware. The software used in CSILEs is specially designed to support group collaboration, communication, and knowledge building through a communal database.

Document sharing   Many groupware applications provide document-sharing functionality. Document sharing allows users to store, share, and retrieve large files. Such sharing is especially useful when two or more people are working on the same project. It allows users to collaborate without the hassle of dealing with large e-mail attachments. Authors collaborating on a document may use tools to help plan and coordinate the authoring process, such as mechanisms for locking parts of the document or linking separately authored documents (Brink, 1998). Document-sharing software is available in varying degrees of sophistication. Certain word processors provide asynchronous support by identifying authorship and by allowing users to track changes and make annotations to documents. Review Manager (http://www.cc-ims.net/RevMan/) is another example of document-sharing software. This product also offers foreign language text compatibility. Lotus Notes (http://www.lotus.com) is another example of a software tool that supports document sharing.

Listservs   Listservs refer to computer-managed mailing lists. When e-mail is sent to a Listserv, it automatically goes to everyone who has subscribed to the list. The Listserv is "a software product that manages email among a group of people" (M. M. Driscoll, 1998, p. 109). A Listserv keeps a list of people's names and e-mail addresses on a computer server. A Listserv as an educational tool is most effective when it is highly moderated. It can be used to stimulate ongoing conversation among learners.

IRC (internet relay chat)   IRC (Internet relay chat) is an Internet technology that allows people to type messages to each other through a text-based "network" in real time, or what is known as the *synchronous mode*. To access the network, users must have a client program that handles IRC. Users log onto a special IRC server and join the IRC stream, or channel, of their choice. IRC provides "the ability to conduct a conversation among a group of learners by typing back and forth" (M. M. Driscoll, 2001, p. 179).

Videoconferencing   Videoconferencing, sometimes called *teleconferencing,* combines the benefits of television and the traditional classroom (Picciano, 2001). Videoconferencing is a technology that allows students in one location to interact in real time with the teacher and other students in another location. The students can see the instructor, and the instructor can see the students. An audio capability also allows students to ask the instructor or each other questions. Some videoconferencing systems are equipped with electronic blackboards and other imaging systems, which allow the instructor to display illustrations or notes. Newer videoconferencing systems allow for classes at multiple sites to participate. Delivery technologies for videoconferencing include telephone systems, satellite, cable, fiber-optic networks, and even desktop computers.

Web-based videoconferencing allows for the transmission of audio and video images to multiple learners through the Internet or intranet (M. M. Driscoll, 1998). Numerous vendors offer Web-based videoconferencing solutions at varying degrees of sophistication. Some systems broadcast the instructor's video only one way to learners. In this situation, the instructor and the learners can hear each other; however, the instructor cannot see the learners, and the learners cannot see one another. Many Web-based videoconferencing packages offer built-in tools useful for educational environments, such as quizzing and document sharing.

Virtual chat   Virtual chat uses software that leverages Internet technology to give users online "rooms" where they can gather to converse and exchange ideas, often using graphical identities ("Virtual Chat Rooms," 1997). Educational applications of online chat use the technology to create online communities in which classroom activities, such as listening to a lecture or chatting with teachers and other students, can occur virtually. Virtual chat rooms are often built around topics or themes.

Delivery models or applications that support dialogic learning environments Using the synchronous and asynchronous technologies just discussed, learners can interact in large- and small-group contexts to support their learning. Examples of online learning delivery models or applications that support dialogic learning environments are MUDs and MOOs. MUDs and MOOs are knowledge networks that emphasize social interaction and negotiation through role-playing. A MUD (multiple user domain, or multiple user dimension) is a "complete virtual world in which you become the body of a character you adopt to navigate that world" (R. Hall, 2001, p. 55). Users explore the virtual world in real time and typically at the same time as other users who are also controlling characters. Users can talk to one another and form teams. Theme, content, and style vary from one MUD to the next. MUDs originated in a game called *Dungeons and Dragons*, which was developed for multiusers on the Internet. In educational settings, MUDs are used as a collaborative tool for students. "In Web-based learning, simulated role portrayal can be facilitated through Multi-User Dialogue (MUD) environments, in which instructors create a multi-user space with a central theme, characters and artifacts" (Khan, 2001, p. 81). A MOO (multiuser domain—object oriented) is a type of MUD that gives users the opportunity to experience virtual worlds as players of a game or explorers of a theme or course. One essential difference between MOOs and MUDs is that MOOs make use of multimedia, whereas MUDs are primarily text based. In addition, MOOs developed into social spaces, lending themselves more readily for use as a virtual classroom or as spaces for conferences and meetings (Walker, 1997). Tapped In (http://ti2.sri.com/tappedin/) is a knowledge network that supports the implementation of MUDs and MOOs in classroom contexts. Seventh graders in a prealgebra class at Portola Middle School, in El Cerrito, California, became the first middle school students in the district to use a MOO. See the following scenario.

The M.A.R.E. MOO

(http://ti2data.sri.com/info/teachers/mare.html)
(Scenario developed by Hulda Nystrom)
Portola Middle School had embarked that year on a schoolwide theme called *M.A.R.E., Marine Activities, Resources, and Education*. M.A.R.E. is a cross-curricular marine studies theme out of the University of California–Berkeley's Lawrence Hall of Science. We were just getting our feet wet with this theme when a variety of grants came through that allowed us to upgrade our Internet access from a single telephone line to a high-speed, fractional T-1 link. Now we had the world open to us to explore islands in the sixth grade, coral reefs in the seventh, and the polar regions in the eighth.

Earlier in the year, we had subscribed to a virtual field trip called *Blue Ice: Focus on Antarctica*, which gave students access to people in a variety of fields who had expertise in matters relating to the scientific, journalistic, and lay study of the South Pole. However, we were just getting our sea legs as this opportunity came and went.

With full Internet access in a lab of 30 computers, we were able to use the articles, guest appearances, and e-mail question-and-answer sessions from

Blue Ice as resources for an online "deep sea" exploration of a variety of human and nonhuman forces at work in one of the planet's most important ecosystems. The M.A.R.E. MOO project took the form of a debate among several "characters" on the question Should human activity, including drilling for oil, whaling, tourism, and scientific exploration, be banned or limited in and around Antarctica? The characters were as follows:

- WhaleWilly, representing the whale community
- PattyPenguin, representing the penguin community
- EcoEdith, representing ecologist William Fraser and organizations such as Greenpeace
- ExplorerEdward, representing Antarctica explorers, past and present
- ReSearcher, representing scientists and researchers in and outside Antarctica
- NSF, representing national and international, governmental and nongovernmental organizations
- IndustryIrving, representing oil companies and the food and whaling industries
- TouringTracy, representing the tourist industry, including ecotourism

Each character was "played" by a team of four to five students. Each team's task was to understand the perspective of their character to such an extent that they could represent that point of view in an online debate. The teams were given the archived e-mails from Blue Ice as resources for "building" their character. They each selected a keyboarder to input their contributions to the debate. The event took place in a "room" described as "a meeting room of the U.N. Subcommittee on Antarctica of the Environmental Affairs Committee."

Mr. Hulse and Computer Resource teacher Hulda Nystrom shared the role of moderator, calling the participants to introduce themselves, state their positions, and, at the end, make their closing statements. The debate sessions were logged for later review and analysis.

Reflect on the preceding example. Which learning technologies were used to implement this MOO? Which theoretical constructs apply? Which instructional characteristics are relevant? Consult Table 5.2 and the instructional characteristics of dialogic pedagogical models (listed in the Constructivist-Based Pedagogical Models section of this chapter) to assist you in developing your answers.

Additional online learning models or applications that embody the characteristics of dialogic learning environments include asynchronous learning networks (ALNs), learning or knowledge networks, telelearning, and knowledge portals. These models were defined in Chapter 1. Examples of more specific instructional strategies and activities that support dialogic learning environments in online learning are presented in Chapter 6.

Integrational Learning Environments

Integrational learning environments are based on the recent emergence of Web-based authoring tools (e.g., Dreamweaver and FrontPage) and course management systems (e.g., WebCT, Learning Space, and Blackboard). These integrative tools or systems allow elements of the instructional attributes of exploratory and dialogic learning environments to be merged into Web-based courseware, online learning environments, and e-learning knowledge portals that can be created without extensive programming knowledge. Web-based authoring tools and course management systems present users with the opportunity to incorporate various instructional strategies, by using the available software features, into a holistic course design. More specifically, they do the following:

- Provide a central location for delivery of course content
- Provide related information or links
- Provide models of assignments
- Allow communication between instructors and students
- Facilitate a group process for development of shared projects
- Permit development of Web-based products

For example, these integrated technological capabilities can facilitate the delivery of hypermedia and multimedia instructional content and provide the communicative means for a group process and mechanisms for the development of Web-based projects all in one centralized tool to support a collective and distributed learning experience. In addition, course management systems can support highly integrative instructional efforts of these types while supplementing face-to-face interaction or supporting delivery of courses at a distance. A detailed discussion of Web-based authoring tools and course management systems and their applications in online learning contexts is presented in Chapters 8 and 9. The classification of pedagogical models into exploratory, dialogic, and integrational learning environments should be perceived as a taxonomy in which integrational learning environments subsume dialogic and exploratory learning environments.

Return to the scenarios presented at the beginning of this chapter. Do you think they are examples of exploratory, dialogic, or integrational learning environments? To make an informed decision, think about the various learning technologies that are needed to facilitate the implementation of these instructional contexts in online learning. Revisit Table 5.2.

CHAPTER SUMMARY

In this chapter, we provided a theory-based approach for mapping personal beliefs about teaching and learning to grounded pedagogical models. Three knowledge acquisition models that have an impact on learning and instruction were discussed. A table was provided in which the major learning theories in the field of instructional design and technology were summarized according to their epistemological orientation, the instructor's and learner's roles, and instructional implications. We then discussed specific pedagogical models grounded in constructivist epistemology and provided instructional characteristics and authentic examples for each model. We classified these pedagogical models into three broad categories of learning environments—exploratory, dialogic, and integrational—to provide a more meaningful structure for understanding the models and their characteristics. Examples of learning technologies and theoretical constructs that relate to each category were also provided to help you associate the instructional characteristics of these models with learning technologies and begin thinking about how to implement these models in online learning contexts.

LEARNING ACTIVITIES

1. Visit the Theory Into Practice database at the companion Web site for this book (http://www.prenhall.com/dabbagh) and find additional knowledge acquisition models and/or pedagogical models that align with your beliefs about teaching and learning. Use Table 5.1 to classify the models you selected along the continuum of objectivism to constructivism and discuss their implications for instruction.

2. Visit the Instructional Design Knowledge Base (IDKB) at the companion Web site for this book (http://www.prenhall.com/dabbagh). Click on "Doing an Instructional Design Project" and then on "Models/Theories." Locate a theory or model under behaviorism or cognitivism and discuss how its implications for instruction differ from those for the models presented in this chapter. Repeat this exercise for other theories or models.

3. Locate the scenarios presented at the beginning of this chapter at the companion Web site for this book (http://www.prenhall.com/dabbagh). To do so, click on the link to this chapter (Chapter 5) and look in the section entitled "Scenarios with Solution Examples." Browse the solutions to these scenarios (or one of the solutions) and analyze how they have been implemented online. Use the Prototype Review Form provided on the Web site to describe how the prototype solution implements a given pedagogical model. Instructions are provided on the form. This activity could also be implemented as a group.

4. Select a different scenario from the Scenarios with Solution Examples section of the companion Web site. Use the Prototype Review Form to analyze this prototype solution. This activity could also be implemented as a group.

5. Select an unsolved scenario related to your instructional context (i.e., higher education, professional or corporate, or K–12) from the Additional Scenarios to Explore section of the companion Web site. Use the Solution Design Form to identify a pedagogical model that best fits this scenario. Instructions are provided on the form. Repeat this exercise for different scenarios as needed. Keep your Solution Design Forms. You will use them in Chapter 6. This activity could also be implemented as a group.

RESOURCES

Explore additional resources at the companion Web site (http://www/prenhall.com/dabbagh) for additional examples of online learning environments and learning technologies that support the pedagogical models discussed in this chapter.

REFERENCES

Barrows, H. S. (1985). *How to design a problem-based curriculum for the preclinical years*. New York: Springer Publishing.

Brink, T. (1998). *Groupware: applications*. Retrieved October 21, 2002, from the Usability First Web site at http://www.usabilityfirst.com/groupware/applications.txl

Cognition and Technology Group at Vanderbilt (CTGV). (1992). Technology and the design of generative learning environments. In T. M. Duffy & D. Jonassen (Eds.), *Constructivism and the technology of instruction: A conversation* (pp. 77–89). Hillsdale, NJ: Erlbaum.

Coleman, S. D., Perry, J. D., & Schwen, T. M. (1997). Constructivist instructional development: Reflecting on practice from an alternative paradigm. In C. R. Dills & A. J. Romiszowski (Eds.), *Instructional development paradigms* (pp. 269–282). Englewood Cliffs, NJ: Educational Technology Publications.

Collins, A. (1991). Cognitive apprenticeship and instructional technology. In L. Idol & B. F. Jones (Eds.), *Educational values and cognitive instruction: Implications for reform* (pp. 121–138). Hillsdale, NJ: Erlbaum.

Dede, C. (1996). Emerging technologies and distributed learning. *American Journal of Distance Education, 10*(2), 4–36.

Driscoll, M. M. (1998). *Web-based training: Using technology to design adult learning experiences*. San Francisco: Jossey-Bass/Pfeiffer.

Driscoll, M. M. (2001). Developing synchronous Web-based training for adults in the workplace. In B. H. Khan (Ed.), *Web-based training* (pp. 173–183). Englewood Cliffs, NJ: Educational Technology Publications.

Driscoll, M. P. (1994). *Psychology of learning for instruction*. Boston: Allyn & Bacon.

Driscoll, M. P. (2000). *Psychology of learning for instruction* (2nd ed.). Needham Heights, MA: Allyn & Bacon.

Duffy, T. M, & Cunningham, D. J. (1996). Constructivism: Implications for the design and delivery of instruction. In D. H. Jonassen (Ed.), *Handbook of research for educational communications and technology* (pp. 170–198). New York: Simon & Schuster/Macmillan.

Fitzgerald, G. E., & Semrau, L. P. (1996, April). *Enhancing teacher problem solving skills in behavioral disorders through multimedia case studies*. Paper presented at the American Educational Research Association (AERA) annual conference, New York.

Follows, S. B. (1999). Virtual learning environments. *T.H.E. Journal, 27*(4), 100–106.

Grabowski, B., Koszalka, T., & McCarthy, M. (1998). *Web-enhanced learning environment strategies* (WELES handbook). The Pennsylvania State University/NASA Dryden Flight Research Center.

Hall, B. (1997). *Web-based training cookbook*. New York: Wiley.

Hall, R. (2001). Glossary of terms in web-based training. In B. H. Khan (Ed.), *Web-based training* (pp. 51–58). Englewood Cliffs, NJ: Educational Technology Publications.

Hannafin, M. J. (1992). Emerging technologies, ISD, and learning environments: Critical perspectives. *Educational Technology Research & Development, 40*(1), 49–63.

Hutchins, E., & Hollan, J. (1999) *COGSCI: Distributed cognition syllabus*. Retrieved November 14, 1999, from http://hci.ucsd.edu/131/syllabus/index.html

Jonassen, D. H. (1988, November/December). Designing structured hypertext and structuring access to hypertext. *Educational Technology*, pp.13–16.

Jonassen, D. H. (1991). Objectivism versus constructivism: Do we need a new philosophical paradigm? *Educational Technology Research & Development, 39*(3), 5–14.

Jonassen, D. H. (1996). *Computers in the classroom: Mindtools for critical thinking* (Chap. 10, pp. 237–253). Upper Saddle River, NJ: Merrill/Prentice Halll.

Khan, B. H. (2001). A framework for Web-based training. In B. H. Khan (Ed.), *Web-based training* (pp. 75–97). Englewood Cliffs, NJ: Educational Technology Publications.

Moore, D. R., & Lockee, B. B. (2001). Design strategies for Web-based training: Using bandwidth effectively. In B. H. Khan (Ed.), *Web-based training* (pp. 271–274). Englewood Cliffs, NJ: Educational Technology Publications.

Nardi, B. A. (1996). Studying context: A comparison of activity theory, situated action models, and distributed cognition. In B. A. Nardi (Ed.), *Context and consciousness: Activity theory and human-computer interaction* (pp. 69–102) Cambridge: MIT Press.

Oubenaissa, L., Giardina, M., & Battacharya, M. (2002, July–September). Designing a framework for the implementation of situated online, collaborative, problem-based activity: Operating within a local and multi-cultural learning context. *International Journal on E-Learning, 1*(3), 41–46.

Penrod, J., & Perry, B. (2003, March 30–April 1). *Virtual University—A higher education administration simulation and learning tool*. Paper presented at the Eighth Annual Mid-South Instructional Technology Conference, Teaching, Learning, & Technology, Murfreesboro, TN.

Picciano, A. G. (2001). *Distance learning: Making connections across virtual space and time*. Upper Saddle River, NJ: Merrill/Prentice Hall.

Rieber, L. P. (1992). Computer-based microworlds: A bridge between constructivism and direct instruction. *Educational Technology Research & Development, 40*(1), 93–106.

Rogers, Y. (1997, August). *A brief introduction to distributed cognition*. Retrieved November 11, 1999, from http://www.cogs.susx.ac.uk/users/yvonner/papers/dcog-brief-intro.pdf

Salomon, G. (1993). *Distributed cognitions: Psychological and educational considerations*. New York: Cambridge University Press.

Scardamalia, M., & Bereiter, C. (1994). Computer support for knowledge-building communities. *The Journal of the Learning Sciences, 3*(3), 260–283.

Scardamalia, M., Bereiter, C., McLean, R. S., Swallow, J., & Woodruff, E. (1989). Computer-supported intentional learning environments. *Journal of Educational Computing Research, 5*(1), 51–68.

Schrum, L., & Berenfeld, B. (1997). *Teaching and learning in the Information Age*. Boston: Allyn & Bacon.

Software systems and their development. (2002). Retrieved October 21, 2002, from The Open University, Computing Department Web site: http://mcs.open.ac.uk/Computing/html/new_courses/m301/glossary.htm

Spiro, J. R., Feltovich, P. J., Jacobson, M. J., & Coulson, R. L. (1992). Knowledge representation, content specification, and the development of skill in situation specific knowledge assembly:

Some constructivist issues as they relate to cognitive flexibility theory and hypertext. In T. M. Duffy & D. H. Jonassen (Eds.), *Constructivism and the technology of instruction* (pp. 121–128). Hillsdale, NJ: Erlbaum.

Stein, D. (1998). *Situated learning in adult education.* Columbus, OH: ERIC Clearinghouse on Adult Career and Vocational Education. (ERIC Document Reproduction Service No. ED418250)

Streaming media. (2002). Retrieved October 21, 2002, from the Whatis.com Target Search, the TechTarget Network Web site: http://whatis.techtarget.com/definition/0, , sid9_gci753540,00.html

Virtual chat rooms useful for DL. (1997, September). *T.H.E. Journal Online: Technological Horizons in Education.* Retrieved October 27, 2002, from http://www.thejournal.com/magazine/vault/A1967.cfm

Walker, J. R. (1997). *Center for Teaching Enhancement Workshop on Synchronous Communication.* Retrieved May 2003 from http://www.cas.usf.edu/english/walker/papers/cte/commands.html

The WebQuest page. (1997). Retrieved July 1997 from http://webquest.sdsu.edu/webquest.html

Wilson, B., & Cole, P. (1991). A review of cognitive teaching models. *Educational Technology Research & Development, 39*(4), 47–64.

INSTRUCTIONAL STRATEGIES AND THEIR ROLE IN DESIGNING AUTHENTIC LEARNING ACTIVITIES FOR ONLINE LEARNING

6

After completing this chapter, you should understand the following:

- The relationship among instructional strategies, pedagogical models, and learning theory

- The significance of authentic learning activities and their impact on instructional strategies

- The types of instructional strategies that support constructivist-based pedagogical models

- The intersection and alignment of exploratory, dialogic, and supportive instructional strategies

- How to implement exploratory, dialogic, and supportive instructional strategies in online learning environments

- How to map instructional strategies to pedagogical models, Web-based technologies, and Web-based features

CONSIDER THE FOLLOWING SCENARIO:

Naming John Doe: The Forensic Pathology Examiner, by Tina Minor[1]

Television, detective novels, and the media have glamorized the profession of forensic pathology—so much so that high school students interested in seeking a career in this field have no realistic appreciation of its methods or its role in crime solving. Investigative agencies like the Federal Bureau of Investigation (FBI) have a need for skillful dedicated forensic pathologists and have developed a workshop to introduce high school seniors with a strong science background to the realities and challenges of the field of forensic science.

Students participating in this workshop will be divided into small groups and given an authentic case of a "John Doe"—the skeletal remains of an unidentified person. The case, background, and resources will be presented through the Web. A software assistant, "Dr. Y. C. Bones," will provide students with guidance as they research the case. After completing their background research, the high school students will visit an FBI crime laboratory, where they can perform a "forensic examination" using a skeletal mock-up and diagnostic equipment. A forensic examiner will guide the groups through the examination process. The groups will then present their findings to the class and their mentor forensic examiner. Required findings include determining the gender, approximate age, height, and ethnicity of the deceased, and estimating the time of death. On the basis of their findings, the students must select a likely positive identification of the deceased from a mock list of missing persons. The examiner and the class will critique each finding and allow the groups to defend their findings. Students will also be required to explain the reasoning process that led them to the solution of the case.

Learning Outcomes

Students completing the workshop will do the following:

- Develop a realistic appreciation of the forensic pathologist's role
- Understand the processes, methods, tools, and equipment used to gather and analyze criminal evidence related to skeletal remains
- Comprehend the relevance of sciences such as biology, physiology, and anthropology to forensic science

---

[1] *Disclaimer:* This work was created by Tina Minor as partial requirements for the course EDIT 732 in the fall of 1999 under the direction of Dr. Nada Dabbagh for the Graduate School of Education at George Mason University. This project is fiction and is not endorsed by or in any way affiliated with the Federal Bureau of Investigation (FBI). The organization, the FBI, is used to "authenticate" a real-world context used in this scenario. Use of and reference to the Federal Bureau of Investigation (FBI) was for educational purposes only. There are references to actual places and locations in the state of Virginia. The scientific and specific forensic information relating to the skeletal remains in the scenario are based on a true case. However, any names, characters, and incidents discussed in this scenario are either the product of the author's imagination or used fictitiously, and any resemblance to actual persons, living or dead, or actual events is entirely coincidental.

- Use appropriate data-gathering and documentation methods
- Collect and analyze supporting evidence needed to make a positive identification of skeletal remains and to link the remains to missing persons
- Develop critical thinking skills by critiquing the other students' findings and reflecting on their own findings on the basis of such critiques

Take a moment and think about how you might implement this scenario as an online learning environment. Which of the pedagogical models discussed in Chapter 5 would you select? Which instructional strategies apply? Which online learning technologies would you use to implement these instructional strategies? Which Web features are emphasized?

This chapter covers the second key component of online learning: instructional strategies. Also covered is their relation to pedagogical models and learning theory and their implications for the design of online learning environments.

INTRODUCTION

In Chapter 5, we discussed constructivist-based pedagogical models and their instructional characteristics and classified these models into three types of learning environments—exploratory, dialogic, and integrational—to facilitate an association between the instructional characteristics of these models and learning technologies. In this chapter, we continue to elaborate on the enactment phase of the Integrative Learning Design Framework (ILDF) for Online Learning by discussing the selection of specific instructional strategies that align with the characteristics of constructivist-based pedagogical models and the enactment of these strategies by using features of online delivery systems. A process that synthesizes the instructional characteristics of the models discussed in Chapter 5 into selected instructional strategies is provided. We begin this process by further examining the Naming John Doe scenario.

The Naming John Doe scenario has all the attributes or instructional characteristics of problem-based learning (PBL). Do you agree? In Table 6.1, we restate these characteristics and map elements of the scenario to each characteristic. On the basis of the mapping shown in Table 6.1, are you convinced that this scenario aligns with the characteristics of PBL? If not, select another pedagogical model from Chapter 5 and repeat the mapping exercise to determine whether the instructional characteristics of the model you selected better fit the elements of this scenario. Either way, the important question is this: How can you implement this model as an online learning environment to ensure that the students will achieve the stated learning outcomes? To implement this model or any pedagogical model in an online learning context, you need to identify specific instructional strategies that support the model characteristics and to enact these strategies by using Web-based technologies. We begin by defining instructional strategies and discussing their relation to pedagogical models and learning theories.

Table 6.1   Mapping the Instructional Characteristics of Problem-Based Learning to the Naming John Doe Scenario

Instructional Characteristics of Problem-Based Learning (see Chapter 5)

1. Promote ownership of the learning process (the problem context motivates students to "own" the problem; students must define the problem).

    The problem context is authentic and related to students' interests (students who enroll in this workshop are already thinking about a career in forensic science). Therefore, the problem context should motivate them to own the problem.

2. Assume no formal prior knowledge in the content area(s) for which the problem is intended.

    Students have no prior knowledge in forensic science.

3. Promote a student-centered, group learning environment.

    Students can complete all the proposed activities in groups and engage in group discussions about the problem issues.

4. Promote self-directed learning (students have to set their own learning goals and choose strategies for achieving these goals).

    Because the case, background, and resources are presented through the Web and Dr. Y. C. Bones will provide guidance, students can individually research the case information, setting their own learning goals and strategies for achieving these goals (e.g., which resources to browse, in what order, what additional information they determine is needed).

5. Promote authentic learning through real-world problems that are ill structured (do not have one solution or solution path).

    The problem is a real-world problem, and no solutions are apparent. On the basis of how each group of students analyzes the case information and the results of their forensic examination, different solutions and solution paths may be formulated. The problem is therefore ill structured.

6. Emphasize problem solving as the primary learning goal by allowing the problem to serve as the center for instruction.

    The scenario emphasizes problem-solving skills. Students learn about forensic pathology while researching the problem information and using the tools of the trade to arrive at a viable solution.

7. Promote self-reflection as the primary assessment tool.

    This characteristic may not be as apparent as the others from just reading the brief scenario introduction. However, the fact that students are gathering information and performing investigative tasks to solve the problem implicitly means that students are reflecting on their findings as they proceed with the investigation and are critically judging the results. In addition, when students are asked at the end to explain to their peers and mentor their reasoning process that led to the identification of the skeletal remains, they are reflecting on their learning process and on how they arrived at their final solution.

8. Allow students to generate hypotheses, set their learning goals, apply their own learning strategies, and solve the problem through searching for and identifying relevant resources.

    This is scenario lends itself to this characteristic. Students are generating hypotheses individually and in groups each time they research the problem data and perform related tasks. This is one of the hallmarks of problem-based learning.

Table 6.1   Mapping the Instructional Characteristics of Problem-Based Learning to the Naming John
Doe Scenario (*Continued*)

9. Allow learners to integrate, use, and reuse newly learned information in context.
    Again, this scenario lends itself well to this characteristic, allowing students to integrate information from several sources and to reuse information relative to the hypothesis generated. Students are continuously revisiting the hypothesis in light of the new information collected or derived.

10. Support recursive, iterative cycling through a reasoning process until a hypothesis is reached (provide scaffolding for learning a reasoning process).
    This characteristic is supported in this scenario for the same reasons as in Item 9. The final solution is reached inductively through a recursive process of reasoning through the data collected.

11. Promote facilitation and scaffolding through instructor guidance (the instructor serves as a tutor and coach).
    The scenario allows for two coaches: a computer coach (Dr. Y. C. Bones) and a human coach (the mentor forensic examiner). Both these experts act as coaches, guiding the students in the problem-solving process.

WHAT ARE INSTRUCTIONAL STRATEGIES?

Instructional strategies are what instructors or instructional systems do to facilitate student learning. Jonassen, Grabinger, and Harris (1991) described instructional strategies as "the plans and techniques that the instructor/instructional designer uses to engage the learner and facilitate learning" (p. 34). Instructional strategies operationalize pedagogical models. In other words, they put the models into practice. When implications of learning theory for education are discussed, instructional strategies are the specifics of how these implications are to be translated into instructional procedures (Shuell, 1980) so that the result is "a plan, method, or series of activities, aimed at obtaining a specific goal" (Jonassen et al., 1991, p. 31). Instructional strategies are therefore derived from pedagogical models, which in turn are derived from learning theory.

To illustrate, we provided in Table 5.1 five examples of learning theories and their implications for instruction. For example, given behaviorism as the learning theory, the implications for instruction revealed three specific instructional strategies: **shaping**—teaching a goal behavior by reinforcing successive approximations to this behavior; **chaining**—establishing complex behaviors made up of discrete, simpler behaviors already known to the learner; and fading—reducing, or fading out, **discriminative stimuli** used to initially establish a desired behavior (Driscoll, 2000). In addition, principles of reinforcement (e.g., positive and negative reinforcement to strengthen or weaken the desired behavior) were identified as important instructional implications for behaviorism and are considered instructional tactics that facilitate the implementation of the three key strategies of shaping, chaining, and fading.

In the case of Ausubel's **meaningful reception learning (MRL),** also known as *subssumption,* or *assimilation, theory,* the instructional implications included (a) activating the learners' prior knowledge, (b) using analogies and metaphors, (c) using **advance organizers,** and (d) making instructional materials meaningful (see Table 5.1). These four instructional implications can be described as instructional strategies derived from this learning theory. For example, instructors who want to adopt an MRL approach to teaching can use advance organizers such as lesson objectives, outlines, and summaries to present content. The focus of this chapter is on the instructional implications of situated cognition and constructivism because their principles align with our conceptualization of online learning as defined in Chapter 1.

PEDAGOGICAL MODELS AND INSTRUCTIONAL STRATEGIES

The pedagogical models resulting from situated cognition theory and constructivism outlined in Table 5.1 included (a) learning communities, or knowledge-building communities; (b) cognitive apprenticeships; (c) anchored instruction, or situated learning; (d) PBL; (e) microworlds, simulations, and virtual learning environments; (f) cognitive flexibility hypertexts; and (g) computer-supported intentional learning environments (CSILEs). As discussed in Chapter 5, all these models subscribe to the following five main instructional conditions or design principles (Driscoll, 2000):

1. Embed learning in complex, realistic, and relevant contexts.
2. Provide for social negotiation as an integral part of learning.
3. Support multiple perspectives and the use of multiple modes of representation.
4. Encourage ownership in learning.
5. Nurture self-awareness of the knowledge construction process. (p. 382)

In this chapter, these instructional implications and the specific instructional characteristics identified for each of the seven models described in Chapter 5 are synthesized into a set of explicit instructional strategies to provide a blueprint of how the online learning developer can implement constructivist-based pedagogical models in an instructional context. The chapter also covers how these instructional strategies can be operationalized, or enacted, through the use of learning technologies that support online learning and Web-based instruction (WBI).

The first instructional implication of constructivist-based pedagogical models is to "embed learning in complex, realistic, and relevant contexts." This feature is also an instructional characteristic of PBL (see Characteristic 5 in Table 6.1). In the Naming John Doe scenario, this instructional characteristic is supported through the provision of an authentic learning activity (in this case, identifying the skeletal remains of John Doe). Promoting authentic learning activities is an instructional characteristic of all constructivist-based models discussed in Chapter 5. So, what are authentic learning activities? Why are they emphasized in constructivist-based models, and what instructional strategies are instantiated when we provide authentic learning activities in instructional contexts?

AUTHENTIC LEARNING ACTIVITIES

Authentic learning activities are learning tasks anchored in a realistic setting in which the focus is on solving a problem rather than learning a body of content. Students apply their current body of knowledge and adapt it to new situations and problems, and, by doing so, they extend their body of knowledge in meaningful ways. Reeves, Herrington, and Oliver (2002, p. 2) identified the following 10 attributes of authentic learning activities:

1. Authentic activities have real-world relevance.
2. Authentic activities are ill defined, which requires students to define the tasks and subtasks needed to complete the activity.
3. Authentic activities comprise complex tasks for students to investigate during a sustained time period.
4. Authentic activities provide the opportunity for students to use a variety of resources to examine the task from different perspectives.
5. Authentic activities provide learners with the opportunity to collaborate.
6. Authentic activities provide students with the opportunity to reflect and involve their beliefs and values.
7. Authentic activities can be integrated and applied across different subject areas and extend beyond domain-specific outcomes.
8. Authentic activities are seamlessly integrated with assessment.
9. Authentic activities create polished products valuable in their own right rather than as preparation for something else.
10. Authentic activities allow competing solutions and diversity of outcomes.

These 10 attributes suggest that authentic learning activities support problem solving, collaboration, reflection, exploration, and exposure to multiple perspectives. For example, the second attribute of authentic learning activities is this: "Authentic activities are ill defined, with requires students to define the tasks and subtasks needed to complete the activity." This statement is an articulation of a problem-solving process. Ill-defined activities do not clearly specify all aspects of the situation or the information needed to solve the situation (Jonassen, 1997). Therefore, students need to define the problem space (make assumptions about the constraints or current state of the situation and the criteria of an acceptable goal state) and the initial tasks and subtasks needed to manipulate the problem space (transform the initial state to a goal state), such as identifying learning needs and action plans (van Merrienboer, 1997).

In PBL, problem solving is a primary learning goal (see Characteristic 6 in Table 6.1). The Naming John Doe scenario engages students in problem solving through the provision of an authentic learning activity (identifying the skeletal remains of John Doe). Students are provided with background information about the case, relevant resources, investigative tools, and expert coaching to help them *solve* the problem. In addition, problem-solving activities promote collaboration among peers, encourage a sense of community, and emphasize approaching the problem from different directions and multiple perspectives. Students in the Naming John Doe scenario are divided into groups and asked to reason through the problem together, during which time they generate a hypothesis, reflect on their findings, and negotiate solutions. The students are also exposed to multiple perspectives within their groups (from different individuals) and across groups (when students are asked to critique each other's solutions at the end). See Characteristics 3, 7, 8, 9, and 10 in Table 6.1.

The preceding analysis suggests that providing authentic learning activities should be a primary consideration when practitioners are designing learning environments that subscribe to a constructivist-based pedagogy. Authentic learning activities, if designed with the 10 attributes in mind, should promote collaboration, reflection, problem solving, multiple perspectives, and hypothesis generation, as well as other exploratory and dialogic (conversational) learning activities. This analysis leads us to the identification of 13 instructional strategies that we believe are essential for effectively implementing constructivist-based pedagogical models. These strategies are also supported by the research findings given in Chapter 3. These strategies and their alignment and intersection are presented in the next section.

INSTRUCTIONAL STRATEGIES THAT SUPPORT CONSTRUCTIVIST-BASED PEDAGOGICAL MODELS

The following 13 instructional strategies embody the instructional characteristics and implications of constructivist-based pedagogical models and align with our conceptualization of online learning as defined in Chapter 1:

1. Promote authentic learning activities.
2. Promote problem solving.
3. Promote collaboration and social negotiation.
4. Promote exploration.
5. Promote hypothesis generation.
6. Promote role-playing activities.
7. Promote articulation.
8. Promote reflection.
9. Promote multiple perspectives.
10. Promote modeling and explaining.
11. Promote coaching.
12. Promote scaffolding.
13. Promote self-directed learning.

The reason for using the word *promote* in the preceding list is to remind you that instructional strategies are what instructors or instructional systems *do* to facilitate student learning. The concept of *doing* is what differentiates strategies from the characteristics or attributes of the models presented in Chapter 5. Characteristics or attributes are static; they describe a concept. However, strategies are dynamic; they invoke action, enactment, or implementation. In addition, these instructional strategies are not discrete. They are highly interdependent and intersect vertically and horizontally, which provides a hierarchical and lateral alignment. Figure 6.1 demonstrates this relationship.

Figure 6.1 Intersection and Alignment of Instructional Strategies That Support Constructivist-Based Pedagogical Models

Figure 6.1 shows that promoting authentic learning activities is a focal or core instructional strategy that supports or enables all other instructional strategies. Figure 6.1 also shows that promoting self-directed learning is a consequence, or an outcome, of the collective implementation of all instructional strategies. Figure 6.1 shows that instructional strategies converge toward promoting authentic learning activities and diverge toward promoting self-directed learning. This convergent–divergent dynamic represents the hierarchical intersection or alignment of these instructional strategies. In addition, three clusters or groups of instructional strategies can be seen in Figure 6.1. These clusters overlap. The overlap represents the lateral intersection or alignment of these instructional strategies. The first cluster—exploratory strategies—includes strategies that promote exploratory-type activities (engaging students in problem solving, exploration, hypotheses generation, and role-playing). The second cluster—dialogic strategies—includes strategies that promote dialogic, or discursive, activities (engaging students in articulation, reflection, collaboration, and multiple perspectives). These two clusters align with the organization of the constructivist-based pedagogical models presented in Table 5.2, which represents a mapping between models, learning technologies, and theoretical constructs. The third cluster—supportive strategies—includes strategies typically enacted by the expert, coach, mentor, instructor, or embedded performance support system, with the goal of modeling the desired performance, skill, or process and observing and supporting learners during their execution of a learning task. As depicted in Table 5.1, the instructor's role in constructivist learning environments is to provide scaffolding and create a resource-rich learning environment to support learning. This is the goal of supportive strategies.

The main idea represented in Figure 6.1 is that authentic learning activities, if designed appropriately according to the 10 attributes identified previously, should engage learners in problem solving, collaboration, social negotiation, exploration, reflection, and consideration of multiple perspectives. When learners are engaged in such activities by design, other activities are invoked, such as role-playing, hypotheses generation, and articulation. In addition, for authentic learning activities to be sustained, the learning environment should include coaching, modeling and explaining, and scaffolding. Collectively, the enactment of these instructional strategies will lead to self-directed learning, which is an important characteristic of the successful online learner, as discussed in Chapter 2. Therefore, these instructional strategies are highly interdependent.

So, how does the online learning developer implement these instructional strategies in online learning or Web-based instructional contexts? In the following subsections, we define each of the instructional strategies illustrated in Figure 6.1 and describe how each strategy can be supported or implemented by using online learning technologies. The selection or promotion of instructional strategies should be grounded in the characteristics of pedagogical models applied to the specific instructional or training context. Learning technologies are then used to enact the selected instructional strategies. The companion Web site for this book (http://www.prenhall.com/dabbagh) provides an interactive interface that allows you to navigate through these 13 instructional strategies and view examples of how each strategy can be enacted in online learning through the use of course management systems (CMSs) such as WebCT and Blackboard. In Chapter 9, we discuss CMSs and their features in detail. We recommend that you read Chapter 9 prior to browsing the interactive Web site if you are not familiar with CMSs and their features.

Promotion of Authentic Learning Activities: A Core Instructional Strategy

As discussed previously, promoting authentic learning activities is the core of all instructional strategies. An authentic activity engages the learner in a realistic and meaningful task that is relevant to the learner's interests and goals. Engaging learners in meaningful and relevant tasks allows them to see the direct implications of their actions and to apply the knowledge they gain in real-world situations (Wilson & Cole, 1996). In general, authentic learning tasks are presented in a learning environment through the use of scenarios, cases, or problems, similar to the scenario presented at the beginning of this chapter and to others provided in Chapter 5. Cases, problems, or scenarios that are used as a stimulus for authentic activity must have some of the important characteristics of real-life problem solving, including ill-defined and complex goals, an opportunity for the detection of relevant versus irrelevant information, active or generative engagement in finding and defining problems as well as in solving them, involvement of the student's beliefs and values, and an opportunity to engage in collaborative interpersonal activities (Young, 1993, p. 45). These attributes mirror the 10 attributes of authentic learning activities identified by Reeves et al. (2002).

If you reflect on the scenarios presented in Chapter 5, you will find that most of them possess these attributes. You can use the 10 attributes identified by Reeves et al. as a checklist for determining the extent to which these scenarios or other scenarios reflect these attributes. Jonassen (1999) recommended that, to design such scenarios, instructional designers examine what experienced practitioners in the field of study do rather than what textbooks preach. For example, if chemistry is the subject of study, the instructional developer should examine what chemists do in the real world (e.g., where they work, the types of tasks they engage in, the pressing research issues in the field). Examining what practitioners do can provide a variety of ideas for designing an authentic learning activity. Another important consideration is ensuring that the authentic activity aligns with the characteristics of the target audience who will interact with the activity. For example, each scenario presented in Chapter 5 was intended for a specific audience. Some of the scenarios were intended for middle school and high school students, others for college students, others for adult learners, and still others for corporate trainees. Therefore, understanding the characteristics of the target audience is paramount because the authentic activity should align with the target audience's interests, goals, and prior knowledge. In addition, understanding the learning outcomes and the instructional content is important. These three considerations are largely determined in the exploration phase of the IDLF for Online Learning presented in Chapter 4.

Last, the online learning developer should understand the learning technologies that support the development and delivery of authentic learning activities. Therefore, with this last consideration in mind, which learning technologies or features do you think are appropriate for designing authentic learning activities such as scenarios, problems, or cases?

In Chapter 5, we described several learning technologies that support the implementation of exploratory learning environments. These technologies included hypertext and hypermedia, graphics, animation, direct manipulation interfaces, and digital video and audio. All these technologies are powerful tools for presenting authentic cases, problems, and scenarios online. For example,

- The online learning developer can use graphics to present elements of the case to make it more realistic (e.g., a picture of the skeletal remains of John Doe would make the Naming John Doe case more authentic).
- The online learning developer can use **digital audio and video** to bring the case to life (e.g., a narrator's voice describing how the skeletal remains of John Doe were found, or a video segment on how an archaeological dig revealed skeletal remains of a historical ruler, would make the case more authentic).
- The online learning developer can use animation to add context to the case (e.g., an animated slide show in which a pointer points to all the tools and diagnostic equipment can show what a forensic examination laboratory looks like).
- The online learning developer can use hypertext and hypermedia to provide elaboration on key text items in the case narrative (e.g., the words *Dr. Y. C. Bones, forensic examiner,* and *FBI* can be linked to a description or a picture of each).
- The online learning developer can develop a direct manipulation interface by using authoring tools (see Chapter 8) to allow learners to immerse themselves in, and manipulate, certain aspects of the case environment (e.g., learners using such an interface can "virtually walk through" a forensic lab and "grab" diagnostic tools and equipment, test their functions on skeletal remains, and observe their impact).

Examples of Web-based cases or scenarios that have been developed with the preceding learning technologies are provided at the companion Web site for this book (http://www.prenhall.com/dabbagh). Note that the underlying or inherent features of the Web that enable the implementation and delivery of authentic learning activities are hypermedia, multimedia, and interactivity. A discussion of the inherent features of the Internet and the World Wide Web and the distinction between Web features and Web technologies is provided subsequently in this chapter.

Exploratory Instructional Strategies

Exploratory instructional strategies include promoting problem solving, exploration, hypothesis generation, and role-playing. In the following subsections, we define each of these strategies and provide examples of their implementation in online learning environments.

Promoting problem solving   Problem solving can be defined as a heuristic search process in a problem space (Newell & Simon, 1972) or as "any goal-directed sequence of cognitive operations" (Anderson, 1980, p. 257). Problem-solving activities place more emphasis on learning how to learn than on learning specific content. In problem-solving activities, the process of problem solving—such as the learner's ability to form a hypothesis, find and sort information, think critically about information, ask questions, and reach a resolution or solution—becomes more important (Roblyer, Edwards, & Havriluk, 1996). When problem-solving activities are placed in an authentic context, learners learn how to apply their knowledge under appropriate conditions. Learners see the implications of new knowledge and are more likely to retrieve the newly acquired knowledge in the same real-world, problem-based situation (Wilson & Cole, 1996). Examples of pedagogical models that emphasize problem-solving activities are PBL and anchored instruction. These models were also classified as exploratory learning environments in Chapter 5.

Learning technologies that support problem-solving activities include asynchronous and synchronous communication technologies, groupware and document-sharing technologies, hypertext and hypermedia, search engines, and online databases and knowledge repositories. The following learning activities are examples of how problem solving can be facilitated in online learning environments:

- The online learning developer can present a Web-based case or problem in which elements of the case are linked to resources or additional data through **hypermedia linkage.**
- The online learning developer can provide an asynchronous discussion forum in which each team can discuss the case or challenge.
- The online learning developer can provide a synchronous discussion area where each team can discuss case issues that require real-time brainstorming and information sharing.

- The online learning developer can provide, using document-sharing technologies or groupware, a Web-based area where groups can work on a document that articulates their solutions to a case or a problem.
- The online learning developer can provide links to **online databases** and **knowledge repositories**, where students can search for relevant case information.

The underlying Web features that enable the implementation and delivery of problem-solving activities are asynchronous and synchronous communication, hypermedia, archivability (the Web is considered an archive of information), and online searching.

Promoting exploration Exploration encourages "students to try out different strategies and hypotheses and observe their effects" (Collins, 1991, p. 135). In exploratory learning, the instructor provides limited instruction and guidance and the emphasis is on student-generated learning through exploring and discovering information. "This puts students in control of problem solving" (Collins, 1991, p. 135). Therefore, exploration and problem solving are closely related. In addition, Collins claimed that through exploration, students learn how to set achievable goals and manage the pursuit of these goals. They learn to set and try out hypotheses and to seek knowledge independently. Exploration can also be considered a comprehension-monitoring learning strategy (Weinstein & Mayer, 1986) because it forces students to monitor their own learning through predicting, hypothesizing, and experimenting. These activities support self-directed learning.

Real-world exploration is always an attractive option for promoting this instructional strategy. However, constraints of cost, time, and safety sometimes prohibit exploratory learning in realistic settings (Wilson & Cole, 1996). Simulations, microworlds, WebQuests, and virtual learning environments are excellent examples of how exploratory activities can be implemented by using technology to minimize the risks and costs of real-world exploration. Examples of these technologies were provided in Chapter 5. In addition, situated learning and PBL models promote exploratory learning by engaging students in discovery, or inquiry-based, learning. In discovery learning, learners are provided with a scientific-like inquiry or an authentic problem in a given content area and asked to generate a hypothesis, gather relevant information from a variety of resources, and provide solutions, action plans, recommendations, and interpretations of the situation. Cognitive flexibility hypertexts (CFHs) also support exploratory learning by enabling learners to browse multiple perspectives of a complex issue in a hypermedia learning environment using cases and themes. Therefore, promoting exploration is largely supported through the provision of authentic activities or tasks as described previously in this chapter.

In addition to the examples provided under promoting authentic activities, the following learning activities promote exploration through the use of Web-based technologies:

- The online learning developer can use Web-based authoring tools and **scripting languages** to develop self-contained instructional modules such as microworlds, simulations, and virtual learning environments that engage students in exploratory-type activities.

- The online learning developer can provide Web-based resources through hypermedia and multimedia links to support students' exploratory activities.
- The online learning developer can provide a link to a search engine at the course Web site to enable students to search for and explore Web-based resources.
- The online learning developer can provide links to online databases and knowledge repositories that provide real-time data such as up-to-date weather information and other scientific data and statistics.

The underlying Web features that enable the implementation and delivery of exploratory learning activities are hypermedia, multimedia, online searching, and interactivity.

Promoting hypothesis generation Promoting hypothesis generation is an instructional strategy that supports concept acquisition by setting forth tentative hypotheses about the attributes that seem to define a concept, then testing specific instances against these hypotheses (Bruner, Goodnow, & Austin, 1956). For example, when students are learning about the concept of the *density of elements,* they are often asked to hypothesize about what would happen when oil and water are mixed in a container. Does the oil sink to the bottom? Why? Or, when learning about the concept of *gravity,* they might be asked to hypothesize which object falls to the ground faster, a stone or a feather. Therefore, the creation of hypotheses is a type of formal scientific reasoning that is facilitated through scientific inquiry (Mayer, 1987). If an adequate and variant number of "what if" examples are provided, hypothesis generation can lead to concept learning because learners can generalize their findings, which results in a working model or concept that can be further refined and compared with expert models.

In schools, science labs have been the conventional setting in which students are encouraged to generate and test hypotheses when they are learning about science concepts. However, with the recent advances in technology, a variety of educational software, such as games, simulations, and microworlds, is now available for students to use to generate hypotheses and test their ideas. In addition, hypothesis generation is no longer limited to learning science concepts. For example, SimCity is a simulation or game in which students can learn about what is involved in building a city. Students can manipulate variables such as the budget, infrastructure, housing, population, zoning restrictions, electricity, public facilities, hospitals, and so forth, and make decisions about the quantity, quality, and architectural design implications of these variables and their interdependencies. When students make unsound decisions, the simulation prompts them to reconsider their decisions on the basis of credible and real-world consequences. In SimCity, students can play out "what if" scenarios, experience the implications of their scenarios, receive informative feedback, readjust variables, make mistakes, learn from their mistakes, and apply what they have learned, all in a virtual environment that is as close as possible to the real thing. Students take ownership of the learning process by assuming authentic roles and taking charge of the responsibilities associated with these roles. The complexity of the learning environment in a game or simulation such as SimCity depends on the sophistication of the underlying program, which controls the number of variables available for manipulation and the scope of interaction among the variables.

Promoting hypothesis generation is accomplished mainly by using exploratory- or inquiry-type pedagogical models, which include microworlds, simulations, immersive virtual learning environments, WebQuests, PBL, and other exploratory-type models discussed in Chapter 5. Promoting hypothesis generation and promoting exploration work hand in hand to help students acquire problem-solving and decision-making skills.

In Web-based or online learning environments, promoting hypothesis generation can be facilitated through the following learning technologies:

- The online learning developer can provide links for **plug-ins**—such as the Macromedia plug-in Shockwave—to engage students in a self-contained instructional module such as a microworld that has been developed with an **authoring tool**.
- The online learning developer can use Web-based animation technology and graphics to present different images or animation plays of a scientific phenomenon and ask students to hypothesize which animation sequence or image applies and why.
- The online learning developer can use digital audio and video to present unfinished excerpts of real-world events and occurrences so that learners can provide an ending to the scenario and a rationale for why they think it should end the way they envisioned.
- The online learning developer can use **dynamic Web pages** to provide students with the ability to query information databases and predict events.

The underlying Web features that enable the implementation and delivery of hypothesis generation are hypermedia, multimedia, online searching, and interactivity.

Promoting role-playing Promoting role-playing is an instructional strategy that allows learners to assume practitioner and professional roles—such as scientists, physicians, historians, and salespersons—and act out situations that these professionals face in the real world. Learners can imagine that they are other people in different situations then make decisions as situations change (Heinich, Molenda, & Russell, 1993). The Virtual University simulation example (http://www.virtual-u.org; Penrod & Perry, 2003) and the Cell WebQuest scenario (both presented in Chapter 5) are examples of situations in which learners assume real-world roles to demonstrate and practice their skills. Role-playing allows learners to practice their knowledge and skills in a simulated real-world situation and immediately observe the results of their actions, which prompts reflection and meaningful learning. Learners bring their experiences into the role-playing situation and consequently gain "ownership" of the learning process. The goal is for the learner to accomplish a mission or task associated with his or her role in the scenario. To survive in a "role," the learner must acquire particular skills and knowledge. At this point, learning occurs. The learning environment that supports role-playing activities is often fictitious or metaphorical but also engaging enough that it captivates and sustains the learner's attention. In addition to learning the particular skills and knowledge of the "role," the student acquires social skills, communication skills, and interpersonal skills, which are characteristics of self-directed learning.

In Web-based or online learning, simulated role-playing can be facilitated through learning technologies or delivery models such as a multiuser domain (MUD) or a multiuser domain—object oriented (MOO), as described in Chapter 5. Tapped In (http://www.tappedin.org) is an example of a knowledge network that supports MUD and MOO models (see Chapter 5). Another example of a MOO is a 3-D educational world created by using Activeworlds. Activeworlds is a software application that allows users to build a 3-D virtual world on the Internet for other users to visit and engage in a powerful interactive experience. Educators can build a 3-D "educational world" complete with social spaces, buildings, rooms, and all sorts of objects and artifacts. Students participating in these virtual worlds can take field trips, perform experiments, design products, explore content, and debate issues by taking on specific roles and interacting in real time over the Internet.

Examples of such "educational worlds" include science labs and clinical practice labs (e.g., Virtual Veterinary Clinic). Students assume roles as scientists, chemists, lab technicians, and veterinarians, and they interact with one another and the learning tasks within these 3-D virtual environments. Appropriate roles can be predetermined for each "virtual world" so that when students enter a world, they must select a role from a pull-down menu list to participate. These roles are known as *avatars*. Avatars are identities, or personae, that identify the participant in a virtual world. Avatars can be programmed to run, jump, fly, dance, and express a host of emotions (e.g., smile, cry, etc.). (Visit the companion Web site—http://www.prenhall.com/dabbagh—for more examples.)

Pedagogical models discussed in Chapter 5 that support role-playing activities are communities of practice, CSILEs, cognitive apprenticeships, and virtual learning environments, among others. In addition to being facilitated by MOOs and MUDs, role-playing activities can be implemented in online learning through the use of digital audio and video, discussion forums, groupware, computer conferencing, videoconferencing, and animation technologies. The underlying Web features that enable the implementation of role-playing activities include synchronous and asynchronous communication, multimedia, and interactivity.

Dialogic Instructional Strategies

Promoting articulation   Promoting articulation involves "having students think about their actions and give reasons for their decisions and strategies, thus making their tacit knowledge more explicit or overt" (Wilson & Cole, 1996, p. 606). In other words, when students are provided with opportunities to articulate their knowledge or understanding of something, they are explaining to others what they know. As students articulate their knowledge to one another, they share multiple perspectives and generalize their understanding and knowledge so that it is applicable in different contexts (Collins, 1991).

Articulation can also be described as a complex elaboration strategy (Weinstein & Mayer, 1986). Weinstein and Mayer presented the following learner activities or tasks as means of articulating personal knowledge: summarizing, paraphrasing, creating analogies, engaging in generative note taking (note taking initiated by the learner rather than directed by the teacher), and answering questions. Of these activities, creating analogies, engaging in generative note taking, and answering questions are most relevant to learning in a CFH (see Chapter 5).

Promoting articulation can also be achieved by various other means, which include working in groups, discussing and debating the issues, reporting back, presenting findings, and negotiating and defending knowledge acquired through learning environments (Oliver, Herrington, & Omari, 1996). In the Naming John Doe scenario, all these activities are supported. *Can you identify the specific elements of the scenario that support these activities?*

Pedagogical models that particularly emphasize or promote articulation are **dialogic learning environments** (see Table 5.2) because the focus of such environments is on discourse, dialogue, and social negotiation. Learning technologies that support the implementation of articulation include e-mail, bulletin boards, discussion forums, Listservs, computer-conferencing tools, document-sharing tools, groupware, virtual chat, Internet relay chat (IRC), MOOs, and MUDs. These technologies can all be subsumed under asynchronous and synchronous communication technologies (see Chapter 2) and are powerful tools for promoting articulation in online learning environments. For example,

- The online learning developer can design an activity that engages students in online discussions through **bulletin boards** or discussion forums. Structured online discussions can be designed to engage students in discussing a subject matter area or a related topic for a finite time period. Facilitators (moderators) of online discussions are assigned to post engaging questions, prompt meaningful responses, keep the discussion focused on the topic, and provide a synthesis of the discussion at the end. Students engaged in online discussions are articulating their understanding of the issues (making tacit knowledge explicit) by answering questions and explaining to others what they know. Protocols and rubrics for structuring and evaluating online discussions are provided in Chapter 7.

- The online learning developer can design activities that engage groups in brainstorming tasks during **virtual chat** sessions. Students working in a group to solve a case or problem can begin strategizing and teaming in real time by sharing their ideas, hypotheses, and action plans collectively.

- The online learning developer can provide, using document-sharing technologies or groupware, a Web-based area where groups can work on a document that articulates their solutions to problems.

- The online learning developer can provide an **e-mail** area at a course Web site designated specifically for students to ask the instructor questions about emergent problems and ad hoc issues (issues that arise).

The underlying Web features that enable the implementation and delivery of the preceding learning activities are asynchronous and synchronous communication.

Promoting reflection   Reflective thinking involves analyzing and making judgments about what happened in the past as a way to give a situation new meaning. Promoting reflection, or reflective thinking, involves asking students to review what they have done, analyze their performance, and compare it with that of experts and peers (Collins, 1991). Reflection and articulation are closely related. Wilson and Cole (1996) pointed out that reflection is like articulation, except it is pointed backward to previous tasks. In traditional learning environments (non Web-based or face-to-face environments), reflection usually occurs through imitation and replay (Collins, 1991). For example, if a batting coach demonstrates a proper swing and contrasts it with the student's swing, this is reflection through *imitation*. The student is reflecting on his or her swing by comparing it with an expert's swing and imitating it. Reflection through *replay* occurs when the batting coach videotapes the student's swing and plays it back, critiquing and comparing it with an expert's swing (Wilson & Cole, 1996, p. 606).

When intellectual or cognitive skills are the learning goals, reflection can occur when, for example, students are asked to keep a journal about a learning experience and then revisit this journal at the end of the experience to reflect on their learning process and reconstruct what they have learned, which gives new meaning to the situation. Another example of reflection in this context is when students enrolled in a writing course are asked to write a paper about a topic at the beginning of the course and revise it at the end of the course. By engaging in this type of activity, students are analyzing what they wrote in the past, making a judgment about their paper, and applying newly gained knowledge to revise it.

In the Naming John Doe scenario, students are engaged in reflective thinking when their case solutions are critiqued by their peers and by the forensic expert and when they are asked to articulate the reasoning process underlying their solutions. Reflection can be considered a comprehension-monitoring strategy (Weinstein & Mayer, 1986) in which learners are checking for comprehension failures by questioning themselves, asking the expert, taking notes, and negotiating with other students. Therefore, reflection is a metacognitive strategy that requires learners to monitor their own learning, which promotes self-directed learning.

Pedagogical models that particularly emphasize reflective-thinking practices are PBL, situated learning, cognitive apprenticeships, CFHs, and CSILEs (see Chapter 5). In Web-based or online learning environments, learners can be engaged in reflective tasks in a variety of ways, using a variety of Web-based technologies. For example,

- The online learning developer can provide students with a **Web posting area** and appropriate tools with which they can **publish** their work (e.g., draft papers and problem solutions). Students can then engage in peer evaluation of one another's work, which prompts reflective thinking.
- The online learning developer can design an activity that engages students in keeping an online journal in which they reflect on their understanding of the reading material for the course. Students can be provided with a private Web posting area to which they can upload their journal entries. Providing a framework or a set of questions to guide students in structuring this journal is important. The online instructor will have access to these journals and can provide feedback to each student through e-mail. Students can look back on their journal entries at the end of the

course and analyze the evolvement of their learning and thinking process, using the instructor's feedback and the course goals as a benchmark.

- The online learning developer can design an activity that engages students in online discussions through bulletin boards or discussion forums. In addition to promoting articulation, these discussion areas can later be revisited by the student to enable reflection on his or her postings and analysis of his or her learning performance.

The underlying Web features that enable the implementation and delivery of the preceding reflective-thinking activities are asynchronous and synchronous communication and the archivability attribute of the Web.

Promoting collaboration and social negotiation   Collaborative learning is a well-established instructional strategy in the traditional classroom. In its simplest form, a collaborative strategy is an instructional strategy that encourages interaction between or among two or more learners to maximize their own and one another's learning. In traditional classroom environments, students are typically paired or grouped in small numbers to work on projects and assignments in and out of class. Group members are actively involved in researching the information they are tasked with learning, organizing it into a meaningful body of knowledge, explaining it to one another, presenting it to the class and their teacher, and relating it to what they know. Through this process, they integrate the knowledge into their existing knowledge structures. Therefore, collaboration engages students in reflection, articulation, exploration, and problem solving.

From a constructivist or situated cognition perspective, collaborative learning can be defined as a collection of activities that emphasize (a) joint construction of knowledge (e.g., joint problem solving by mutual refinement); (b) joint negotiation of alternatives through argumentation, debate, and other means; and (c) student reliance on both other students and teachers as learning resources (see Chapter 2). Therefore, social negotiation is an integral component of collaboration. As Duffy and Cunningham (1996) stated,

> In collaboration and social negotiation the goal is to share different viewpoints and ideas and to collaborate on problem-solving and knowledge building activities. Groups are formed to provide variation in classroom activity (face-to-face or virtual), share work-loads (permitting larger projects), and promote peer tutoring. (p. 187).

In addition, collaboration supports scaffolding and multiple perspectives, which are defined subsequently in this chapter.

Pedagogical models that particularly emphasize collaborative learning are dialogic learning environments such as communities of practice, knowledge building communities, and CSILEs, as well as PBL, situated learning, and cognitive apprenticeships (see Chapter 5). In Web-based or online learning environments, collaboration and social negotiation are supported mainly through the use of asynchronous and synchronous communication technologies as well as document-sharing tools and groupware. These technologies further advance the effectiveness of collaborative learning by bringing students into contact with learning peers from around the world, which provides a richer learning experience than that of traditional face-to-face collaboration (Lea,

Rogers, & Postmes, 2002). Following are examples of how this instructional strategy can be facilitated in online learning:

- The online learning developer can set up online group discussion areas focused around a topic or specific activity, goal, or project, such as a case study, by using asynchronous discussion forums, to promote collaboration and social negotiation. Some group discussion areas can be open ended and unmoderated to allow students to solicit information from one another, whereas others can take the form of a structured online discussion, as in the examples provided previously.
- The online learning developer can design activities that allow group members to share documents related to a group project. Sharing documents online is a collaborative activity and can range from simply displaying the document in a designated Web posting area to having group members work simultaneously on a document by using groupware (an application sharing tool). If the document is displayed, group members can discuss its content through e-mail, videoconferencing, or chat. If groupware is used, group members can coedit the document online and annotate the document if the groupware has built-in annotation systems.
- The online learning developer can engage students in data collection and organization activities when they are working on a group project by setting up a shared online database using **database-driven Web sites** (dynamic Web pages) and learning objects technology. Shared databases allow each group member to contribute data individually to the database in the form of references (e.g., a URL), contact information, pictures, and text documents and to retrieve data from it as needed. CSILEs are an example of a pedagogical model that implements the concept of a shared, or communal, database to support collaborative learning (see Chapter 5).
- The online learning developer can engage students in synchronous communication activities by using virtual chat and videoconferencing. Real-time collaborative activities allow groups to brainstorm ideas, debate problems, and develop action plans in a short, finite time period.

The underlying Web features that enable the implementation and delivery of collaborative learning activities are asynchronous and synchronous communication, online searching, multimedia, and the archivability attribute of the Web.

Promoting multiple perspectives Promoting multiple perspectives is an instructional strategy that emphasizes the construction of flexible knowledge. Exposing students to multiple points of view with regard to understanding or judging things or events allows learners to rearrange information to construct new knowledge and acquire flexible and meaningful knowledge structures (Duffy & Cunningham, 1996, p. 178). Essentially, promoting multiple perspectives involves presenting information in a variety of ways to encourage learners to view the knowledge base from multiple viewpoints and find their own connections and explanations (Jacobson, 1994). The goal of promoting multiple perspectives is to generate cognitive dissonance so that, first, learners become aware of multiple perspectives on an issue, which is the case in real-world situations, and, second, learners become engaged in exploring each perspective to seek a meaningful resolution to the issue at hand, which allows them to construct new meaning in the context of their own experiences and knowledge.

Case-based learning is a powerful approach for promoting multiple perspectives. Students learn how to reason through multiple, authentic cases, much as real-world practitioners do, building a repertoire of knowledge that prepares them to think and reason like experts. A pedagogical model that particularly emphasizes multiple perspectives, using cases, themes, and multiple sources and resources, is a CFH. In addition, as mentioned previously, collaborative learning and articulation support the promotion of multiple perspectives.

In Web-based or online learning, promoting multiple perspectives can be supported mainly through the use of hypermedia technology, digital audio and video, search engines, and asynchronous and synchronous communication tools. Following are examples of how this instructional strategy can be enacted in online learning:

- The online learning developer can use hypermedia to provide Web links to cases that articulate different perspectives on an issue. For example, in the Watchers on the Web scenario in Chapter 5, students are faced with a dilemma about privacy in the digital age and are learning about how to address the balance between personal privacy and freedom of speech, and national security. They will be presented with several cases representing different perspectives on the issue and asked to judge the relevance of the cases to legal, political, constitutional, ethical, practical, technological, or cultural considerations. These cases and themes can be organized by using hypermedia links to facilitate purposeful exploration.
- The online learning developer can include audio and video to certain aspects of a case to provide real-world relevance.
- The online learning developer can include a search engine on the course Web site so that learners can seek additional information relative to their learning task.
- The online learning developer can include a discussion forum to encourage students to articulate their viewpoint on an issue, hear other students' viewpoints, and ask questions.
- The online learning developer can provide an "ask the expert" e-mail link or listserv for students to use when they are seeking expert opinions and perspectives about the issue at hand.

The underlying Web features that enable the implementation and delivery of multiple perspectives are hypermedia, multimedia, asynchronous and synchronous communication, interactivity, and online searching.

Supportive Instructional Strategies

Promoting modeling and explaining   Modeling and explaining are time-tested instructional strategies made most evident in trade apprenticeships. Modeling and explaining provide learners with an example of the desired performance by focusing on the expert's performance (Jonassen, 1999). Traditional modeling and explaining consists of "integrating both the demonstration and explanation during instruction," including false starts, mistakes, and dead ends, so that students can see how a process is handled (Wilson & Cole, 1996). Essentially, modeling shows how a process unfolds, whereas explaining involves giving reasons why it happens that way. For example, when teachers model and explain, they verbalize internal information processing and reasoning while performing the procedures involved in a task. Teachers often use think-aloud protocols to model problem-solving strategies. Similarly, experts show and tell which strategies are being used in solving problems.

Modeling and explaining internal processes is an effective way to scaffold students' performance. By experiencing a teacher's or an expert's cognitive processes, students are better able to adopt the expert's mode of thinking (Gorrell & Capron, 1990). Therefore, explaining the thought processes behind an action or a decision is key in modeling expert performance. However, experts sometimes have difficulty articulating their covert thought processes because they form mental models or schemata of their problem-solving skills, which cannot be easily broken down into explicit or overt sequences or action scripts. Expert systems technology and modeling software have been instrumental in assisting instructional designers to capture expert performance to make it available to novices.

A pedagogical model that specifically emphasizes modeling and explaining is cognitive apprenticeship. As described in Chapter 5, cognitive apprenticeship is "the showing and telling characteristic of apprenticeship" (Collins, 1991, p. 124). The showing is the modeling strategy, and the telling is the explaining. The combination of showing and telling results in the development of conditionalized or situated knowledge—that is, knowledge about where and when knowledge should be used to solve problems (Clark & Kazinou, 2001; Wilson & Cole, 1996). Cognitive apprenticeships emphasize cognitive skills and technology-enabled reflection, articulation, and exploration (Collins, 1991).

In Web-based or online learning, modeling and explaining can be supported mainly through dialogic learning environments in which teachers and students use synchronous and asynchronous communication technologies to articulate their understanding of issues and overtly explain their thought processes through think-aloud protocols. Multimedia technology can also support modeling and explaining because it can capture an expert's performance and replay it as audio or video. Modeling and explaining can also take the form of providing worked examples of problems and models of best practices through Web-based delivery methods. For example,

- The online learning developer can provide access to a Web-based area or Web site where solutions to problems or instructional challenges that have been deemed exemplary by teachers or experts are posted for others to peruse.
- The online learning developer can provide a listserv address to which experts subscribe so that students can ask experts questions about difficulties they are encountering in understanding a procedure or concept. Experts can then model their internal thought processes through this listserv or provide prompts and cues as to how students should approach a problem-solving task.
- The online learning developer can use digital audio and video to capture an expert's performance while he or she is performing a real-world task.

- The online learning developer can provide access to a synchronous chat area where experts can use think-aloud protocols to walk students through a problem-solving process. When students are privy to such a process, they are actively listening to the strategies that the experts are using to rationalize their decisions and actions.

The underlying Web features that support modeling and explaining are asynchronous and synchronous communication, archivability, hypermedia, interactivity, and multimedia.

Promoting coaching   Coaching means observing or monitoring student performance when students are completing a task and providing guidance and help when appropriate (Wilson & Cole, 1996). The purpose of coaching is to improve learners' performance. Hence, a good coach motivates learners, monitors and analyzes their performance, provides comments and feedback, and promotes reflection and articulation on new information learned (Jonassen, 1999). When implementing coaching strategies, practitioners must not stifle learner exploration and problem solving, which can easily happen when coaches or coaching systems provide too much guidance too quickly.

Essentially two approaches to coaching can be taken. The first is the expert–novice approach, and the second is the mentor–protégé approach. The difference is in the relationship between the coach or expert and the student. In the first approach, the relationship is unidirectional, which means that "the student observes and mimics or follows the instructions of the coach" (Duffy & Cunningham, 1996, p. 184) with the goal of replicating the coach's behavior. In the second approach, the relationship is bidirectional, which means that the skills and knowledge of both the coach and the learner are taken into consideration and the goal is to arrive at a reasonable understanding of each other's views (Duffy & Cunningham, 1996). The first approach supports the objectivist view of learning, in which knowledge is an entity to be transmitted from coach to learner. The second approach emphasizes the constructivist view of learning, in which knowledge is a shared entity that is socially negotiated through discourse and mediation of alternative views.

Whichever approach is used, coaching should include the following four instructional attributes (Collins, 1991, p. 127): (a) provide help directed at real difficulties, (b) provide help at critical times, (c) provide as much help as needed to accomplish tasks, and (d) provide "new eyeglasses" for the student (help the student see the process from different perspectives). Pedagogical models that support the instructional strategy of coaching include cognitive apprenticeships, situated learning, PBL, and communities of practice. In Web-based or online learning environments, coaching can be implemented through the following learning technologies:

- The online learning developer can provide a self-contained instructional module that monitors students as they engage in a learning task and provides hints or advice at critical moments.
- The online learning developer can provide a **frequently asked question (FAQ)** Web-based area where students can seek help when they encounter difficulties while completing a learning task.

- The online learning developer can provide hypermedia links to Web sites that provide guidance on how to accomplish learning tasks.
- The online learning developer can provide a synchronous chat area where experts can coach students how to problem solve, negotiate a situation, or accomplish other learning tasks.
- The online learning developer can provide a Web-based area where students can post self-explanations of how they approached solving a problem or completing a learning task, which prompts learners to reflect on their performance and compare it with the performance of others.

The underlying Web features that support coaching activities are hypermedia, multimedia, asynchronous and synchronous communication, interactivity, and archivability.

Promoting scaffolding Scaffolding (see also Chapter 2) involves supporting novice learners by limiting the complexities of the context and gradually removing these limits (a concept known as *fading*) as learners gain the knowledge, skills, and confidence they need to cope with the full complexity of the context (Young, 1993). Assistance is provided to learners on an as-needed basis, and as their task competence increases, assistance is gradually faded to allow learners to complete the task independently (Jarvela, 1995; Pressley, Hogan, Wharton-McDonald, Mistretta, & Ettenberger, 1996).

Scaffolding is originally a Vygotskyan (Lev Vygotsky, 1896–1934) concept based on the idea of providing supportive assistance to the learner within the parameters of a learner's **zone of proximal development (Zo-ped, or ZPD;** Wood, Bruner, & Ross, 1976). The ZPD is a measure of a learner's current ability and knowledge—what he or she is able to perform with no assistance—and the learner's expected or anticipated ability and knowledge—what the learner can be challenged to accomplish with supportive assistance (Vygotsky, 1978). Providing the appropriate level of supportive assistance in a learning environment is a challenge for instructors and instructional designers. Novice students and students who have a significant knowledge base require different levels and types of support to push them to perform at the their potential development zone. Therefore, a layered structure to scaffolding is recommended in which novice learners get the support and information they need to help them engage in the learning task without slowing advanced students who may not need the same level and type of support (Dabbagh, 2003).

Scaffolding can be achieved through various activities and related instructional strategies. In a traditional classroom setting, scaffolding is often achieved through one-on-one collaboration with the teacher, an expert, or a more competent learner. This is only one example of how scaffolding is achieved: through coaching. One-on-one mentoring works exceptionally well when different students have different needs. Scaffolding can also be achieved through modeling and explaining. When experts model their internal thought processes, as discussed previously, students are prompted to reflect on their own performance, compare it with that of the expert's, and improve their performance. Scaffolding can also be achieved by providing appropriate and varied resources and tools to support learning. Overall, the goal is to create a learning culture in which collaboration, learning with self-awareness, multiple perspectives, and self-management are promoted, and in which the teacher's role is reciprocal, supportive, and communicative as it is responsive to learner needs (McLoughlin & Oliver, 1999).

In Web-based or online learning environments, scaffolding can be supported through the following learning technologies:

- The online learning developer can structure the online course so that one-on-one mentoring and guidance is provided through the use of e-mail.
- The online learning developer can provide a link to a search engine so that students are encouraged to search for information as they need it.
- The online learning developer can provide hypermedia links to **embedded online tools,** such as a calculator, a spreadsheet or database program, or other cognitive tools (e.g., the ability to draw a concept map or diagram), that can either perform part of the task for the learner to reduce its complexity or assist the learner in performing the task.
- The online learning developer can provide a discussion or chat area where students can seek help on how to perform certain tasks.
- The online learning developer can provide an online index and/or a glossary of important terms and their definitions.
- The online learning developer can provide hypermedia links to carefully selected Web-based resources that support the learning task.
- The online learning developer can provide hypermedia links to worked examples of learning tasks or samples of previous projects to clearly communicate to the learners the task or project requirements.

The underlying Web features that support scaffolding activities are hypermedia, multimedia, asynchronous and synchronous communication, interactivity, online searching, and archivability.

Summary   Before we present the last instructional strategy, it is appropriate to end this section with a quote that effectively summarizes the relationship among the instructional strategies of modeling, coaching, and scaffolding. "Modeling is focused on the expert's performance. Coaching is focused on the learner's performance. Scaffolding is a more systemic approach to supporting the learner, focusing on the task, the environment, the teacher, and the learner" (Jonassen, 1999, p. 234).

Promotion of Self-Directed Learning

In Chapter 2, we defined self-directed learning as the skill of learning how to learn or being metacognitively aware of your own learning, and we described it as an important characteristic of the online learner. In this chapter, we discuss self-directed learning as an instructional strategy and describe how it can be promoted or supported in online learning environments to help the learner acquire self-directed learning skills such as time planning and management, comprehension monitoring, and self-evaluation.

Self-directed learning is a process in which learners take the initiative, with or without help from others, to analyze their learning needs, state learning goals, identify resources for learning, choose and implement learning strategies, and evaluate learning outcomes (Lowry, 1989). A closely related construct to self-directed learning, albeit interchangeable, is self-regulated learning. Self-regulated learning has its roots in social cognitive theory. Self-regulation refers to the degree to which students can become metacognitively, motivationally, and behaviorally active participants of their learning process (Zimmerman, 2000). Among the key self-regulatory processes affecting student achievement and motivational beliefs are goal setting, self-monitoring, self-evaluation, use of task strategies (e.g., rehearsing and memorizing, and organizing and transforming), help seeking, and time planning and management (Kitsantas, 2002; Zimmerman, 2000).

In traditional face-to-face classroom settings, the instructor can exercise significant control over the learning process and can monitor student self-regulatory processes closely. However, in Web-based or online learning environments, students must learn how to monitor their own learning process to accomplish their learning goals (Besser & Bonn, 1997; Dabbagh & Kitsantas, 2004). Therefore, helping students become self-directed is critical to their success in online learning environments.

Promoting self-directed learning in online learning environments can be achieved by considering each self-regulatory process just identified (e.g., goal setting, self-monitoring, self-evaluation) and using appropriate Web-based technologies to support it. For example,

- E-mail can assist learners in setting specific, process-oriented goals to achieve a learning task by communicating such goals to the instructor and receiving feedback on the implementation and appropriateness of these goals for successfully achieving the task. Students articulate their goals, and instructors provide coaching.
- Asynchronous discussion forums can assist learners in keeping track of their progress (self-monitoring) by engaging them in reflecting on previous postings and making necessary adjustments that are in alignment with their learning goals.
- The use of hypermedia links to provide explicit rubrics and evaluation criteria for course assignments supports students' self-evaluation by allowing them to compare their performance with the stated criteria. The instructor is scaffolding student learning by providing clear expectations and requirements for learning tasks. Hypermedia links can also be used to provide worked examples of the desired performance. In this case, the instructor is modeling and explaining expert behavior.
- The use of multimedia (e.g., graphics, audio, and video) can greatly enhance students' learning by engaging them in alternative and multiple forms of processing the instructional content. Students use task strategies to help them accomplish their learning goals. The instructor is scaffolding student learning by providing alternative forms of processing the content.
- The use of asynchronous and synchronous communication technologies to support **collaborative problem-solving activities** can support students' help seeking. Students articulate their understanding of the learning task by posting messages or drafts of task reports to an online group area and seeking feedback from their peers to set appropriate learning goals.

The preceding examples demonstrate how the collective enactment of exploratory, dialogic, and supportive instructional strategies promotes self-directed learning. When students are using Web-based technologies to articulate their understanding of the learning content and reflect on their performance, they are engaging in goal setting, self-monitoring, and self-evaluation. When students are using Web-based technologies to engage in collaborative and problem-solving activities, they are exposed to multiple perspectives and are using different task strategies to process the learning task. Last, when instructors are using Web-based technologies to coach, scaffold, model, and explain expert behavior, they are supporting the student self-regulatory processes of help seeking, goal setting, self-monitoring, and self-evaluation.

MAPPING INSTRUCTIONAL STRATEGIES TO WEB FEATURES

For each instructional strategy described in the preceding section, we provided examples of how the strategy can be facilitated in online learning by using Web-based technologies. In addition, at the end of each set of examples, we listed the underlying Web features that enable the implementation and delivery of the strategy in online learning. These Web features included asynchronous and synchronous communication, archivability, online searching, hypermedia, multimedia, and interactivity. Web features are inherent technological characteristics of the World Wide Web, and Web technologies enable these features (Khan, 1997). For example, asynchronous communication is a Web feature that is enabled by e-mail and other asynchronous communication technologies such as discussion forums and bulletin boards. Online searching is a Web feature that is enabled through search engines. Multimedia is a Web feature that is enabled though computer graphics and digital video and audio.

The distinction between Web features and Web technologies is important because it provides the online learning developer with an understanding of the underlying characteristics or features of the Web as a delivery medium and the learning affordances or opportunities that are applicable through the use of Web-based technologies. As Kozma (1994) suggested, each delivery medium has a unique set of characteristics, and understanding the ways in which students use the capabilities of the medium is essential to understanding the influence of the medium on learning. By capitalizing on the inherent features of the Web, the instructional developer can design effective online learning environments through the use of learning technologies that enable these features. Table 6.2 provides a guideline for the enactment of the instructional strategies discussed in this chapter in online learning environments based on Web features and technologies. The table maps instructional strategies to pedagogical models, Web technologies, and Web features. The first and last instructional strategies discussed in this chapter are not included in Table 6.2 because promoting authentic learning activities forms the core of all other instructional strategies and promoting self-directed learning is the expected outcome of the collective enactment of exploratory, dialogic, and supportive instructional strategies.

Table 6.2   Mapping Instructional Strategies to Pedagogical Models, Web Technologies, and Web Features

INSTRUCTIONAL STRATEGY	SUPPORTING PEDAGOGICAL MODEL	ASSOCIATED WEB TECHNOLOGIES	WEB FEATURES
EXPLORATORY STRATEGIES			
Promoting problem solving	Problem-based learning, anchored instruction	Hyperlinks, asynchronous and synchronous discussion forums, document-sharing technologies, groupware, online databases, knowledge repositories	Hypermedia, online searching archivability, synchronous, asynchronous
Promoting exploration	Simulations, microworlds, virtual learning environments, WebQuests, problem-based learning, anchored instruction, cognitive flexibility hypertexts	Hyperlinks, search engines, online databases, scripting languages, Web-based authoring tools, self-contained instructional modules	Hypermedia, multimedia, online searching, interactivity
Promoting hypothesis generation	Simulations, microworlds, virtual learning environments, WebQuests, problem-based learning, anchored instruction	Plug-ins, Web-based authoring tools, Web-based animation, digital audio and video, dynamic Web pages (database-driven Web sites)	Hypermedia, multimedia, online searching, interactivity
Promoting role-playing	Cognitive apprenticeships, communities of practice, virtual learning environments, simulations, CSILEs, problem-based learning	MOOs, MUDs, Internet chat, videoconferencing, computer conferencing, groupware	Asynchronous, synchronous, multimedia, interactivity
DIALOGIC STRATEGIES			
Promoting articulation	Knowledge networks, CSILEs, communities of practice, cognitive apprenticeships, problem-based learning	Bulletin boards, discussion forums, virtual chat sessions, document-sharing technologies, groupware, e-mail, Web posting areas	Asynchronous, synchronous
Promoting reflection	Problem-based learning, cognitive apprenticeships, CSILEs, anchored instruction	Web posting areas, bulletin boards, discussion forums, e-mail, note-taking tools	Asynchronous, synchronous, archivability

Table 6.2 Mapping Instructional Strategies to Pedagogical Models, Web Technologies, and Web Features (*Continued*)

DIALOGIC STRATEGIES			
Promoting collaboration and social negotiation	CSILEs, problem-based learning, anchored instruction, communities of practice	Asynchronous and synchronous discussion forums, bulletin boards, groupware, document-sharing technologies, video conferencing technologies, chat, shared databases	Asynchronous, synchronous, online searching, multimedia, archivability
Promoting multiple perspectives	Cognitive flexibility hypertexts, communities of practice, CSILEs	Hyperlinks, graphics, digital video and audio, Listservs, asynchronous discussion forums, search engines	Hypermedia, multimedia, asynchronous, synchronous, interactivity, online searching
SUPPORTIVE STRATEGIES			
Promoting modeling and explaining	Cognitive apprenticeships, simulations, CSILEs, communities of practice	Asynchronous and synchronous discussion forums, graphics, animation, videoconferencing, digital audio and video, Web posting areas, e-mail	Hypermedia, multimedia, asynchronous, synchronous, interactivity, archivability
Promoting coaching	Microworlds, simulations, cognitive apprenticeships, anchored instruction, problem-based learning	E-mail, hyperlinks, asynchronous and synchronous discussion areas, self-contained instructional modules, Web-based authoring tools	Hypermedia, multimedia, asynchronous, synchronous, interactivity, archivability
Promoting scaffolding	CSILEs, cognitive apprenticeships, cognitive flexibility hypertexts, problem-based learning, microworlds	Hyperlinks, e-mail, search engines, asynchronous and synchronous discussion areas, online databases	Hypermedia, multimedia, asynchronous, synchronous, interactivity, online searching, archivability

Note. CSILEs = computer-supported intentional learning environments; MOOs = multiuser domains—object oriented; MUDs = multiuser domains.

CHAPTER SUMMARY

In this chapter, we discussed the relationship among instructional strategies, pedagogical models, and learning theory, and the enactment of instructional strategies in online learning environments. Synthesizing the characteristics of constructivist-based pedagogical models discussed in Chapter 5, we identified 13 instructional strategies and described their interdependence, alignment, and intersection. Specifically, promoting authentic learning activities was emphasized as a core instructional strategy leading to the identification of 11 instructional strategies that were classified into three categories: exploratory, dialogic, and supportive. Promoting self-directed learning was identified as an instructional strategy resulting from the collective enactment of exploratory, dialogic, and supportive instructional strategies. Examples of how each instructional strategy can be implemented through the use of online learning technologies were provided. The chapter also provided a table that maps instructional strategies to associated pedagogical models, Web technologies, and Web features. This table (Table 6.2) can help guide the online learning developer in implementing instructional strategies in online learning.

LEARNING ACTIVITIES

1. Return to the Naming John Doe scenario provided at the beginning of this chapter. Review the questions you were asked. Use Tables 6.1 and 6.2 to help you identify the instructional strategies, Web technologies, and Web features that support the implementation of this scenario in an online learning context. Develop a table that maps the learning outcomes listed in the scenario to instructional strategies, Web technologies, and Web features.

2. Visit the companion Web site for this book (http://www.prenhall.com/dabbagh) and click on the link to this chapter (Chapter 6). You will find links to each of the 13 instructional strategies discussed in this chapter. Each link takes you to an interactive table that demonstrates how the instructional strategy can be implemented by using the features of a CMS such as WebCT or Blackboard. Follow the instructions provided on the Web site to complete an activity related to these tables. You will need the Solution Design Form that you created in Chapter 5 (see Learning Activities for Chapter 5). Be sure to keep the results of this activity as well. You will use these in Chapter 9.

3. Revisit the suggested instructional strategies and activities for each of the online learning research categories provided in Chapter 3. Map these strategies and activities to the 13 instructional strategies provided in this chapter. In other words, which suggested strategies and activities in Chapter 3 promote scaffolding? modeling? problem solving? and so forth.

4. Visit the Instructional Design Knowledge Base (IDKB) at the companion Web site for this book (http://www.prenhall.com/dabbagh). Click on "Doing an Instructional Design Project" and then on "Strategies/Tactics." Browse through the list of strategies listed under behaviorism or cognitivism and pick a strategy with which you are familiar. Think about how you might implement this strategy in an online context by using the Web-based technologies described in this chapter.

5   Visit the Instructional Design Knowledge Base (IDKB) at the companion Web site for this book (http://www.prenhall.com/dabbagh). Click on "Doing an Instructional Design Project" and then on "Strategies/Tactics." Pick the link "Gagné's events of instruction" listed under cognitivism. Pick a familiar learning task or instructional context and develop a table, similar to Table 6.2, to map Gagné's events of instruction to Web technologies and features, providing specific examples of learning activities as demonstrated in this chapter.

RESOURCES

Explore additional resources at the companion Web site (http://www.prenhall.com/dabbagh) to learn more about how to promote the different types of instructional strategies discussed in this chapter by using Web-based technologies.

REFERENCES

Anderson, J. R. (1980*). Cognitive psychology and its implications*. San Francisco: Freeman.

Besser, H., & Bonn, M. (1997). Interactive distance-independent education: Challenges to traditional academic roles. *Journal of Education for Library and Information Science, 38*(1), 35–42.

Bruner, J. S., Goodnow, J. J., & Austin, G. A. (1956). *A study of thinking*. New York: Wiley.

Clark, R., & Kazinou, M. (2001). *Promoting metacognitive skills among graduate students in education*. Retrieved June 20, 2002, from http://et.sdsu.edu/RClark/ET640/RCMKPOPS2.htm

Collins, A. (1991). Cognitive apprenticeship and instructional technology. In L. Idol & B. F. Jones (Eds.), *Educational values and cognitive instruction: Implications for reform* (pp. 121–138). Hillsdale, NJ: Erlbaum.

Dabbagh, N. (2003). Scaffolding: An important teacher competency in online learning. *TechTrends, 47*(2), 39–44.

Dabbagh, N., & Kitsantas, A. (2004). Supporting self-regulation in student-centered Web-based learning environments. *International Journal on E-Learning, 3*(1), 40–47.

Driscoll, M. P. (2000). *Psychology of learning for instruction* (2nd ed.). Needham Heights, MA: Allyn & Bacon.

Duffy, T. M., & Cunningham, D. J. (1996). Constructivism: Implications for the design and delivery of instruction. In D. H. Jonassen (Ed.), *Handbook of research for educational communications and technology* (pp. 170–198). New York: Simon & Schuster/Macmillan.

Gorrell, J., & Capron, E. (1990). Cognitive modeling and self-efficacy: Effects on preservice teachers' learning of teaching strategies. *Journal of Teacher Education, 41*(2), 15–22.

Heinich, R., Molenda, M., & Russell, J. (1993). *Instructional media and the new technology of learning* (4th ed.). New York: Macmillan.

Jacobson, M. J. (1994). Issues in hypertext and hypermedia research: Toward a framework for linking theory-to-design. *Journal of Educational Multimedia and Hypermedia, 3*(2), 141–154.

Jarvela, S. (1995). The cognitive apprenticeship model in a technologically rich learning environment: Interpreting the learning interaction. *Learning and Instruction, 5,* 237–259.

Jonassen, D. H. (1999). Instructional design models for well-structured and ill-structured problem-solving learning outcomes. *Educational Technology Research & Development, 45*(1), 65–94.

Jonassen, D. H. (1999). Designing constructivist learning environments. In C. M. Reigeluth (Ed.), *Instructional-design theories and models: A new paradigm of instructional theory* (Vol. II, pp. 215–239). Mahwah, NJ: Erlbaum.

Jonassen, D. H., Grabinger, R. S., & Harris, N. D. C. (1991). Instructional strategies and tactics. *Performance Improvement Quarterly, 3*(2), 29–47.

Khan, B. H. (1997). Web-based instruction (WBI): What is it and why is it? In B. H. Khan (Ed.), *Web-based instruction* (pp. 5–18). Englewood Cliffs, NJ: Educational Technology Publications.

Kitsantas, A. (2002). Test preparation and test performance: A self-regulatory analysis. *Journal of Experimental Education, 70*(2), 101–113.

Kozma, R. B. (1994). A reply: Media and methods. *Educational Technology Research & Development, 42*(3), 11–14.

Lea, M., Rogers, P., & Postmes, T. (2002). Side-view: Evaluation of a system to develop team players and improve productivity in Internet collaborative learning groups. *British Journal of Educational Technology, 33*(1), 53–63.

Lowry, C. M. (1989). *Supporting and facilitating self-directed learning.* Columbus, OH: ERIC Clearinghouse on Adult Career and Vocational Education. (ERIC Document Reproduction Service No. ED312457)

Mayer, R. E. (1987). *Educational psychology: A cognitive approach.* Boston: Little, Brown.

McLoughlin, C., & Oliver, R. (1999). Pedagogic roles and dynamics in telematics environments. In M. Selinger & J. Pearson (Eds.), *Telematics in education: Trends and issues* (pp. 32–50). Kidlington, Oxford, UK: Pergamon Press.

Newell, A., & Simon, H. A. (1972). *Human problem solving.* Upper Saddle River, NJ: Prentice Hall.

Oliver, R., Herrington, J., & Omari, A. (1996). *Creating effective instructional materials for the World Wide Web.* Paper presented at the 1996 Australian World Wide Web Conference (AusWeb). Retrieved November 14, 2002, from http://ausweb.scu.edu.au/aw96/educn/oliver/index.htm

Penrod, J., & Perry, B. (2003, March 30–April 1). *Virtual University— A higher education administration simulation and learning tool.* Paper presented at the Eighth Annual Mid-South Instructional Technology Conference, Teaching, Learning, & Technology, Murfreesboro, TN.

Pressley, M., Hogan, K., Wharton-McDonald, R., Mistretta, J., & Ettenberger, S. (1996). The challenges of instructional scaffolding . . . the challenges of instruction that supports student thinking. *Learning Disabilities Research and Practice, 11,* 138–146.

Reeves, T. C., Herrington, J., & Oliver, R. (2002, April). *Authentic activity as a model for Web-based learning.* Paper presented at the annual meeting of the American Educational Research Association, New Orleans, LA, Session 41.06.

Roblyer, M. D., Edwards, J., & Havriluk, M. A. (1996). Learning theories and integration models. In M. D. Roblyer, J. Edwards, & M. A. Havriluk (Eds.), *Integrating educational technology into teaching* (pp. 54–79). Upper Saddle River, NJ: Merrill/Prentice Hall.

Shuell, T. J. (1980). Learning theory, instructional theory, and adaptation. In R. E. Snow, P. A. Federico, & W. E. Montague (Eds.), *Aptitude, learning and instruction* (Vol. 1, pp. 277–301). Hillsdale, NJ: Erlbaum.

van Merrienboer, J. (1997). *Training complex cognitive skills: A four component instructional design model for technical training.* Englewood Cliffs, NJ: Educational Technology Publications.

Vygotsky, L. (1978). *Mind in society*. Cambridge, MA: Harvard University Press.

Weinstein, C. E., & Mayer, R. E. (1986). The teaching of learning strategies. In M. C. Wittrock (Ed.), *Handbook of research on teaching* (pp. 315–327). New York: MacMillan.

Wilson, B. G., & Cole, P. (1996). Cognitive teaching models. In D. H. Jonassen (Ed.), *Handbook of research for educational communications and technology* (pp. 601–621). New York: Simon & Schuster/Macmillan.

Wood, D., Bruner, J., & Ross, G. (1976). The role of tutoring in problem solving. *Journal of Child Psychology and Psychiatry, 17*, 89–100.

Young, M. F. (1993). Instructional design for situated learning. *Educational Technology Research & Development, 41*(1), pp. 43–58.

Zimmerman, B. J. (2000). Attaining self-regulation: A social-cognitive perspective. In M. Boekaerts, P. Pintrich, & M. Seidner (Eds.), *Self-regulation: Theory, research, and applications* (pp. 13–39). Orlando, FL: Academic Press.

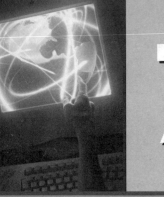

7

EVALUATION FOR ONLINE LEARNING: A PROCESS MODEL

After completing this chapter, you should understand the following:

- The characteristics of constructivist evaluation

- A process model for evaluation

- The importance of incorporating a variety of methods and levels in evaluations of online learning

- Kirkpatrick's levels of evaluation and their relationship to online learning

- The basic elements of several types of formative evaluation testing

- Different methods and measurement approaches in a selected sample of online instruction or training evaluation efforts

CONSIDER THE FOLLOWING THREE SCENARIOS:

True Colors: Tom is often frustrated after teaching a unit on photosynthesis to his class of fourth graders. A creative and innovative teacher, Tom devises a way to combine hands-on activities with computer-based activities to engage the students. His students will investigate how leaves change color and link this activity to a simple representation of the photosynthesis process. Tom is inspired by exploratory pedagogical models that promote discovery learning approaches. He creates the lesson with guidance from Bernie Dodge's Web site on WebQuests and hands-on activities he finds on the Web. Tom hopes this unit will promote learning, engage students, impress his teacher colleagues, and adhere to the science standards. He has one only problem. How does he show results to his principal and colleagues?

War and Peace: Professor Hughes teaches an undergraduate course on nonfiction writing. Inspired by the multiple perspectives represented in the debate on the war in Iraq, she decides to include several assignments in her online course that incorporate argumentation strategies and realistic writing activities. Presenting a six-stage model of an argument—claims, grounds, warrants, backing, qualifiers, and rebuttals—Professor Hughes requires her students to apply these stages to online debates and writing assignments. She associates this approach with dialogic learning strategies that promote articulation, social interaction, and multiple perspectives. One of the writing assignments is for the students to write an editorial to *The Washington Post* on their position on the war in Iraq. Dr. Hughes uses the capabilities of Lotus Notes to provide multiple authentic information resources, including video, audio, media reports, and images, in her online course. To support their positions, students need to gather evidence, identify and evaluate sources, and articulate their reasoning. Professor Hughes thinks her idea is so good that she would like to find a way to collect data and evaluate the online course so that she can write an article about it. However, she is not sure how to evaluate online learning activities.

A Risk Management Community: During the last 6 months, Beth has been charged with designing and developing an online learning community that will capture and represent knowledge on risk management for her employer. The online learning community provides a virtual space where members can locate, synthesize, and contribute to knowledge resources on the systematic process of risk management to help employees manage risk. The system was built according to the instructional characteristics of the pedagogical model of communities of practice and includes instructional strategies related to modeling, scaffolding, and collaboration. It encompasses a process of planning for risk, assessing risk areas, developing risk-handling options, monitoring risks to determine how risks have changed, and documenting overall risk management. Beth, with her team, designs and develops a highly usable learning community that contains contact resources, learning resources, announcements, events, presentations, tools, and case studies related to risk management. The initial launch of the risk management online learning community is successful. However, Beth needs to quickly devise a way to demonstrate this success to her boss.

Choose a scenario and think about how you would approach evaluating the online instruction or training represented. Where would you begin? What process would you use? How would you determine what to evaluate?

In this chapter, we provide a systematic process model for implementing the evaluation phase of the Integrated Learning Design Framework (ILDF) for Online Learning. We also present an overview of evaluation methods and measurement approaches used in online learning.

INTRODUCTION

Evaluation has been characterized as a process used to judge the "worthwhileness" of something in order to make decisions (R. E. Clark, 2000). Judging the worthwhileness of an online course or module can be as simple or as complex as the developer's goal for evaluating the value of the enacted design. In Chapters 2 and 4, we outlined the multiple roles that an online developer can assume and competencies that the online instructor might have. An evaluator, or a researcher, is a person who engages in the process of careful, studious inquiry or examination of a particular phenomenon. Using this definition, a teacher, trainer, or professor who studiously or systematically examines the creation and implementation of his or her online learning materials may be engaged in an evaluative process.

Evaluation is a crucial part of every design and development effort because it can determine the worth or value of the instruction or training as well as its strengths and weaknesses (Tessmer, 1993). A common assumption is that evaluation processes can be applied only in a formal manner by using experimental research methods. These methods traditionally involve participants who are randomly assigned to groups that interact with treatment or learning materials that vary on a specific element and the use of statistical methods to determine whether that element demonstrates differences in learning beyond the level of chance. Although experimental research methods are one way of examining the impact of online learning, these formal evaluation methods are not always the best way to determine the worth or value of online instruction (Bernard, de Rubalcava, & St. Pierre, 2000). Many other methods are available for a practitioner to evaluate online learning materials, and the commonality among the different approaches and methods is the overall goal of contributing to or improving learning effectiveness. As Reeves (1997) stated,

> The purpose of evaluation within instructional design is not crunching numbers, telling stories or deconstructing meaning, but supporting the overall goals of the ID effort, improving human learning and ultimately the human condition. (p. 176)

Through evaluation, practitioners may begin to better understand the impact of instructional strategies on learning and the nature of instruction and training delivered through online technologies. However, to accomplish this, practitioners need to first adopt a systematic process of evaluation that includes these four steps:

1. Clearly determine the purpose, desired results, and methods of evaluation.
2. Formatively evaluate the design and development prior to launching the online course.
3. Revise the online materials according to the results of the formative evaluation.
4. Implement the online learning experience and evaluate the results according to the identified goals.

The evaluation phase of the ILDF for Online Learning outlines this process for determining the worthwhileness or value of instructional strategies enacted through online technologies. The evaluation phase promotes an iterative, systematic approach to designing and developing online learning through testing enacted designs as a way to inform current or future development. Evaluation can be conducted at multiple points in the process. However, it is most commonly conducted after the instruction or training has been implemented online.

Several types of evaluation are considered in the evaluation phase of the ILDF for Online Learning. Planning for *summative evaluation* is the focus of the first stage of the evaluation phase. In this type of evaluation, the impact of the online materials is examined after they are finalized. *Formative evaluation* and *revision* processes are implemented in the second and third stages and are focused primarily on determining the strengths and weaknesses of the instruction during development, while the opportunity to improve the instruction or training still exists (Tessmer, 1993). Assessment of learning outcomes (or student performance on tests, assignments, etc.) can inform both types of evaluation (George & Cowan, 1999). Gray (1989) advocated a broad view of assessment and evaluation that might include all these forms to promote self-awareness, change, and self-renewal and provide useful information to inform a wide range of decisions. Given the complexity of online learning environments, considering a range of evaluation and assessment strategies is useful.

Evaluation efforts can be categorized on a continuum of informal to formal approaches and methods. R. C. Clark and Mayer (2003) differentiated between two types of evaluations or research: informal studies, in which conclusions are based primarily on student observations or feedback, and more formal experimental studies or clinical trials. In the ILDF for Online Learning, differences in formal or informal evaluation approaches are determined by the developers' goals and the social and cultural context. The teacher, professor, or trainer determines the level of formality of the evaluation processes most appropriate for the context and selects and adapts these processes for his or her purposes. Figure 7.1 illustrates our view of the continuum from informal to formal evaluations, based on a range of methods that inform conclusions and the desired impact of the results.

Evaluation efforts discussed in this book reflect both formal efforts (demonstrated by the research studies outlined in Chapter 3) and more informal evaluation efforts

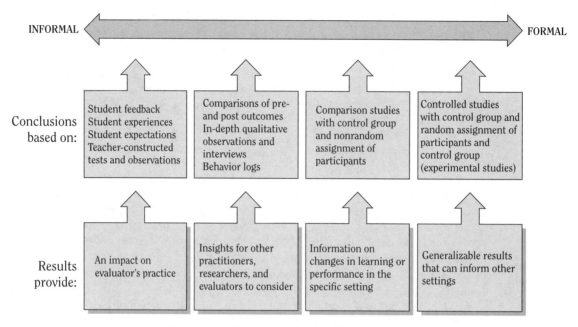

Figure 7.1   Informal to Formal Evaluation Continuum

(many are highlighted in this chapter). Our purpose in the evaluation phase of the ILDF for Online Learning is to provide a logical, systematic process through which the online learning developer can consider the range of evaluation approaches and methods. The specific challenges of evaluating instructional technology such as online learning and constructivist-based learning environments are discussed next.

> *Where on the continuum of informal to formal evaluation methods presented in Figure 7.1 would you place each scenario presented at the beginning of this chapter? Do you think Tom's situation requires formal or informal evaluation methods? What about Professor Hughes's situation? Think about whether Beth should conduct her evaluation of the risk management community in either an informal or a formal manner.*

ISSUES RELATED TO EVALUATION OF INSTRUCTIONAL TECHNOLOGY

Practitioners in the field of instructional technology have struggled with determining appropriate evaluation methods for technology-enabled instruction or training. The advent of distance learning and the complex nature of online delivery media have reintroduced the debate and discussion. At issue is whether evaluation efforts should separately examine the technology delivery media and the instructional strategies that can be embedded in many technology delivery systems or should examine the combination of media delivery systems and the instructional strategies that they afford.

R. E. Clark's (2000) position is that when a practitioner is asking evaluation questions related to distance education and online learning, all evaluations should explicitly investigate *either* the delivery technology (e.g., Web course authoring system, multimedia system) *or* the instructional technology (e.g., instructional sequencing, structure, or strategies) but not both. According to Clark's view, the technology system is only a vehicle for delivering instructional strategies. Therefore, evaluation efforts should focus either on the impact of the technology system on the access to, use of, or reliability of the technology *or* on issues related to implementing instructional strategies such as the achievement of program objectives and learning.

In addition, R. E. Clark (2000) believes that all instructional technologies (e.g., the instructional strategy or method) can be delivered by any online or distance education delivery medium. An example of this position is the contention that instructional strategies encompassed in a problem-based learning approach (discussed in Chapters 5 and 6) could be delivered by using any technology delivery system, including course management systems such as Blackboard or WebCT (discussed in Chapter 9), or could be delivered by stand-alone, non-Web-based multimedia instruction or classroom instruction. Clark's point is that online learning developers should focus their evaluation efforts on the impact of the instructional strategies rather than on the technological features of the system or focus evaluation efforts on the impact of technology on the use of or access to the system. The results of many current evaluation efforts in online learning claim that technology attributes impact learning rather than the instructional strategies.

Kozma (2000) has taken the opposing view: that evaluation efforts in educational and online technology should focus on the intersection of delivery media and the instructional strategy or method—not just one or the other exclusively. Kozma strongly advocates considering the connection between the instructional design or technology (e.g., instructional strategy or method) and the delivery technology (e.g., online learning system), as well as how these elements intersect in the specific learning context. Kozma contends that, for research and evaluation purposes, educational technologists or online developers need to examine the relationship between instructional strategies and delivery technologies in order to determine how learning occurs and the overall value of online instruction or training. R. E. Clark's (2000) sole emphasis on instructional strategies, in Kozma's (2000) perspective, ignores the interrelationship between the technology delivery system and how the instructional strategies support instructional goals.

Other researchers' positions seem to mediate the opposing views of Clark and Kozma. Most notably, Gibbons, Lawless, Anderson, and Duffin (2000) stated how specific online delivery systems can facilitate or place constraints on the instructional strategies that can be delivered and evaluated. For example, formally evaluating the instructional strategy of collaborative learning in the classroom is more difficult because it involves recording and/or transcribing the interaction that occurs so that it can be analyzed later. In contrast, many online learning tools include the ability to automatically record all text-based interaction, which allows the preservation of relevant data for immediate analysis. Carefully considering the convergence between the online developer's intended instructional strategies and the features and capabilities of the online learning system can promote the consideration of different evaluation methods. The examples presented in this chapter (and in Chapter 4 in the evaluation section) represent different emphases in on-line evaluation, including a focus on the instructional strategies, the delivery system, or the convergence of the two. The ILDF for Online Learning promotes clearly determining the focus of the evaluation effort. The ongoing debate between instructional technology theorists and researchers will not be solved in this book. However, the issues raised about what to evaluate during examination of online learning systems are important to consider, and practitioners need to take into account the developer's specific goals and the online learning social and cultural context, particularly when they are attempting to evaluate online constructivist learning environments.

EVALUATION OF CONSTRUCTIVIST OR OPEN-ENDED LEARNING ENVIRONMENTS

As stated in Chapter 2, a constructivist learning environment is "a place where learners may work together and support each other as they use a variety of tools and information resources in their guided pursuit of learning goals and problem-solving skills" (Wilson, 1996, p. 5). Online learning systems are often associated with constructivist learning environments and provide a virtual space where learners can construct knowledge through learning activities, designed by developers, that capitalize on the capabilities of the online tools. Evaluating constructivist learning activities presents challenges in determining appropriate methods that best align with the assumptions of learning that constructivism promotes. Adding to this challenge is determining appropriate evaluation methods for carefully examining how constructivist-based pedagogical models and strategies are enacted with online learning tools. For example, Gunawardena, Lowe, and Carabajal (2000) stated that traditional evaluation methods do not support the "open-ended nature of online learning, the multiple threads of conversation and fluid participation patterns" (p. 1) and that online learning environments present and pose significant challenges for evaluation. These researchers seemed to align themselves with Kozma and stated that to conduct an evaluation, practitioners need to understand the unique characteristics and social and ecological structure of the online learning environment and develop new principles for evaluation of these constructivist environments.

Jonassen (1991) pointed out that different assumptions about learning and the processes that support learning underlie constructivism than those underlying traditional instructional design or traditional teaching approaches. Therefore, different evaluation methods should be considered for determining the value and impact of constructivist learning environments. Jonassen suggested that to evaluate constructivist learning environments, evaluators should focus on higher order thinking skills such as problem solving and how learners build knowledge rather than focusing on a single indicator or product of learning such as a test. Gunwardena et al.'s (2000) study illustrated this in their examination of how knowledge is constructed in online learning networks through the process of social communication and negotiation by using a variety of methods (see Chapter 3 for more details on this study).

Jonassen (1991) also recommended that evaluation occur in contexts that are as rich and complex as the instructional environments. In other words, evaluation methods should be implemented in an online environment, reflecting the complexity and authentic characteristics of the online instructional tasks. For example, in a formal evaluation study, Hara, Bonk, and Angeli (2000) wanted to examine how cognitive processing and interaction occurred for participants in online computer conferencing. The evaluation was structured to analyze how often the participants responded to one another in the computer conferencing environment, the interaction patterns that occurred, and the social cues that were present. The researchers then categorized the level of cognitive skills in the messages. This evaluation occurred in the same context as the instruction because the complex nature of online communication, including the rate, pattern, and nature of interaction that took place in that environment, was thoroughly examined. Although many evaluation efforts are not as formal, aligning evaluation methods with the nature of the instruction is a worthy goal.

According to Jonassen (1991), another consideration for evaluating constructivist learning is the incorporation of multiple perspectives. According to constructivist theory, learners form their own understandings of instruction or training. Therefore, evaluators will also form their own unique perceptions and understandings that impact an evaluation effort. Perhaps one of the best ways to evaluate online learning materials is to involve multiple evaluators or participants, who can contribute multiple perspectives on the value and impact of the online learning instruction or training. Involving evaluators and participants from different levels and types of experience—such as experts, novices, learners, colleagues, and other online learning developers—may provide rich information for the evaluation. In Kanuka and Anderson's (1998) evaluation efforts, they wanted to determine whether the online environment promoted more than social interaction and induced higher level thinking about the issues discussed with 25 managers of workplace learning centers across Canada. These researchers examined the communication in the asynchronous computer conference and surveyed selected participants to determine their perspectives on the effectiveness of the online training conference in promoting higher level thinking about the issues discussed (see results reported in Chapter 3). These evaluation methods supported gathering and analyzing multiple perspectives on the online learning experience from participants as a way to analyze the impact and value of the online discussion.

In addition to including multiple perspectives, involving multiple products is important in conducting evaluations of constructivist learning environments. Evaluation efforts that target a single outcome measure such as one test or one survey present only one facet of the training or learning experience. Online learning experiences typically include multiple instructional strategies and activities, such as online discussions, individual reflections, small-group activities, papers, projects, and others. Jonassen (1991) suggested valuating learning products as a portfolio. For example, the portfolio approach was used in evaluating a graduate-level course that incorporated online learning methods to support an authentic instructional design and development experience. In the course, students posted their design document products at each stage of the experience (e.g., needs analysis, objectives, instructional strategies, evaluation methods), which ultimately resulted in a comprehensive design document or portfolio. Students also held small-group online discussions around the production of these materials. To assess student learning, the instructor evaluated a Web-based portfolio of the design products, along with group discussions, individual reflections on the experience, and self- and peer evaluation reports on group processes. After several semesters, these products were evaluated across multiple groups of students in a comprehensive, in-depth qualitative evaluation of the course.

Perhaps the best approach to evaluating constructivist learning activities in online learning environments is to use a variety of evaluation methods when possible. Particularly with emerging online instructional and training environments, multiple methods may be useful for determining the value and impact of constructivist-based online instruction or training. Bernard et al. (2000) stated that using a variety of evaluation and research methods is important, especially

- when a field of study is still in its infancy and little "strong theory" exists;
- when it is still unclear what factors influence learning and what outcome measures are most appropriate, given what level of learning is intended;
- when interactions among learners are complex and subtle;
- when the most interesting and important outcomes of the learning experience lie within these complex and subtle interactions. (p. 272)

EVALUATION PHASE OF THE ILDF FOR ONLINE LEARNING

The evaluation process presented in the ILDF for Online Learning incorporates multiple methods and perspectives on evaluation. Our philosophy is that formal or informal methods may be appropriate at different points in online learning design, development, and implementation and that the online learning developer needs to consider and carefully select from a range of evaluation approaches. Incorporating multiple methods (e.g., formal and/or informal), multiple perspectives (e.g., learner, colleague, stakeholder, management, administration), and multiple levels (learner's reactions, learning, behavior, and organizational results) can result in an effective evaluation of online learning. R. E. Clark (2000) also emphasized these ideas by stating that all evaluation efforts need to (a) adopt an early concern for evaluation, (b) use a multilevel evaluation plan, and (c) conduct a cost-effectiveness or impact analysis. The social and cultural factors surrounding the online learning effort often dictate the selection of evaluation methods. The scenarios presented at the beginning of this chapter attempt to portray different social and cultural contexts and are used to illustrate the application of the processes and methods in the evaluation phase across different contexts (highlighted in the next section).

Barksdale and Lund (2001), in their book *Rapid Evaluation*, provided an overarching systematic approach for designing evaluation efforts that incorporate the elements identified by R. E. Clark (2000). We adapted this approach for online learning by streamlining some of the steps originally geared toward business training sessions to align with the ILDF for Online Learning and to address many evaluation contexts. The Barksdale and Lund (2001) rapid evaluation process is primarily embedded in the first step of the evaluation phase of the ILDF for Online Learning: determining the purpose, desired results, and methods of evaluation. The underlying methods of the first step of the evaluation phase are listed next and are described in detail in the following subsections.

1. Clearly determine the purpose, desired results, and methods of evaluation.
   a. Determine the need for evaluation.
   b. Determine the purpose of the evaluation.
   c. Write an evaluation strategy statement.
   d. Determine the objectives of the evaluation strategy.
   e. Consider the social and cultural factors related to the evaluation.
   f. Determine the desired results of the evaluation strategy.
   g. Conduct a multilevel, or balanced, evaluation by using Kirkpatrick's levels of evaluation.
   h. Determine the level of formality or informality of the evaluation methods.
   i. Select evaluation methods congruent with the learning activities.
   j. Determine applicable measurement approaches.

Clearly Determine the Purpose, Desired Results, and Methods of Evaluation

If possible, practitioners should consider evaluation early in the design and development of online instruction or training. Planning for and conducting evaluations early in the process can provide significant information for both design and evaluation efforts (Barksdale & Lund, 2001; R. E. Clark, 2000). Evaluation efforts could include validating the need for online learning prior to design and identifying important elements to include in an online experience. Other evaluation efforts could determine "baseline" information about the set of conditions that will be replaced by online learning (R. E. Clark, 2000) for use in comparison with conditions after implementation. Determining methods early also allows for deliberate alignment of the learning activities with evaluation efforts, which results in meaningful outcomes. If the online learning developer can consider his or her evaluation purposes and needs in the enactment phase, then he or she can shape the learning activities to produce the most useful results for his or her evaluation purposes.

Determine the need for evaluation   Although we believe that evaluation efforts provide significant advantages for online learning development, many developers are unsure whether to conduct an evaluation effort because they perceive it to be too difficult or time consuming. Research shows that evaluation seldom occurs in instructional design efforts; therefore, developers cannot benefit from what might be learned (Tessmer & Wedman, 1995). Evaluation is a critical phase in the ILDF for Online Learning and can greatly contribute to practitioners' knowledge of the effectiveness of the pedagogical models and instructional strategies enacted online. Considering both informal and formal evaluation approaches may encourage online learning developers to incorporate evaluation processes in their design and development efforts, to share their findings with others, and to contribute to the improvement of the field of online learning.

   Determining the specific need for evaluation assists the developer in targeting the appropriate strategy and methods that can most benefit his or her online learning efforts. The specific need for evaluation can be determined by answering questions from Barksdale and Lund (2001) that are adapted in this chapter for online learning:

- Do you need to know whether your learners or employees think the online course or lesson is warranted or necessary? Has a need for the course or lesson been identified? Is evidence available to support the decision to conduct the course or lesson online?
- Do you need to know how the online materials might be improved?
- Do you need to know what additional elements need to be included to enhance the online experience?
- Do you need to know whether the skills or knowledge obtained in the online learning instruction or training are applied or used in another context?
- Do you need to provide evidence of the knowledge and skills gained by learners or employees to meet established standards of learning, accreditation, certification, or other purposes?
- Do you need to link the online learning experience to business, school, or organizational goals?
- Do you need to assess whether the online learning experience meets or exceeds best practices?
- Are you interested in collecting data to help develop future online learning design and development?

These questions are important for the developer to answer to determine his or her specific needs for evaluation, which can then direct the purpose and strategy for the particular online learning context.

Determine the purpose of the evaluation   Given an identified need, the practitioner must determine the overall purpose of the evaluation. Evaluation efforts can have multiple and varied goals, such as the following:

1. Determining the perceived value of online learning
2. Assessing the learning of specific knowledge or skills

3. Determining how what is learned may be applied in other contexts
4. Identifying the need for course improvements
5. Identifying the need for additional support and feedback for the learner
6. Determining whether the online course meets the organization's goals

Clearly identifying the purpose of the evaluation effort along with the desired results and methods is crucial in effectively judging the value or worth of online learning for the developer, learners, and organization.

Revisit the three scenarios at the beginning of this chapter. What are Tom's need and purpose for evaluating the online WebQuest activity? What about Professor Hughes? What are her stated need and purpose for evaluation? Which of the questions related to determining the need for online learning are most applicable to Beth's situation?

Write an evaluation strategy statement   Barksdale and Lund (2001) suggested writing a one- to three-statement paragraph that defines the purpose of the evaluation strategy. The evaluation strategy statements provide a mechanism with which the practitioner can begin to target the methods and measurement approaches that best align with an evaluation effort. Examples of evaluation strategy purpose statements are as follows:

- The purpose of the evaluation strategy is to provide information about my students' and colleagues' reactions to the online WebQuest entitled "How and Why Leaves Change Color," which explores photosynthesis. The evaluation will investigate how students integrate, synthesize, and understand resources on photosynthesis in a WebQuest activity, which will improve the development of my next online activity. The evaluation effort should also help position this unit within the state standards for fourth-grade science.
- The purpose of the evaluation strategy is to determine whether undergraduates demonstrate the use of argumentation strategies in the online nonfiction writing course examining the multiple perspectives on the war in Iraq. The evaluation will also solicit the students' perspectives on the online activities to contribute to our review of how the Web course authoring system supports these writing strategies.
- The purpose of the evaluation strategy is to determine the impact of the online learning community and knowledge management system on risk management and their use in risk management. In addition, the evaluation effort will examine members' perspectives on the community, how members interact with one another, how they apply what they have learned from the community, and any cost savings for the company related to the implementation of risk management procedures.

Determine the objectives of the evaluation strategy   Once an evaluation strategy statement has been written, the next step is to determine related objectives for conducting the evaluation. For example, the science teacher's evaluation strategy may require the development of a method for gathering his students' and colleagues' reactions to incorporating WebQuests as a new instructional strategy. This method could take the form of an online survey, a paper-based activity that asks for their opinion about the WebQuests, or even a classroom discussion documented by the teacher's reflective memos or notes.

In contrast, the university professor evaluating the online course on nonfiction writing skills needs to develop ways for her students to demonstrate the use of the argumentation strategies in the online writing activities. She might want to consider some learning activities that would allow her to preserve their attempts to apply the strategies as they progress through the class—such as online debates, role-plays, critiques, rebuttals, position papers, expert interviews, panels, and so forth. If she had planned her evaluation prior to the delivery of her course, this professor would have been able to shape the learning activities to yield useful information for her evaluation and assessment purposes.

The objectives of the developer of the online learning community on risk management are to determine an appropriate method for assessing members' reactions, use, application, and organizational impact. The developer needs to determine how she might collect this information. She might want to collect some of the information off-line as well as construct mechanisms within the online community system to collect other information. Objectives like these represent the tasks that the online developer might need to accomplish to conduct the evaluation.

Consider the social and cultural factors related to the evaluation   Barksdale and Lund (2001) recommended that when a practitioner is determining an evaluation strategy, he or she should consider what the evaluation needs to accomplish, the impact on the participants, and the overall payoff to the organization as a whole. Linking the evaluation to organizational or business goals strives to align the evaluation strategy with established organizational objectives and culture. Similarly, establishing an evaluation strategy for an online course that is compatible with program and university goals or intended learning outcomes can support the overall effectiveness of the educational system (Huba & Freed, 2000). The alignment of intended learning outcomes for an online or blended course with academic program and university goals and a compatible evaluation strategy also provides a solid direction for design and evaluation that will be valued in the social and cultural context (see Table 7.1).

In addition to taking into account the explicit organizational goals and outcomes, the online developer needs to consider the more implicit social and cultural factors present in an organization that may significantly contribute to and impact the evaluation strategy. As you can see by reading the preceding evaluation strategy statements, each evaluation effort serves a different purpose according to the specific cultural and social factors involved. For teachers in school settings, evaluating online learning may involve social interaction with students, teacher colleagues, and/or school administration. Not only can the multiple perspectives garnered from students, peers, and supervisors provide valuable input on how learning materials should be structured in a school-based setting, but they can also provide perspectives on the effectiveness of the online materials at the individual learner and school organizational levels.

Individuals involved in evaluating online courseware have relevant and varied perspectives to offer in all phases of designing and developing online instruction and training.

Table 7.1   Alignment of Online Evaluation Strategy with University, Program, and Course Outcomes

Institutional outcome
George Mason University will provide students with "a superior education enabling students to develop critical, analytical, and imaginative thinking" (George Mason University, 1994)

Academic program outcome
(Instructional Technology program)
Students can apply knowledge, skills, analytic thinking, and creativity to craft effective solutions to instructional challenges, including the design and development of instructional materials, by using the latest information technologies.

Course outcome (blended online and face to face)
Students can analyze, design, develop, and evaluate multimedia and Web-based instruction or training through the application of the instructional design process and authentic interaction with project stakeholders and the student design team.

Evaluation strategy
The purpose of the evaluation strategy is to analyze online group interaction and dialogue related to the application of the instructional design process to the project to glean evidence of critical and analytic thinking in design. The strategy will also determine individual analytic and creative contributions to the team design and development efforts through posted Web-based project products as well as professional interaction with stakeholders and clients.

For example, assessing the perspectives of stakeholders (e.g., management, or school or university administration) relevant to the online course prior to any design and development (e.g., during the exploration phase) would assist in directing the design and evaluation efforts. Similarly, evaluating learners', colleagues', and experts' reactions to a prototype of online learning materials would prevent costly revisions later in the enactment phase. Determining the overall payoff of online instruction or training for a specific organization requires knowledge of the political and financial factors important to the administration or management and is typically conducted during the final evaluation phase of the project.

The culture of an organization can also directly impact evaluation goals. In some school, corporate, and higher education settings, evaluation efforts are valued and encouraged, whereas in others such efforts are not. Justifying the benefit of conducting an evaluation of online learning is not an easy task in any setting. However, the benefits of systematic evaluation have been shown to improve instructional materials and to induce learning (Tessmer, 1993). An online learning developer can investigate the specific culture of the organization to determine the best case for conducting an evaluation. In the school scenario, teachers sharing their results with other teachers can improve both their own and their colleagues' professional practice. In higher education, faculty who implement evaluative processes in their online courses and publish the results can significantly contribute to the field of online learning and their own discipline. In business, companies benefit from the results of evaluative efforts related to online learning that are published through training organizations such as the American Society for Training & Development or are shared at professional conferences. Considering the specific social and cultural context related to online learning and evaluation can improve evaluative efforts, prevent obstacles, and encourage sharing and dissemination of useful results.

Determine the desired results of the evaluation strategy After identifying the need, purpose, strategy, objectives, and social and cultural factors related to the evaluation effort, determining the outcome or the desired results of the evaluation strategy can assist in further clarifying or focusing the effort. This step involves describing the learning objectives, desired outcomes, and learning environment; identifying the participants; assessing their needs; and determining the desired results or outcomes of the instruction or training (see Table 7.2).

Determining the desired results of the online instruction or training for participants in the evaluation helps to guide developers toward applicable evaluation methods. Often, multiple participants in an evaluation effort have different needs, which results in a multilevel evaluation. Evaluation efforts may involve stakeholders such as learners, trainees, teachers, trainers, colleagues, experts, clients, and so forth. Considering who might be impacted by the evaluation and the results the developer would like to see provides guidance for the selection of appropriate methods.

Analyzing the documentation from previous phases of the ILDF for Online Learning can assist the online learning developer in identifying participants to involve and clarifying the desired results of the evaluation on the basis of their needs. For example, one recommendation in the exploration phase is to document or describe the participants and stakeholders involved in the course and their knowledge, preferences, and attitudes about the online course prior to design and development. This documentation could serve as baseline information about who might participate in the evaluation effort and possibly provide additional data for comparison after the online course or training has been conducted. The enactment phase also results in identification of specific instructional strategies based on pedagogical models that result in a description of the instructional goals or intended learning outcomes. Documenting learning processes, pedagogical models, and instructional strategies selected and enacted with online technologies provides a rich, analytic description of the instructional or training methods that can then be evaluated (see Table 7.2).

Conduct a multilevel, or balanced, evaluation by using Kirkpatrick's levels of evaluation Addressing multiple levels of evaluation in online learning provides the developer with comprehensive knowledge about the impact of the instruction or training. Barksdale and Lund (2001) referred to this process as "balancing" the evaluation to include the customer view, the organization view, and evidence of learning and performance improvement to provide a comprehensive evaluation strategy.

Kirkpatrick's (1998) levels of evaluation permit the distinction of many of these views and their incorporation into an overall evaluation effort. A process that originated in 1959 and has been written about extensively in corporate human resources literature, Kirkpatrick's levels of evaluation are appropriate for all evaluation efforts, whether

Table 7.2 Alignment of Instruction or Training, Participants and Their Needs, and Desired Results of
Online Learning Evaluations

INSTRUCTION OR TRAINING	PARTICIPANTS AND NEEDS	DESIRED RESULTS
True Colors WebQuest: How and Why Do Leaves Change Color? Fourth-grade students engage in group-based authentic learning activity through hands-on activities and integrating and synthesizing information from various online resources to understand photosynthesis. This unit will cover photosynthesis through exploring leaves that are changing color and the importance of trees for our environment. Students will synthesize and present the findings in a multimedia presentation.	*Primary participants* Fourth-grade students need more learner-centered and engaging methods of studying photosynthesis. *Secondary participants* Fourth-grade teachers need to understand how their students are integrating and synthesizing information on photosynthesis. Fourth-grade teachers need to ensure alignment of classroom activities with science standards of learning	• Increased interest and engagement in learning about photosynthesis • Valued teaching approach by fourth-grade teachers in the school • Rich description of how students integrate and synthesize information on photosynthesis in a combination of hands-on and WebQuest activities, to guide future instruction • Alignment of instructional activities with state standards
War and Peace: An Online Nonfiction Writing Course Undergraduates participate in a situated learning experience, applying argumentative strategies in online writing activities. Students use argumentation strategies to establish and	*Primary participants* Undergraduate students who are required or elect to take a course to improve their professional writing skills *Secondary participants* Undergraduates who desire to take a writing course conducted primarily online	• Application of argumentation strategies taught in the course to writing exercises and assignments • In-depth investigation of the issue and exploration of multiple perspectives • Effective use of the online learning environment to support writing strategies

(Continued)

INSTRUCTION OR TRAINING	PARTICIPANTS AND NEEDS	DESIRED RESULTS
defend their position on the war in Iraq through various writing activities including debates, position papers, editorials, and so forth.		
A Risk Management Community: An Online Community of Practice Online learning community and knowledge management system that provides knowledge and learning resources on risk management. Program managers review, contribute, collaborate, and participate in an online community of practice to improve their knowledge of risk management processes and procedures.	*Primary participants* Program managers who are required to plan for potential future problems in the organization, not just current problems, in order to reduce risks and costs *Secondary participants* Subject matter experts who have experienced unexpected emerging risks and provide guidance to program managers to help them identify potential emerging risk events in their projects	• Distributed knowledge in risk management across the organization • Promotion of the application of risk management processes to emerging risk situations • Increasing participation and use of online learning community resources • Linkages from real-world problems to information and knowledge gained in the online learning community • Guidance provided to program managers through online coaching by subject matter experts experienced in risk management • Determination of cost–risk analysis from previous assessments

conducted in education, business, or industry settings. The four levels integrated with online learning are as follows:

Level 1: Reaction, or how learners perceive online instruction or training
Level 2: Learning, or the extent to which learners change attitudes, gain knowledge, or increase skill in online learning or training
Level 3: Behavior, or how learners have changed their behavior as a result of online instruction or training
Level 4: Results, or the final results that have occurred at the organizational level as a result of the delivery of online instruction or training

Kirkpatrick (1998) noted that evaluation efforts become more complex and time consuming as you advance through the levels. The Kirkpatrick evaluation model provides guidance for promoting a balanced evaluation strategy and can assist the online developer in targeting appropriate evaluation methods for his or her needs. Table 7.3 provides an illustration of the desired results of evaluation, aligned learning activities, and specific evaluation methods and measurement approaches according to Kirkpatrick's levels.

Level 1: Reaction At Level 1 of Kirkpatrick's model, the reaction or satisfaction of the individuals involved in the online instruction or training is evaluated. Evaluating learner reactions provides feedback that can assist developers in evaluating the effectiveness of the individual online program and can provide information for the improvement of online design and development efforts in general. Such evaluation can be accomplished in various ways, including the use of forms, surveys, interviews, or group discussions. Regardless of the method used for gathering information, ensuring a positive reaction to the online learning experience is important for supporting learning. Kirkpatrick (1998) indicated that a positive reaction to learning or training materials may not guarantee learning, but a negative reaction can reduce learning.

Level 2: Learning The second level of Kirkpatrick's model involves the more complex effort of evaluating learning. Knowledge learned, skills developed, or attitudes changed constitute learning in Kirkpatrick's (1998) view. Determining the intended learning outcomes of an online course or training is crucial at this level. Huba and Freed (2000) suggested asking the following questions:

> If I provide the best possible course for students, creating a stimulating environment for learning with opportunities to explore central ideas,
>
> - What will my students know?
> - What will they understand?
> - What will they be able to do with their knowledge at the end of the course? (p. 93)

The online learning developer needs to determine clear learning outcomes that align with learning activities to provide the foundation for selecting appropriate evaluation methods. Determining the desired learning results, or what students should know and do at the end of an online course or experience, can explicitly structure the evaluation

Table 7.3 Alignment of Desired Results, Learning Activites, and Evaluation Methods

DESIRED RESULTS OF EVALUATION	LEARNING ACTIVITIES	EVALUATION METHOD
True Colors WebQuest • Increased interest and engagement in learning about photosynthesis • Valued teaching approach by fourth-grade teachers in the school • Rich description of how students integrate and synthesize information on photosynthesis in a combination of hands-on and WebQuest activities, to guide future instruction • Revised classroom tests aligned with the instructional activities, students' and teachers' perceptions, and state standards	• Answer these guiding discussion questions: What would happen if there were no trees? How do trees stay alive? Why do leaves change color? • Draw and describe the process of how leaves change color. • Participate in a hands-on activity: watching leaves change color when they are exposed to light. • Locate Web resources that describe photosynthesis, and produce a multimedia presentation, using text and graphics to provide an explanation.	• *Level 2 (Learning):* Preassessment—Before and after the lesson, individual drawings of how leaves change color • *Level 3 (Behavior):* Documented observations of class interaction when the students are exploring resources and integrating hands-on activities in the WebQuest activity • *Level 1 (Reaction):* A survey of students' attitudes about the WebQuest activity • *Level 1 (Reaction):* A survey of teacher colleagues' attitudes about their implementation of the WebQuest activity and how the activity maps to science standards • *Level 2 (Learning):* A review of the multimedia products for their content accuracy according to a teacher-constructed rubric based on standards
War and Peace: An Online Nonfiction Writing Course • Application of argumentation strategies taught in the course to writing exercises and assignments • In-depth investigation of the issue and understanding of multiple sides of the issue through writing • Effective use of the online learning environment to support writing strategies	• Participate in online debates (with guidelines) about the issue. • Identify the presence or absence of the presented stages of an argument in an online debate. • Analyze and annotate sources that support the multiple perspectives on the issue. • Post key issues and join a group forum to further examine a selected key issue. • Articulate an individual hypothesis or claim about a selected key issue. • Gather evidence, evaluating sources and processing information, to support the hypothesis or claim.	• *Level 2 (Learning):* Preassessment: Analysis of students' initial arguments according to identified stages • *Level 2 (Learning):* Qualitative analysis of the online discussion and writing assignments for evidence of argumentation strategies after presentation of the identified stages • *Level 3 (Behavior):* Tracking of student usage of online tools and resources, as well as the amount of participation in the online course, through computer logs • *Level 1 (Reaction):* Solicitation

Table 7.3 Alignment of Desired Results, Learning Activites, and Evaluation Methods (*Continued*)

	• Write an editorial constructing the argument that demonstrates sound reasoning and the connection of evidence to claims through warrants and backing.	of students' perceptions of learning about the issue and multiple perspectives on the issue through the use of online conference tools • *Level 1 (Reaction):* An online form students use to rate the effectiveness of the online environment for the assignments
A Risk Management Community: An Online Community of Practice • Distributed knowledge in risk management across the organization • Promotion of the application of risk management processes to emerging risk situations • Increasing participation and use of online learning community resources • Linkages from real-world problems to information and knowledge gained in the online learning community • Guidance provided to program managers through online coaching by subject matter experts experienced in risk management • Determination of cost–risk analysis from previous assessments	• Across the company, access important resources and contact information related to risk management. • Connect with others involved in risk management processes. • Share information and knowledge through online discussions, case studies, shared events, and resources. • Learn processes through learning resources, tools, and collaborative discussions.	• *Level 1 (Reaction):* A member survey assessing the perceived value prior to use and the actual value after participation for several weeks in the online community • *Level 1 (Reaction):* An online member survey assessing the perceived value prior to implementation and the actual value of online coaching and mentoring by a subject matter expert after several weeks of implementation • *Level 2 (Learning):* Solicitation, from members, of case studies of the application of risk management processes related to information garnered from the site • *Level 3 (Behavior):* Tracking of the overall use of the site, as well as the number of contributions and generation of new ideas, at defined intervals • *Level 3 (Behavior):* Assessment of a unit's risk management procedures and knowledge prior to use of the online learning community and several months after to determine any behavior change • *Level 4 (Results):* Participants' cost–risk analyses that estimate, document, and evaluate the dollar costs required to perform tasks, compared with the actual costs to determine the effectiveness of the risk management process

method. For example, in Table 7.2, in the War and Peace: An Online Nonfiction Writing Course entry, the learning outcome is for the undergraduate students to apply argumentation strategies to their writing. The desired results of the evaluation are to determine how these students apply these particular strategies by analyzing their arguments before and after the instructional lesson teaching these strategies. The learning outcome is clearly identified and closely matches the desired results of the evaluation. The method of comparing student work prior to and at the end of the lesson on the argumentation strategies reflects a typical Level 2 learning evaluation.

Examining learning outcomes provides direction for evaluating knowledge, skills, and attitudes in an online environment. Drafting the desired results of the evaluation effort early in the process can also help the developer to formulate intended learning outcomes. The most formal evaluation efforts in Level 2 involve experimental studies with random assignment of participants and tight control of factors that might influence learning. Examples of this type of evaluation can be found in Chapter 3 (see Jacobson, Maouri, Mishra, & Kolar, 1996). Kirkpatrick (1998) emphasized evaluation designs that are less formal, promoting comparisons across groups (including a control group that does not receive the instruction or training if possible) but not requiring random assignment of participants, to determine any changes in learning. Evaluation methods like these are more demanding to conduct in an online context but can yield informative results if carefully planned.

Learning can also be examined through what Robson (2002) referred to as "flexible designs," which include case studies and other types of qualitative research designs that do not require "tight pre-specification of the design prior to data collection" (p. 164). Qualitative evaluation involves the intensive study of the background, status, and environmental interactions of a social system at the individual, group, institutional, or community level (Isaac & Michael, 1990). In many examples of evaluation in online learning qualitative research design (see, for example, Pena-Shaff, Martin, & Gay, 2001, described in Chapter 3) or a combination of experimental and qualitative techniques (see, for example, Barab, Thomas, & Merrill, 2001, described in Chapter 3) has been used.

Less formal methods of evaluating learning might include documenting differences in student learning through classroom tests, learning products produced, or observations of changes in student behavior. This type of evaluation is often described as "action research," which involves teachers' reflections on their professional practice (Arhar, Holly, & Kasten, 2001). As an example of this form of action research evaluation, Lewis (2002) promoted the use of "lesson studies," which originated in Japan, as a more informal type of collaborative evaluation that could be adapted to online learning. In lesson studies, teams of teachers closely study the administration and impact of a particular lesson. Teachers work in teams in which one teacher is involved in teaching while the other teacher gathers evidence of student learning and development. The lesson and evidence are presented, evaluated, and discussed among a group of teachers for the purposes of improvement and dissemination of valuable teaching techniques. This evaluation method has much to offer in the online context for peer collaboration and feedback on online course design and implementation.

Chou (2001) used a similar method in the evaluation of an online WebCT course addressing online computer-mediated communication by having several doctoral students observe student behavior and learning. The observers provided insights into student development across the course, instructor–student interaction, and course elements such as online discussions, journals, and general postings. This example demonstrates a less formal but valuable evaluation of an online environment that could be categorized as a Level 2 evaluation.

Level 3: Behavior   Kirkpatrick's (1998) third level of evaluation addresses the transfer of knowledge or skills to another context as evidence of a change in performance or behavior. This level of evaluation is much more difficult to determine and to attribute directly to online instruction or training. However, evaluating the behavior related to the identified knowledge, skills, and attitudes prior to and after online instruction or training can help to identify any change that may have occurred (Kirkpatrick, 1998). The Thomson Job Impact Study (NETg, 2003, See Chapter 4) highlighted in Chapter 4 provides an example of this level of evaluation. The evaluation required participants to rate their own level of proficiency with Microsoft Excel before and after blended training that included online methods. Supervisors were also asked to rate the participants' proficiency on this real-world task. Data on the participants' accuracy on the Excel tasks and time on task were collected and showed behavioral differences among the groups participating. The application of knowledge or skill can be evaluated in multiple ways, through observations, surveys, or interviews that might involve teachers or trainers, their students or subordinates, and administrators or supervisors. Using multiple sources of information and multiple perspectives can assist developers in detecting behavioral change and in considering how such change might be related to the online learning experience.

Incorporating formal qualitative and quantitative research designs in evaluation can provide useful information about learning. However, less formal evaluation methods may also be used to determine the worthwhileness of online learning. The evaluation process may also include the practical objectives of delivering a product or accomplishing specific goals, applying skills, and creating feedback mechanisms to determine progress toward these goals (Isaac & Michael, 1990).

Level 4: Results   Determining the organizational impact of online instruction or training, Kirkpatrick's (1998) fourth and final level of evaluation, may be the most difficult to achieve. Showing the broad impact of an online learning effort may be difficult in some cases because the content and process of learning that is addressed may not contain easily quantifiable, tangible evidence. Evaluating the overall impact of a specific online learning effort requires identification of relevant factors such as the reduction of accidents, an increase in sales volume, an increase in employee retention, an increase in student recruitment and attendance, or financial savings for the company, school, or university that might be influenced by online learning materials. Although attributing any organizational level change exclusively to online training may be impossible, Level 4 evaluations attempt to provide useful information that point to necessary changes in the instructional and training context (Kirkpatrick, 1998).

R. E. Clark (2000) advocated evaluating cost-effectiveness in all distance education or online training efforts by comparing the cost of two or more technology options and assessing the monetary and time costs of teaching or learning. Various models exist for considering factors related to organizational impact and return-on-investment models and may be useful for conducting Level 4 evaluations (see, for example, Horton, 2001; Levin, 1983).

Determine the level of formality or informality of the evaluation methods   The ILDF for Online Learning promotes consideration of a multilevel evaluation strategy. Table 7.3 highlights examples that combine different levels of evaluation (reflected in Kirkpatrick, 1998). For example, the True Colors WebQuest involves learning products produced (student drawings reflecting how the leaves change color before the WebQuest experience and student-generated multimedia representations of this process after) in the classroom. The teacher in this scenario also documented his observations of how students integrated and synthesized the hands-on activities with the WebQuest activities. In addition, he conducted a survey of his students to determine their reactions. In contrast with the results of the Thomson study (NETg, 2003, see Chapter 4), the results of the True Colors WebQuest evaluation were limited to impacting only his fourth-grade classroom, and the evaluation was conducted in a much less formal manner than that of the Thomson study. However, the systematic evaluation process that the teacher used provided rich information for his purposes. The selection of formal or informal methods depends on the developer's evaluation strategy, desired results, and the social and cultural context of the evaluation.

Less formal evaluation methods can provide useful information on online learning design and development efforts. For example, incorporating informal feedback mechanisms such as online self-assessment, reflection, peer or group feedback, and portfolio reviews may be just as useful as tests, surveys, interviews, and other formal research methods in particular cases. The same evaluation methods can also be implemented at different levels of formality. For example, learning logs or journals either can provide informal feedback for an instructor to review so that he or she can think about changes for the course or can be used as a data source for more rigorous qualitative analysis. Implementing a systematic approach such as the ILDF for Online Learning affords different methods and levels of formality that the developer can select from according to his or her goals and context.

Select evaluation methods congruent with the learning activities   A useful strategy is to examine the learning activities to determine whether the evaluation methods are congruent with what the learner will be doing in the online context during the instruction or training. Learning activities provide the developer with opportunities to collect embedded online feedback and other data (e.g., text responses, discussions, surveys, assignments, projects). For example, in the A Risk Management Community scenario, detailed in Table 7.3, the evaluation method that involved tracking site usage by the number of participant contributions and ideas generated was congruent with the intended learning activity of sharing information and knowledge in the community. By using the power of the online system to quickly generate activity logs, the online developer was able to measure how much information and knowledge sharing occurred.

Mapping learner activities to evaluation methods allows the developer to take advantage of the unique characteristics online delivery media afford for conducting evaluation efforts. Online learning activities can provide useful data for summative evaluation purposes in formal experimental, comparative, or qualitative evaluations. Other activities can provide informal feedback or continuous assessment of the learner's progress for formative evaluation purposes. Table 7.4 provides a sampling of learning activities that can be incorporated into online learning environments for evaluation and assessment purposes (Morgan & O'Reilly, 1999). Morgan and O'Reilly's (1999) methods for assessing learners online include instructional strategies (e.g., critical thinking, problem solving) and learning activities (e.g., essays, reports, reflective journals) that are enacted or embedded in technology-based environments and can be used for evaluation purposes.

Determine applicable measurement approaches   One of the most difficult challenges in creating an evaluation plan is determining how to measure the results of a systematic study. Determining the appropriate measurement approach for online learning is the next step in the evaluation phase of the ILDF for Online Learning. A *measure* is a standard, an instrument, or an approach used to assess the results of a learner's performance or learning. Barksdale and Lund (2001) suggested that the measurement approach should be selected prior to designing the instruction or training. Integrating and aligning the measurement approach with instruction or training is the key to successful and effective evaluation processes. As an example of a policywide focus on the integration of instruction and evaluation, efforts, The Pennsylvania State University established a set of principles for learner assessment in online learning or distance education courses. These principles include the following four:

1. Assessment instruments and activities should be congruent with the learning goals and skills required of the learner throughout a distance education program or course.
2. Assessment and measurement strategies should be integral parts of the learning experience—enabling learners to assess their progress, to identify areas for review, and to reestablish immediate learning or lesson goals.
3. Assessment and measurement strategies should accommodate the special needs, characteristics, and situations of the distance learner.
4. Distance learners should be given ample opportunities and accessible methods for providing feedback regarding the instructional design of the distance education program. (The Pennsylvania State University, n.d.)

Although these principles seem to be directed primarily toward learner assessment and formative evaluation, the guidelines could also be applied to summative evaluation. The evaluation phase of the ILDF for Online Learning provides guidance for mapping the evaluation strategies to learning activities to prompt creative solutions for measurement approaches in online learning. The online learning context provides features that can integrate continuous assessment or measurement approaches that provide information on the learner's progress, such as ungraded activities or tests; feedback; self-assessment quizzes and tests; formal feedback from the instructor, peers, or workplace colleagues; and informal dialogue with instructors, peers, or others

Table 7.4   Learning Activities and Types of Online Assessment

---

Critical thinking
- Essays
- Reports
- Reflective journals
- Discussions

Problem solving
- Multimedia or text-based scenarios
- Simulations using CD-ROM

Demonstrating techniques
- Videoconferencing
- Verification by workplace mentor or site monitor

Self-management
- Journal
- Autobiography
- Portfolio
- Learning contact

Information access/management
- Database development
- Bibliography
- Problem solving

Demonstrating knowledge
- Written exam with local proctors
- Quick feedback through multiple choice
- True/false matching
- Short answer tests

Designing or creating
- Portfolios
- Projects using video or the Web

Communicating
- Debate
- Role-play
- PowerPoint presentation
- Report journal
- Essay

Teamwork and collaboration
- E-mail
- Listserv
- Conferencing discussion or debate

Note. From *Assessing Open and Distance Learners* (pp. 49–53), by C. Morgan and M. O'Reilly, 1999, London: Kegan Page.

or workplace colleagues; and informal dialogue with instructors, peers, or others (Morgan & O'Reilly, 1999). The American Association for Higher Education (n.d.) advocates ongoing or continuous assessment or evaluation through a linked series of activities rather than an isolated "one-shot" assessment. Integrating opportunities for learners to demonstrate what they have learned at frequent points in the online course by capitalizing on the embedded features of the technology provides an opportunity to synthesize learning and to provide valuable feedback to both the learner and the developer for evaluation.

Other informal measurement approaches can include rubrics, checklists, and self-evaluation embedded in an online course to provide the learner and the developer with consistent guidelines for accomplishing online instructional or training tasks and valuable information on learner progress and attitudes. Many course management tools integrate features that permit the creation of tests, surveys, or usage data for an individual learner. Preserving asynchronous and synchronous discussions automatically captures qualitative data that can be carefully analyzed either during or after the conclusion of the course. These tools are used to measure the reaction, learning, behavioral, and organizational impact of online learning. Many of these methods encompass both formal and informal approaches to evaluation. Examples of some informal measurement approaches used for formative and summative online learning evaluation efforts are described in Table 7.5, and several are elaborated on later in this chapter.

Formatively Evaluate the Design and Development Prior to Launching the Online Course

Methods of formative evaluation   The ILDF for Online Learning promotes the integration of formative evaluation methods into the online development or evaluation effort. Formative evaluation is characterized as "a judgment of the strengths and weaknesses of instruction in its developing stages for the purposes of revising the instruction to improve its effectiveness and appeal" (Tessmer, 1993, p. 11). This purpose is different but complementary to the purpose of summative evaluation efforts, in which the effectiveness of the online instruction or training is evaluated after the online course is delivered and will not be revised. Formative evaluation procedures can be conducted in a variety of ways. According to Tessmer (1993), prominent methods of formative evaluation include the following:

- Expert review—experts review the instruction with or without the evaluator present. The experts can be content experts, technical experts, designers or instructors.
- One-to-one evaluation—one learner at a time reviews the instruction with the evaluator and comments upon it.
- Small group—the evaluator tries out the instruction with a group of learners and records their performance and comments.
- Field test—the evaluator observes the instruction being tried out in a realistic situation with a group of learners. (p. 15)

Table 7.5   Informal Evaluation Measurement Approaches

INFORMAL MEASUREMENT APPROACHES	LEARNER ACTIVITIES	DESCRIPTION AND EXAMPLES
Group evaluation by learners	• Use of online forms for group reports analyzing Web sites and integrating design guidelines • Use of online forms for individual reflection on design guidelines, with model answers provided • Application of the design guidelines in group Web development projects	Collis (1998) presented a model for ongoing, or continuous, evaluation activities in an online group-based experience in which were applied design guidelines to multimedia development. Evaluative mechanisms included individual examinations and group projects using self-, peer, and instructor evaluations. Students commented on peer evaluations and compared them with their own evaluations. Instructors implemented regular, periodic opportunities for peer feedback on projects and student evaluation of the course, often using the same forms and materials.
Instructor self-evaluation or reflection	• Identification of electronic resources on health topics • Evaluation, summarization, and annotation of electronic resources • Implementation of guided search strategies (formative assessment activity) • Publication of resources for sharing in discussion forum	Orsini-Jones and Davidson (1999) integrated a systematic and reflective approach for implementing a health science course by using WebCT. A cycle of iterative instructor planning, action, and reflection was implemented, which revealed that students required additional support in areas such as Internet searching. In response, the instructor incorporated an additional formative assessment activity that showed that students could evaluate resources but required support in search strategies. These results informed the next cycle of course development.
Group evaluation by instructors	Teacher participants • Study and improve the best available lessons • Think deeply about their long-term goals for students • Collaboratively plan lessons • Carefully study student learning	Lewis (2002) used collaborative peer feedback to prompt teachers to systematically study and determine lesson, unit, and subject area goals. Based on Japanese lesson study, this evaluation method involves collecting evidence of learning,

Table 7.5   Informal Evaluation Measurement Approaches (*Continued*)

INFORMAL MEASUREMENT APPROACHES	LEARNER ACTIVITIES	DESCRIPTION AND EXAMPLES
	and behavior • Develop powerful instructional knowledge • See their own teaching through the eyes of students and colleagues	increased interest or motivation, or students' treatment of one another in the classroom. This information is collected by a team of two teachers when one of them is engaged in teaching. The other team member gathers evidence of student learning and development. The lesson and evidence are presented, evaluated, and discussed to improve teaching. This evaluation technique has the potential to be applied in an online context for online instructors to collaboratively review, evaluate, and refine online teaching.
Portfolios	• Contributions to a Web portfolio to support development of personal theories of learning, promote reflection, and facilitate connections among theory and practice	Avraamidou and Zembal-Saul (2002) investigated how Web-based portfolio development supported reflective thinking by preservice elementary teachers in a professional development school. The results of examining teaching philosophies, reflection statements, and understanding of student-centered science learning revealed rich understanding, self-reflection, and self-evaluation with time.
Checklists	• Evaluation of distance and online learning materials	Clarke (2001) presented a checklist to use to examine distance and online learning materials for key features such as their timeliness, objectives, learning strategies, suitability, and quality. Evaluation methods included independent review of the materials. Expert and learner reviews are also suggested.
Rubrics	• Required online discussion partici-	Dabbagh (2003) constructed several rubrics addressing the level and *(Continued)*

Table 7.5 Informal Evaluation Measurement Approaches (*Continued*)

INFORMAL MEASURMENT APPROACHES	LEARNER ACTIVITIES	DESCRIPTION AND EXAMPLES
	pation • Facilitation and moderation of online discussions incorporating evidence of critical thinking and synthesis	quality of online postings and evaluating student moderation and facilitation of discussions for an instructional design course. A protocol for posting threads, guidelines for contributions, a rubric for determining the quantity and responsiveness of timely contributions, and criteria with which to judge student facilitation and moderation of online discussions were used for evaluation of student performance in the course.
Survey questionnaires	• Posting of discussions • Tracking of participation and use of computer tools, such as content creation, student tracking, and synchronous and asynchronous tools • Pre- and postcourse surveys	Peled and Rashty (1999) examined precourse questionnaires on student characteristics and expectations in the online environment and postcourse questionnaires focused on the effectiveness of the course along with quantitative data from computer log files and qualitative data from discussions, to evaluate the Introduction to Political Science course in Jerusalem. Student use of course areas showed more passive than active participation in the course, and questionnaire responses confirmed what computer tracking logs showed: that most students were satisfied with the online course and that confidence increased as the course progressed.
Computer tracking and data logs	• Online posting of an action plan for application of lockout procedures, for others' review • Application of learned procedures to the case study	Pappas, Lederman, and Broadbent (2001) monitored student performance in a 2-week Web-based course for the manufacturing industry. Tracking the amount and quality of participation in online discussions during the 2-week course and mapping participation to final case study responses provided formative and summative information for feedback and final evaluation purposes.

These methods can be incorporated into the design and development of online instruction or training at multiple points. Nieveen (1997) identified four stages and suggested modes of formative evaluation that might be applicable at each stage. The first stage is the *design specification stage,* in which only a description of the program or online learning environment exists. This stage correlates with the exploration stage of the ILDF for Online Learning and might include the use of theory or expert-based reviews to determine whether the plan for the online instruction or training is congruent with the identified problem or task. According to Nieveen, the second stage is the *global program stage,* in which only a few elements of the design have concrete form. This stage correlates with the early enactment phase, and formative evaluation might focus on expert review of the enacted instructional strategies and the feasibility or practicality of implementing the remaining design. In the third stage, the *partially detailed stage,* a segment of the online instruction or training has been developed in detail and can be tested with learners in the field as well as with experts. This stage correlates with the later enactment phase, in which some instructional strategies are implemented in detail by using online technologies and can then be evaluated. The fourth stage, the *extrinsic quality stage,* focuses on the implementation of a close-to-final version of the online instruction or training and promotes formative evaluation efforts involving realistic conditions and multiple settings.

A systematic effort is also required in formative evaluation to identify the purpose and nature of the evaluation. For example, Chou (2001) conducted a systematic investigation of an online course, using formative evaluation methods to examine synchronous computer-mediated communication (CMC) systems in order to (a) examine the characteristics of several synchronous tools, (b) identify features that were conducive to online interactions, (c) understand how novice learners adapt to synchronous CMC systems, and (d) investigate features that would be central to the design of synchronous learning systems based on a constructivist design. The focus of the course was on exploring theories and applications for CMCs and consisted of group-moderated discussions that involved searching, for and choosing a topic, discussing the class procedures, and providing background information for the class to read, as well as intensive online writing activities. The students were provided with guidelines for conducting and participating in student-centered discussions and implemented the assignments with various CMC synchronous systems, including WebCT chat, Netscape CoolTalk, CU-SeeMe, Activeworlds, and The Palace. The formative evaluation methods included observer logs by four doctoral candidates who observed the course for student development, instructor–student interaction, and course elements. The observers read student postings, journals, and conference transcripts, and field-tested functions of the CMC synchronous systems. Students rated their skills in CMC environments at the beginning, middle, and end of the semester, using a Likert-type scale, and rated the CMC synchronous systems on social presence, communication effectiveness, and communication interface.

These multiple sources of data in the formative evaluation provided rich information on the participants' reactions and activity. A review of previous course data showed that the students used the synchronous tools in a playful, nonfocused manner. However, the student-centered guidelines for online discussions introduced in this course produced more focused discussions. A positive attitude change was noted as the course progressed, and skill improvement was noted in pre-, mid-, and end-semester self-reports. Interestingly, the students complained most about WebCT in their journals during the first week of using the system. However, the WebCT system received the highest ratings at the end of the semester. The Palace was rated second because of its inclusion of affective components such as avatars, voice activation, and bubble messages. CU-SeeMe and CoolTalk were rated lower as a result of poor audio and video transmission during the semester. After examining the multiple sources of data for this formative evaluation, Chou (2001) created the following list of suggested features for a synchronous learning environment:

- *Low bandwidth:* Participants preferred fast-loading conferencing tools.
- *Ease of navigation:* Clear navigation presents frustration.
- *Accessibility:* Excessive technical steps should be avoided.
- *Nonintrusiveness:* The environment should afford separate and private communication spaces.
- *Affective affirmation:* Affective affirmation allows positive feedback from the system through avatar facial expressions, which indicate moods, or tone of voice from other students.
- *Fun and pleasure:* The environment should have a relaxing, gamelike atmosphere with graphical representations.
- *Humanizing and sensitive qualities:* Students need to be able to represent themselves through avatars and nonverbal cues sensitive to gender and cultural differences.
- *Good audio and video quality:* Students require a high level of quality to stay engaged.
- *Support tools for knowledge construction:* The environment should have built-in functions such as conferencing, transcript recording, whiteboards, file transfer, brainstorming, note taking, and voting to facilitate online conversations.
- *Community building:* The environment should promote small-group collaboration on tasks to help establish a sense of community.

Usability testing A specific type of formative evaluation that focuses primarily on the effectiveness of the instructional or training materials is usability testing. Rubin (1994) outlined a systematic approach to conducting usability testing that examines the integration of user-centered design and product design. Usability testing, as a type of formative evaluation that capitalizes on the user's perspective, provides useful information for ensuring the effective design of online learning environments. Rubin described user-centered design as the practice of designing products so that users can perform required use, operation, service, and supportive tasks with a minimum of stress and maximum efficiency. Space limitations prevent a detailed description of this methodology (see Rubin, 1994, for a full discussion of this method). However, many of the considerations in usability testing are similar to other evaluative efforts. According to Rubin, the six basic steps or elements of usability testing are as follows:

1. Develop a problem statement.
2. Use a representative sample of end users.
3. Engage end users in actual instruction or a training environment.
4. Observe and probe the end users' experience.
5. Collect (and analyze) qualitative or quantitative performance and preference measures.
6. Recommend improvements to the design.

Methods and measurement approaches for usability testing can be as varied as other evaluation efforts. Rubin (1994) recommended techniques such as participatory design, in which one or more representative users are included on the design team to provide input and evaluate in-progress design efforts. Focus groups, groups of user representatives, are typically used in the early stages of design to provide formative evaluation input. Other methods include (a) surveys to determine user preferences, (b) walk-throughs to explore early concepts or designs, (c) tests to assess user understanding of navigation elements, (d) expert evaluations to review the system for a specific purpose, and (e) field studies in which users try out the materials after they are significantly developed. These methods focus specifically on the usefulness, effectiveness, and operation of an online system, as well as on the users' perceptions and general impressions. Incorporating several cycles of formative evaluation and/or usability testing best guarantees a usable and an effective online course.

Revise the Online Materials According to the Results of the Formative Evaluation

Conducting formative evaluations of instructional materials results in improved instruction and increases in student learning (Nathenson & Henderson, 1980). Tessmer (1993) indicated that these types of improvements are found in all types of instruction, including computer-based and multimedia instruction or training, that capitalize on formative evaluation methods. Formative evaluation (including usability testing) can identify the major and minor target areas for revision in online learning materials. Rubin (1994) suggested a quick preliminary review of the formative evaluation testing results to determine problems that online developers can begin work on immediately. An online learning development team may need a written report that compiles, summarizes, and communicates the data and results to all team members, whereas an individual developer may require only a bulleted list of elements to address.

Rubin (1994) also suggested prioritizing the problems by criticality. Determining the severity of the problem and the probability of its occurrence provides a determination of the criticality. For example, during the creation of an online learning community, usability testing revealed that participants could not locate the log-in prompt and did not realize they needed to log in with a user name and password until they could not access other parts of the site. The frustration expressed by all users, the repeated occurrence of this problem, and the importance of the log-in for accessing the rest of the site made this the most severe and critical problem to address. Once the log-in screen was revised and placed more prominently on the screen, these problems were eliminated.

Implement the Online Learning Experience and Evaluate the Results According to the Identified Goals

The ILDF for Online Learning promotes both formative and summative evaluation as valuable and complementary methods that can provide useful results to inform the application of instructional strategies (based on pedagogical models) in the online learning context. By implementing sound evaluation processes relevant to identified goals and sharing findings with others through academic journals, teacher discussion groups, corporate presentations' or other methods, each practitioner can significantly contribute to the improvement of the field of online learning.

The evaluation cases described next depict a limited but informative sample of a range of evaluation implementation efforts in online learning. The evaluation purpose and methods may vary, but all involved a systematic process for implementing an online learning experience and then evaluating it. We encourage you to identify your own examples of implemented online learning evaluations, or, better yet, to conduct one.

Group learning   Many evaluation methods detailed in the online learning literature provide descriptive data based on a single course. These efforts typically do not extend beyond Kirkpatrick's Level 1 evaluations but can include valuable and informative qualitative or quantitative data. For example, Collis (1998) described a model for continuous evaluation in an online group–based experience applying design guidelines to multimedia development. The learning activities in the online course included group reports analyzing Web sites according to specific design guidelines, as well as individual reflections and application of the guidelines in a group-based multimedia development project. The evaluation methods were congruent with the learning activities and included individual examinations and group projects evaluated by self-evaluation, peer-evaluation, and instructor evaluation online forms. The instructors implemented continuous evaluation through regular and periodic opportunities for students to receive online feedback on their projects from their group members, as well as a required self-evaluation of the project for whole-class review. Instructors used the same online evaluation form that provided criteria for application of design guidelines to inform their final evaluations for the course. Although in this example, primarily reaction-level data were examined, the methods described provide a good example of incorporating multiple perspectives on student work into online evaluation. For detailed procedures and results, refer to the original study cited in the References.

Computer logs and online survey questionnaires   Many online course authoring tools permit tracking of an individual student's activity on the site and allow for instantaneous review of survey or questionnaire data. Incorporating this descriptive information into evaluation efforts can provide useful data for summative evaluation. Peled and Rashty (1999) integrated Level 1 and Level 3 evaluation methods, examining survey questionnaire responses and online discussion transcripts that evaluated reactions, as well as computer log files of student activity. These researchers implemented a precourse questionnaire that collected information on student characteristics and expectations of the online Introduction to Political Science learning course. The postcourse survey focused on the effectiveness of the course related to student confidence. The Web-based learning environment automatically collected information on the amount of participation, students' preferred learning tools, and the use of discussion groups. All this information was integrated to show the behavior of students in the online course related to their location, gender, and self-reported level of computer confidence and satisfaction. This example highlights the ease of collecting course data by using current Web tools to better understand student behavior.

Collaborative and individual instructor reflections Evaluation efforts can incorporate perspectives from instructors as well as from students or participants. Lewis (2002) championed this idea through her evaluation of Japanese lesson-study cycles, which encompass a collaborative peer feedback system. In lesson studies, teachers work in teams: One teacher is involved in teaching, while the other teacher gathers evidence of student learning and development. The data are presented, evaluated, and discussed among a group of teachers for the purposes of dissemination and improvement of teaching techniques. As stated previously, this evaluation method has much to offer in the online context for peer collaboration and for feedback on the online course design and implementation.

Orsini-Jones and Davidson (1999) implemented a similar approach with an individual instructor who used a systematic process of planning, action, and reflection in multiple cycles of her WebCT-based health sciences course. Learning materials were adapted and created on the basis of the instructor's reflections. In response to a student's request for additional guidance on Internet search strategies, the instructor created and posted a formative assessment exercise. The exercise revealed that students could evaluate Web resources in health science but required additional support in searching for them. This information was used to formatively revise the course for the next implementation cycle.

The preceding examples typify the more informal, yet powerful evaluation methods supported by the documentation and reflection cycles in the ILDF for Online Learning. Typically, these efforts rely on Level 1 reaction data from multiple sources, including other instructors and students, but can also incorporate Level 2 learning information related to qualitative and quantitative evidence of student progress and attitudes.

Mixed quantitative and qualitative methods More formal evaluation efforts can incorporate extensive quantitative and qualitative data collection and analysis in an experimental study. Uribe, Klein and Sullivan (2003) described a study of the effects of collaborative learning on solving authentic problems by using a computer-mediated environment with a Reserve Officer Training Corps (ROTC) class. The learning activities that were implemented included students' progression through a Web-based instructional program on problem-solving strategies and student application of the problem-solving strategies to realistic scenarios. The students interacted with the instructional materials on either an individual or a collaborative basis (groups of two with a high-ability student paired with a low-ability student) by using Blackboard. The measurement approaches were highly congruent with the learning activities and included an embedded knowledge quiz assessing student learning of the problem-solving process, as well as a researcher-constructed rubric to evaluate the scenario essay responses. Additional measurement approaches included a 10-item attitude survey and qualitative analysis of online collaborative discussions. These evaluation methods depict a formal multilevel study that incorporates Level 1 student reactions assessed through quantitative surveys and two open-ended responses. The researchers also implemented a Level 2 evaluation of learning through a researcher-constructed rubric assessing application of the problem-solving knowledge to authentic scenarios, time on task, and qualitative analysis of the related online discussions. The study showed that collaborative dyads performed significantly better on the tests and spent more time on the instruction than did participants who worked alone. This study illustrates a multilevel, formal experimental evaluation strategy using multiple methods to reveal the impact of collaborative learning on problem solving in a Web-based course environment.

Qualitative observation and Usage   Evaluation efforts can examine the impact of instructor perspectives on student actions and behavior in the online environment by using formal qualitative methods. Fishman (2000) examined how teachers' expertise with and attitudes toward online learning activities influenced secondary (9th, 10th, 11th, and 12th-grade) students' use of online tools. The learning activities involved the use of several asynchronous communication systems, including e-mail, Usenet news discussion groups, and a computer-conferencing system, and a multimedia authoring tool. Many of these features were integrated into an online "collaboratory notebook" to support group projects in earth science.

The evaluation effort examined the students' online activities with regard to number of e-mail messages sent, news messages posted, and notebook pages created, across 13 classes. In addition, one-on-one interviews were conducted with teachers, who discussed how the online tools supported the activities. The teachers rated their own skill and comfort with the online tools. This information provided a detailed description of the patterns of student use and how they are influenced by a teacher's actions and intentions in an individual classroom. This study incorporated Level 1 data from the teachers by evaluating their reaction to their use of online tools in science lessons and Level 3 data by depicting weekly intervals of student behavior, through the use of asynchronous tools. Although this study did not specifically measure changes in online student behavior in individual classrooms, it did provide an informal evaluation of the observed usage of online tools across several classrooms.

CHAPTER SUMMARY

In this chapter, we addressed issues and processes related to the evaluation of online instruction and training environments. An evaluation process model adapted for online learning environments was presented, along with an overview of multiple evaluation methods and measurement approaches. Kirkpatrick's (1998) levels of evaluation were presented and described. Finally, examples of the implementation of different evaluation methods were presented to illustrate the levels of evaluation and the range and scope of formative and summative evaluation approaches in online learning. As these evaluation examples demonstrate, multiple levels and methods can be incorporated into evaluation efforts in the online context. The unique capabilities of online tools can provide rich information for evaluating online instruction or training. Most important, a well-formed evaluation strategy that incorporates a thoughtful, systematic approach can provide a wealth of information related to the "worthwhileness" of online courses. Using the systematic approach of the ILDF for Online Learning and sharing the results with a wider community of teachers, professors or trainers may ultimately improve the practice of online learning, design, and development.

LEARNING ACTIVITIES

1. Locate a few published evaluations related to online learning and determine the methods and measurement approaches used and the level of evaluation according to Kirkpatrick's levels.
2. With the articles and sites obtained in Activity 1, map the evaluation efforts to Figure 7.1 and discuss where the studies may fall on the informal to formal evaluation continuum.
3. Also with the articles and sites obtained in Activity 1, determine which studies seem to be formative evaluation efforts and which seem to be summative evaluation efforts.
4. Visit the companion Web site for this book (http://www.prenhall.com/dabbagh) and access the sample of research studies associated with Chapter 3. Determine how many studies use experimental methods, qualitative methods, mixed methods, or other methods. Discuss your results.
5. Create a table that reflects the desired results of your online learning evaluation, the learning activities, and the evaluation method. Share this table with a partner to determine whether the elements are congruent.
6. Document how you would conduct an evaluation of your online instruction or training. Create a table describing briefly how you would complete the following steps:
   a. Clearly determine the purpose, desired results, and methods of evaluation.
   b. Formatively evaluate the design and development prior to launching the online course.
   c. Revise the online materials according to the results of the formative evaluation.
   d. Implement the online learning experience and evaluate the results according to the identified goals.

RESOURCES

Books

The following books are critical to understanding the theoretical underpinnings of the evaluation process model and methods discussed in this chapter. These books may be consulted for further elaboration as needed.

Arhar, J. M., Holly, M. L., & Kasten, W. C. (2001). *Action research for teachers: Traveling the yellow brick road.* Upper Saddle River, NJ: Merrill/Prentice Hall.

Mann, C., & Stewart, F. (2000). *Internet communication and qualitative research: A handbook for researching online.* London: Sage.

Maxwell, J. (1996). *Qualitative research design: An interactive approach.* (Vol. 41, Applied Social Research Methods Series). Thousand Oaks, CA: Sage.

Robson, C. (2002). *Real world research: A resource for social scientists and practitioners* (2nd ed.). Malden, MA: Blackwell.

Additional Resources

Explore additional resources at the companion Web site (http://www.prenhall.com/dabbagh) to learn more about how to evaluate online learning. Especially see the Online Discussion protocols and rubrics for information on how to structure and evaluate asynchronous discussion forums. These protocols and rubrics have been widely used nationally and internationally in various online learning contexts.

REFERENCES

American Association for Higher Education. (n.d.) *Assessment forum: 9 principles of good practice for assessing student learning.* Retrieved September 29, 2003, from http://www.aahe.org/assessment/principl.htm

Arhar, J. M., Holly, M. L., & Kasten, W. C. (2001). *Action research for teachers: Traveling the yellow brick road.* Upper Saddle River, NJ: Merrill/Prentice Hall.

Barab, S. A., Thomas, M. K., & Merrill, H. (2001). Online learning: From information dissemination to fostering collaboration. *Journal of Interactive Learning Research, 12*(1), 105–143.

Barksdale, S., & Lund, T. (2001). *Rapid evaluation.* Alexandria, VA: American Society for Training & Development.

Bernard, R. M., de Rubalcava, R., & St. Pierre, D. (2000). Collaborative online distance learning: Issues for future practice and research. *Distance Education, 21*(2), 260–277.

Chou, C. C. (2001). Formative evaluation of synchronous CMC systems for a learner-centered online course. *Journal of Interactive Learning Research, 12*(3/4), 173–192.

Clark, R. C., & Mayer, R. E. (2003). *E-learning and the science of instruction.* San Fransisco: Jossey-Bass/Pfeiffer.

Clark, R. E. (2000). Evaluating distance education: Strategies and cautions. *The Quarterly Review of Distance Education, 1*(1), 3–16.

Clarke, A. (2001). *Assessing the quality of open and distance learning materials.* Leicester, UK: National Institute of Adult Continuing Education. (ERIC Document Reproduction Service No. ED459362).

Collis, B. (1998). Building evaluation of collaborative learning into a WWW-based course: Pedagogical and technical experiences. *Indian Journal of Open Learning, 7*(1), 67–77.

Dabbagh, N. (2003). *Online discussion protocols and rubrics.* Retrieved from http://mason.gmu.edu/~ndabbagh/wblg/online-protocol.html

Fishman, B. (2000). How activity fosters CMC tool use in classrooms: Reinventing innovations in local contexts. *Journal of Interactive Learning, 11*(1), 3–27.

George, J., & Cowan, J. (1999). *A handbook of techniques for formative evaluation.* London: Kegan Page.

George Mason University. (1994). *Faculty and staff handbook.* Retrieved from http://www.gmu.edu/facstaff/handbook/preamble.html

Gibbons, A. S., Lawless, K., Anderson, T. A., & Duffin, J. R. (2000). The Web and model-centered instruction. In B. Khan (Ed.), *Web-based instruction* (Vol. 7; pp. 137–146). Englewood Cliffs, NJ: Educational Technology Publications.

Gray, P. J. (1989). *Achieving assessment goals using evaluation techniques: New directions for higher education.* San Francisco: Jossey-Bass.

Gunawardena, C. N., Lowe, C., & Carabajal, K. (2000, February). *Evaluating online learning: Models and methods.* Paper presented at the Society for Information Technology and Teacher Education (SITE) Conference, San Diego, CA.

Hara, N., Bonk, C. J., & Angeli, C. (2000). Content analysis of online discussion in an applied educational psychology course. *Instructional Science, 28*(2), 115–152.

Horton, W. (2001). *Evaluating e-learning.* Alexandria, VA: American Society for Training & Development.

Huba, M. E., & Freed, J. E. (2000). *Learner-centered assessment on college campuses: Shifting the focus from teaching to learning.* Needham Heights, MA: Allyn & Bacon.

Isaac, S., & Michael, W. B. (1990). *Handbook in research and evaluation: A collection of principles, methods, and strategies useful in the planning, design, and evaluation of studies in education and the behavioral sciences* (3rd ed.). San Diego, CA: EdITS.

Jacobson, M., Maouri, C., Mishra, P., & Kolar, C. (1996). Learning with hypertext learning environments: Theory, design and research. *Journal of Educational Multimedia and Hypermedia, 5*(3/4), 239–281.

Jonassen, D. H. (1991). Evaluating constructivist learning. *Educational Technology, 31*(9), 28–33.

Kanuka, H., & Anderson, T. (1998). Online social interchange, discord and knowledge construction. *Journal of Distance Education, 13*(1), 57–74.

Kirkpatrick, D. L. (1998). *Evaluating training programs.* San Francisco: Berrett-Koehler.

Kozma, R. (2000). The relationship between technology and design in educational technology research and development: A reply to Richey. *Educational Technology Research & Development, 48*(1), 19–21.

Levin, H. H. (1983). *Cost effectiveness: A primer.* Beverly Hills, CA: Sage.

Lewis, C. (2002). *Lesson study: A handbook of teacher-led instructional change.* Philadelphia: Research for Better Schools.

Morgan, C., & O'Reilly, M. (1999). *Assessing open and distance learners.* London: Kegan Page.

Nathenson, M. B., & Henderson, E. S. (1980). *Using student feedback to improve learning materials.* London: Croom Helm.

NETg. (2003). *Thomson Job Impact Study: Final results: The next generation of corporate learning: Achieving the right blend.* Retrieved from http://www.netg.com/Upload/uk_ThomsonJobImpactStudy.pdf

Nieveen, N. (1997). *Computer support for curriculum developers: A study on the potential of computer support in the domain of formative curriculum evaluation.* Unpublished doctoral dissertation, Faculty of Educational Science and Technology, University of Twente, The Netherlands.

Orsini-Jones, M., & Davidson, A. (1999). From reflective learners to reflective lecturers via WebCT. *Active Learning, 10,* 32–38.

Pappas, G., Lederman, E., & Broadbent, B. (2001). Monitoring student performance in online courses: New game–new rules. *Journal of Distance Education, 16*(2), 66–72.

Peled, A., & Rashty, D. (1999). Logging for success: Advancing the use of WWW logs to improve computer mediated distance learning. *Journal of Educational Computing Research, 21*(4), 413–431.

Pena-Shaff, J., Martin, W., & Gay, G. (2001). An epistemological framework for analyzing student interactions in computer-mediated communication environments. *Journal of Interactive Learning Research, 12*(1), 41–68.

The Pennsylvania State University. (n.d.). *An emerging set of guiding principles and practices for the design and development of distance education.* University Park, PA: Author. Retrieved from http://www.cde.psu.edu/DE/IDE/guiding_principles/

Reeves, T. C. (1997). Established and emerging evaluation paradigms for instructional design. In C. R. Dills & A. J. Romiszowski (Eds.), *Instructional development paradigms* (pp. 163–198). Englewood Cliffs, NJ: Educational Technology Publications.

Robson, C. (2002). *Real world research: A resource for social scientists and practitioners* (2nd ed.). Malden, MA: Blackwell.

Rubin, J. (1994). *Handbook of usability testing: How to plan, design and conduct effective tests.* New York: Wiley.

Tessmer, M. (1993). *Planning and conducting formative evaluations: Improving the quality of education and training.* London: Kegan Page.

Tessmer, M., & Wedman, J. (1995). Context-sensitive instructional design models: A response to design research, studies and criticism. *Performance Improvement Quarterly, 8*(3), 38–54.

Uribe, D., Klein, J., & Sullivan, H. (2003). The effect of computer-mediated collaborative learning on solving ill-defined problems. *Educational Technology Research & Development, 51*(1), 5–19.

Wilson, B. (1996). What is a constructivist learning environment? In B. G. Wilson (Ed.), *Constructivist learning environments: Case studies in instructional design* (pp. 3–8). Englewood Cliffs, NJ: Educational Technology Publications.

AUTHORING TOOLS: PARADIGMS, USAGE, AND FUTURE IMPLICATIONS

8

After completing this chapter, you should understand the following:

- The general principles and features of authoring tools

- Why hypermedia is a critical feature of authoring tools

- The pedagogical implications of authoring tools as they relate to designing hypermedia learning environments

- The differences among multimedia authoring tools, Web-based authoring tools, course management systems (CMSs), and content management systems

- The evolution of authoring tools from technological and pedagogical perspectives

- The leading authoring tools in higher education, K–12, and corporate sectors

- The future implications of authoring tools

CONSIDER THE FOLLOWING THREE SCENARIOS:

Classified Training, by Greta Ballard: Managers of a federal organization want to train their personnel on a classified procedure. The procedure involves preparing trainees to assume the roles of on-the-job-training (OJT) instructors or OJT program managers in district offices across the United States. The training must follow specific standards outlined in the *OJT Guide*. Because of the high security surrounding this training program, Web-based training (WBT) has been ruled out as an option. Stand-up training has also been ruled out as a result of the complexities associated with scheduling such training in a timely manner at the various district offices. In addition, because procedures and roles are dictated in the *OJT Guide* and there are correct and incorrect ways of accomplishing the job, the team assigned to develop this training decided that the theoretical grounding of the training will be mainly objectivist. Given these constraints, the team decided that **computer-based instruction (CBI)** is the most appropriate format for designing, developing, and delivering this training. The questions facing the team now are as follows: What authoring tool should we use to develop this training? and Which features should we be looking for in an authoring tool to ensure effective and efficient CBI development? The team members set out to study the characteristics of authoring tools so that they can select a tool that best fits their needs.

Web-Enhanced Instruction: A professor in a higher education institution wants to develop a Web site to support the Introduction to Astronomy class that he teaches. The professor would like to include on this Web site online resources for students to explore so that they can better understand the principles and concepts under study and stay current with the latest developments in the field. He would also like students to discuss the course content online in small groups and collaboratively create Web sites that inform the general public about recent developments in astronomy. Which authoring tool should this professor be considering? Should the professor use a Web development tool or a CMS?

Course Management or Content Management System?: An instructional designer working for a large university has been tasked with identifying an off-the-shelf CMS that has the following features: (a) a powerful search engine, (b) a user-friendly interface, (c) the ability to generate and store learning objects, (d) the ability to generate and store complex queries, (e) the capability for users to browse the knowledge base, and (f) the ability to generate documentation on user demand. The instructional designer has extensive experience with CMSs and their features but is not familiar with content management systems. The instructional designer prepares the following questions to research: What is the difference between a CMS and a content management system? Are content management systems an extension of CMSs? Are there other names for these tools on the market? and What are learning objects? To get started, the instructional designer posts these questions to an educational technology Listserv.

As you begin reading this chapter, think about these scenarios and your experi-
ence with authoring tools or CMSs. For example, have you ever had to compare
and contrast authoring tools to make an appropriate selection for your organi-
zation? If so, which features did you consider in this comparison? technical? cost?
pedagogical? ease of use? Have you used an authoring tool to develop instruction?
What were some of the pedagogical features of the instructional product? Have
you used a CMS as an instructor or a student? What were some of the features
that you found particularly useful?

This chapter covers the general characteristics of multimedia and Web-based
authoring tools and provides a thorough description of their features and instructional
implications. The chapter also includes a description of the evolution of authoring tools
from technological and pedagogical perspectives and an introduction to CMSs as a class
of authoring tools specifically designed to develop and deliver online learning. Content
management systems are also introduced as tools that facilitate the development of
learning objects. The chapter concludes with a discussion of the future implications of
authoring tools and CMSs.

WHAT ARE AUTHORING TOOLS?

Authoring tools are software tools that enable instructional designers, educators, teachers, and learners to design interactive multimedia and hypermedia learning environments without knowledge of programming languages. "The premise behind authoring
tools is the absence of a programmer or the ability of designers with little or no programming experience to develop and design instructional applications" (Hedberg &
Harper, 1998). For example, *multimedia* authoring tools (also known as *CD-ROM-based*
authoring tools) facilitate the development of CBI by masking the programming layer,
and Web-based authoring tools facilitate the development of Web-based instruction
(WBI) by masking the HTML scripting layer (Craney, 1996). Examples of multimedia authoring tools include Hypercard (by Apple), ToolBook (by Click2learn), and Authorware
(by Macromedia), and examples of Web-based authoring tools include Dreamweaver (by
Macromedia), Claris HomePage (by Apple), and FrontPage (by Microsoft). In essence, an
authoring tool is an accelerated application or a simplified form of programming that includes preprogrammed elements for the development of interactive multimedia and the
deployment of a point-and-click user interface to activate these elements (Siglar, 1999).

HISTORY OF AUTHORING TOOLS

Authoring tools can be traced to the 1960s, when "computer-assisted instruction was
viewed as an economically viable way to distribute teaching expertise" (Huntley & Alessi,
1987, p. 259). Authoring specialists and programmers used authoring tools to convert
paper-based instructional designs into learning programs by assembling text, graphics,

media, and animations and sequencing them into interactive programmed instruction modules (Hall, 2001). In 1993, more than 165 authoring tools were available, many of which no longer exist. Those that survived have been adapted for delivery of training over the Internet and are sometimes referred to as *Internet*-enabled authoring tools because traditional authoring tools were not initially designed to author content for the Web.

In 1997, Kozel reported that about 50 commercial multimedia authoring tools were available, not counting highly specialized niche tools. Most of the market share at that time was spread among the most popular tools: IconAuthor (by Aimtech), SuperCard (by Allegiant Technologies), Quest (by Allen Communication), the ToolBook II line (by Asymetrix, which is now Click2learn), Director and Authorware (both by Macromedia), and mTropolis (by mFactory; Kozel, 1997). Macromedia claimed to own 80% of the authoring market between its two tools (Director and Authorware), and Director possibly dominated the market share. Other tools with a loyal following included Hypercard (by Claris, which is now Apple), Oracle Media Objects, MediaTool (by Apple), and CourseBuilder (by Discovery Systems).

METAPHORS AND PARADIGMS UNDERLYING AUTHORING TOOLS

Authoring tools accomplish their tasks through the use of a certain methodology or paradigm that requires a type of heuristic or algorithmic thinking similar to that of programming languages (Siglar, 1999). Examples of these paradigms include the **scripting metaphor;** the **card-scripting metaphor; iconic, or flow, control;** the **frame metaphor;** hypermedia linkage; the **hierarchical object metaphor; tagging** and the **cast-score metaphor;** (Kozel, 1997; Siglar, 1999; see Table 8.1).

You can think of each paradigm as an organizational structure that facilitates the design of instructional materials and learning activities. Depending on the paradigm of a specific authoring tool, the design approach, development time, instructional capabilities, and learning curve (ease of use) could vary widely from those of other authoring tools. Hedberg and Harper (1998) emphasized this point by stating, "The organizing metaphor of the authoring system has become critical to the effective design of the final learning environment" (p. 1). However, Kasowitz (1998) insisted that the value of an authoring tool is measured by how well it can support a particular designer's task, regardless of its strength or approach. In other words, the value of an authoring tool can best be measured by examining its pedagogical effectiveness and the types of instructional and learning strategies it supports (Dabbagh, Bannan-Ritland, & Silc, 2001). For example, the first scenario presented at the beginning of this chapter explicitly states that there are correct and incorrect ways to perform the job of OJT instructor. Therefore, the authoring tool should be able to keep track of a trainee's progress by documenting correct and incorrect responses to performance questions and should enable the designer to adapt the instruction to each trainee's progress on the basis of this information. The third scenario—Course Management or Content Management system?—requires that the authoring tool be able to generate learning objects (discussed later in

Table 8.1 Authoring Paradigms

Authoring paradigm	Description of paradigm	Examples of authoring tools
Scripting metaphor	Resembles a programming language in that it involves specifying all media elements by file name and interactions by coding	TenCORE Language Authoring System
Card-scripting metaphor	Uses an index card structure or a book metaphor to link elements	Hypercard, SuperCard, HyperStudio, TenCORE, ToolBook II
Iconic, or flow, control	Uses icons to represent interactions and links them sequentially in a flow line that depicts the result	CourseBuilder, Authorware, IconAuthor, Authorware Attain
Frame metaphor	Uses icons to specify interactions and links them conceptually to provide a structural flow	StorySpace, Digital Chisel, Astound, Quest, Multimedia Fusion
Hierarchical object metaphor	Uses an object metaphor such as object-oriented programming, which is visually represented by embedded objects and iconic properties	Dazzler Deluxe, Docent, mTropolis, MediaSweets, ToolBook II Instructor, Quest, Net +, Oracle Media Objects
Hypermedia linkage	Uses a hypermedia navigation metaphor to link elements	FrontPage, Dreamweaver, HomeSite, Claris HomePage
Tagging	Uses tags in text files to link pages, provide interactivity, and integrate multimedia elements	**SGML**, HTML, **VRML**
Cast-score metaphor	Uses horizontal tracks and vertical columns to synchronize media events in a time-based fashion	Director, Flash, **Javascript,** Java

this chapter) and complex queries to its knowledge base. Accomplishing these requirements may depend on the organizing paradigm or scripting metaphor of the tool. However, it also depends on the ability of the tool to support the pedagogical requirements of a learning task. Regardless of which heuristic paradigm an authoring tool uses, all authoring tools share the following general characteristics or features:

- A point-and-click interface with **drop-down menus** and **toolbars**
- A hypermedia-linkage capability allowing media linking and navigation control
- The ability to monitor your progress while you are working, by toggling between an author mode and a user mode
- The ability to focus more on instructional design features and less on technical features

- The ability to integrate multimedia elements such as graphics, sound, and video
- The ability to import existing files and graphics and export files to other systems
- The ability to format the look and feel of the screen
- The ability to perform a range of editing functions such as copying, pasting, moving, inserting, and deleting elements
- The ability to represent information in multiple formats (e.g., linear, nonlinear, option controlled, performance-response controlled)

HYPERTEXT AND HYPERMEDIA AS A FUNDAMENTAL PRINCIPLE OF AUTHORING TOOLS

As the second characteristic in the preceding list indicates, all authoring tools have a hypermedia-linkage capability allowing media linking and navigation control. This capability is based on the concept of *hypertext*, which Ted Nelson originated in the early 1970s as a vision of what computers could allow us to do with the written word (Nelson, 1974). Nelson defined *hypertext* as a form of "nonsequential writing" allowing multiple reading paths and diffusing the boundaries between author and user. Since Nelson's conception of the term, many other definitions have permeated the literature, ranging from a specific technical perspective to a more encompassing cognitive perspective. For example, a 1990 definition of *hypertext* by Tripp and Roby espousing the cognitive perspective states, "Hypertext is a nonlinear, multidimensional, semantic structure in which words are linked by associations" (Roblyer, Edwards, & Havriluk, 1997, p. 196). This structure is said to mimic the ability of the brain to store and retrieve information by referential links for quick and intuitive access (keep & McLaughlin, 1995).

Fiderio's 1988 definition integrates both the technical and the cognitive perspectives of hypertext as follows:

> Hypertext, at its most basic level, is a database management system (DBMS) that lets you connect screens of textual information using associative links. At its most sophisticated level, hypertext is a learning environment for collaborative work, communication, and knowledge acquisition. (p. 237)

Hypertext is also a natural technique for supporting multimedia interfaces because it is based on interlinking nodes that may contain different media—hence the term *hypermedia*. "Hypermedia includes all characteristics of hypertext plus the capabilities of video, audio, and animation displays" (Roblyer et al., 1997, p. 196). Many people use the terms *hypertext* and *hypermedia* interchangeably. In this chapter, we use the term *hypermedia* to refer to the hypermedia-linkage capability of authoring tools and the term *hypermedia learning environments* to refer to instructional products generated by the use of authoring tools.

Authoring tools (Web based and non–Web based) enable designers to create hypermedia links ranging from a simple sequence of words to a branching system of textual and nontextual elements with both internal and external links that a user can interact with to access information. The user–content interaction generated by the use of hypermedia links in computer-based instruction or computer-assisted instruction (CBI/CAI) is often referred to as *interactivity*. Hypermedia has played a fundamental role in generating interactivity in CBI/CAI, allowing the user to exercise some control over the learning environment by selecting menu items, clicking on objects, and selecting linear or nonlinear paths in a lesson (Chou, 2003). With the move to Internet and Web-based communications technologies, interactivity took on a new meaning, which extended interaction to learner–learner and learner–group modes as discussed in Chapter 1. In addition, learner–content interaction has been expanded to include Web resources in a variety of formats providing a richer learning experience.

PRIMARY CLASSES OF AUTHORING TOOLS

Authoring tools can be classified according to several variables—for example, type of author or adopter (e.g., corporate developer vs. teacher educator), type of delivery medium (e.g., CD-ROM vs. Internet), type of operating system (Windows vs. Macintosh), type of scripting metaphor, cost, ease of use, range of user base (e.g., learners, instructors, developers), level of technical support, type of interface, market share, media capabilities, and instructional design capabilities. In this chapter, we classify authoring tools according to the type of delivery medium (CD-ROM vs. Web based) and the type of instruction produced relative to the specific features of the delivery medium (e.g., CBI vs. WBI). Figure 8.1 represents this classification.

CD-ROM-Based Authoring Tools   **Web-Based Authoring Tools**

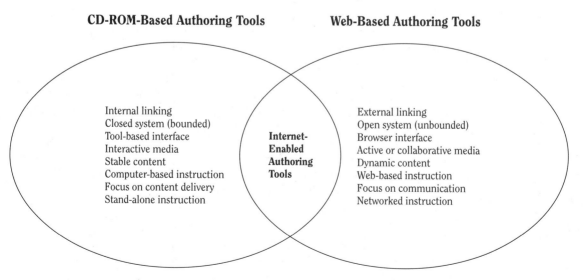

Internal linking
Closed system (bounded)
Tool-based interface
Interactive media
Stable content
Computer-based instruction
Focus on content delivery
Stand-alone instruction

Internet-Enabled Authoring Tools

External linking
Open system (unbounded)
Browser interface
Active or collaborative media
Dynamic content
Web-based instruction
Focus on communication
Networked instruction

Figure 8.1   Classes of Authoring Tools

According to Figure 8.1, two primary classes of authoring tools exist: CD-ROM-based authoring tools (also known as *multimedia authoring tools*) and Web-based authoring tools. From an instructional product perspective, CD-ROM-based authoring tools are primarily used to develop CBI, and Web-based authoring tools are primarily used to develop WBI. CBI is instruction or courseware typically delivered on a CD-ROM or from a mainframe computer to a desktop computer through a local area network (LAN) rather than over the Internet (Hall, 2001). CBI is considered the precursor to WBI, which is instruction or courseware delivered over the Internet or the Web. CBI and WBI can be contrasted according to several instructional variables, such as stability of learning content, type of instructional activities, and scope of interaction, among others. In Table 8.2, we provide examples of the instructional attributes of CBI and WBI by comparing the features and instructional products associated with the use of CD-ROM-based and Web-based authoring tools. We also include in this table the features & instructional products associated with the use of course management systems (CMS) which are discussed in the next section. Although the future of most CD-ROM-based

Table 8.2   Features of Authoring Tools

CATEGORY	GENERAL FEATURES	INSTRUCTIONAL PRODUCTS OR MODELS
CDROM-based authoring tools (Examples include Hypercard, Authorware, ToolBook II, Director)	• Have a tool-based interface • Are used with CD-ROM and videodisc technologies • Have a **closed system** (does not allow the user to go beyond the boundaries of what is there) • Have generally stable content • Have mostly internal linking; could have external links requiring firing up a browser • Can be Internet-enabled through plug-ins • Require installation; therefore, are operating system dependent • Require a steep learning curve for the developer to take full advantage of their features • Are used mostly by developers and instructional designers to produce instructional software • Do not have specific instructor or learner tools (only developer tools)	• Computer-based or computer-assisted instruction (CBI/CAI) • Simulations • Games • Microworlds • Tutorials • Individualized instruction • Programmed instruction • Self-contained interactive modules • **Mastery learning** • "Canned" or stand-alone instructional products • Standard testing programs (e.g., SAT) • Criterion-based testing

Table 8.2 Features of Authoring Tools (Continued)

CATEGORY	GENERAL FEATURES	INSTRUCTIONAL PRODUCTS OR MODELS
Web-based authoring tools (Examples include FrontPage, Dreamweaver, Claris HomePage, HomeSite)	• Have a browser interface • Are used with Internet-based technologies • Have an **Open system** (allows the user to go beyond the boundaries through external linking to the World Wide Web) • Are extensible (potential for extending the functionality of existing features without jeopardizing the performance of the tool) • Have dynamic content • Enable active or collaborative media • Require a steep learning curve for the developer to take full advantage of their features • Are used by a variety of users to develop Web sites for multiple purposes • Do not have specific instructor or learner tools • Have a browser interface	• Single Web pages and integrated Web sites for information presentation to support classroom instruction • Structured Web sites resulting in a variety of formats for Web-based instruction (WBI) • Personal and institutional home pages • Web publishing • Organization of Web-based resources • Complex animations and interactions when used with high-level scripting languages (e.g., Java, Javascript, **C++**)
Course management systems (Examples include WebCT, Blackboard, TopClass, Virtual-U, LearningSpace)	• Are used with Internet-based technologies • Have an open system • Are easy to use • Have dynamic content • Enable active or collaborative media • Have specific tools for instructors, learners, and administrators • Have embedded communication tools (e-mail, discussion forums, group tools) • Are used primarily to manage and deliver online learning in educational institutions and e-learning in corporate settings	• Distance education programs • Courseware (WBI) • Knowledge networks • Asynchronous and synchronous learning environments • Distributed learning environments

authoring tools is to be able to have Web delivery capabilities (Web-delivered CBI) or Internet "play" capabilities through the use of plug-ins, CD-ROM-based authoring tools were not originally designed to take advantage of the inherent and unique features of the Internet and the Web, such as connectivity, asynchronous and synchronous communication, and global **accessibility**. Therefore, Internet-enabled authoring tools are not a separate class of authoring tools but an extension of traditional or CD-ROM-based authoring tools and are represented in Figure 8.1 as the intersection of the two primary classes.

Take a moment and reflect on the first scenario presented at the beginning of the chapter. Which class of authoring tools should the project team be considering for developing the training program? Look at the characteristics of the two classes of authoring tools listed in Figure 8.1 to determine which list best fits the training goals.

COURSE MANAGEMENT SYSTEMS

Another class of authoring tools, known as *course management systems* (*CMSs*; also known as *learning management systems,* or *LMSs,* and/or *courseware*), emerged when Web-based authoring tools became increasingly used to create Web-based courses for online delivery. The need for a more integrative structure to manage the delivery of such courses and facilitate the migration from face-to-face classroom instruction to WBI resulted in the development of "one stop, one shop" commercial applications (also known as **turnkey applications**) such as WebCT and Blackboard. Unlike previous Web-based authoring tools, CMSs include instructor tools, learner tools, and administration tools, which allow for different types of users (an extended user base) and for a multitude of Internet and Web-based activities embedded within the tool. CMSs are discussed in depth in Chapter 9. However, statistics on usage and examples of the most prominent CMS tools in higher education and the corporate sector are provided later in this chapter.

Table 8.2 lists the three classes of authoring tools just described, the general features of each class, examples of authoring tools in each class, and associated instructional products or models.

EVOLUTION OF AUTHORING TOOLS

Table 8.2 clearly shows that authoring tools have evolved from technological and pedagogical perspectives. From a technological perspective, authoring tools have evolved on several fronts: **networkability** (connectivity), hypermedia **extensibility**, level of use (extended user base), and ease of use. From a pedagogical perspective, authoring tools have evolved from authoring-bounded, program-controlled learning systems to authoring-open-ended, learner-centered environments. In the following subsections, we discuss the technological and pedagogical implications of authoring tools as they relate to the three classes presented in Table 8.2.

Technological Implications

Connectivity   CD-ROM-based authoring tools were primarily designed for software developers and became popular mechanisms for supporting the production of CBI, in which learners interact primarily with an instructional program to gain mastery of a certain skill or knowledge (Koswitz, 1998). As discussed previously in this chapter, the Internet shifted the focus of interactivity from interaction with an instructional program to interaction with other learners across time and place (Kearsley & Shneiderman, 1998). This shift from local or predefined interaction to global interaction gave birth to the principle of globalization discussed in Chapter 1. Globalization is a consequence of the networked configuration of the Internet, which enabled increased connectivity and access to resources, events, and various tasks through the use of e-mail, discussion boards, and other Internet-based technologies that facilitate asynchronous learning and information delivery. Subsequently, authoring tools evolved to accommodate the shift to global interaction. For example, CMSs now include Internet-based communications technologies under an integrated structure, which makes designing collaborative activities that are time and place independent easier and widens the scope of teacher–learner and learner–learner communication. As a result of these capabilities, pedagogical models such as distributed learning, knowledge networks, asynchronous learning networks, and virtual communities (discussed in Chapter 1) began emerging.

Hypermedia extensibility   The Web has also dramatically altered the concept of *hypermedia*, which is a crucial attribute of the interface of an authoring tool, as discussed previously in this chapter. Hypermedia has evolved from a predetermined, finite internal linking structure contained within the boundaries of a learning system to an infinite external linking structure that knows no boundaries. This technological development greatly impacted the nature of instructional content and instructional resources. CD-ROM-based authoring tools have commonly relied on stable content to organize and structure instruction, which is mainly why the resulting learning system is bounded and program centered. The Web shifted the focus from accessing materials on bounded delivery media, such as CD-ROMs, to accessing unbounded, or dynamic, information through a network of global resources on the Web (Clark & Lyons, 1999; Hedberg, Brown, & Arrighi, 1997). CMSs now include features and components that allow instructors and learners to modify content and contribute resources, which has resulted in flexible and active information structures. As a result of these capabilities, the nature of instructional content and instructional resources has changed from a well-defined and stable knowledge base to an unfiltered and dynamic information base. (See Chapter 1 for a comparison of traditional and Web-based learning environments.)

Given the preceding discussion, do you think the Classified Training scenario presented at the beginning of this chapter calls for a well-defined and stable knowledge base or a dynamic information base? Can the instructional designer predetermine hypermedia structures within this knowledge base? In the second scenario, Web-Enhanced Instruction, is the professor relying on stable or dynamic content? Can the professor predetermine hypermedia linking structures within this knowledge base?

Level and ease of use   The advent of the Web also created the need for tools to develop Web pages, which began with simple text editors that created HTML files and evolved to Web-based authoring tools that continued to grow in functionality and integrated more user features and Internet-based technologies. With the launching of CMSs, the learning curve dropped sharply as the interface became more template controlled ("choose-it-and-we'll-do-it-for-you") and the functions more context sensitive. With little or no prior experience in authoring, instructors, learners, university administrators, and corporate developers can easily explore the potential of these integrated tools to create, engage in, manage, and deliver online learning.

Pedagogical Implications

The technological implications discussed in the preceding section suggest more flexibility in the design of online learning environments. For example, depending on how the instructor and the learners use the features of an authoring tool in an online course, the pedagogical philosophy underlying the course design can range from a strict **instructivist** approach to a radical constructivist approach (Reeves & Reeves, 1997). A strict instructivist approach typically results in a Web-based course that has a tutorial structure in which the content is organized by the instructor and delivered or imparted to the students. In contrast, a radical constructivist approach typically results in a learner-centered pedagogy in which students use Web features as tools to construct their own knowledge representations by restructuring content and creating and contributing resources to the course structure (Bannan & Milheim, 1997; Reeves & Reeves, 1997). With the inclusion of learner tools in CMSs, online learning environments are becoming increasingly learner centered. Learners can create and organize information in a meaningful way and in the process learn how to take responsibility for their own learning. For example, CMSs now include note-taking tools, development tools, self-assessment tools, communication tools, and collaborative tools. These tools encourage continuous dialogue (interaction) between the user and the courseware and between the user and other users so that the learner is productively and continuously active. This dialogic view of interactivity aligns well with situated cognition and learning as a social process, as discussed in Chapters 1 and 5. According to the tenets of situated cognition, knowledge is situated in and distributed across the interactions learners have with other learners, instructional content, and learning tools.

Therefore, courses initially designed for traditional learning environments (see Chapter 1) and later transformed to a Web-based format using a CMS will more likely undergo a pedagogical reengineering that is more constructivist and less instructivist (Dabbagh & Schmitt, 1998). The presence of Internet-based communication tools, collaborative tools, and Web publishing tools in CMSs is making such pedagogical implications possible. However, the use of CMSs, or any authoring tool, could still result in a strict instructivist approach if the potential of the tool features is not effectively integrated into the learning design. As Tiedemann (2002) contended, "The challenge is not so much in selection and infrastructure implementation as it is in the appropriate design and use of the selected tool" (p. 9). For example, a Web-based course can be designed that is self-contained and requires minimal instructor intervention and interaction with other learners. Practice and feedback activities can be embedded in a Web-based course much as they would be in CBI/CAI, and learners can proceed through linearly sequenced tutorial-like content presentations at their own pace, which results in a program-centered, or instructivist, learning environment. Caution must therefore be exercised to ensure that WBI is not just CBI delivered over the Web. Given that CBI is primarily developed by using CD-ROM-based authoring tools and WBI is primarily developed by using Web-based authoring tools, the type of delivery medium (i.e., CD-ROM vs. Web) has played an important role in determining the instructional designs that are possible. As Clark and Lyons (1999) suggested, "The lesson that we have learned over decades of technological evolution is that each new medium provides instructional capabilities that are unique. And each medium demands a new approach to exploit its capabilities for promoting learning" (p. 52).

Given the preceding discussion, take a moment and think about the second scenario presented at the beginning of this chapter: Web-Enhanced Instruction. What class of authoring tools should the professor be considering for the types of learning activities he is envisioning for his students? Do you think that the astronomy course will undergo a pedagogical transformation now that the professor is thinking of including online resources and collaborative activities? If the professor wanted only to include a resource Web site to support the course content, would a CMS be the appropriate authoring tool or would a Web-based authoring tool be sufficient?

LEADING AUTHORING TOOLS

Usage Statistics and Ratings of Web-Based Authoring Tools

In a survey conducted by SecuritySpace in July 2000 on Web authoring tool usage, the following Web-based authoring tools were listed in descending order of percentage of usage: Microsoft's FrontPage, Netscape Composer, Adobe PageMill, NetObjects Fusion, Softquad's HoTMetal Pro, IBM Homepage Builder, NetObjects Authoring, Macromedia's Dreamweaver, Allaire's HomeSite, and IBM NetObjects TopPage (SecuritySpace.com,

2000).[1] However, when taking the mind-set of a professional Web developer responsible for a medium-sized company's Web efforts, Oliver Rist of *InternetWeek* (1998) selected three Web-based authoring tools that were deemed powerful enough to develop cutting-edge pages yet visual enough to do so quickly and easily. The three tools were Microsoft's FrontPage, Adobe's PageMill, and Macromedia's Dreamweaver. FrontPage ranked first in terms of being an all-in-one professional-level design and management tool, and PageMill and Dreamweaver followed closely behind. In a 2000 roundup of Web-based authoring tools, Dreamweaver was given first place by the editors of *PC Magazine* (Mendelson, 2000) for advanced site design, with an average user rating of 9/10, and FrontPage was given first place for basic site design, with an average user rating of 7/10. Allaire's HomeSite received an honorable mention in the same issue and, because of its thorough code-editing tools, was highly recommended for developers who prefer complete control over their HTML code.

In a more recent survey conducted by SecuritySpace in January 2004, the following Web-based authoring tools were listed in descending order of percentage of usage: BBEdit, Macromedia's Dreamweaver, Arachnophilia, StarOffice, HTMLed, Allaire's HomeSite, Frontier, and Analog (SecuritySpace.com, 2004). The SecuritySpace survey was based on a sample size of 12,662,942 pages downloaded from 1,493,576 Web sites. However, authoring tool usage was detected on only 315,080 sites (21.1% of all sites visited) because, as in the 2000 survey, the names of Web-based authoring tools are not always inserted into the Web page META tag generator and thus may not have been picked up by the survey. Therefore, keep in mind that usage statistics are not always accurate. In addition, as new Web-based authoring tools continue to emerge, new ratings and market shares will emerge as well.

Usage Statistics and Ratings of CMSs

CMSs represent yet another share of the market that clearly lies in the education sector because the main goal of these tools is to facilitate the management and delivery of on-line courses to support e-learning and distance education programs. A survey conducted by the U.S. Department of Education's National Center for Educational Statistics (NCES; Lewis, Farris, Snow, & Levin, 1999) revealed that the number of distance education programs increased by 72% from 1994–1995 to 1997–1998 and that an additional 20% of the institutions surveyed at the time planned to establish distance education programs within the next 3 years. The NCES also reported that 1.6 million students were enrolled in distance education courses in 1997–1998. In an October 2000 industry research report, Eduventures.com Inc., a leading independent e-learning industry analyst firm, projected that the higher education e-learning market would grow from $4 billion to $11 billion by 2003 (Stokes, Evans, & Gallagher, 2000). In 2003, the NCES reported that, since the mid-1990s, distance education course enrollments had nearly doubled, to about 3.1 million (Waits & Lewis, 2003).

---

[1] The usage survey tool was determined by examining the Web page META tag generator. META tags are HTML tags that describe the contents of a Web page. The names of Web-based authoring tools are not always inserted into META tags.

Not surprisingly, institutions and faculty members are feeling pressure to offer Web-based courses to meet economic and student demands. The recent proliferation of CMSs is in answer to these demands. Examples of CMSs and LMSs that cropped up to meet e-learning education and training demands in both the higher education and the corporate sectors include WebCT, Blackboard, Convene, Embanet, Element K, Real Education, eCollege.com, Docent, KnowledgePlanet, Centra, SmartForce, SkillSoft, Symposium, TopClass, WebMentor, eWeb, Web Course in a Box, Internet Classroom Assistant, Ingenium, Lotus LearningSpace, SoftArc's FirstClass, Serf, Eduprise.com, and Virtual-U. Landon (2000) reported that as many as 109 course management software packages were on the market. However, many of the e-learning providers have been bought out through mergers and acquisitions or have collapsed as a result of fickle markets and untried business models (Harris, 2002). For a more comprehensive list of authoring tools and a comparative analysis of their technical features, visit the EduTools Web site at http://www.edutools.info/course/.

Usage Statistics in Higher Education

In the higher education sector, WebCT (WebCT.com, 2000) was the world's leading provider of integrated e-learning systems for higher education, serving more than 2,600 colleges and universities in more than 80 countries worldwide. At that time, Blackboard also claimed that it was the leading provider of Internet infrastructure software for e-education, with 2,300 clients and a user base of more than 5.4 million individuals worldwide (Blackboard.com, 2000). In the October 2000 industry report mentioned previously, Eduventures.com reported that Blackboard had established the strongest market position in the higher education e-learning industry (Stokes et al., 2000). The same report also indicated that WebCT had reached a sizable share of this market and that with its partnership with Thomson Learning, it was in an excellent position to match or even surpass Blackboard in the coming months. However, in 2003, Blackboard was named the most popular e-learning platform in U.S. higher education, with 46% of the market, compared with 35% for WebCT (Dun & Bradstreet, 2003). According to this market analysis, WebCT and Blackboard have clearly emerged as the top commercial online learning providers in higher education, which has resulted in what Blackboard Chairman Matthew Pittinsky described as "good rivalry" (Olsen, 2001).

Usage Statistics in the Industry

The statistics are not as clear in the corporate learning sector. According to Eilif Trondsen, director of the Learning on Demand program at SRI Consulting Business Intelligence, the e-learning industry is so fragmented that the largest e-learning vendor does not have even a 5% market share (Harris, 2002). Harris (2002) added that the e-learning market is "feverishly seeking to develop credibility" and that "products and services are so new that many customers can't define their own needs," which is why e-learning vendors are "gambling and often losing on untried business models" (p. 28).

Despite this uncertainty, Trondsen argued that SmartForce has emerged as an industry leader in LMSs because of its smart acquisition strategy (Harris, 2002). Since 1999, SmartForce has acquired several e-learning vendors and providers, ranging from those that support interactive technologies and collaborative tools to those that manage content by using learning objects technology (discussed subsequently in this chapter). Trondsen claimed that through such acquisitions and mergers, SmartForce can promote an architecture that integrates and manages three platforms simultaneously—technology, content, and services—realizing that customers want a total e-learning solution (Harris, 2002).

What Is a Killer Application?

With SmartForce possibly emerging as a dominant corporate e-learning provider and Blackboard and WebCT currently perceived as dominant higher education online learning providers, the question remains whether a "killer" application will emerge or whether the technology will keep changing to introduce yet new e-learning products. Rosenberg (2001) defined a *killer application* as a "breakthrough application that can give an organization a quantum leap in learning and in competitiveness" (p. 144). In other words, it is an e-learning application that is so effective and innovative that it redefines e-learning in an organization. In simpler terms, a killer application is a "program that gives average people the capability to use technology to solve everyday problems and enrich their lives" (Harrsch, 2003). For example, e-mail was the first killer application.

As far as e-learning applications are concerned, Eduventures.com predicted in the October 2000 report that in the next 18 to 24 months the higher education e-learning business would be dominated by two or three large applications or maybe even one killer application (Stokes et al., 2000). At the time we wrote this book, WebCT and Blackboard dominated the market as the leading providers of integrated e-learning systems in higher education. However, no single killer application had emerged since the publication of the October 2000 report. Late 2003 technology publications such as *The Technology Source* and *ComputerWorld* indicated that RSS (really-simple-syndication, or RDF site summary, depending on the source) technology may be the next killer application. RSS technology is a Web publishing format designed to help the average user distribute and receive information in a convenient way such as receiving news feeds to your desktop without having to subscribe to newsgroups or Listservs. In addition, several CMS application providers are teaming up with other e-learning industry training leaders to embrace a more open and flexible architecture and a new technology in the development of education and training materials known as *open source content*, or *learning objects technology*.

Learning Objects Technology

Learning objects technology is rooted in the object-oriented paradigm of computer science, which values the creation of digital components (called *objects*) that can be reused in multiple contexts (Wiley, 2002). The idea is to adopt some or all of the nonproprietary technical standards that Massachusetts Institute of Technology (MIT), Stanford, and others are developing as part of the Open Knowledge Initiative. This initiative involves developing online teaching technologies and course materials that are shareable and reusable so that they can be delivered to the learner on an as-needed and just-in-time basis. In addition, these technical standards will enable LMSs and CMSs to handle all types of digital content. For instructional designers, this means building small instructional components (knowledge objects) that can be reused multiple times in different learning contexts (Wiley, 2002). The instructional and training benefits of learning objects technology include (a) increased efficiency with regard to training development cycle times, (b) the potential for increased effectiveness and personalization of training, and (c) consistency in design and development tasks (Bannan-Ritland, Dabbagh, & Murphy, 2002).

Content Management Systems

As a result of learning objects technology, a new breed of authoring tools, known as *content management systems,* or *learning content management systems (LCMSs),* has emerged. The emphasis of LCMSs is on managing content through the creation of learning objects, instead of managing courses, which is the primary goal of a CMS. LCMSs are now allowing practitioners to create and manage learning objects that can be served to the learner at the appropriate time, which makes them a "must-have" tool in the e-learning industry (Chapman & Hall, 2001). Examples of LCMSs include TopClass (by WBT Systems), LEAP Learning Development System (LDS; by Intellinex), ePath Learning (by ePath Learning, Inc.), and Docent Outliner and Docent Content Delivery Server (by Docent). The third scenario presented at the beginning of this chapter is an example of the capabilities of LCMSs. For more information on LMSs and LCMSs, visit Brandon Hall's Web site at http://brandon-hall.com/.

CLASSES OF AUTHORING TOOLS REVISITED

With the introduction of content management systems, or LCMSs, four classes of authoring tools now exist, as depicted in Figure 8.2. These classes are (a) CD-ROM-based authoring tools, (b) Web-based authoring tools, (c) course management or learning management systems (CMSs or LMSs), and (d) content management systems, or learning content management systems (LCMSs). Figure 8.2 portrays the four classes of authoring tools in concentric circles, which indicates that new classes of authoring tools or LMSs are maintaining many of the general features and characteristics of traditional authoring tools. What is mostly changing is the **authoring paradigm** underlying the architecture of the tool, the delivery medium for the instructional products, the primary target users, and the type of instructional product (e.g., Web page vs. knowledge object). In addition, with each emerging class of authoring tools, new features are being added that increase the functionality of the tool in terms of integrating new learning

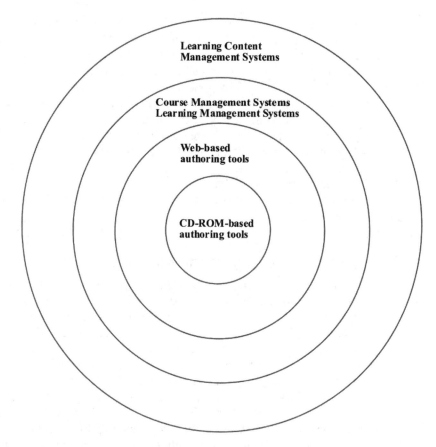

Figure 8.2 Four Classes of Authoring Tools

technologies (e.g., synchronous and asynchronous communication tools) and extend its user base and instructional design capabilities.

FUTURE IMPLICATIONS OF AUTHORING TOOLS

As discussed at the beginning of this chapter, the aim of traditional authoring tools (i.e., CD-ROM-based authoring tools) is to automate entirely or partially the courseware construction process by supporting tasks such as the ability to create screens and screen objects such as menus and buttons, link content to other content, and sequence material (Bell, 1998). However, the lack of specific design principles often restricts the kinds of instructional designs these tools support, which leads largely to the creation of simplistic drill and practice programs or uninteresting tutorials (Hodger, 1985). "The result is a tool that supports a broad range of possible instructional applications, some of which may be good, and some of which are likely to be poorly executed, but none of which will have been created with much guidance from the tool itself" (Bell, 1998, p. 76). Murray (1998) further emphasized this shortcoming of traditional authoring tools by stating that "commercial authoring systems excel in giving the instructional designer tools to produce visually appealing and interactive screens, but behind the presentation screens is a shallow representation of content and pedagogy" (p. 6). Thus, the question is How do we preserve the level of usability and the instructional development methods that instructional designers have become familiar with and add tools, features, and authoring paradigms that will allow more powerful and flexible learning systems to be built? Two approaches attempt to answer this question: the **intelligent tutoring system (ITS)** approach and the object-oriented approach. Both are based in an information technology perspective. Next, we briefly discuss each approach and its implications for designing effective hypermedia we learning environments.

The ITS Approach to Authoring Systems

The first approach proposes that ITSs should be embodied by authoring tools to allow additional levels of abstraction, modularity, and visualization of the design process so that more powerful and flexible authoring paradigms can be achieved (Bell, 1998; Murray, 1998). ITSs are inference-making systems that seek to continuously improve each learner's learning by prescribing instruction that has a high probability of preventing learner error or misconception and by continuously adapting this instruction according to moment-to-moment diagnosis (Tennyson & Christensen, 1988). In the case of authoring tools, the goal of an ITS would be to support the designer of the learning environment instead of the learner. For example, an intelligent instructional design expert system would be embedded in the authoring tool to allow designers to spend more time designing at the conceptual and pedagogical level instead of focusing on the features of the tools, so that more engaging instructional designs could be produced (Robson, 2000).

The Object-Oriented Approach to Authoring Systems

The second approach proposes that new metaphors for authoring tools need to be developed to match current instructional practices and theory (Hedberg & Harper, 1998). Hedberg and Harper (1998) added that, currently, most authoring tools limit the designer to the preprogrammed modules of the tool and to the underlying assumptions of highly structured instructional design models. In other words, the paradigm or metaphor of an authoring tool can guide or restrict the types of instructional designs possible. For example, authoring tools for the construction of Web documents (Web-based authoring tools) offer a page metaphor with hypertext as the dominant linking structure, which enables more of a top-down design process than that of the screen metaphor of more traditional, or less complex, multimedia authoring tools such as HyperStudio, which supports a more linear or sequential design process (Hedberg et al., 1997). Therefore, the need for new authoring metaphors that are less restrictive and that allow users to implement more flexible instructional design is imminent.

According to Kozel (1997), "Of all the metaphors likely to survive, objects [the object-oriented metaphor] stand the greatest chance because they reflect an evolutionary improvement in the software engineering world" (p. 42). The object model or authoring metaphor represents an inevitable evolution in application development because interactive multimedia are both created in and delivered as software, which makes authoring complex programs easier by thinking of interactive elements as objects. Authoring tools are already moving toward this direction. With the introduction of learning objects technology, LCMSs are now paving the way for a new authoring paradigm that supports the design of more flexible and efficient learning environments.

In addition, learning objects technology is allowing practitioners to introduce a pedagogical or conceptual layer to an authoring tool, which enables the design of more intelligent and flexible learning environments. This layer is added primarily by representing instructional strategy and instructional content separately and by modularizing the instructional content for multiple use and reuse (Murray, 1998). Separating pedagogy and content will allow practitioners to embed the pedagogy in the intelligent tutor (expert system) for the proponents of the ITS approach and in the properties of objects for the proponents of the object-oriented model. Such authoring tools can facilitate the design of instructional actions by modifying the behavior of an intelligent tutor (in the ITS case) or by specifying the relationship between objects (in the object model) according to the learner's specific needs or the pedagogical characteristics of the content being taught.

Furthermore, the traditional systematic instructional design process does not allow instructors to effectively communicate their content, which requires instructional designers to see a lot of content before they can understand what the instructor wants (Robson, 2000). An object-oriented approach would resolve this problem because instructors could more easily translate their content into learning resources or pedagogical elements (e.g., I use lectures, assessment items, resources, etc.) and instructional designers can then create a prototypical environment matching the instructor's expectations without seeing any content (Robson, 2000). This approach aligns well with the Integrated Learning Design Framework for Online Learning presented in Chapter 4. It puts the instructional designer and/or the online instructor in control of the design process. Both the pedagogical elements and the content can be stored as learning objects in a database and accessed for multiple uses in multiple contexts. The idea is to define learning objects or resources such that each learning resource has specific instructional properties enabling its pedagogical integration with other resources. Authoring systems will be designed for the creation of generically encoded reusable information, which will allow the design process to proceed by specifying learning resources, creating links among the resources, and authoring content independently of format (Davidson, 1993; Robson, 2000).

Learners as Producers of Hypermedia Learning Environments

Another critical factor that could impact the pedagogical use of authoring tools is whether the learner is perceived as the user or the producer of hypermedia learning environments. The *learners as producers* concept supports a generative, or constructivist, approach to learning, in which learners are using technology tools as cognitive tools to generate their own learning and construct knowledge (Sims, 1995). Hedberg et al. (1997) argued that if the learner's activities are regarded as the central focus in an educational context, learners should be thought of as software (courseware) producers rather than software users in the development of educational software for both bounded CD-ROM titles and unbounded Web-based resources. These researchers proposed the integration of learner tools into authoring systems that allow users, for example, to organize information in a meaningful way by positioning elements on the screen, creating new links, and generating multimedia objects.

Such cognitive tools could include a notebook in which to copy, edit, and format text; a visual graphics tool with which to create marker buttons that point to multimedia elements such as video, audio, or pictures and enable the learner to manipulate these elements; and a cognitive mapping tool (concept-mapping tool) that allows flexible information representation (Hedberg & Harper, 1998). Many CMSs include a range of learner tools that are often underused because of the vendors' insistence on promoting the instructor and administrative capabilities of the system. Chapter 9 covers learning tools at length and provides several examples of how learners can use these tools as cognitive tools to guide their learning and understanding. However, current CMSs need to greatly improve to include the learner functionality that Hedberg and Harper proposed.

Learning objects technology has the potential to support this generative learning approach by placing the authoring system or tool that supports the development of learning objects in the hands of the learner instead of the designer (Bannan-Ritland et al., 2002). With regard to a specific learning goal, the learner could be instructed to define, configure, adapt, and generate learning objects and thereby contribute to the design of an educational or a training application, and, in the process, construct new knowledge and understanding of related content. As mentioned previously, companies producing CMSs are beginning to support the construction of learning objects by teaming up with pioneers in the e-learning industry who have taken on the challenge of managing content through LCMSs and/or by extending the capabilities of their current authoring system to support the creation and delivery of learning objects. Depending on who creates, assembles, and links these objects, the pedagogical philosophy of the learning environment can vary from an instructivist approach to a constructivist approach, which results in either a directed or an open-ended learning environment.

SUMMARY

Whatever the current state of authoring tools may be, the pedagogical goal of an authoring tool, according to Harasim (1999), is "to provide a flexible framework to support advanced pedagogies based on active learning, collaboration, multiple perspectives, and knowledge building" (p. 45). CMSs include several features and components that enable learners to engage in active learning processes such as reflective and collaborative practices. They also enable instructors to engage in modeling and scaffolding techniques to support the active construction of knowledge. In the last chapter of this book, we focus on how CMSs can be used to support these teaching and learning practices. We selected four CMSs that we believe represent the current uses of CMSs in higher education, K–12, and the corporate sectors. They are WebCT, Blackboard, Virtual-U, and Lotus LearningSpace. Chapter 9 covers the features and functions of these tools and provides examples of how these features support the implementation of the instructional strategies and models discussed in Chapters 5 and 6.

CHAPTER SUMMARY

This chapter covered the general features and principles of authoring tools and the metaphors and scripting paradigms underlying their functionality. Hypermedia was distinguished as a fundamental principle that characterizes authoring tools by their ability to produce hypermedia learning environments such as computer-based instruction (CBI) and Web-based instruction (WBI). Two primary classes of authoring tools were identified: CD-ROM-based authoring tools and Web-based authoring tools. The evolution of authoring tools was discussed from technological and pedagogical perspectives, leading to the development of course management systems and learning content management systems. A table was provided listing the general features and associated instructional products of CD-ROM-based authoring tools, Web-based authoring tools, and course management systems. The chapter also provided a market analysis of the leading authoring tools in these three categories. Last, future implications of authoring tools were discussed in terms of (a) the potential of intelligent tutoring systems, (b) learning objects technology, and (c) the concept of learners as producers of hypermedia learning environments, for supporting the development of more powerful and flexible authoring systems.

LEARNING ACTIVITIES

The URLs for the Web sites referred to in the following activities are available from the companion Web site for this book: http://www.prenhall.com/dabbagh.

1. Go to the Stardust Web site and The Blackout Syndrome Web site. Interact with these instructional modules with a classmate or on your own. Do you think these modules are examples of CBI? WBI? or perhaps CBI delivered over the Web? If you need help determining how to characterize these instructional modules, revisit Table 8.2 and compare the instructional features of each module with the features and products listed in columns 2 and 3 of the table. Also, examine whether each module capitalizes on the inherent features of the Web (see Table 6.2 for a list of these features). Could either Stardust or The Blackout Syndrome have been delivered on a CD-ROM without losing any of its instructional effectiveness?

If the links to these Web sites are broken or no longer available, go to the home page of The JASON Project or the home page of The Mystery Spot (see the companion Web site for these URLs) and pick another learning module with which to conduct this activity. Your response may differ depending on the module you select.

2. Visit the ThinkQuest Web site and look at some of the winning sites that were created through ThinkQuest competitions and programs. Determine which pedagogical approach these learning challenges are based on (i.e., instructivist or constructivist). Develop a list of instructional attributes for one of these learning challenges and determine which class of authoring tools was most likely used to develop these modules.

3. Visit the EduTools Web site. Click on the Compare Products tool and choose the By Product Name tool to compare Blackboard and WebCT or any other two CMSs of your choice. Discuss the results of your comparison with your classmates or instructor. Do you think the comparison features used at this site are conclusive? If you were charged with selecting one of these CMS products, do you think you have enough information with which to make a decision? Why or why not? Repeat the process for other tools of your choice.

4. Visit Brandon Hall's Web site, click on the Publications button, and find the *LMS 2003: Comparison of Enterprise Learning Management Systems* report. Find the online demonstration of the LMS Selection Tool provided with this report and study its questions. What additional questions might you add to this tool to help your organization find an appropriate CMS?

5. Conduct a search on learning content management systems (LCMSs), using a Web-based search engine, and compile a list of features of this authoring tool to help the instructional designer portrayed in the third scenario at the beginning of this chapter better understand content management systems. Additional key words to use in this search are *content management*, *learning objects*, and *knowledge objects*.

RESOURCES

Explore additional resources at the companion Web site (http://www.prenhall.com/dabbagh) for selected authoring tools and CMSs to learn more about their technical features, costs, and instructional development capabilities.

REFERENCES

Bannan, B., & Milheim, W. D. (1997). Existing Web-based instruction courses and their design. In B. H. Khan (Ed.), *Web-based instruction* (pp. 381–388). Englewood Cliffs, NJ: Educational Technology Publications.

Bannan-Ritland, B., Dabbagh, N. H., & Murphy, K. L. (2002). Learning object systems as constructivist learning environments: Related assumptions, theories, and applications. In D. A. Wiley (Ed.), *The instructional use of learning objects* (pp. 61–98). Bloomington, IN: Agency for Instructional Technology (AIT)/Association for Educational Communications and Technology (AECT).

Bell, B. (1998). Investigate and decide learning environments: Specializing task models for authoring tool design. *Journal of the Learning Sciences, 7*(1), 65–105.

Blackboard.com. (2000). About Blackboard. Retrieved July 13, 2001 from BB.com.

Chapman, B., & Hall, B. (2001). *Authoring tool strategies: Choosing tools that match your company's e-learning initiative.* Sunnyvale, CA: brandon-hall.com.

Chou, C. (2003). Interactivity and interactive functions in Web-based learning systems: A technical framework for designers. *British Journal of Educational Technology, 34*(3), 265–279.

Clark, R. C., & Lyons, C. (1999). Using Web-based training wisely. *Training, 36*(7), 51–56.

Craney, L. (1996). Web page authoring tools: Comparison and trends. In D. I. Raitt & B. Jeapes (Eds.), *Online Information 96: Proceedings of the 20th International Online Information Meeting, London* (pp. 447–452). Oxford, UK: Learned Information. (ERIC Document Reproduction Service No. ED411867)

Dabbagh, N. H., Bannan-Ritland, B., & Silc, K. F. (2001). Pedagogy and Web-based course authoring tools: Issues and implications. In B. Khan (Ed.), *Web-based training.* (pp. 343–354). Englewood Cliffs, NJ: Educational Technology Publications.

Dabbagh, N. H., & Schmitt, J. (1998). Redesigning instruction through Web-based course authoring tools. *Educational Media International, 35*(2), 106–110.

Davidson, W. J. (1993). SGML authoring tools for technical communication. *Technical Communication, 40*(3), 403–409.

Dun & Bradstreet. (2003). *Sales and marketing solutions.* Retrieved August 30, 2003, from http://www.zapdata.com/

Fiderio, J. (1988). A grand vision: Hypertext mimics the brain's ability to access information quickly and intuitively by reference. *Byte, 13*(10), 237–244.

Hall, B. (2001). *Authoring tools 2001: A buyer's guide to the best e-learning content development applications.* Retrieved August 27, 2002, from http://www.brandon-hall.com

Harasim, L. (1999). A framework for online learning: The Virtual-U. *IEEE Computer, 32*(9) 44–49.

Harris, P. (2002). E-learning: A consolidation update. *T + D Magazine, 56*(4) 27–33.

Harrsch, M. (2003, July/August). RSS: The next killer app for education. *The Technology Source.* Retrieved August 8, 2003, from http://ts.mivu.org

Hedberg, J., Brown, C., & Arrighi, M. (1997). Interactive multimedia and Web-based learning: Similarities and differences. In B. H. Khan (Ed.), *Web-based instruction* (pp. 47–58). Englewood Cliffs, NJ: Educational Technology Publications.

Hedberg, J., & Harper, B. (1998). *Visual metaphors and authoring.* Retrieved March 29, 1998, from http://www.immll.uow.edu.au/~JHedberg/ITFORUM.html.

Hodges, J. O. (1985). Developing your own microcomputer courseware with authoring tools. *Social Education, 49*(1), 59–62.

Huntley, J. S., & Alessi, S. M. (1987). Videodisc authoring tools: Evaluating products and a process. *Optical Information Systems, 7*(4), 259–281.

Kasowitz, A. (1998). *Tools for automating instructional design.* Syracuse, NY: ERIC Clearinghouse on Information and Technology. (ERIC Document Reproduction Service No. ED420304)

Kearsley, G., & Shneiderman, B. (1998). Engagement theory: A framework for technology-based teaching and learning. *Educational Technology, 38*(5), 20–23.

Keep, C., & McLaughlin, T. (1995). *The electronic labyrinth: The rhetoric of link traversal.* Retrieved January 16, 2001, from http://jefferson.village.virginia.edu/elab/hfl0044.html

Kozel, K. (1997). The classes of authoring programs. *Emedia Professional, 10*(7), 28–34, 36–43.

Landon, B. (2000). *Course management systems.* Retrieved May 2000 from http://www.edutools.info/course/index.jsp

Lewis, L., Farris, E., Snow, K., & Levin, D. (1999, December 17). *Distance education at postsecondary education institutions: 1997–98.* Washington. DC: National Center for Education Statistics, Institute of Education Sciences, U.S. Department of Education. (NCES No. 2000-013). Retrieved March 2000 from http://nces.ed.gov/surveys/peqis/publications/2000013/

Mendelson, E. (2000, May 23). Design a great site? *PC Magazine, 19*(10), 134–152.

Murray, T. (1998). Authoring knowledge-based tutors: Tools for content, instructional strategy, student model, and interface design. *Journal of the Learning Sciences, 7*(1), 5–64.

Nelson, T. H. (1974). *Computer lib/dream machines.* Sausalito, CA: Mindful Press.

Olsen, F. (2001). Getting ready for a new generation of course-management systems. *The Chronicle of Higher Education, 48*(17), 25–30.

Reeves, T. C., & Reeves, P. M. (1997). Effective dimensions of interactive learning on the World Wide Web. In B. H. Khan (Ed.), *Web-based instruction* (pp. 59–66). Englewood Cliffs, NJ: Educational Technology Publications.

Rist, O. (1998, April 13). HTML tools: Visual Web authoring. *InternetWeek.* Retrieved from http://www.internetwk.com/reviews/rev041398.htm

Roblyer, M. D., Edwards, J., & Havriluk, M. A. (1997). *Integrating educational technology into teaching.* Upper Saddle River, NJ: Prentice Hall.

Robson, R. (2000). *Object-oriented instructional design and Web-based authoring.* Retrieved September 26, 2000, from http://www.eduworks.com/robby/papers/objectoriented.html

Rosenberg, M. J. (2001). *E-learning: Strategies for delivering knowledge in the digital age.* New York: McGraw-Hill.

SecuritySpace.com. (2000, August 1). *Web authoring tools report.* Burlington, Ontario, Canada: E-Soft Inc. Retrieved February 2004 from http://www.securityspace.com/s_survey/data/man.200007/webauth.html

SecuritySpace.com. (2004, February 1). *Web authoring tools report.* Burlington, Ontario, Canada: E-Soft Inc. Retrieved February 2004 from http://www.securityspace.com/s_survey/data/man.200401/webauth.html

Siglar, J. A. (1999, April 4). *Multimedia authoring systems FAQ.* Retrieved March 30, 2000, from http://www.tiac.net/users/jasiglar/faq_index.html

Sims, R. (1995). Interactivity: A forgotten art? (ITForum Paper No. 10). Retrieved November 5, 1999, from http://itech1.coe.uga.edu/itforum/paper10/paper10.html

Stokes, P., Evans, T., & Gallagher, S. (2000, October). *After the Big Bang: Higher education e-learning markets get set to consolidate.* Boston: Eduventures.com, Inc.

Tennyson, R. D., & Christensen, D. L. (1988). MAIS: An intelligent learning system. In D. H. Jonassen (Ed.), *Instructional designs for microcomputer courseware* (pp. 247–274). Hillsdale, NJ: Erlbaum.

Tiedemann, D. A. (2002). Distance learning development and delivery applications. *Educational Technology & Society, 5*(1).

Waits, T., & Lewis, L. (2003, July 18). *Distance education at degree-granting postsecondary institutions: 2000–2001.* Washington, DC: National Center for Education Statistics, Institute of Education Sciences, U.S. Department of Education. (NCES No. 2003-027). Retrieved June 2003 from http://nces.ed.gov/surveys/peqis/publications/2003017

Wiley, D. A. (2002). Connecting learning objects to instructional design theory: A definition, a metaphor, and a taxonomy. In D. A. Wiley (Ed.), *The instructional use of learning objects* (pp. 3–24). Bloomington, IN: Agency for Instructional Technology (AIT)/Association for Educational Communications and Technology (AECT).

9

COURSE MANAGEMENT SYSTEMS: PEDAGOGICAL FEATURES, SELECTION, AND LIMITATIONS

After completing this chapter, you should understand the following:

- The pedagogical and technological features of course management systems (CMSs)

- The categories within which these features can be classified

- The distinguishing features of specific CMSs

- The types of instructional and learning activities that can be implemented by using the features of CMSs

- How to select a CMS from institutional, pedagogical, and technological perspectives

- The limitations of CMSs

CONSIDER THE FOLLOWING THREE SCENARIOS:

Virtual Communities: Educators at a higher education institution that offers both resident (face-to-face) and online instruction want to help students become more enculturated in the campus community. More specifically, they would like students who are taking online courses to stay apprised of campus activities and administrative services, to be able to participate in virtual clubs, and to communicate more actively with resident students. The educators want to use a course management system (CMS) that supports synchronous and asynchronous discourse, communication, and collaborative activities to form virtual communities that provide both a social and an academic atmosphere for students that extends beyond the boundaries of the physical institution.

New Product Rollout: The organizational development group of a large industry is charged with training all supervisors on how to use a new computerized employee evaluation system. The training is mandatory; however, many of the supervisors are in the field at different locations and have different work schedules and operational responsibilities. A learning management system (LMS) is needed to deliver and manage this training efficiently and effectively. The LMS should provide the supervisors with tools to use to customize the evaluation materials to their employees' specific job responsibilities. In addition, the LMS should be able to track who completed this training and keep a record of past and future training requirements for each supervisor.

AP Chemistry: A high school teacher who teaches advanced placement (AP) chemistry courses has been asked by the county school district to make the course available to other high schools that do not have enough students to justify expending the resources for an on-site AP chemistry class. The teacher is faced with the challenge of selecting a CMS with which to deliver and manage the course. The teacher does not want to spend an excessive amount of time redesigning her course for online delivery and wants to be able to upload her existing syllabus, lectures, assignments, resources, quizzes, and tests to a secure Web site that students can access to successfully complete the course online. The CMS should have features that facilitate the development, delivery, and evaluation of multiple-choice quizzes and tests similar to the AP exam. Students should also be able to monitor their progress and receive timely feedback on the quizzes and tests.

Before proceeding, reflect momentarily on the preceding scenarios. What do they have in common? How do they differ? Does each scenario have specific requirements? If so, what type of requirements are they? institutional? pedagogical? technological? administrative? How would you go about selecting the appropriate CMS or LMS for each context?

This chapter covers the technological and pedagogical features of CMSs and the use of CMSs in the design and development of online learning. The chapter also includes a discussion on what distinguishes one CMS from another, how to select a CMS from institutional and administrative perspectives, and the technological and pedagogical limitations of CMSs.

COURSE MANAGEMENT SYSTEMS

A course management system (CMS) is a collection of Web applications that integrate technological and pedagogical features of the Internet and the World Wide Web into a single, template-based authoring and presentation system that facilitates the design, development, delivery, and management of Web-based courses and online learning environments. As discussed in Chapter 8, CMSs emerged when a comprehensive system that integrated all the components and tools needed to support Web-enabled curriculum delivery became necessary to support novice faculty in making the leap to online learning. Before then, Web authoring tools like Dreamweaver and FrontPage required technical skills with which most faculty members were unfamiliar or uncomfortable. In addition, administrators at higher education institutions did not have enough staff to train or support faculty in the use of such tools for the delivery of Web-based instruction (WBI) on a large scale. These Web development tools also lacked built-in functionality associated with course administration, collaboration, and student assessment. CMSs were therefore designed to enable faculty members to quickly learn one software package that delivers WBI, which consequently decreased the need to train faculty to use multiple software products to accomplish the same task (Hazari, 2001; Kubarek, 1999).

PEDAGOGICAL AND TECHNOLOGICAL FEATURES OF CMSs

According to Maslowski, Visscher, Collis, and Bloemen (2000), CMSs should do the following:

a. Extend the benefits of the good instructor and fine campus environment
b. Increase the flexibility of participation in the faculty's courses
c. Increase the level of activity and engagement of students in the learning process
d. Increase the contact between instructors and students via more personal communication and less lecturing. (p. 9)

CMSs accomplish these goals through various pedagogical and technological features, including Web links, search engines, synchronous and asynchronous communication tools, course announcement areas, student posting areas, the ability to track student records and interactions, assessment tools, management of course information, tools for collaborative work, Web-based development capabilities, and multimedia and resource development capabilities. The goal is to provide a central location where course content can be delivered, related information or links can be listed, models for assignments can be provided, instructors and students can communicate, and groups can develop shared projects in the form of Web-based products. These integrative development and delivery systems present an opportunity for practitioners to incorporate various pedagogical models and instructional strategies, such as those discussed in Chapters 5 and 6, by using the available software features and components. Specifically, CMSs facilitate the design and delivery of integrational learning environments (see Chapter 5). Furthermore, students can learn to use these systems fairly quickly and can access course content and participate in engaging and meaningful learning activities remotely. With a relatively flat learning curve and simple system requirements, CMSs can facilitate online learning without imposing insurmountable technological barriers. Their multipurpose functionality and multiuser-base attribute have led to their ubiquitous adoption, as discussed in the following subsections.

Multipurpose Functionality

CMSs "combine database and Web functionalities in order to support the efficient management of Web-based support in the teaching and learning process of an institution" (Maslowski et al., 2000, p. 5). This means that a CMS has two layers of functionality: (a) a back-end layer that system administrators can access to control certain features such as system security and the assignment of access rights and privileges to different user categories (e.g., course instructors vs. students), and (b) a front-end layer that instructors and students can manipulate not only for teaching and learning purposes, but also for general course administration, delivery, and management. As a result of this multipurpose functionality, CMSs include instructor tools, learner tools, and administrative tools, which allows for different types of users and for multiple Internet and Web-based activities embedded within the overall system.

Multiuser Base

The multiuser-base structure of CMSs provides an advantage over the structures of previous authoring tools, which to a large extent demanded the technical skills of programmers, Webmasters, and server administrators for effective management of instructional Web sites, especially with regard to maintaining security and tracking students' progress and assignment submissions. CMSs placed the process of developing, delivering, and managing online instruction in the hands of the content expert and the instructor, which resulted in the widespread use of such tools in higher education settings, school settings, and industries.

Ubiquitous Adoption

Evidence of the ubiquitous adoption of CMSs in higher education institutions was provided by the results of a survey conducted in The Campus Computing Project (Green, 2001). These results indicated that in 21% of all college courses in 2001, CMSs were used to support instruction (Olsen, 2001). This figure had increased 15% from the year 2000. Industry evidence of the use of CMSs (or LMSs as these tools are known in the e-learning industry) is not as clear. According to a market analysis of the 2002 U.S. e-learning industry (Adkins, 2002), e-learning is being more widely adopted across all sectors, and government and academic markets are leading the way. A 2001 comprehensive analysis of employer-sponsored training in the United States by the editors of *Training* magazine (Galvin, 2001) revealed that 11% of all industry training was delivered by computer (a decline of 2% from the figure for the year 2000). Of this computer-delivered training, 22% occurred online through the Internet, and 30% occurred online through an intranet (an internal computer network). According to these statistics, you could infer that approximately 6% of all industry training in the United States is online. However, whether this online training is being delivered by means of LMSs, learning content management systems (LCMSs), or a combination of Web-based applications is unclear (see Chapter 8 for examples of leading CMSs and LMSs and additional usage statistics).

EXAMPLES OF CMSs

In this section, we provide brief descriptions of four CMSs—WebCT, Blackboard, Virtual-U, and Lotus LearningSpace—to familiarize you with a sample, or a snapshot in time, of commercial CMS and LMS products and their general features and components. Our selection of these four products was not based on any particular strategy but on our familiarity with these systems and the courseware produced (Dabbagh, Bannan-Ritland, & Silc, 2001). Subsequently in the chapter, a more formal strategy is provided to assist you in selectively distinguishing CMSs from one another on the basis of their specific features and components. This strategy will allow you to select a CMS that meets your needs and the needs of your institution or business. The CMS products featured in this chapter are described as they existed at the time of this writing. These descriptions are not intended as user documentation but as overviews for understanding the pedagogical implications of CMSs and the application of CMSs to the design and development of online learning and WBI. We acknowledge that these CMS products may change before this book is published. However, many academic institutions will probably still be using some of the product versions described next, and most of the features discussed in this chapter will probably still be current.

WebCT

WebCT (http://www.webct.com) currently has three editions: a standard edition, a campus edition, and an enterprise edition. The standard edition is ideal for practitioners who want a robust, pedagogically sound course platform but do not need extensive features for enhanced scaling or integration with campus systems. The campus edition offers a total online learning solution to administrators who want to integrate their online courses with campuswide portals and student information systems. The enterprise edition is designed to support the existing structure, operations, and work flow of higher education institutions, presenting a business transactional system in addition to managing online courses and student information systems. Our focus in this chapter is on the standard edition. In addition to facilitating the organization of course material on the Web, WebCT's standard edition provides various tools and features that can be used within a course to increase its interactivity. Examples include a conferencing system, online chat, student progress tracking, group project organization, student self-evaluation, grade maintenance and distribution, access control, navigation tools, automarked quizzes, automatic index generation, a course calendar, student home pages, embedded e-mail, and course content searches and glossaries.

Blackboard

Blackboard (http://www.blackboard.com) offers four levels of its online development software: (a) Blackboard Learning System, (b) Blackboard Content System, (c) Blackboard Portal System, and (d) Blackboard Transaction System. Blackboard Learning System is an improvement over previous versions of Blackboard, which included features such as content organization, class discussions, group communication tools, an online quizzes tool, e-mail, an announcements posting area, and a digital drop box. Blackboard Learning System includes content-sharing capabilities that provide instructors with more capability and control, a new assessment creation system for deploying tests and surveys, a new Gradebook interface, improved discussion boards and virtual classroom tools, and improved capabilities for integration with student information, identity management, and authentication systems.

Blackboard Content System is aligned with the goals of content management systems, which emphasize managing content rather than managing courses (see Chapter 8). Blackboard Content System supports the development of shareable and reusable learning objects (see Chapter 8), e–portfolio management, virtual hard drive management, and library digital asset management (see http://www.blackboard.com for more information on the capabilities of this system).

Blackboard Portal System includes customizable institutionwide portals and online campus communities. Its advanced architecture allows easy integration of multiple administrative systems in addition to course management and content management.

Blackboard Transaction System is similar to the enterprise edition of WebCT. It facilitates the integration of business and financial transactions such as e–debit processing, Web deposits, auditing capabilities, and other auxiliary services that help colleges, universities, and corporations leverage their e-learning investment on an as-needed basis.

Our focus in this chapter is on Blackboard Learning System and the features of this system that facilitate course management. Overall, Blackboard has a reputation for being easy to use, particularly by novice faculty members. "Call it guidance or micromanagement, Blackboard does help you get a course up and running very quickly" (Caplan-Carbin, 2003).

Virtual-U

Virtual-U (http://www.vlei.com) is an online learning application made up of various integrated components. These components include the VGroups conferencing system, which enables instructors to easily set up collaborative groups and define structures, tasks, and objectives; the Workspace and the Course Syllabus (known as *course structuring tools*), which enable instructors without programming knowledge to create complete courses online; the Gradebook, which allows student performance tracking; and system administration tools. A unique feature of Virtual-U is its pedagogical advisement layer, which is embedded in the tool to coach instructors on how to effectively integrate active and collaborative activities in online learning. The developers of Virtual-U also incorporated utilities that capture usage data so that users can examine the following processes and considerations in relation to the design, delivery, and management of online learning: instructional design, impact on instructor and learner workload, satisfaction and practice, quality of learning, and assessment issues. More than 150 instructors and 230 courses from 30-plus disciplines in all fields of knowledge are involved in testing Virtual-U in Canada and internationally to determine the effectiveness of this CMS for delivering online learning.

Lotus LearningSpace

Lotus LearningSpace (http://www.lotus.com) is IBM's e-learning technology, which is primarily geared toward the industry. Current Lotus LearningSpace systems include Lotus LearningSpace 5, Lotus Learning Management System, and Lotus Virtual Classroom (previously known as *Lotus LearningSpace Forum*). Lotus LearningSpace 5 supports self-paced, collaborative, and virtual classroom learning. It includes features such as the Schedule, which provides a means for structuring course assignments; the MediaCenter, a tool for creating and managing the knowledge base of a LearningSpace course and that works in conjunction with the Multimedia Library; and the CourseRoom, an interactive, facilitated environment for secure student-within-team, student-to-peer, and student-to-instructor collaboration. Chat, e-mail, discussions, and document-sharing capabilities are some of the features that allow students to collaborate easily as they learn.

Lotus Learning Management System provides a single platform for managing classroom-based and e-learning resources in an effort to streamline corporate learning programs and deliver training resources to employees as needed. For example, it provides reporting and tracking techniques to support decision making and human capital management, and the development of competency-based learning solutions to help increase worker productivity and reduce training costs.

Lotus Virtual Classroom is designed to deliver real-time learning to employees, customers, suppliers, and business partners located anywhere in the world (see http://www.lotus.com for more information). Using the latest Sametime technology, this system includes record and playback functions, broadcast capabilities, and real-time breakout sessions to support teamwork.

Our focus in this chapter is on Lotus LearningSpace 5. This system includes many of the features of Lotus Learning Management System and Lotus Virtual Classroom.

Other CMSs and LMSs

For a comprehensive list of CMSs and LMSs and a comparative analysis of their technical features, visit the EduTools Web site at http://www.edutools.info/course.

INTEGRAL FEATURES AND COMPONENTS OF CMSs

Several common features are integral to all course management software (Barron & Liskawa, 2001):

- Asynchronous communication
- Synchronous communication
- Online testing
- Home pages (for students and instructors)
- Security features (e.g., password protection and level of usability)
- Course design and management
- Student management
- Student and site tracking

An alternative classification of common features proposed by the Center for Curriculum Transfer and Technology (2000) includes Web browsing, asynchronous and synchronous sharing, student tools, resources, a lesson, course data, administration, a help desk, and technical information. Although these categories capture the integral features of CMSs, they do not provide a pedagogical classification of the specific components or tools that support such features. For example, what are the tools that support synchronous and asynchronous communication, course design and management, and online testing? What are their pedagogical functions? How are these tools used in an instructional context?

To answer these questions, we developed a broader and more pedagogically oriented classification of CMS features. We also provided specific examples of the various components and tools within each category by using the four CMS or LMS products we selected. These examples should enable you to assess the pedagogical potential of a CMS and to understand how instructors and learners can use the individual components of a CMS to engage students in meaningful online learning. The five classes or categories of pedagogical tools embedded in a CMS are as follows:

1. **Collaborative and communication tools**
2. **Content creation and delivery tools**
3. **Administrative tools**
4. **Learning tools**
5. **Assessment tools**

Next, we describe each class of tools and provide five tables that list the specific tools belonging to each category for WebCT, Blackboard, Virtual-U, and Lotus LearningSpace.

Collaborative and Communication Tools

Collaborative and communication tools include asynchronous communication tools, synchronous communication tools, and group tools. Asynchronous communication allows instructors and learners to "post messages, read and respond to messages, reflect on responses, revise interpretations, and modify original assumptions and perceptions" (Chamberlin, 2001, p.11). These actions are possible because of the time-delayed nature of asynchronous communication. Asynchronous communication is an inherent feature of Internet-based communications technology and has become an essential facility for online learning. CMSs have incorporated asynchronous communication through components or tools such as e-mail, threaded discussion forums, and bulletin boards, which have enabled one-to-one, one-to-many, and many-to-many interactions. In addition, tools such as Profiles in Lotus LearningSpace, Personal Information in Blackboard, and Student Homepages in WebCT allow students to post biographies and share personal and background information and experiences, which prompts meaningful communication and socialization.

Synchronous communication gives participants the ability to interact in real time (as in face-to-face learning). Students and instructors log on at the same time and are virtually present together. They can discuss an issue, present information on a topic (using PowerPoint, for example), collaborate on a task or a project, model or explain a procedure or a concept, and engage in brainstorming or hypothesis generation activities. Synchronous communication is more informal and spontaneous than asynchronous communication is. CMSs have incorporated synchronous communication through features or tools such as virtual chat, electronic whiteboards, instant messaging, screen sharing, and audio- and videoconferencing.

Group tools support both asynchronous and synchronous communication to enable groups of students to work and learn as a team. CMSs can generate group discussion areas and provide groups with document-sharing and -editing tools to engage students in completing group assignments and tasks. Group tools can support formal (e.g., presenting the final product of collaborative work) and informal (e.g., work-in-progress) types of group activities. Examples of group tools include group discussion forums, virtual chat areas, file exchange tools, group posting areas, breakout sessions, and group e-mail.

Some group tools also allow learners to create their own learning communities with peers and/or others outside the course, in contrast to groups or teams defined by the instructor. For example, Blackboard has User Directory, a tool or feature that connects learners with all users of Blackboard on campus, irrespective of the courses in which they are enrolled. Blackboard also has Class Roster, a tool with e-mail links so that learners can contact one another and form virtual study groups. Virtual-U has a synchronous tool called *Café* that allows students to socialize in an informal setting. Table 9.1 provides more examples of collaborative and communication tools listed by product.

Table 9.1 Examples of Collaborative and Communication Tools

BLACKBOARD	LEARNINGSPACE	VIRTUAL-U	WEBCT
Address Book	Breakout Session	Café	Chat
Chat	Broadcast	E-mail	Discussions
Discussion Board	Chat	Instructor Profile	E-mail
Edit Your Homepage	CourseRoom	Resources and Conferences	Student Homepages
E-mail	Discussion Board	VGroups	Whiteboard
Group Pages	E-mail	VU-Chat	
Personal Information	Follow Me	Whiteboard	
Roster	Live Session		
Staff Information	Profiles		
User Directory	Question and Answer		
Virtual Classroom	Screen Sharing		
Whiteboard	Virtual Classroom		
	Whiteboard		

Note. The names of the tools listed in this table may not adhere to the exact terminology used in the course management systems (CMSs), particularly depending on the versions of the CMSs used.

To understand the specific functions of the preceding features and the instructional and learning activities afforded by this class of tools, visit the companion Web site for this book (http://www.prenhall.com/dabbagh) and click on each CMS listed under Features and Components of Course Management Systems located in Chapter 9.

Content Creation and Delivery Tools

Content creation and delivery tools include tools that enable instructors to deliver course content and resources, and tools for learners that enable them to contribute course content, submit assignments, and interact with course resources. For example, Blackboard has tools such as Course Information and Course Documents that enable instructors to post the course syllabus and documents related to course assignments. Instructors can upload documents as Word, HTML, or PDF files. The files appear as links for students to click on and download to their computer or to view as HTML files in their browser. Blackboard also has an External Links feature that enables instructors to provide students with Web links (hypermedia links) related to the course content.

WebCT has tools such as Add URLs, Add Page or Tool, Content Module, and Manage Files that allow instructors to organize the course content in a variety of formats ranging from a linear, or sequential, format in which learners view the content as though turning the pages of a book, to a more random, or nonlinear, format in which students view the content in any order they choose. The Content Assistant feature in WebCT provides instructors with help and options on how to generate course content.

Table 9.2   Examples of Content Delivery and Creation Tools

BLACKBOARD	LEARNINGSPACE	VIRTUAL-U	WEBCT
Assignments	Activity	Course Content	Add URLs
Books	Assignments	Course Editor	Add Page or
Course Content Areas	Content Creation	Course Syllabus	Tool
Course Documents	Course Planner	General Information	Assignments
Course Information	Interface Customization	Portfolio	CD-ROM
Course Tasks	MediaCenter	Submission Box	Content Assistant
Digital Drop Box		Units/Topics	Content Module
External Links			Goals
Learning Units			Image Database
Resource Center			Language
			Manage Files
			Presentations
			Syllabus
			References

Note. The names of the tools listed in this table may not adhere to the exact terminology used in the course management systems (CMSs), particularly depending on the versions of the CMSs used.

Examples of student content creation tools include a student presentation area in WebCT, which allows students to post their assignments, reflection journals, and solutions to case studies. Student presentation areas also enable students to contribute additional course resources for exploration by peers. Students (or the instructor) create an HTML file (called the *index file*) that serves as a menu of hyperlinks to the documents that students upload to their designated area. WebCT also has an Assignments feature that allows instructors to post an assignment or a class activity, assign points to the activity, and list start and end dates for the assignment. Students can download the activity and submit their solution to a designated area for the instructor to grade and/or provide feedback about. Blackboard has a similar feature, called *Course Tasks,* for activities and assignments. Table 9.2 provides more examples of content creation and delivery tools listed by product.

To understand the specific functions of the preceding features and the instructional and learning activities afforded by this class of tools, visit the companion Web site for this book (http://www.prenhall.com/dabbagh) and click on each CMS listed under Features and Components of Course Management Systems located in Chapter 9.

Administrative Tools

Administrative tools include (a) tools to manage students and student information, such as importing the class roster from the institution's registration system, updating or editing student information, assigning user IDs and passwords, removing users, generating

Table 9.3 Examples of Administrative Tools

BLACKBOARD	LEARNINGSPACE	VIRTUAL-U	WEBCT
Area Availability	Registration	Course Space Manager	Course Recycler
Categorize Course	Security	Set Options	Course Homepage
Course Availability	Schedule	Regular Events	Register (students,
and Guest Access	Announcements		instructor, teacher's
Course Recycler			assistant)
Course Settings			Change Settings
Enrollment Options			Security
Announcements			Manage Course
Course Calendar			Course Calendar

Note. The names of the tools listed in this table may not adhere to the exact terminology used in the course management systems (CMSs), particularly depending on the versions of the CMSs used.

presentation areas, and generating an e-mail list; (b) tools to manage teaching assistants, such as adding teaching assistants, graders, and course designers to the course and providing guest access; and (c) tools to manage group work, such as generating student groups, group work areas, and presentation areas at which to post group work. For example, in WebCT, instructors can generate a Student Presentations area by assigning one area per student or group. Student Presentations can be considered a content creation and delivery tool from a student standpoint and an administrative tool from an instructor standpoint.

Administrative tools also include functions such as setting the duration of the course, controlling enrollment options, categorizing the course in the course catalog, and setting the course availability (access to the course). Table 9.3 provides more examples of administrative tools listed by product.

To understand the specific functions of the preceding features and the instructional and learning activities afforded by this class of tools, visit the companion Web site for this book (http://www.prenhall.com.dabbagh) and click on each CMS listed under Features and Components of Course Management Systems located in Chapter 9.

Learning Tools

Learning tools include tools primarily for learners that enable them to interact meaningfully with course content. In the process of exploring course content, working on assignments, and participating in learning activities, students can apply learning and organizational strategies to process the content in a meaningful way and organize their learning experience. Learning tools can be thought of as tools that enable learners to manipulate content online and create personalized experiences during the learning process, in contrast to tools that allow students to post the products of their learning in a presentation area or a drop box. The abilities to annotate text while exploring course content, take notes (online), link information, and build a personal folder of relevant material are examples of learning tools.

Several types of learning tools are embedded in CMSs:

- *Collection-type tools*, such as bookmarks, personal folders, and a compile feature that enables individual compilation of course materials and discussion forums for later use
- *Expository-type tools*, such as diary or journal-type note-taking tools that are generally not shareable; Post-it or annotation-type features that can be directly associated with course materials and can be shared; and student calendars that learners can use to organize tasks and define schedules
- *Exploratory-type tools*, such as open-ended search tools that can scan course materials, the entire course site, or the Web; and customizable portals that students can use to explore sites for prespecified information or news
- *Scaffolding-type tools*, such as a glossary, help tools, an index, and a course map or a navigation map, that support learners in finding course information and navigating through course content

Table 9.4 provides more examples of learning tools listed by product.

Table 9.4 Examples of Learning Tools

BLACKBOARD	LEARNINGSPACE	VIRTUAL-U	WEBCT
Collect	Annotations in the	Bookmarks	Bookmarks
Course Map	CourseRoom	Course Calendar	Compile Pages
Manual	Help	Course Viewer	Course Map
Personal Calendar	My Favorites	Glossary	Glossary
	Personal Folder in		
Personal Tasks	MediaCenter		
Electric Blackboard	Search Discussion Board	Library, Laboratories	Help
	Search MediaCenter	Navigation Map	Index
	Tool Tips	Personal Workspace	My Bookmarks
			My Notes
			Personal Calendar
			Resume Course
			Search
			Student Tips
			WebCT.com

Note. The names of the tools listed in this table may not adhere to the exact terminology used in the course management systems (CMSs), particularly depending on the versions of the CMSs used.

To understand the specific functions of the preceding features and the instructional and learning activities afforded by this class of tools, visit the companion Web site for this book (http://www.prenhall.com/dabbagh) and click on each CMS listed under Features and Components of Course Management Systems located in Chapter 9.

Assessment Tools

The last category of tools includes assessment tools primarily for instructors to use, although the tools can engage learners in self- and peer-assessment activities depending on the pedagogical orientation of the course. Most CMSs integrate objectivist assessment tools, such as the ability to create programmed quizzes or tests that are generally true–false, multiple-choice, matching, ordering, or fill-in-the-blank assessments. These forms of assessment are electronically scored and can provide instant feedback to the student. Questions can also be randomized from a pool of questions or a question bank to ensure that students are not simply memorizing the test.

Additional forms of assessment include comprehension essay-type tools in which the student submits a text-based assignment directly to the assessor through a communications component or a submission box–type feature such as the Digital Drop Box tool in Blackboard. Essay-type tests or assignments are more subjective and can be used to assess higher order learning skills. Grading essay-type tests with an intelligent *parser* (a program that can search text and match or compare results against preestablished text parameters set by the instructor) might be possible. However, currently CMSs do not have embedded intelligent agents or parsers, and instructors must grade such assignments by using traditional grading methods and provide feedback to students through a communication tool such as e-mail.

Assessment tools can also be used to develop self-assessment tests. Self-assessment tests are an example of authentic assessment that allows students to monitor their comprehension and learning. WebCT has a specific Self Test tool that instructors can use to construct self-assessment tests. Authentic assessment can also be implemented by using content creation and delivery tools. For example, instructors can engage students in peer-assessment activities by developing rubrics for assignments, posting such rubrics by using a content delivery tool, and requiring students to use these rubrics to evaluate one another's work. Peer evaluations can be submitted by using a communication tool or a content delivery tool such as Student Presentations in WebCT. Instructors can also promote self-assessment by requiring students to submit reflection journals and to create electronic portfolios to demonstrate their learning. Then, instructors can use the e-mail feature to provide constructive feedback on such assignments. Surveys can also be generated so that instructors can assess individual contributions to group work and collect student feedback about the course for formative evaluation.

Assessment tools also include tracking features that allow instructors and students to track and monitor their progress. For example, WebCT allows instructors to track the number of times students accessed the course, which content pages students accessed, what time students accessed these pages, and for how long. WebCT also provides

Table 9.5   Examples of Assessment Tools

BLACKBOARD	LEARNINGSPACE	VIRTUAL-U	WEBCT
Assessment Manager	Assessment Manager	Assignment Manager	Monitor
Course Statistics	Check Progress	Assignments, Tests and Activities	My Grades
My Grades	Portfolio in Profiles	Gradebook	My Progress
Online Gradebook		Log Miner	Quiz
Pool Manager			Self Test
Quiz			
Survey			

Note. The names of the tools listed in this table may not adhere to the exact terminology used in the course management systems (CMSs), particularly depending on the versions of the CMSs used.

instructors with tools to use to track the number and time of postings per student and to search discussion forums by student name, user ID, date, and/or discussion topic.

Most CMSs include tools for reporting grades, which result in My Grades or Check Progress tools that allow learners to track their progress by checking their grades periodically. Instructors can generate grading columns for each assignment, assign the number of points for each column, and record the points for each student after an assignment is submitted and graded. Instructors have the option of hiding, revealing, or releasing grades when appropriate. The grading columns operate like a spreadsheet, providing class averages per assignment and totals per student as well as other informative statistics. Instructors can also download grading areas as a single file and import the file into a database or a spreadsheet program for further analyses. Table 9.5 provides more examples of assessment tools listed by product.

To understand the specific functions of the preceding features and the instructional and learning activities afforded by this class of tools, visit the companion Web site for this book (http://www.prenhall.com/dabbagh) and click on each CMS listed under Features and Components of Course Management Systems located in Chapter 9.

Summary

Thinking about CMSs in terms of the categories or classes of tools described in the preceding sections can be helpful in making the most out of the features a CMS provides. For example, if you want to emphasize collaboration and communication in an online course that you are developing, you can examine the specific collaborative and communication tools of the CMS you are using to design appropriate instructional and learning activities. If assessment is a key component of your course design, you can examine the capabilities of the assessment tools of the particular CMS to ensure that you can deliver the evaluation instruments or strategies that you are envisioning for your audience. If you want to emphasize the use of learning strategies to help learners become more self-directed and take ownership of the learning process, you can examine whether the CMS has an appropriate selection of learning tools so that you can design appropriate activities. If the emphasis is on delivering specific instructional content in a variety of formats, the capabilities of content creation and delivery tools can be explored. By using this approach, you can support your personal pedagogical orientation to the design and development of a Web-based course. In addition, these categories of tools can help distinguish one CMS product from another to facilitate the selection of a CMS. This distinction is discussed in the next section.

DISTINGUISHING FEATURES OF SELECTED CMSs

On examining Tables 9.1 through 9.5 and the supporting functions and instructional examples at the companion Web site, you will notice that some CMSs have distinguishing features under certain categories that are worth noting. For example, Virtual-U has distinguishing features in the collaborative and communication tools category, such as VGroups, VU-Chat, Café, and Conferences. Although other CMSs include similar features, Virtual-U emphasizes these tools both in its interface design and in its pedagogical advisement layer, which prompts adopters to capitalize on these features and redesign their courses to accommodate the use of such features. Virtual-U's collaborative and communication tools enable the design of more spontaneous or generative learning activities that subscribe to constructivist learning models, such as communities of practice (CoP) and knowledge-building communities. This feature is consistent with the underlying pedagogical orientation of Virtual-U, which is to support active learning and interaction through collaborative course designs. Linda Harasim (1997), who pioneered the development of Virtual-U as both a CMS and a research tool, identified four criteria that should be adopted when you are designing online courses by using CMSs. They are (a) ensuring active participation by students, (b) ensuring peer interaction, (c) providing multiple perspectives, and (d) providing a spatial or visual metaphor of academic institutions to facilitate the transition from face-to-face learning to online learning. Virtual-U was developed to support these criteria.

WebCT can be perceived as having a more comprehensive set of features under the content creation and delivery tools category. Features such as Add URLs, Add Page or Tool, Content Assistant, and Content Module enable several organizational and sequencing formats for delivering course content. In addition, the Manage Files feature enables access to personal and system files, which allows direct HTML editing and manipulation of the file structure. Other tools do not provide as much flexibility in supporting the organization of course content and may not provide access to the personal and system files storage area so as not to burden users with an added layer of complexity. WebCT also has unique content creation and delivery tools for students, including the Student Presentations area (listed as Presentations in Table 9.2). This tool enables learners individually or in groups to create and contribute shareable content. WebCT also has a good range of learning tools. Students can compile discussion forums for further reflection; use the course index, course glossary, and search tools for quick content searches; and use the My Notes tool to monitor their learning.

Blackboard can be perceived as having distinguishing features under the administrative tools and assessment tools categories and an overall balanced distribution of features across all other categories. Blackboard can be considered more structured and balanced in terms of providing a range of traditional teaching tools, which is perhaps why Blackboard has a reputation of being more user friendly than most other CMSs. However, the trade-off may be that this CMS is not as flexible in terms of the instructional designs it supports. Blackboard's new Building Blocks architecture, though, promises to be a breakthrough in CMS technology (Blackboard, Inc., 2003). It will allow campus learning environments to integrate existing software applications by using an administrative interface for installing and monitoring additional tools and a full user interface for delivering these tools as seamlessly as a core Blackboard CMS feature. This development will provide the potential for more engaging instructional designs.

Lotus LearningSpace is presented as more of an adult peer-to-peer (collaborative) learning tool. For example, one distinguishing feature is Screen Sharing. It allows users to access, from their desktop, a new computer application that their company is implementing and to interact with the application remotely. This feature may be effective for companies who are rolling out a new product and want their employees to learn how to use this product from a remote location. Lotus LearningSpace also has a Breakout Session feature that provides the capability of organizing participants into small conferencing groups to maximize interaction in a synchronous mode. This feature can be used along with the Screen Sharing feature to elicit group participation. These two features make Lotus LearningSpace more conducive to real-time group work. Lotus LearningSpace also has unique tools under the learning tools category, such as the Annotations tool in the CourseRoom. Students can use this tool to annotate course material and choose whether or not they want to share their annotations with their peers. This learning tool is extremely powerful because the student is personalizing his or her learning experience by directly and meaningfully manipulating the content. Another unique learning tool in Lotus LearningSpace is the Personal Folder tool. This tool can be used to collect documents for further study.

Take a moment and think about the scenarios provided at the beginning of this chapter in relation to this discussion. Which class of tools is emphasized in the Virtual Communities scenario? New Product Rollout? AP Chemistry? In the Virtual Communities scenario, collaboration and communication seem to be highly emphasized. Which CMS has the most variety of collaboration and communication tools? Visit the companion Web site to explore more examples of instructional and learning activities for each class of tools. In the New Product Rollout scenario, the emphasis seems to be on learning tools in addition to content delivery and assessment. The supervisors should be able to customize the training content to their own context. Therefore, tools that enable users to manipulate the content and organize it in meaningful ways are necessary. In the AP Chemistry scenario, the emphasis seems to be on content delivery and assessment. On the basis of this analysis, which CMS or LMS is most suitable for each scenario?

SELECTION OF A CMS

Despite the pedagogical and comparative benefits of classifying CMS features into five categories and identifying related instructional and learning activities (see the companion Web site and related activities at the end of this chapter), selecting a CMS is becoming an increasingly complex task from an institutional perspective. Campus information technology executives, as well as chief learning officers (CLOs) in the corporate sector, are facing daunting challenges as a result of rising user expectations, an expanding user base, tight budgets, and difficult staffing requirements. In addition, these individuals face technological challenges that include integrating a CMS with student information systems (or an LMS with enterprise systems) and keeping up with network infrastructures that are transitioning to wireless technologies, which pose considerable security risks (*Syllabus e-Newsletter*, 2003). However, certain practices have guided the selection of a CMS or an LMS.

For example, common practice has been for developers at academic institutions to select a single, user-friendly CMS and establish a comprehensive suite of services around it. The primary reason is that the goal in higher education institutions is often to get faculty on board and convince them that using a CMS will enhance their teaching and provide students with more access to course materials and a wider range of learning tools. Another reason is that instructional support units at educational institutions cannot support individual authoring, updating, and administering of course Web pages (Kubarek, 1999). Unlike the corporate, government, and industry sectors, in which large sums of money may be paid for training development and these functions are often outsourced to e-learning specialists, higher education institutions need the tool to be placed in the faculty's hands because the faculty are primarily responsible for designing their courses and teaching them. Administrators at some higher education institutions may be interested in launching a series of online degrees to increase enrollment and cut costs, in which case a viable option may be to outsource the development and delivery of online learning to e-learning specialists and vendors. However, more often than not, administrators at academic institutions move at a more cautious pace and begin using a CMS to integrate technology into the teaching and learning process.

Alternatively, corporate executives may want an LMS for centralizing the delivery of all their training materials, whether off the shelf or developed in-house. They may also be interested in LMSs that feature a wide array of collaborative and communication tools to enhance team-building and project management skills among employees in different geographic locations. An LMS that can update employee records upon training completion is an added bonus.

No matter what the situation, choosing a CMS or an LMS can be a daunting task from an administrative standpoint. In 2002, Hall contended, "There is no single authoring tool or authoring method that is the definitive correct approach for every situation. . . . The answer is always it depends." In other words, it depends on the organization's specific e-learning requirements. So that a developer can understand an organization's e-learning requirements, Hall suggested starting with a few questions that help cut to the bottom line quickly:

1. Do the managers of the organization envision converting all current training to e-learning? If not, how many hours of e-learning are envisioned?
2. How many courses or modules need development? Will these courses be developed from scratch or do existing print-based materials need to be converted to digital form?
3. What types of instructional strategies and models are envisioned?
4. Who will develop the training (team vs. individuals), and how many developers will be on a team?
5. Will the organization managers have purchased content or computer-based instructional modules with the expectation of delivering this content through a CMS?
6. Who is the audience and how will they be accessing the training (e.g., high-speed modem, Internet, intranet)? What equipment and software will they be using (e.g., videocams, microphones, and speakers; Windows or Macintosh operating systems; Internet Explorer or Netscape Navigator)?
7. What is the organization's budget?
8. Does the organization have existing information systems that need to interface with this training?
9. Do learner performance results from the training need to be tracked?

Several other researchers and practitioners have offered similar guidelines and recommendations. For example, Zvacek (2000) recommended involving as many stakeholders as possible in the selection process, especially faculty members, both novices and prodigies (i.e., both those who have not yet made the leap to online instruction and those who are comfortable with high-tech applications). Zvacek reported that involving representatives from a variety of academic disciplines and academic support services is perhaps the most effective way to help administrators at an institution select and adopt a CMS. Zvacek also recommended preparing a comprehensive list of possible evaluation criteria, then prioritizing them according to the users' needs, administration's goals, and long-term institutional practices and policies.

Kubarek (1999) suggested that essential or basic criteria must be considered, along with supplementary or additional criteria. Among the basic criteria are the ease of use of the tool, its overall functionality (quantity and quality of features and components embedded in it), and its quality of rapport with the developers. Other criteria include (a) **scalability** (e.g., increases in the number of course Web sites would not require a corresponding increase in support and staff), (b) degree of user ownership (i.e., enabling faculty to be responsible for creating and administering their own course Web sites), and (c) user-friendliness (i.e., the degree to which novice technology users can build and maintain a course Web site without getting frustrated with the technology.

On the basis of the preceding recommendations, we offer an expanded list of general questions and criteria to guide the selection of a CMS or an LMS. We divide these criteria into four dimensions: institutional, pedagogical, technological, and user support. Keep in mind that these criteria can be prioritized to fit the needs of the organization whose administrators are interested in designing and delivering online learning, WBI, or e-learning.

Institutional Issues

Institutional issues begin with consideration of why the administrators of an organization want to adopt a CMS or an LMS: To improve employee performance? to cut training costs? to increase enrollment? to provide certificates and degrees through distance learning? or to integrate technology into the teaching and learning process? These are a few of the questions aimed at discovering the underlying goal of administrators who are considering adopting a CMS. Other institutional issues to consider are as follows:

- *What is the established customer base of the tool?* This consideration helps developers to facilitate collaborative activities with other institutions (e.g., faculty at different institutions could teach a course to students at different institutions). For the corporate sector, this could mean the ability to share existing online courseware and training modules.
- *What is the organization's budget?* Once this is determined, find out how the vendor is charging for the CMS. Some vendors charge by user, others by site license, and yet others have different charges for the basic version of the system, which has limited functionality, compared with those for the full version. Consider also hardware, software, and installation requirements, and annual and maintenance fees. Typical questions to ask include the following (Guest & Juday, 2001):
  - Does the pricing address consulting fees, training fees, and annual maintenance costs?
  - Are future upgrades and system components included in the initial contract?
  - Does the pricing include the addition of future users?
  - *Does the institution have an adequate technological infrastructure to support Online learning applications?*

    Planning for a technological infrastructure to support online learning means planning for the network or hardware infrastructure, planning for the software and services from external providers, and planning for the people to manage these systems (Boettcher & Kumar, 2000). The network infrastructure needs to be (a) scalable, to accommodate a growing number of users and programs; (b) reliable (i.e., available on a mission-critical basis); and (c) secure. The infrastructure also needs to support asynchronous and synchronous learning, on-campus and distant learners, and collaboration across space and time. This type of infrastructure requires both technological and human-based support to help maintain the momentum of an online learning environment and provide the necessary instructional and counseling support, technical support, and troubleshooting (Khan, 2001).

An effective way of thinking about the infrastructure required to deliver online learning would be along three dimensions: technology, organization, and policy (Boettcher & Kumar, 2000). Technology planning implies planning for connectivity (the network and its associated hardware and software components, as just discussed), organization implies planning for instructional and technical support, and policy implies planning for how membership in an online community is defined and the extent of access to resources such as library resources, as well as issues related to software licensing, authentication, authorization, and security.

Pedagogical Issues

Pedagogical issues are primarily instructional design issues. The individual (or team) charged with selecting a CMS should study the following issues in this category: (a) the type of content and the learning outcomes expected; (b) the instructional strategies and pedagogical models envisioned; (c) the features and components of the tool (to determine whether it accommodates the design and delivery of these strategies and models); (d) the expertise of the faculty or facilitators who will be conducting the instruction or training, both from a technological perspective and a pedagogical perspective; and (e) learner profiles and backgrounds. These issues were discussed at length in previous chapters of this book. Following are some specific questions to consider under the pedagogical dimension:

- *Instructional design models and strategies:* Which instructional design models and strategies are envisioned for this instruction or training? Are opportunities available for teamwork and collaborative activities, or will the training be mostly instructor driven? Is the training critical for job performance? What type of learning outcomes are the learners expected to master? problem-solving skills? procedural skills? declarative knowledge?
- *Features and components of the tool:* What type of features and components does the tool have? What classes of tools are well represented? not well represented? Examine the features of the tool, using the five classes of tools described in this chapter. Does the tool have any unique features that are congruent with your pedagogical needs? Do these features support the instructional models and strategies envisioned for the online learning environment?
- *Faculty and student pedagogical profiles:* What is the pedagogical orientation of the faculty, instructors, or trainers at the organization (e.g., objectivist vs. constructivist)? Do the faculty support student-centered learning? What is their technical expertise? What is the pedagogical orientation of the students or trainees? What is their technical expertise? These issues were discussed in detail in Chapter 2.

Technological Issues

The technological dimension includes hardware, software, and installation requirements; **compatibility** and **interoperability** with existing software; ease of use; accessibility; and the extent to which the CMS can accommodate more users (scalability), content, and functions (extensibility). Following are some specific questions to consider along these lines:

- *Hardware, software, and installation requirements:* Does the CMS require special operating systems, back-end databases, storage space?
- *Compatibility:* How does the CMS interface with existing online courseware that your institution or organization currently supports or uses? Consideration of this criterion will ease **migration** from one format to another.
- *Interoperability:* What is the potential of the CMS for extensive integration with the institution's administrative and information software?
- *Ease of use or tool functionality:* How flexible is the CMS in terms of supporting existing course content? How does the CMS support novice technology users? How does the CMS support expert technology users? Is there an acceptable medium for the user base?
- *Accessibility:* How accessible is the CMS from remote locations? Are any **firewalls** used that might prevent users from accessing the content? What is the required bandwidth for optimum access?
- *Scalability:* Is the CMS scalable? In other words, does it have the ability to add users and/or increase access time without the need to increase technical or human support?
- *Extensibility:* Is the CMS extensible? In other words, does it have the ability to add more features and functionality without the need to change the tool architecture?
- *Migration to newer versions:* When you upgrade to a new version, can the current courses be migrated without manual adjustments?

User Support Issues

The user support dimension ensures that adequate technical, administrative, and instructional support exists for the successful implementation of online learning. The issue of user support was discussed in Chapter 2 from the perspective of the online instructor and the online learner. In this section, we discuss user support from an institutional perspective. In the absence of other defining selection criteria, this dimension may be the one that could steer an organization toward one CMS more than another. Issues to consider under this dimension include the following:

- *Technical support (also known as* product support*) both from the CMS vendor and from the organization's in-house Help Desk, systems administrators, and programmers:* Questions to ask are as follows: What type of technical documentation is available from the vendor? Is the documentation print based? Web based? Is human vendor support available for technical problems? If so, what are the hours of technical support assistance? Does technical support cost extra? What is the level of technical support? Is the technical support for students? faculty? administrators? Does the CMS provide an e-mail list for the users so that system administrators can post announcements about server outages, software updates, backups, and so forth? Does the organization have an in-house technical support system? If so, what are its current duties? What are its areas of expertise? Can it support the implementation of a CMS?

- *Instructional support:*   What type of paper documentation is available to support the use of the CMS? Is training or consulting available to assist you in learning the basic features of the CMS (e.g., How to generate a course site? add course content? perform common administration functions?)? Is a support site available for quick reference and timely information? Is a frequently asked question (FAQ) document on the vendor's Web site that is frequently updated?

When researching the user support dimension, you must keep in mind that many organizations have developed their own technical and instructional support units to facilitate user support tasks. However, these units need to communicate with the vendor on an ongoing basis to remain apprised of new technical and instructional CMS features and to ensure that the full potential of the CMS is being used. In addition, including personnel from such in-house units in the decision-making process is crucial.

LIMITATIONS OF CMSs

Although CMSs greatly facilitate the design, development, delivery, and management of online learning and WBI, as demonstrated in this chapter, these learning technologies have limitations that must be addressed before you can fully understand their educational potential. The last section of this chapter covers the pedagogical and technological limitations of CMSs. Also provided are suggestions and alternatives for users who are looking for specific or unique features that do not require the integrative and comprehensive nature of CMSs or for users who want more flexibility and control in authoring their own Web-based content and learning interactions.

Pedagogical Limitations

Oliver (2001) stated that "a major concern of online course management systems is that they emphasize faculty dissemination tools over student processing tools, even though the latter are more likely to promote student interaction and engagement" (p. 47). Oliver added that CMSs may therefore impede the design of online learning environments that support inquiry-based learning, problem solving, and knowledge building. Other researchers share similar perspectives. For example, Carl Berger, Director of Advanced Academic Technology and Professor of Science and Technology Education at the University of Michigan at Ann Arbor, suggested that CMSs were not meant to be a pedagogical tool, but rather a productivity tool for handling the administrative tasks of teaching (Olsen, 2001). In addition, George Blakeslee, Professor of Education at Lesley University in Cambridge, Massachusetts, pointed out that many professors at Lesley who are avid technology users prefer to use sophisticated Web tools such as Dreamweaver, Drumbeat, and other Web editors to build their course Web sites and instructional activities. Consequently, they relegate the use of CMS to posting announcements and assignments and setting up occasional discussion forums (Olsen, 2001).

Perhaps this behavioral trend can be attributed to the perception that most CMSs lack the flexibility to support certain instructional activities satisfactorily (e.g., group-based production of academic deliverables) and/or fail to include certain features instructors may want (e.g., seamless integration with other software; Klemm, 2001). Klemm also added that CMSs enforce conformity as a result of their template-based architecture. This inherent characteristic of CMSs is, on the one hand, what facilitates their use and, on the other hand, what perhaps leads to less engaging instructional designs. To expedite the development of online courses, users often choose the most obvious and easily accessible components and features of a CMS, which compromises sound pedagogy (Harvey & Lee, 2001).

For example, Harvey and Lee (2001), conducted research on how the use of CMSs affects the instructional design process. These researchers found that CMSs engender a certain type of instructional structure that mimics the typical functioning of traditional face-to-face classroom learning and concluded that these tools seem to impede the design of more learner-centered, constructivist course designs. Marra and Jonassen (2001) concurred with these conclusions and added three specific pedagogical limitations of CMSs that, in their view, "create significant barriers to implementing constructivist learning principles in online courses" (p. 304). These limitations are the inability of CMSs to support (a) multiple forms of knowledge representation, (b) authentic forms of assessment, and (c) the use of distributed tools that assist students in knowledge construction and meaning making.

Although the preceding criticisms are credible and well supported, we maintain that a comprehensive examination of the features and components of CMSs and the careful integration of the instructional activities afforded by these features as described in this chapter, will yield flexible and effective instructional designs, including learner-centered and constructivist designs. We believe that if faculty and course designers take the time to redesign their existing courses when they are using a Web-based course management tool, much of the replication of traditional face-to-face classroom instruction can be avoided, and instructional designs that take advantage of the inherent features of the Web will emerge. Pedagogical gains have been documented when professors have taken the time to redesign their courses before putting them online (Dabbagh & Schmitt, 1998; Olsen, 2001).

However, in certain situations, developers will inevitably overlook augmenting the use of CMSs with other Web tools and software applications better suited for designing specific pedagogical models or providing sophisticated learning tools such as concept-mapping software and visualization and modeling tools. For example, authoring tools such as Dreamweaver and FrontPage may be better suited for developing online courseware when the integration of multimedia (e.g., audio, video, multimedia libraries, and digital libraries) must be customized. Likewise, if the course pedagogy calls primarily for knowledge building based on group activity, online collaborative tools that support data collection, creation of databases, analysis of data, and co-construction of Web-based products may be more suitable than CMSs are. Centra, Pensare, and Lotus software are examples of such tools in the corporate learning sector. Centra Software is the dominant U.S. synchronous collaboration provider, recently acquired by SmartForce (Harris, 2002). Pensare is a content-collaboration platform optimized for captive audiences both in higher education and in corporate learning, and Lotus software, a product of IBM Mindspan Solutions (http://www.lotus.com), is a leader in collaborative technologies.

Tapped In (http://www.tappedin.org) and Knowledge Forum (http://www.knowledgeforum.com) are examples of such tools in higher education. Tapped In is an online workplace (multiuser domain) that allows education professionals from around the world to engage in professional development programs and informal collaborative activities (see Chapter 5). Knowledge Forum is a type of concept-mapping software that allows students to create notes, attach media to these notes, and visually display them in a Web browser so that other individuals can build on the concept under discussion by linking to the notes to form elaborate information webs. Both these tools were discussed in Chapters 5 and 6 with regard to constructivist-based pedagogical models and strategies. Also available are sophisticated annotation tools (e.g., Harvard's Annotation Engine; Berkman Center for Internet & Society, 2000) that allow students to annotate Web pages, and sophisticated search engines (e.g., VisIT; Visualization of Information Tool, University of Illionis) that allow students to conduct online searches and visually organize the results into meaningful structures (using folders) or concept maps (Beckman Institute for Advanced Science and Technology, 2000).

Although these tools have powerful capabilities to support visualization, modeling, and knowledge-building processes, they often require a steep learning curve and special installation procedures. Perhaps this is why their use is not as ubiquitous as that of CMSs. It is beyond the scope of this book to discuss these learning technologies; however, if you are interested in learning more about these technologies, the references at the end of this chapter are a good starting point. Overall, despite their pedagogical limitations, CMSs can support a range of instructional models that subscribe to behaviorist, cognitivist, and constructivist learning theories.

Technological Limitations

Critiques of CMSs have also revealed technological concerns that are worth noting. For example, Jeffrey Weiss, Professor of Economics at the City University of New York, reported that Blackboard is "very multimedia-unfriendly" (Olsen, 2001). Weiss was unable to run Java programs within Blackboard's system. Other individuals reported that uploading documents to the student presentation and assignment areas in WebCT is frustrating for students because of the unintelligent procedure (Dabbagh, 2000). Additional technological concerns include the following:

- The architecture of the tools is not robust enough to support the kind of teaching to which we are committed (McKenna, Lesley University, cited in Olsen 2001).
- Courses are not **portable** from one management system to another (you can take the files, but you must reorganize the content and the course structure using the tools and features of the new system; Mathews, University of California at Davis, cited in Olsen, 2001).
- Users are unable to develop tutorials, simulations, and realistic cases and problems because CMSs cannot adequately support multimedia tools (Oliver, 2001).
- Providing access to cognitive tools to scaffold students' learning and supporting the learning of such tools are difficult (Marra & Jonassen, 2001).
- CMSs require a third-party administrator for many functions (Klemm, 2001).

- CMSs risk obsolescence when better technology comes along (Klemm, 2001).
- The visual metaphor (Web interface) is not designed according to instructional design principles, and some of the icons can be misleading to some students (Harvey & Lee, 2001).
- The navigation layout is not designed from a student's point of view (the links are not interrelated, which causes students to fully exit course spaces before entering others and consequently lose focus or view the interaction as mediocre; Harvey & Lee, 2001).

These technological limitations are valuable to know and further inform users and potential adopters of CMSs of the potential of CMSs in developing customized online learning environments. As with all educational software and new learning technologies, evaluations of such systems should be based on their strengths and weaknesses and on the careful analysis of the institution's goals, and the pedagogical, technological, and user support dimensions discussed in this chapter.

CHAPTER SUMMARY

This chapter provided a general overview of course management systems (CMSs), with WebCT, Blackboard, Lotus LearningSpace, and Virtual-U used as examples. The chapter covered the general features and components of CMSs and provided a pedagogical classification of their features consisting of five classes: collaborative and communication tools, content creation and delivery tools, learning tools, administrative tools, and assessment tools. The chapter also included a discussion on distinguishing features of WebCT, Blackboard, Lotus LearningSpace, and Virtual-U and provided specific guidelines for selecting a CMS. These guidelines were grouped under four dimensions: institutional, pedagogical, technological, and user support. Last, limitations of CMSs were discussed from pedagogical and technological perspectives.

LEARNING ACTIVITIES

1. Return to the scenarios at the beginning of this chapter. Review the questions you were asked about these scenarios while reading the chapter. Consult the tables at the companion Web site for this chapter (http://www.prenhall.com/dabbagh). Finalize your decision about which CMS is best suited for each scenario. Select one of the scenarios and prepare a list of the CMS features that are most applicable in supporting the instructional context of the scenario.
2. Refer to the Solution Design Form you created in Chapter 6. Locate the CMS features you identified as part of your solution design. Using the tables in this chapter (or at the companion Web site), classify each feature according to the five classes or categories of tools described in this chapter. Which class of tools did you use most?

3. Review the results of your analysis from Activity 2. Did you select features from several CMSs? Did any one CMS have all the features you needed? Examine the tables at the companion Web site for this chapter to see if you can find one that does. Select the CMS that is the "best fit" for your design. Justify your selection on the basis of the concepts discussed in this chapter.

4. Visit the companion Web site and click on the link to this chapter (Chapter 9). Pick a CMS and describe how you would use its features to design an online learning environment that subscribes to some of the models discussed in Chapter 5. For example, assume that you would like to design a cognitive apprenticeship to help your students learn the skills and attributes of an expert school principal. Or, if you want a more corporate-oriented scenario, assume that an investment firm would like its newly hired interns to experience the culture of investment banking by getting firsthand advice from the pros and following their day-to-day behavior. How would you use a CMS to design such a model? Which instructional or learning activities would you emphasize? Use the instructional characteristics of cognitive apprenticeships presented in Chapter 5 to guide your decisions.

5. In this chapter, you were exposed to a list of nine general questions and four dimensions of criteria suggested as guidelines for selecting a CMS. Examine these nine questions and try to distribute them across the four dimensions. Can you find a place for each question under each of these dimensions? If not, what new dimensions or categories do you think should be added to accommodate these questions?

6. Generate your own set of questions and/or categories for selecting a CMS based on your institution's goals and policies for online learning.

7. Visit Brandon Hall's Web site (see the companion Web site for this book— http://www.prenhall.com/dabbagh—for the URL for this Web site), click on the Publications button, and find the *LMS 2003: Comparison of Enterprise Learning Management Systems* report. Find the online demonstration of the LMS Selection Tool provided with this report. Answer the questions to the best of your knowledge or consult with your organization's administrators responsible for selecting learning technologies. Compare this list with the list you developed in Activity 6.

RESOURCES

Explore additional resources at the companion Web site (http://www.prenhall.com/dabbagh) to learn more about the CMSs described in this chapter.

REFERENCES

Adkins, S. S. (2002). *Market analysis of the 2002 U.S. e-learning industry: Convergence, consolidation and commoditization.* Retrieved June 2002 from http://www.brandonhall.com/public/execsums/execsum_adkins1.pdf

Barron, A. E., & Liskawa, C. (2001). Software tools for online course management and delivery. In B. Khan (Ed.), *Web-based training* (pp. 303–310). Englewood Cliffs, NJ: Educational Technology Publications.

Beckman Institute for Advanced Science and Technology. (2000). *VisIT: Visualization of information tool*. Retrieved June 2002 from http://lrs.ed.uiuc.edu/students/kauwell/VisIT/

Berkman Center for Internet & Society. (2000). *Annotation Engine*. Retrieved June 2002 from http://cyber.law.harvard.edu/projects/annotate.html

Blackboard, Inc. (2003, July 23). *Blackboard announces industry's first developers workshop*. Retrieved August 25, 2003, from http://www.blackboard.com

Boettcher, J. V., & Kumar, M. S. V. (2000). The other infrastructure: Distance education's digital plant. *Syllabus, 13*(10), 14–22.

Caplan-Carbin, E. (2003). My beloved Blackboard: Teacher empowerment for students' success. *Proceedings of the Eighth Annual Mid-South Instructional Technology Conference: Teaching, Learning, and Technology, Murfreesboro, TN*. Retrieved July 15, 2003, from http://www.mtsu.edu/~itconf/proceed03/111.html

Center for Curriculum Transfer and Technology. (2000). *Online educational delivery applications: A Web tool for comparative analysis*. Retrieved June 2002 from http://www.edutools.info/course

Chamberlin, W. S. (2001, December). Face-to-face vs. cyberspace: Finding the middle ground. *Syllabus 15*(5), 11, 32. Available online at http:www.syllabus.com

Dabbagh, N. H. (2000). The challenges of interfacing between face-to-face and online instruction. *TechTrends, 44*(6), 37–42.

Dabbagh, N. H., Bannan-Ritland, B., & Silc, K. F. (2001). Pedagogy and Web-based course authoring tools: Issues and implications. In B. Khan (Ed.), *Web-based training* (pp. 343–354). Englewood Cliffs, NJ: Educational Technology Publications.

Dabbagh, N. H., & Schmitt, J. (1998). Pedagogical implications of redesigning instruction for Web-based delivery. *Educational Media International, 35*(2), 106–110.

Galvin, T. (2001). Industry 2001 report. *Training, 38*(10), 40–75.

Green, K. C. (2001, October). *eCommerce comes slowly to the campus: The 2001 National Survey of Information Technology in U.S. Higher Education* (also known as *The 2001 Campus Computing Survey*). Encino, CA: Campus Computing. Retrieved December 2001 from http://www.campuscomputing.net/summaries/2001/index.html

Guest, S., & Juday, J. (2001, November). *Guidelines for buying e-learning services*. Retrieved June 2002 from http://www.learningcircuits.org/2001/nov2001/guest.html

Hall, B. (2002). *Authoring tools strategies*. Retrieved June 2002 from http://www.brandon-hall. com/

Harasim, L. (1997, May). *Learning in hyperspace*. Paper presented at the Learning, Teaching, Interacting in Hyperspace: The Potential of the Web workshop, sponsored by the University of Maryland System Institute for Distance Education and the International University Consortium, Adelphi, MD.

Harris, P. (2002). E-learning: A consolidation update. *Training and Development, 56*(4), 27–33.

Harvey, D. M., & Lee, J. (2001). The impact of inherent instructional design in online courseware. *The Quarterly Review of Distance Education, 2*(1), 35–48.

Hazari, S. I. (2001). *Evaluation and selection of Web course management tools*. Retrieved June 2002 from http://sunil.umd.edu/webct

Khan, B. H. (2001). A framework for Web-based learning. In B. H. Khan (Ed.), *Web-based training* (pp. 75–98). Englewood Cliffs, NJ: Educational Technology Publications.

Klemm, W. R. (2001, May/June). Creating online courses: A step-by-step guide. *The Technology Source*.

Kubarek, D. (1999). On the Internet: Introducing and supporting a Web course management Tool. *Syllabus, 12*(10), 52–55.

Marra, R. M., & Jonassen, D. H. (2001). Limitations of online courses for supporting constructive learning. *The Quarterly Review of Distance Education, 2*(4), 303–317.

Maslowski, R., Visscher, A. J., Collis, B., & Bloemen, P. P. M. (2000, May/June). The formative evaluation of a Web-based course-management system within a university setting. *Educational Technology, 40*(3), 5–19.

Oliver, K. (2001). Recommendations for student tools in online course management systems. *Journal of Computing in Higher Education, 13*(1), 47–70.

Olsen, F. (2001, December 21). Getting ready for a new generation of course-management systems. *The Chronicle of Higher Education, 48*(17), A25.

Syllabus e-Newsletter. (2003, July 29). Retrieved July 29, 2003, from Syllabus@101communications-news.com (e-mail address)

Zvacek, S. M. (2000). Decisions, decisions: Choosing a Web course development package. *The Quarterly Review of Distance Education, 1*(4), 337–344.

Accessibility The degree to which software, such as a course management system, is available to all users, especially those using the course from remote locations such as off campus.

Accretion A schema theory construct in which the process of learning is described as integrating facts into an existing schema. (*See also* **Restructuring** and Tuning.)

Administrative tools Course management system tools used to manage all course users, especially students and student information, such as importing the class roster from the institution's registration system, updating or editing student information, and creating student groups. (*See also* **Course management system.**)

Advance organizers Instructional strategies or materials—such as lesson objectives, outlines, and summaries—used to present content and focus the student on the lesson goals. A technique developed in **meaningful reception learning** (MRL) theory.

Affordances Possibilities or opportunities for action.

Anchored instruction A pedagogical model in which authentic learning activities are promoted as a way to ensure that learning is situated in contexts that reflect the way the knowledge will be useful in real-life situations (Collins, 1991). Also known as *situated learning.*

Animation A technique used to create the illusion of movement or interactivity. It can be used to simulate software, describe physical processes, or simply gain students' attention (B. Hall, 1997).

Architecture The technical design of a system, such as a course management system, and the functional capabilities, requirements, and limitations this design implies.

Articulation A learning activity that encourages the learner to make tacit knowledge explicit. Articulation can be achieved through various activities, such as working in groups, discussing and debating the issues, reporting back, presenting findings, and negotiating and defending knowledge acquired through learning environments (Oliver, Herrrington, & Omari, 1996).

Assessment tools Course management system tools that instructors can use to help them evaluate student learning. These tools also include self-assessment and peer-assessment tools.

Asynchronous A communication technology that does not rely on timed data transmissions to connect two or more computers, which results in delayed-transmission interactions such as e-mail. (*See also* **Synchronous.**)

Asynchronous communication tools Communication technologies that support delayed interactions in an online learning environment. Examples are e-mail and threaded discussions. Such tools can be contrasted with chats or whiteboard communications, which take place in real time. (*See also* **Synchronous communication tools.**)

Authentic learning activities Learning tasks that are anchored in a realistic setting and in which the focus is on solving a problem rather than on learning a body of content. A central instructional strategy that supports or enables other constructivist instructional strategies.

Authoring paradigm A metaphor or a model used in an authoring package as an interface to assist instructional designers in developing courseware,

Authoring tool A software tool that enables instructional designers, educators, teachers, and learners without knowledge of programming languages to design interactive multimedia and hypermedia learning environments.

Avatars "Personalities" assumed by users in a virtual reality environment for role-playing or fantasy purposes or as a way to conceal the users' true identities.

Behaviorism A theory in which learning is described as the process of stimulus response that begins and ends in the environment that is external to the learner. The instructor's goal is to elicit desired behaviors by providing appropriate stimuli.

Bulletin boards Asynchronous communication tools or Web services that provide people with a virtual way to connect and read or "post" messages. Similar to cork bulletin boards you might find on a wall (R. Hall, 2001).

C++ A popular object-oriented programming language for graphical applications such as games and simulations.

Card-Scripting metaphor An authoring paradigm in which an index-card structure or a book metaphor is used to link elements. (*See also* **Authoring paradigm.**)

Cast-score metaphor An authoring paradigm in which horizontal tracks and vertical columns are used to synchronize media events in a time-based fashion. (*See also* Authoring paradigm.)

Chaining An instructional strategy in which complex behaviors are taught by first instilling simpler responses in the learner and then encouraging the learner to combine the simpler behaviors into more complex interactions.

Chat An informal real-time or synchronous online conversation between two or more users via networked computers. A user typically enters a chat room and types a message that will appear on the monitors of all the other users who have entered the same chat room. (*See also* Synchronous and Synchronous communication tools).

Chat whispering Sending a private message to a user in a chat room using the "whisper" command, which results in "whispered" text that only the designated user can see.

Chunking An instructional strategy in which complex concepts are taught by dividing them into manageable "chunks" or units of instruction that can be easily assimilated and memorized and ultimately combined to construct the complex concept.

Closed system An application that does not allow users to go beyond the boundaries of what is included in the system. Users are unable to interact with external elements, such as pages on the Internet.

Coaching An instructional strategy involving observing or monitoring student performance and providing guidance and help when appropriate (Wilson & Cole, 1996).

Cognitive apprenticeship A pedagogical model in which learners are invited into the real-life practices of a knowledge domain and are asked to perform these practices as apprentices or interns. As they assimilate the skills modeled by experts in the practice, the learners assume additional responsibilities and authority within the group.

Cognitive characteristics Aspects of the learner, including his or her learning style, motivation, prior knowledge, degree of self-direction, metacognitive skills, and social learning skills.

Cognitive flexibility hypertext (CFH) Hypermedia learning environment that provides learners with several nonlinear paths of traversing content through the use of cases, themes, and multiple perspectives. Based on the principles of cognitive flexibility theory.

Cognitive flexibility theory An integrated theory of learning, mental representation, and instruction. Emphasizes advanced knowledge acquisition in ill-structured domains and the flexible use of preexisting knowledge.

Cognitive information processing (CIP) An example of the information-processing theory of knowledge and cognition that portrays the mind as having structures and functions analogous to those of a computer.

Cognitive Load A theory related to the relationship between short-term and long-term memory stating that optimum learning occurs when the load on working memory is minimized.

Cognitive strategies Learning strategies, including organizing, elaborating on, structuring, analyzing, and restructuring information, used to solve a problem or achieve a cognitive goal.

Collaboration Interaction between or among two or more learners to maximize their own and one another's learning. Instructional strategies can promote collaboration through the use of group projects in either a face-to-face or an online environment.

Collaborative and communication tools Course management system asynchronous communication tools, synchronous communication tools, and group file-sharing and communication tools.

Collaborative learning A collection of perspectives that emphasize the joint construction of knowledge, social negotiation, and student reliance on peers and teachers as learning resources. Promotes social learning skills, discursive and dialogic skills, reflection skills, and self- and group-evaluation skills.

Combinatorial Learning A meaningful reception learning construct in which the process of learning is described as relating new ideas to existing analogous ideas. (*See also* Meaningful reception learning.)

Communities of practice (CoPs) Groups of learners or professionals with a common goal who congregate to share information and resources, ask questions, solve problems, and achieve goals, and, in doing so, collectively build new knowledge and evolve the practices of their community. A CoP is also considered a pedagogical model.

Compatibility The ability of a software application such as a course management system to work with other existing online courseware and server-based applications that your institution or organization supports. (*See also* **Interoperability.**)

Computer-assisted instruction (CAI) Computer-based instruction that exposes learners to small chunks of content material, allows self-pacing, and provides immediate knowledge of the correctness of a response.

Computer-based instruction (CBI) Any instructional program that uses the computer as the primary mode for delivery of instruction.

Computer conferencing Online conferencing. Involves interactive dialogue over the Internet.

Computer-mediated communication (CMC) Communication features facilitated by computer, such as e-mail, chat, or Web conferencing, for the purpose of teaching at a distance in synchronous or asynchronous time.

Computer-supported intentional learning environment (CSILE) A collaborative learning environment in which networked computers are used to enable students to build knowledge representations comprising text, pictures, audio, and video, and to support shared access to these knowledge representations through a communal database. Supports generative learning activities.

Constructivism An epistemology encompassing the following assumptions: Reality is constructed by the knower, meaning is negotiated, and multiple viable truths or viewpoints exist. Also known as the *constructivist paradigm*.

Content analysis techniques Techniques for examining communication symbols (characters, words, paragraphs, etc.) in an attempt to infer meaning from the context of the study.

Content creation and delivery tools Course management system tools for instructors that enable them to deliver course content and resources. Also tools for learners that enable them to contribute course content, submit assignments, and interact with course resources.

Conversational Relating to informal speech. An informal discussion of an issue. (*See also* **Discursive** or **Dialogic.**)

Conversational media Asynchronous and synchronous communication tools. An example is **threaded discussion forums.**

Copyright The legal right of an author (or an owner) of an original creation to have exclusive rights to its use, with certain exceptions (including the **fair use** exception). The principles of U.S. copyright law are identified in the Copyright Act of 1976.

Correspondence study Distance education delivered primarily through print media. The learning content is segmented into manageable units to provide a lot of structure and thus ensure success.

Course management system (CMS) A Web authoring tool that integrates technological and pedagogical features of the Internet and the World Wide Web into a single, template-based authoring and presentation system that facilitates the design, development, delivery, and management of Web-based courses and online learning environments. Examples of CMSs include WebCT, Blackboard, Lotus LearningSpace, FirstClass, and WebMentor. Also known as a *Web-based course management system*.

Courseware Software designed for educational use.

Data-driven Web sites *(also known as dynamic Web pages)* Web sites that access a database to display information on the basis of a user request. The Web page is dynamically created from information requested from the database (Kurtus, 2000).

Delivery technologies Technologies that provide a multitude of instructional services and functions that, prior to their advent, could be accommodated only in face-to-face settings. Digital video, audio, and message transport technologies provide collaboration, communication, informational, instructional, and analytic services to learners at distant locations.

Dialogic Relating to a dialogue. (*See also* **Dialogic instructional strategies.**)

Dialogic instructional strategies Instructional strategies that promote discursive student activities (students are engaged in articulation, reflection, or collaboration or are exposed to multiple perspectives).

Dialogic learning environments Learning environments in which the emphasis is on social interaction through dialogue and conversation supported by asynchronous and synchronous communications technologies.

Digital audio and video A form of media in which audio and video recordings are converted to digital (electronic) format so that they can be transmitted by a computer.

Digital media Electronic recordings of video, audio, graphical, or textual objects for transmission and playback over computer systems.

Directed learning environments (or directed approach) Learning environments in which the instructor is teaching an identifiable body of knowledge to the students by using methods grounded in behavioral and early cognitive learning theory.

Direct manipulation interface An instructional screen with a drag-and-drop-type functionality in which learners can use the mouse to move objects on the screen to accomplish an instructional objective.

Discourse Conversation or connected speech or writing.

Discriminative stimuli Events or objects used to initially establish a desired behavior.

Discursive Ranging across numerous topics, especially in an orderly or coherent way. (*See also* **Dialogic** or **Conversational.**)

Discussion forum *See* **Threaded discussion forums.**

Distance learning The deliberate organization and coordination of distributed forms of interaction and learning activities to achieve a shared goal.

Distributed cognition A learning theory or knowledge acquisition model in which cognition is thought of as a distributed phenomenon, one that goes beyond the boundaries of a person to include the environment, artifacts, social interactions, and culture. (*See also* **Situated cognition.**)

Distributed learning Learning that is distributed across space, time, and various media (including face-to-face interaction).

Document sharing A software feature that allows multiple authors to collaborate on a document or another type of file or allows multiple documents to be linked. (*See also* **Groupware.**)

Drop-down menu A collection of items listed in a field on a computer screen. The user can select the collection by clicking on the field name.

Dynamic Web pages (*See* Data-driven Web sites.)

Electronic networks   Networks that connect computers to facilitate information transfer. The Internet is a global electronic network.

Electronic performance support system (EPSS)   A computer-based instructional application designed to run simultaneously with another application, or embedded within another application, to provide user support. An EPSS typically provides just-in-time, context-sensitive assistance to users to help them accomplish specific tasks.

Embedded online tools   Computer applications or tools that are integrated into Web sites or a course management system so that users can access such tools without having to switch to another program.

Enactment phase   The second phase of the Integrative Learning Design Framework for Online Learning, characterized by operationalizing or acting out models of teaching and learning through appropriate instructional strategies or activities and embedding these strategies in the selected learning technology.

Encoding   A cognitivist construct in which learning is described as relating new concepts to existing concepts as a way to strengthen the new concepts in memory.

Enculturation   Understanding how knowledge is used by a group of practitioners or members of a community.

Epistemology   A branch of philosophy in which the nature of reality and knowledge is studied.

Evaluation phase   A process that guides the evaluation of the effectiveness of instruction or training. Although this phase is commonly identified as the last phase in the systematic process of instructional design, it is a continual process that occurs throughout the exploration and enactment phases within the Integrative Learning Design Framework for Online Learning.

Explaining   An instructional strategy in which expert thought or performance is verbalized. A think-aloud process that often accompanies modeling. (*See also* **Modeling.**)

Exploration   A learning activity and a comprehension-monitoring strategy that encourages students to monitor their learning through predicting, hypothesizing, and experimenting.

Exploration phase   The first phase of the Integrative Learning Design Framework for Online Learning, characterized by the online developer's integration of his or her prior knowledge, others' perspectives, and relevant information related to the instruction or training context.

Exploratory instructional strategies   Instructional strategies in which exploratory learning activities are promoted. Students are engaged in problem solving, exploration, hypothesis generation, and/or role-playing activities.

Exploratory learning environments   Learning environments in which learners are provided with a scientific-like inquiry or an authentic problem in a given content area and asked to generate a hypothesis, gather relevant information using a variety of resources, and provide solutions, action plans, recommendations, and interpretations of the situations. Learners are supported by technologies such as hypermedia, animation, digital audio and video, plug-ins, self-contained instructional modules, search engines, and direct manipulation interfaces.

Extensibility   The ability of a course management system to accommodate additional uses or to have more features or functions added, without the need to change the architecture of the tool. (*See also* **Scalability.**)

Extension courses   Courses that bring the educational resources of university campus to the broader community to provide lifelong opportunities for personal and professional growth.

Fading   An instructional strategy in which desired behaviors are elicited by gradually removing visible cues or learner support as the learner masters the learning task.

Fair use   An exception to U.S. copyright laws that is granted for nonprofit educational activities (or other research or news-reporting activities) that would not jeopardize the copyright holder's "rights to the fruits of his labor." Section 107 of the U.S. Copyright Act of 1976 is commonly known as the *fair use exception*.

Field dependent   A cognitive style characterized as the preference for relating to information serially or in a fixed overall pattern and processing information more globally.

Field independent   A cognitive style characterized as the preference for analytically breaking up information and separating relevant material from its context to distinguish relevant information from incidental information.

Firewalls   Security software or hardware that prevents unauthorized users outside an organization from accessing a private network within the enterprise. (*See also* **Intranet.**)

Formative evaluation   Part of the evaluation phase of instructional design. Formative evaluation enables instructional designers or developers to evaluate the instructional materials and related user performance prior to implementation of the materials. The term may also be used to imply assessment performed while the instructional process or event is still occurring.

Frame metaphor   An authoring paradigm in which the metaphor of a movie frame is used so that timed, or synchronous, interactions or animations can be designed. (*See also* **Authoring paradigm.**)

Gagné's "events of instruction"   A standard sequence of instructional strategies developed by Robert M. Gagné. The events of instruction were derived from early cognitive theory and designed to support all types of learning outcomes.

Generative note Taking   *See* **Generative strategies.**

Generative strategies (or generative learning)   Instructional strategies appropriate for a constructivist learning environment in which scaffolding is used to promote learner self-directedness, not to compensate for a lack of it.

Globalization   The widening, intensifying, speeding up, and growing impact of worldwide interconnectedness.

Graphics   Two- or 3-D pictures that can be in the form of static images, animated graphic files, or video files.

Groupware   Multiuser software that enables synchronous and asynchronous communication and document sharing and production. (*See also* **Document sharing.**)

Hierarchical object metaphor   An authoring paradigm in which an object metaphor, such as object-oriented programming, is used and is visually represented by embedded objects and iconic properties. (*See also* **Authoring paradigm.**)

HTML   Hypertext markup language. A scripting language used to develop Web pages.

Hypermedia   A technology that extends the functionality of hypertext to include graphics, audio, and video elements—some of which may require plug-ins to be viewed.

Hypermedia linkage   An authoring paradigm in which a hypermedia navigation metaphor is used to link elements. (*See also* **Authoring paradigm.**)

Hypertext   A technology that allows the user to access textual information in a nonlinear manner by using hyperlinks. Web pages currently implement this technology through **HTML.** (*See also* **Hypermedia.**)

Hypothesis generation   A learning activity that helps students learn concepts, problem solving, and reasoning skills through the process of scientific inquiry. Instructors can promote hypothesis generation by providing an adequate and variant number of "what-if" examples.

Iconic, or flow, control   An authoring paradigm used by a software package, such as an authoring system, that uses icons to represent interactions and links them sequentially in a flow line that depicts the actual result. (*See also* **Authoring paradigm.**)

Independent study   A type of traditional distance learning in which the program accommodates the students' independence by being more responsive to the students' needs and goals.

Information processing theory   A cognitive learning theory that portrays the human learner as a processor of information in much the same way as a computer is. Information undergoes a series of transformations until it can be permanently stored in memory. (*See also* **Cognitive information processing.**)

Inquiry-based learning (or inquiry-based approach)   A complex set of thinking abilities involving observing, gathering, synthesizing, predicting, and reflecting on the world around us. This approach may involve the use of tools and strategies to measure, observe, and analyze information and to synthesize models. Also considered a pedagogical model. The Integrative Learning Design Framework is an inquiry-based approach to instructional design.

Instructional characteristics   A collection of attributes that characterize a pedagogical model and imply a set of instructional strategies.

Instructional design (ID)   A field of study involving the systematic process of analysis, design, development, implementation, and evaluation of instructional or learning systems. Also known as *instructional systems design (ISD).*

Instructional problem   A situation that can be resolved by instruction provided to one or more learners. One goal of the analysis phase of instructional design or the exploration phase of the Integrative Learning Design Framework for Online Learning is to identify the instructional problem(s).

Instructional strategies   The plans and techniques that the instructor or instructional designer uses to engage the learner and facilitate learning. In the enactment phase of the Integrative Learning Design Framework for Online Learning, instructional strategies are used to operationalize pedagogical models.

Instructivist   A method of instruction involving the use of structured lessons in which the content is organized by the instructor and delivered or imparted to the students.

Integrational   To make into a whole by bringing all parts together. Directed toward integration.

Integrational learning environments   Environments that facilitate the merging of elements of the instructional attributes of exploratory and dialogic learning environments into Web-based courseware, online learning environments, and e-learning knowledge portals. These environments are supported by technologies such as Web-based authoring tools and course management systems.

Integrative Learning Design Framework (ILDF) for Online Learning   A constructivist and inquiry-based approach to the design of online learning consisting of three phases: exploration, enactment, and evaluation. This model attempts to adhere to a systematic view of instructional design but also poses a more dynamic, flexible process that depends heavily on the online developer's knowledge base as well as the social and cultural context in which the online development occurs.

Intellectual property Any item that meets one of these three criteria: (a) an author's original creation expressed in any medium, (b) a new invention that has use, or (c) a text and/or graphic that identifies a provider of services or goods. Each of these has protection under various statutes of intellectual property law. (*See also* **Copyright.**)

Intelligent tutoring system (ITS) An inference-making system that seeks to continuously improve the learning of each learner by prescribing instruction that has a high probability of preventing learner error or misconception, and by continuously adapting this instruction according to moment-to-moment diagnosis (Tennyson & Christensen, 1988).

Interaction Communication or dialogue that occurs between instructors and learners, among learners, or between a user and a technology or computer-based systems.

Interactivity A feature of instructional strategies that emphasizes a two-way communication between the instructor and the learner, or between an instructional program and the learner.

Interface All elements of a computer software program or application that affect the user's or the developer's interaction with the screen design and layout, including menus, buttons, graphics, navigational components, structural components, and content.

Internet The global network of networks that connects millions of computers for the purposes of communication and data sharing. (*See also* **World Wide Web.**)

Internet-based technologies Technologies that use the Internet for connectivity, such as e-mail, Web sites, and search engines.

Internet relay chat (IRC) Computer software that allows multiple parties to participate in synchronous (same-time) text-based communications on the Internet.

Interoperability The ability of a software package such as a course management system to share data with institutional software systems, such as student records, billing, and other information systems.

Intranet A network based on the same technologies as the Internet that resides behind a firewall controlling who can access it. (*See also* **Internet** and **Firewalls.**)

Java A general-purpose programming language developed by Sun Microsystems and used to code small programs called *Java applets* that can be downloaded from a Web server and run on a Java-enabled browser. The predecessor to JavaScript.

JavaScript A scripting language developed by Netscape to enable Web authors to design interactive sites. It is similar to Java but can be run dynamically within the user's browser without the need for downloading.

Knowledge acquisition and representation models Theories of how people learn and how knowledge is constructed, stored, and later retrieved for use.

Knowledge-building communities Learning communities in which communication is perceived as transformative (resulting in a new experience or learning) through knowledge sharing and generation.

Knowledge networks Telecommunication networks initially formed by geographically separated institutions for the purpose of sharing information. Information is linked through electronic transfer or collaborative action to support the production and use of knowledge.

Knowledge portals Originally a service metaphor adopted by the Internet commerce environment to imply a simplified local entry point with links to various services and content within and outside the site to provide diverse visitors with a "one-stop" location for accomplishing a variety of informational and learning objectives.

Knowledge repositories Electronic (digital) databases or libraries of content that leverage a common vocabulary to structure best practices, lessons learned, directories, and other documents and information resources within the context of a professional practice, organization, or learning community.

Learner-centered CAI *See* **Student-centered classroom learning environments.**

Learner control A pedagogical construct that emphasizes student choice and decision making in the learning environment. (*See also* **Pedagogical control.**)

Learning communities Groups of people engaging in a collective sociocultural learning experience in which participation is transformed into a new experience or new learning. The broader umbrella under which communities of practice and knowledge-building communities are defined.

Learning content management systems (LCMSs) Learning management systems with an emphasis on creating and managing learning objects instead of managing learners and learning activities. (*See also* **Learning objects technology.**)

Learning environments "Place[s] where learners may work together and support each other as they use a variety of tools and information resources in their guided pursuit of learning goals and problem-solving skills" (Wilson, 1996, p. 5).

Learning management system (LMS) Synonymous with *course management system.* Used predominantly in the corporate culture. Turnkey software package that includes instructor tools for content creation and learner administration and assessment, as well as learner tools and facilities for the presentation of multiple Internet and Web-based activities embedded within or launched from the system.

Learning objects technology A technology that is grounded in the object-oriented paradigm of computer science, which values the creation of digital components (called *objects*) that can be reused in multiple contexts (Wiley, 2002).

Learning orientation A mix of individual learning differences related to emotions, intentions, and social factors and how they guide the development of cognitive and social processes.

Learning as a social process A social constructivist perspective on learning in which interaction plays an integral part and the emphasis is on acquiring useful knowledge through enculturation.

Learning theory A theory that describes how people acquire, represent, and retrieve knowledge. Informs the development of pedagogical models.

Learning tools Course management system tools that enable learners to manipulate content online and create personalized experiences during the learning process, as well as scaffolding tools that support the learning process.

Listserv A software application that can manage e-mail for special-interest discussion groups so that messages can be easily exchanged among members of a particular group.

Locus of control A learner characteristic correlated with strength of motivation. The tendency of a learner to attribute learning outcomes to his or her personal efforts or to external or uncontrollable factors.

Mastery learning An assessment strategy used in some types of objectivist learning environments that uses student testing to determine whether a student has achieved the learning goals on the basis of whether the student meets or exceeds a cutoff score.

Meaningful reception learning (MRL) Also called *subsumption theory*. A theory in which learning is described as the process of activating prior knowledge in order to assimilate new knowledge with existing knowledge to provide meaning. The instructor's goal is to ensure that the student forms the proper linkages.

Metacognition Awareness, knowledge, and control of your own learning process.

Microworlds Pedagogical models in which computer-generated exploratory and experiential learning environments provide the learner with the observation and manipulation tools necessary to generate, experience, explore, and test hypotheses in order to learn a concept or understand a process. Microworlds are less complex and realistic than simulations.

Migration The process of moving from one software application or information-processing system to another, or of upgrading to a new version.

Modeling An instructional strategy that demonstrates the process of expert performance, including the making of and learning from mistakes. Often accompanied by explaining. (*See also* **Explaining.**)

MOO or **MUD** Multiuser domain (MUD) or multiuser domain—object oriented (MOO). Internet-accessible text-based and object-based shared virtual spaces well suited for creating communities of practice and knowledge-building communities.

Multimedia The blending of multiple media—text, graphics, audio, and video—into a learning or an informational resource.

Multiple perspectives A learning activity that promotes flexible knowledge structures. Instructors provide this experience by exposing learners to multiple view points, understandings, or judgments.

Needs assessment An instructional design process that includes analyses of learners to identify their learning styles, prior knowledge, experience in the use of online learning technologies, collaborative learning skills, time-management and orienting skills, social skills, and self-directed learning skills.

Networkability Connectivity and access to resources, events, and various tasks through the use of e-mail, discussion boards, and other Internet-based applications.

Objectivism An epistemology in which reality is assumed to be external to the learner and to be mind independent and in which knowledge of reality is transmitted from the instructor to the student. Also known as the *objectivist paradigm*.

Object oriented Any item that can be individually selected, reused, modified, and manipulated. Most design and programming systems support object-oriented technologies, which increase developer productivity and facilitate the design of standard applications and interfaces.

Online databases Databases that can be searched through the Internet. For example, search engines allow users to search for information stored in an online database.

Online journaling The process of keeping an electronic journal in which experiences, ideas, or reflections are documented regularly. In an educational context, journaling helps students reflect on their learning process and monitor progress. Web logs are a form of online journaling. (*See* **Web logs.**)

Online learning An open and distributed learning environment in which pedagogical tools enabled by Internet and Web-based technologies are used to facilitate learning and knowledge building through meaningful action and interaction. Examples of online learning environments include knowledge networks, knowledge portals, asynchronous learning networks, telelearning, virtual classrooms, and Web-based instruction.

Online learning technologies   Internet and Web-based tools that learners (and instructors) use to gather information, provide content and context, construct knowledge, and interact and collaborate. Examples are telecommunications technology, hypermedia technology, and Web-based course authoring tools.

Open, or Flexible, Learning   "A new approach to describing distance education where the emphasis shifts from delivering a pre-established curriculum to focusing on individual and local needs and requirements, creating open learning places based on the here and now" (Edwards, 1995, p. 242).

Open system   An application that allows a user to go beyond the boundaries of what is included in the system, such as pages on the Internet or external data elements or programs.

Parallel distributed processing (PDP) model   A knowledge acquisition and representation model that depicts knowledge and cognition as "stretched over," or distributed across, the whole network structure of long-term memory (much like a neural network; hence the "mind as a brain" analogy), not, as is posited in cognitive information processing (CIP), as residing in fixed loci in the brain (Salomon, 1993).

Pedagogical constructs   Instructional contexts such as open, or flexible, learning; distributed learning; learning communities; communities of practice; and knowledge-building communities that embody (formally or informally) one or more pedagogical models.

Pedagogical control   The extent to which the user can meaningfully and consistently communicate with an instructional system. (*See also* **Learner control.**)

Pedagogical models   Cognitive models or theoretical constructs derived from learning theory and enabling the implementation of specific instructional and learning strategies.

Pedagogical reengineering   Reevaluating traditional teaching approaches for online delivery (Collis, 1997).

Plug-ins   Software programs that allow different types of multimedia files and applications to be viewed within a Web browser.

Point-and-click interface   A graphical screen interface that supports user interaction by means of a mouse or another point-and-click device rather than a text-based interface.

Portable   The degree to which a course management system can be moved from one infrastructure, such as a server platform (e.g., Apache or Linux), to another.

Pragmatism   An epistemology in which knowledge is viewed as socially mediated and contextual and is expressed in group interactions, shared views, and common artifacts.

Presentation and visualization tools   Online learning technologies that facilitate the organization and representation of ideas and content through the creation of concept maps and multimedia presentations and products.

Problem-based learning (PBL)   A pedagogical model that engages the learner in a complex problem-solving activity in which the problem drives all learning and no prior knowledge is assumed. The goals are to help students develop collaborative learning skills, reasoning skills, and self-directed learning strategies.

Problem-solving   A learning activity in which the *process* of problem solving—such as the learner's ability to form a hypothesis, find and sort information, think critically about information, ask questions, and reach a resolution or solution—is more important than the solution (Roblyer, Edwards, & Havriluk, 1996).

Programmed instruction (PI)   A pedagogical construct for implementing behaviorist principles of operant conditioning. Predecessor to computer-assisted instruction.

Reflection   A learning activity and metacognitive strategy that includes analyzing and making judgments about what happened in the past as a way to give a situation new meaning. Instructional strategies to promote reflection include journaling and evaluating previous work.

Reinforcement   A behaviorist instructional strategy in which rewards or punishments (positive or negative reinforcements) are used to strengthen or weaken the desired behavior.

Restructuring   A schema theory construct that describes one process of learning as replacing or subsuming an old schema with a new one.

Role-playing   A learning activity that allows learners to practice their knowledge and skills in a simulated real-world situation and immediately observe the results of their actions, which prompts reflection and meaningful learning.

Scaffolding   An instructional strategy used to enhance the learner's metacognitive skills and problem-solving abilities by providing appropriate support to enable achievement of cognitive goals within the learner's **zone of proximal development** (ZPD).

Scalability   The ability of a course management system to accommodate additional demands on its resources, such as the addition of users and/or an increase in access time, without the degradation of performance or the need to increase technical or human support. (*See also* **Extensibility.**)

Schema theory   A theory that describes learning as a process of activating and reconstructing relevant mental models for understanding new knowledge according to perception of the context. The instructor's goal is to ensure that the student forms the proper linkages.

Scripting languages   Computer programming languages designed for "scripting" or automating the operation of a computer. For example, HTML is a scripting language.

Scripting metaphor An authoring paradigm that resembles a programming language in that it involves specifying all media elements by file name and interactions by coding. (*See also* **Authoring paradigm.**)

Search engines "Software application[s] that locate words, phrases, and files on a Web site" (Driscoll, 1998, p. 274). Search engines list links to the Web pages containing the word or phrase sought. By clicking on the link, the user can call up the Web page.

Self-contained instructional modules Computer-based instructional units that support a specific set of learning outcomes, from which learners access information as needed rather than using a larger, more comprehensive instructional program.

Self-directed learning "The skill of learning how to learn or being metacognitively aware of one's own learning" (Olgren, 1998, p. 82).

SGML Standard generalized markup language. A system for organizing and tagging document elements. SGML does not specify any particular formatting; rather, it specifies the rules for tagging elements and is used as the basis for HTML.

Shaping A behaviorist instructional strategy that rewards approximations of desired behaviors to elicit the responses ultimately sought.

Simulations Pedagogical models in which computer-generated exploratory and experiential learning environments that model environments and situations are used. More realistic and complex than microworlds.

Situated cognition A knowledge acquisition model that portrays knowledge representations as dynamic, constantly evolving, and subject to infinite juxtapositions. Also a learning theory that emphasizes learning as a social phenomenon and knowledge as extending beyond an individual's mind to encompass the products of a culture and the processes of groups interacting with one another and the environment (Salomon, 1993). (*See also* **Distributed cognition.**)

Situated learning A pedagogical model in which authentic learning activities are promoted to ensure that learning is situated in contexts that reflect the way the knowledge will be useful in real-life situations (Collins, 1991). Also known as *anchored instruction.*

Social constructivism A learning theory in which learning is viewed as a socially mediated activity emphasizing the social framework or culture surrounding a learning context.

Social discord Lack of agreement among people. Arguments or conflict in social or educational settings.

Social negotiation An interaction between or among two or more learners to achieve consensus and shared meaning. Also referred to as *collaboration.*

Social presence Evidence of social interaction in online communication.

Socioemotional communication Self-generated communication directed toward establishing relationships among learners that can take many forms, ranging from exchanging empathetic messages to self-disclosure (Rovai, 2001).

Storyboard A storyboard documents the interface on a computer screen. It details not only the text, graphics, multimedia, and interactions featured on-screen, but also the processes and logic of the interactions. A design tool used during the enactment phase of the Integrative Design Framework for Online Learning.

Streaming video and audio A Web-based technology (either a plug-in or a stand-alone software application) that plays multimedia files located on a remote server on a local computer without the need to download them.

Student-centered classroom learning environments Learning environments in which students are actively engaged in the learning process and assume primary responsibility for their own learning.

Subsumption A **meaningful reception learning** construct in which the process of learning is described as subsuming new ideas within broader, existing ideas.

Summative evaluation Assessment performed at the conclusion of an instructional event. It is designed to improve the instructional strategies and use of delivery technology within a course or an instructional product or system. (*See also* **Formative evaluation.**)

Superordinate A **meaningful reception learning** construct in which process of learning is described as synthesizing new ideas to subsume existing ideas.

Supplantive strategies Instructional strategies generally provided by the subject-matter expert, coach, mentor, instructor, or embedded performance support system, with the goal of modeling the desired performance and observing and supporting the learners during their execution of a learning task.

Synchronous A communication technology in which timed (synchronized) data transmissions occurring in a steady stream are used to connect two or more computers and thus enable real-time interactions such as online chats. (*See also* **Asynchronous.**)

Synchronous communication tools Communication technologies that support real-time interactions in an online learning environment. Examples are online chats, MOOs, MUDs, or whiteboard and virtual classroom communications. These tools can be contrasted with e-mail and threaded discussions, which take place as delayed interactions. (*See also* **Asynchronous communication tools.**)

Synthetic environments Artificial environments created through computer simulation. (*See also* **Virtual learning environments.**)

Tagging A paradigm used by a software package, such as an authoring system, that uses tags in text files to link pages, provide interactivity, and integrate multimedia elements.

Telecommunications technology Hardware and software systems that support electronic transport of voice, video, and data.

Telelearning "Making connections among persons and resources through telecommunications technologies for learning-related purposes" (Collis, 1996, p. 9).

Threaded discussion forums A type of e-mail communication that facilitates topical discussions. Messages in a threaded discussion are not directed to individual mailboxes but are created in a "public" discussion area. Members of the discussion group reply to the message, which creates a "thread" that chronicles the group's communications.

Three-component model for online learning A model for online learning in which (a) pedagogical models based on learning as a social process inform the design of online learning, and (b) instructional and learning strategies are derived from pedagogical models and implemented through (c) learning technologies. This model forms the basis for the Integrative Learning Design Framework for Online Learning.

Toolbars Collections of icons displayed on a computer screen that represent a set of related functions that the user can invoke by clicking on an icon.

Traditional, or conventional, learning environments Educational environments in which teaching and learning occur primarily in a face-to-face setting or a classroom and in which the teacher is perceived as the expert, the main deliverer of knowledge, and the sole assessor of student learning.

Traditional distance learning environments Traditional learning environments in which the teacher and the learner are geographically separated. (*See also* **Traditional, or conventional, learning environments.**)

Tuning A schema theory construct in which the process of learning is described as revising an existing schema to reflect new experiences.

Turnkey applications Integrative all-in-one software packages.

Usage-centered design An application design in which the needs of the end user are considered paramount. Considered one of the inputs useful during the exploration phase of an instructional design project.

Videoconferencing Technology used to connect multiple parties simultaneously in a conference in which participants can see and hear one another and, depending on the software used, share documents or share a whiteboard space.

Virtual chat An Internet technology that allows multiple users to interact synchronously in a private or a public "space" for social or learning activities. Chat "rooms" may support online communities or be dedicated to special interest topics, or they may support fantasy or role-playing.

Virtual classroom A formal online learning environment that mimics a classroom learning environment, without face-to-face interaction. Students in the virtual classroom use Internet and Web-based technologies to interact with professors, classmates, and learning content.

Virtual learning environments (VLEs) Shared synthetic environments that immerse a student in an authentic situation and allow the student to communicate with others (either real or synthetic) and to jointly or individually manipulate the environment. Similar to simulations. (*See also* **Synthetic environments.**)

VRML Virtual reality modeling language. A specification for displaying 3-D objects on the World Wide Web. Web pages written in VRML currently require a plug-in to be viewed properly.

Web-based authoring tools Application software used to design and deliver online learning and Web-based instruction.

Web-based instruction (WBI) Use of the World Wide Web to deliver instruction and instructional resources, including hypertext, hypermedia, multimedia, and communications technologies.

Web-based publishing and authoring tools A category of online learning technologies that includes software such as HTML editors, Java scripting, database scripting, and other programming languages that facilitate the creation of simple Web pages to complex 3-D animations, information repositories, and virtual reality environments.

Webcasting The transmission of a live event over the Web through a media player.

Web logs Also known as *blogs* or *Weblogs*. Frequent chronological publications of personal thoughts and Web links (Netlingo, n.d.).

WebQuest An exploratory learning environment that consists of "an inquiry-oriented activity in which most or all of the information used by learners is drawn from the Web" (Dodge, 1998).

World Wide Web (WWW) A component of the Internet that provides HTML-based Web documents and multimedia files to users by means of Web browser software. (*See also* **Internet.**)

Zone of proximal development (Zo-ped, or ZPD) A concept introduced by Lev Vygotsky to describe the role of scaffolding as an aspect of social learning that assists the student in completing a cognitive task that the student could not do alone and by doing so, supports the student's intellectual growth.

REFERENCES

Collins, A. (1991). Cognitive apprenticeship and instructional technology. In L. Idol & B. F. Jones (Eds.), *Educational values and cognitive instruction: Implications for reform* (pp. 121–138). Hillsdale, NJ: Erlbaum.

Collis, B. (1996). *Tele-learning in a digital world*. Boston: International Thomson Computer Press.

Collis, B. (1997). Pedagogical reengineering: A pedagogical approach to course enrichment and redesign with the World Wide Web. *Educational Technology Review, 8,* 11–15.

Dodge, B. (1998). *The WebQuest page*. Retrieved July 15, 2003, from http://webquest.sdsu.edu/

Driscoll, M. (1998). *Web-based training: Using technology to design adult learning experiences*. San Francisco: Jossey-Bass/Pfeiffer.

Edwards, R. (1995). Different discourses, discourses of difference: Globalisation, distance education, and open learning. *Distance Education, 16*(2), 241–255.

Hall, B. (1997). *Web-based training cookbook*. New York: Wiley.

Hall, R. (2001). Glossary of terms in Web-based training. In B. H. Khan (Ed.), *Web-based training* (pp. 51–58). Englewood Cliffs, NJ: Educational Technology Publications.

Kurtus, R. (2000). Database-driven Web sites. Retrieved February 2004 from http://www.school-for-champions.com/web/datadriven.htm

Netlingo: The Internet dictionary. (n. d.). Retrieved February 2004 from http://www.marketingterms.com/dictionary/blog/

Olgren, C. H. (1998). Improving learning outcomes: The effects of learning strategies and motivation. In C. C. Gibson (Ed.), *Distance learners in higher education* (pp. 77–96). Madison, WI: Atwood.

Oliver, R., Herrington, J., & Omari, A. (1996). *Creating effective instructional materials for the World Wide Web*. Paper presented at the 1996 Australian World Wide Web Conference (AusWeb). Retrieved November 14, 2002, from http://ausweb.scu.edu.au/aw96/educn/oliver/ index.htm

Roblyer, M. D., Edwards, J., & Havriluk, M. A. (1996). Learning theories and integration models. In M. D. Roblyer, J. Edwards, & M. A. Havriluk (Eds.), *Integrating educational technology into teaching* (pp. 54–79). Upper Saddle River, NJ: Merrill/Prentice Hall.

Rovai, A. P. (2001). Building a classroom community at a distance: A case study. *Educational Technology Research & Development, 49,* 33–48.

Salomon, G. (1993). No distribution without individuals' cognition: a dynamic interactional view. In G. Salomon (Ed.), *Distributed cognitions: psychological and educational considerations.* (pp. 11–138).New York: Cambridge University Press.

Schon, D. A. (1987). *Educating the reflective practitioner: Toward a new design for teaching and learning in the professions*. San Francisco: Jossey-Bass.

Tennyson, R. D., & Christensen, D. L. (1988). MAIS: An intelligent learning system. In D. H. Jonassen (Ed.), *Instructional designs for microcomputer courseware* (pp. 247–274). Hillsdale, NJ: Erlbaum.

Wiley, D. A. (2002). Connecting learning objects to instructional design theory: A definition, a metaphor, and a taxonomy. In D. A. Wiley (Ed.), *The instructional use of learning objects* (pp. 3–24). Bloomington, IN: Agency for Instructional Technology/Association for Educational Communications and Technology.

Wilson, B. (1996). What is a constructivist learning environment? In B. G. Wilson (Ed.), *Constructivist learning environments: case studies in instructional design* (pp. 3–8). Englewood Cliffs, NJ: Educational Technology Publications.

Wilson, B. G., & Cole, P. (1996). Cognitive teaching models. In D. H. Jonassen (Ed.), *Handbook of research for educational communications and technology* (pp. 601–621). New York: Simon & Schuster/Macmillan.

AUTHOR INDEX

SUBJECT INDEX